SENSEX
of Regional Parties

A comprehensive account of regional parties that altered the course of Indian Politics

Now as the Congress high command decided to tie-up with AIADMK Munnetra Kazhagam in Tamil Nadu, then opposing it P. Chidambaram and G.K. Moopanar with their supporters formed a new party on March 29, 1996. Later on, the Congressmen loyal to G.K. Moopanar formed a new regional political Party, the Tamil Nadu Maanila Congress. There were many occasions when G.K. Moopanar was offered the top leadership, yet he suggested the name of some other leader for this and chose to focus on the [illegible] throughout the party. G.K. Moopanar was a supporter of [illegible] K. Kamaraj from the very beginning and K. Kamaraj [illegible] as his political successor. In 1999, Moopanar refused to support the BJP led government's trust vote in the Lok Sabha, which ultimately led to the downfall of the Vajpayee [illegible] government.

[illegible] again made the Finance Minister when the [illegible] was formed in 2004. During this time the [illegible] the government disagreed with him [illegible] In November 2008, he was given [illegible] government was again formed [illegible] On May 15, 2017, the CBI registered an FIR [illegible] company INX. It was alleged [illegible]

SENSEX of Regional Parties

A comprehensive account of regional parties that altered the course of Indian Politics

AAKU SRIVASTAVA

PRABHAT PAPERBACKS

Published by
PRABHAT PAPERBACKS
An imprint of Prabhat Prakashan Pvt. Ltd.
4/19 Asaf Ali Road,
New Delhi-110002 (INDIA)
e-mail: prabhatbooks@gmail.com

ISBN 978-93-5521-236-8
SENSEX OF REGIONAL PARTIES
by Aaku Srivastava

Cover Design
Manoj Sinha

Edition
First, 2022

Price
₹ 500 (Rupees Five Hundred Only)

Printed at
Nakshatra Art

A Word of Gratitude

To all these friends who have by sharing about parties and persons made this book possible.

- **Rajkeshwar Singh**, Ex Information Commissioner, UP Government.
- **K.V. Prasad**, Ex Bureau Chief, Tribune, Delhi.
- **Jagtar Singh**, Sr. Journalist, Indian Express, Chandigarh.
- **Alok Mehta**, Padmashree Awardee, Sr, Journalist.
- **Ratan Mani Lal**, Ex. Editor, Hindustan Times, Lucknow.
- **Ashok Mishra**, Ex Bureau Chief, Hindustan Times, Patna.
- **Ramendra Sinha**, Ex. Resident Editor, Hindustan, Patna
- **Rakesh Rocky**, Sr. Journalist, Tehelka, Delhi.
- **Chandan Mishra**, Sr. Journalist, Ranchi.
- **Om Prakash Ashok**, Sr. Journalist.
- **Sanjay Srivastava**, Sr. Journalist, News18 Network.
- **Vijay Vidrohi**, Sr. Journalist, Jaipur.
- **Harsh Kumar Singh**, Sr. Journalist.
- **Ranjeeb, Sr. Journalist**, Lucknow.
- **Shailesh**, Sr. Journalist, Delhi.
- **Professor Ravi Shukla**, Mumbai.
- **Manoj Kumar Sahu**, Sr. Journalist, Raipur.

and

Jyoti Srivastava

Annadurai, a prominent figure of the Dravidian movement and founder of the DMK. The reason for his burial was also said to be political. Jayalalithaa's Party AIADMK wanted to save her political legacy in the same way as MGR's. It was also reportedly said that the rituals followed in this case were in accordance with the Sri Vaishnava tradition.

[illegible] the politics of the state, there was turmoil between the regional parties, but Karunanidhi also kept moving forward. It was [illegible] a regional party like the DMK a part of an alliance with both the Congress and the BJP in the governments at the Centre. When V.P. Singh's coalition government was formed at the Centre, the weightage of regional parties got enhanced in national politics. During the coalition governments, Karunanidhi's [illegible] in national politics automatically gained prominence. There [illegible] personalities [illegible] politicians who possess [illegible] and aggressive [illegible] in politics also weakened his party. He [illegible] and flamboyant leader. His attitude towards the [illegible] He was a great orator and served [illegible]. Political analysis cannot ignore the [illegible] extended family of politicians. In fact, [illegible] in the central government for 1[illegible] such as the DMK. Karunanidhi had tied up

Contents

PART-1

THE ORIGIN OF REGIONAL PARTIES

1
The Rise of Regional Parties in Indian Politics

The emergence of Regional Parties as major centres of power in the Country's politics is one of the most important events in post-independence history. Due to India's geographical, social and political diversity, foreign intellectuals once opined that as a modern nation, India was so "unnatural that it would not exist for long". That is why the formation of the Indian Union after Independence was an attempt to save that diversity in itself. The effort was to keep regional aspirations flourishing in the federal structure. The main reason for the origin of regional parties is believed to have been general dissatisfaction with the national parties. From unbalanced regional development, competition and ethnicity to the spirit of religion, etc. these all added fuel to the fire. You will see that more than half of the regional parties were formed with the demand of their own region or state. (We shall read more about it in a separate chapter in detail.)

So in the past, after Prime Minister Pt. Jawahar Lal Nehru and later Indira Gandhi, the people felt the need for expansion of regional representation. It, in turn, paved the way for the rise of several regional parties. Indian politics is regionalised on the basis of India's cultural diversity and plurality in terms of class, caste and ethnicity, for example, Jats in Haryana UP and Rajasthan;

Yadav and Kurmi in Bihar, UP; Reddy and Kamma in Andhra Pradesh; Vokkaliga and Lingayat in Karnataka etc. Similarly, the linguistic restructuring of India, led to the emergence of regional identity among the people. Uneven development due to the green revolution, prosperity in some areas and backwardness in others and the Emergency imposed by Indira Gandhi also gave impetus to new parties to emerge. The vested interests of some former maharajas and zamindars, failure of national politics or central government to fulfil regional aspirations, ideologies and political disagreements also led to divisions among large parties. These parties generally function in a State or a particular region with a limited electoral base. They work for the regional interest on ethnic, cultural and linguistic grounds, for example, only for the natives of that State, the demand for reservation of seats in jobs is made. They are usually focused on local and regional issues showing no interest in forming a government at the Centre. They desire more political autonomy in India.

In fact, from 1952-64, there was the Nehru era with the Congress running government in most places, but after Nehru's death, the situation could no longer remain the same in the 1967 elections. In the Lok Sabha elections, the Congress did not get a majority in eight States and its seats in the Lok Sabha were reduced to 54 per cent. During the period 1964-77, the Congress got divided and later the situation worsened with screw-ups by Morarji Desai in Gujarat and Jai Prakash Narayan in Bihar. The situation became grim to a stage that Indira Gandhi had to impose Emergency in 1975. The imposition of the Emergency due to the deteriorating political situation was the first ever and unique in the Country. Even today, whenever there is an adverse situation for a Party, political parties raise the ghost of Emergency and scare them. (We also see this phenomenon in the form of the rule of regional parties. Lalu Prasad Yadav rule in Bihar is often termed as 'Jungle Raj' which Nitish Kumar's supporters often used lest RJD should come in power again.) We also can say at this juncture the era of like-minded parties' governments begins. But this is where the rough patch for the Congress also starts. If several regional parties were formed in the Country between 1980 and 1989, it is attributed to the internal strife within the Congress. Or it can be said that the Congress has been the origin of most of the regional parties. The regional leaders were not happy with the way it functioned and when pushed to the wall they launched their own new Party. A fresh example is Mamata Banerjee and then there is Sharad Pawar we all know. (we would read about them in chapters ahead). From 1952 to 1989, as long as there were one-Party governments at the Centre, regional politics could not dominate the federal system. However, it was not that regional politics was all marginalised. Potti Sriramulu, a freedom fighter from Andhra Pradesh, was the man who, after a 58-day fast and sacrificing his life, forced the then Nehru Government to set up a State Reorganisation Commission in 1953. It was then that States were formed on linguistic grounds.

Different regional parties have been formed in India from time to time and have been playing their part in the parliamentary democracy of the Country. Some parties like Shiromani Akali Dal and Jammu and Kashmir National Conference were formed even before the Country attained independence in 1947. But most of the other regional parties have been formed only post-Independence. The development of parties in the category of regional parties intensified, especially in 1967, when the Indian National Congress Party, which played a key role in the Country's freedom struggle, began to lose its grip on the voters. In the fourth general elections of 1967, the concept of non-Congressism led to the formation of an anti-Congress front in many States. Many Congress leaders formed regional parties. Chaudhary Charan Singh, a well-known farmer leader, created his own mass base with the medium and backward classes of Uttar Pradesh while being in the Congress and formed the Bharatiya Kranti Dal as soon as he parted ways with the Party. After the general elections held in 1967, the Congress government was formed at the Centre, but it got a majority in only 9 States out of 17. In State politics, a round of coalition governments of regional and non-Congress parties thus began.

Regional parties soon gained momentum and posed a challenge to the national parties. They made political and economic neglect of the region or State in the hands of the national parties their ground and marched ahead. From 1989 to 2009, that is, from the 9th Lok Sabha to the 15th Lok Sabha, no national Party was in a position to form a government on its own i.e. without the support of regional parties. In the Assembly elections held in 5 States at the end of 2013, regional parties could not do much, but the emergence of the Aam Aadmi Party in Delhi was a significant event. Aam Aadmi Party's temperament has never been of a regional Party. Efforts were made to contest in other States and in Punjab it also had a huge success in the 2017 elections. If there were no strategic miscalculation, it would have formed the government there. The AAP actually did so in the 2022 elections by registering a historic win in the Punjab Assembly elections. We would see it locking horns in many other States as well.

By the way, the Shiromani Akali Dal, one of the oldest regional parties, was established in 1920 by the Shiromani Gurudwara Prabandhak Committee (SGPC), a religious organisation, during British rule. Similarly, Dravida Munnetra Kazhagam (DMK) was founded in 1949 by C.N. Annadurai in Madras (Chennai). The word Dravidian is a symbol of the Dravidian caste. The word Munnetra means progressive and Kazhagam means organisation. The Party was formed mainly to counter the growing influence of North India in the Southern part of India and of the Brahmin caste. In early 1972, DMK split and in October 1972, M.G. Ramchandran, the superstar from south and also treasurer of the DMK, formed his own Party and named it Anna Dravida Munnetra Kazhagam. The Party was later renamed as All India Anna Dravida Munnetra Kazhagam.

A Party which secures at least 6% of the total votes in Lok Sabha elections or Assembly elections in four States and wins at least four seats in Lok Sabha is recognised as a national Party. A Party which secures at least 6% of the total votes in the election to the Legislative Assembly of a State and wins at least two seats in Lok Sabha is recognised as a State Party.

According to the Election Commission of India, India has more than 2,000 political parties, including eight "recognised national" and more than 50 "recognised State" parties. Besides 8 national parties - Indian National Congress, Bharatiya Janata Party, Nationalist Congress Party (NCP), Communist Party, Bahujan Samaj Party, Rashtriya Janata Dal, All India Trinamool Congress and National People's Party, most of the major parties in the Country have been classified as 'State parties' by the Election Commission. These are commonly known as regional parties. Yet these parties do not have to be regional in their ideology or approach. Some of these parties are all India parties which have till now succeeded only in a few States. There are about two dozen parties which have not been recognised so far. Many of them are in power in their State while some are waiting for their turn. Though some parties may be national as per the Election Commission's calculations, the Nationalist Congress Party (NCP), Bahujan Samaj Party (BSP), Rashtriya Janata Dal (RJD of Bihar), Trinamool Congress (TMC) and National People's Party are as such "national" parties but because they have an impact at the regional level, we will discuss them as regional parties.

The BSP has a great influence in Uttar Pradesh and in the decade after 2000, its number of MPs has been 13 (13th Lok Sabha), 14 (14th Lok Sabha), 21 (15th Lok Sabha) but its influence in the rest of the States has been negligible. The same has been the case with RJD and NCP and they have been dominant in Bihar and Maharashtra respectively. The most interesting story ever is that of the NPP led by P.A. Sangma, which is the parent Party of Meghalaya and also has MLAs in Arunachal and Manipur.

P.A. Sangma's son Conrad Sangma is the Chief Minister from Meghalaya. The total number of votes may be less than the votes of a single major Lok Sabha... and the specialty of our democracy is that today NPP is a national Party. (It is not our intention to consider them inferior by any means.) Another interesting fact is that there are some States where regional parties have no influence on a large scale. There, the fight is directly between the Congress and the BJP. There are some States where the Congress is present only very nominally, like in West Bengal. And similarly, in some States the BJP is present in poor numbers.

It is interesting to observe the balance of politics in the Country tilting since the nineties and subsequent decades and now regional parties are dominant in more than half of India's States. In many States, they have held the reins of power on their own, while in many States they are partnering in government with national parties.

There are many types of regional parties in India to consider. The parties based on regional culture and ethnicity are Shiromani Akali Dal, Jharkhand Mukti Morcha, Mizo National Front etc. The parties formed by division in the national Party boast of a prosperous history. Parties emanating from Congress are ruling in several States. Trinamool Congress (by the way is technically a national Party now), NCP and North East parties are dominant in their respective States. First, Utkal Congress was formed from Congress. Biju Patnaik created a different history in the State. Biju's Party again joined the Janata Dal and later, as we know, his son Naveen Patnaik formed the Biju Janata Dal and is now the Chief Minister of Orissa continuously for the last five terms thus creating a unique history. Kerala Congress is also a Party from the Congress. On the other hand, some parties, which irreparably damaged the roots of the Congress, were based on the charismatic personality of the leader such as the Himachal Vikas Congress and the Haryana Vikas Party, etc. In many States, small parties were formed after breaking up with the Congress. Some survived, some withered after a while. But the political scenario was made interesting by those parties which amalgamated caste with charismatic personality and emerged as big parties. The RJD led by Lalu Prasad Yadav and Mulayam Singh Yadav's Samajwadi Party commanded a different place. With Mulayam advancing in age, Akhilesh Yadav was once the Chief Minister of the Party and Lalu's younger and flamboyant son Tejashwi is the CM in waiting from the RJD.

It was because of the growing existence of regional parties that coalition governments were in existence for nearly two decades before 2014. In the two general elections of 2014 and 2019, breaking the 25-year compulsions of coalition politics, the same Party (BJP) got an absolute majority on its own. However, the government is still formed by a coalition of several political parties. But after the 2019 general elections, the results of the Assembly elections in Maharashtra, Haryana, Jharkhand in December 2020 and West Bengal, Tamil Nadu, Puducherry and Kerala in March-April 2021 firmly established the presence of regional parties and that they are going to last unfazed.

Regional parties believe that only they can bring development to the people of a particular region. One of the characteristics of all regional parties is that all of them run at the behest of a leader who commands unchallenged authority within the Party. In short, they are being run by one leader and his confidants. His family members and relatives are also much involved in the Party's functioning. Therefore, the existence of such parties in general is also very closely linked to the lifespan of the leader running them. In fact, there is also a crisis of survival before regional parties having no family members of the founder to take over the Party leadership. In the past there have been many parties which, along with their founder, ceased to exist or faded away.

The rise of regional parties has undeniably changed the nature of electoral politics in India. A common myth about regional parties is that their rise is, by definition, diminishing and continuously shrinking the stature of national parties. But in fact, after an unprecedented increase in the position of regional parties in the late 1980s and early 1990s, the pattern of electoral competition at the national level has achieved a surprisingly stable balance of power.

In fact, as long as the role of regional parties was confined to the States, the times were different, but the period that lasted for 25 years after 1989, especially after the assassination of Rajiv Gandhi, changed drastically after the leadership crisis in the Congress and the deteriorating economy of the Country. There was a period of politics of beaming alliances in which scenarios went mercurial and kept changing very rapidly. Decisions got difficult to arrive at and implementing them happened to be even more cumbersome. The era of caste and community politics and its pressure grew at the Centre. Many experts called it a proper burst of federalism.

The total vote share won by two truly national parties and the 'rest' in the last five elections, which means mainly regional parties, surprisingly shows that the respective popularity of these two groups is in a stable holding pattern. The share of votes won by regional parties for the first time in 1996 broke 50 percentage points. Then there was fluctuation. By 1999, the vote share of regional parties had fallen to 48 percent. By 2004, their vote share was back to 51 percent, i.e. at the same level as it was eight years ago, before a modest rise in the 2019 elections. The increasingly fragmented vote has affected the share of seats won by regional parties in the Lok Sabha elections in 2019. At present, regional parties occupy 41 per cent of the seats. This is actually a decline from the last two electoral cycles. The vote share of regional parties reached its highest level (53 per cent) in 2009, but the share of seats allotted to regional parties declined due to fragmentation.

In the 2009 general election, Mayawati's Bahujan Samaj Party fielded 500 candidates out of 543 constituencies across

India (incidentally, it is more than any other Party). Still, the Party captured only 21 seats in its stronghold Uttar Pradesh. In fact, the BSP was not a contender even in most of the constituencies in which it entered the fray; Its candidates were in the top two of the 72 constituencies in total. Compare this with the Congress, which contested 440 seats, won 206 seats. The BJP got 116 seats and came second in 110 other seats. Regional parties' hold over States was at the highest during 1997 which is continuously declining.

In 2012, Akhilesh Yadav, when he was just thirty-eight years old, brought his Samajwadi Party (SP) to power in Uttar Pradesh with a single-Party majority. Prior to this, the last years (2003 to 2007) of the SP's power under Mulayam Singh Yadav were marked by blatant corruption and miserable condition of law and order in UP, resulting in the Party's defeat in the 2007 State elections. When Akhilesh's government came in 2012, it was highly expected that Akhilesh would break the image that had been continuing with his father's regime. But it did not happen. Mamata Banerjee, a former Congress leader who left the Party to form her own Trinamool Congress in West Bengal, was also hailed for the change she had promised if she was elected in 2011. Mamata didi continued her threat even in the 2021 Assembly elections. It has also been proved that despite the forceful presence of a strong popular leader like Prime Minister Narendra Modi, victory in the Assembly elections cannot be guaranteed.

Regional leaders like Mulayam Singh Yadav, Mayawati, Anupriya Patel, Lalu Prasad Yadav, Nitish Kumar, Naveen Patnaik, Arvind Kejriwal, Uddhav Thackeray, Parkash Singh Badal, Jayant Singh Chaudhary (son of Ajit Singh) are still popular in a particular class and region. They have been making and distorting the equations of power in their respectives States.

Until the Assembly elections in Uttar Pradesh in 2022 political equations were different. As soon as the results were announced, the dreams of few were shattered while some made a mark for themselves. Those who had entered into an Alliance with a bigger party, may not have fared well if they hadn't done so. Here I would include Jayant Singh's " Rashtriya Lok Dal" also. Asaduddin Owaisi's AIMIM was being touted as a B party for BJP or a big player by itself, but could not put up a good show. In fact it got less votes than even NOTA. On the other hand, seven seats that BJP won, had a victory margin of less votes that AIMIM candidate got, which means had the AIMIM candidate not been there, BJP would have lost the seat. Arvind Kejriwal's Aam Aadmi Party too jumped in the fray but its vote share was .35%, again less than NOTA. It is surprising looking at the historic 80% seat won by AAP in Punjab. Sensing the urgency of the occasion, Suheldev Bharatiya Samaj Party Chief Om Prakash Rajbhar and Jan Adhikar Party's Babu Singh Kushwaha had formed the Bhagidari Sankalp Morcha by joining 8 smaller parties together. It was said to have a good standing in backward class. This front included Suheldev Bharatiya Samaj Party (SBSP), Krishna Patel's Apna Dal (K) besides Jan Adhikar Party, Owaisi's AIMIM, Premchandra Prajapati's Bharatiya Vanchit Samaj Party, Anil Chauhan's Janata Kranti Party (R), and Baburam Pal's Rashtra Uday Party etc. SP joined hands with the Mahan Dal, which was supposed to have a political stronghold in the Bareilly-Badaun and Agra regions. The Janwadi Party's Sanjay Chauhan and Rashtriya Lok Dal led by Jayant Chaudhary went with the Samajwadi Party. Parties like Sanjay Nishad's Nishad Party, O.P. Rajbhar's Suheldev Bharatiya Samaj Party, Anupriya Patel's Apna Dal benefitted by entering into an alliance. They strengthened their base and also enhanced their vote percentage. Apart from these, many other regional parties are ready to try their luck in the electoral battlefield in the elections to come.

By the way, a debate about regional parties keeps doing the rounds frequently and unceasingly. Can regional parties ever pose a challenge to the sovereignty of the nation? This question has often been arising especially in the border States. Barring Jammu-Kashmir and one or two of the States in the North-East, its prospects are hardly conspicuous. Anyway, regional parties are playing an important role in the politics and development of the Country and the States. Therefore, it can be foreseen that they would continue to thrive in the Country.

Context:

1. 'India Speeches and Introduction' - Winston Churchill
2. Indian Governance and Politics – Morris Jones (Translated)

❑

2
Spring of Caste & Regional Aspirations

It is extremely strenuous to accurately fathom the roots of religion and caste-based politics in India. In this part of South Asia, hundreds of years before Christ, when castes formed, there began politics to attain supremacy over others. It is insignificant who survived, which one surfaced or got marginalised. When other religions came to the fore in this field, the politics of uniting people and communities in the name of religion also began. The Kings adopted or patronised different religions periodically with a view to maintain their political supremacy and switched to some other religion without shilly-shallying. But this is not the subject matter of this book. We will discuss here the politics of caste and religion in the post-Independence era and the political parties that thrived on it.

On August 15, 1947, when the first acting government was formed under the leadership of Prime Minister Jawaharlal Nehru, it tried to inculcate all ideologies and religions. However, earlier, Mohammed Ali Jinnah's politics of religion or Quam and community-based nationalism had resulted in partition of the country. The lesson of the ghastly tragedy of partition was soon forgotten and religion and caste-based politics began to germinate. Analysts are of the opinion that the voting trait of a large section of Indians is swayed to vote in favour of one's caste or religion.

There may be many reasons for this, but they feel that the leader of their community is more likely to work in their favour. When the first Lok Sabha elections were held in 1951-52, there were many parties in the electoral arena who tried to make their way into the corridors of politics through caste, region or religion, claiming to protect their rights. Among them were the Bharatiya Jana Sangh, the All India Ram Rajya Parishad, the Hindu Mahasabha calling themselves the Hindu Nationalist Party and raising their voice for rights of the Hindus. Similarly, the Indian Muslim League played the politics of Muslims and the Shiromani Akali Dal in Punjab was talking of Sikh rights. In Tamil Nadu, the Tamil Nadu Toilers Party eyed the Vanniyar votes. To unite and organise Dalits, B.R. Ambedkar's Scheduled Castes Federation was also in the fray. The Justice Party in the south attempted to woo the Dravidians. Similarly, a Depressed Class League was also formed in Punjab. In the North-East, a separate political party in the form of Khasi-Jaintia Darbar tried to woo the Khasi and Jaintia tribal communities. The party named the Cookie National Association was in the fray for the Cookie community.

On the one hand, the Congress was accused of promoting Muslim appeasement from the very beginning and on the other hand, the parties rooted in the politics of Hindu nationalism did not get much success initially. Perhaps one of the reasons for this was Shyama Prasad Mukherjee himself who adorned the Nehru Council of Ministers. That is why Hindu nationalists had to wait for a long time to taste any success. The generation recovering from the pain of partition had more faith in healing. Similarly, the Muslim League, which raised its voice for Muslim rights, could not make much of an impact in national politics. Yes, the Shiromani Akali Dal, which was formed before independence, attained power in Punjab only in 1967.

But the parties that played ethnic politics succeeded rapidly. Dravidian politicians in the south were the first to succeed. The main reason behind this was the awakening created by dignitaries like

E. Periyar among the backward sections of the society. According to Nicholas Drinks' book Castes of Mind: Colonialism and the Making of Modern India Periyar initiated the "Aatm Gauravam' or rather the Self-Esteem Movement in 1944 by creating Dravidar Kashagam to awaken the Dravidian community. It was simply a social movement and not a political Party. Similarly, Gail Omvedt writes in his book Dalit Visions: The Anti-Caste Movement and the Construction on an Indian Identity that the Indian National Congress-affiliated Tamil reformer E.V. Ramasamy Nayakkar was the first to blatantly oppose the Brahmanical leadership of the Congress in 1919. Periyar was also opposed to Brahmin supremacy and keeping the Dravidians at the lower level in Tamil Nadu.

Margaret Ross Burnett's book Prehistory and History of the DMK, which was reviewed in detail by journalist N. Ram in 1977, attributes Periyar's second marriage to the formation of the DMK. In 1949, 72-year-old Periyar married his own Party leader Maniammai, 31. Earlier, it was understood that his nephew, E.V.K. Sanpath was to inherit the legacy of Periyar, but Periyar married the young Maniammaiand passed his legacy to her. Angered by this, many of his followers left Dravidar Kazhagam and joined C.N. Annadurai, who formed a separate Party called Dravida Munnetra Kazhagam (DMK). The party caught the nerve of the people of Tamil Nadu by agitating against Hindi in the State. As a result, the DMK government was formed in Madras province in 1967. After Annadurai, the party continued to gain strength under M. Karunanidhi. Noted actor M.G. Ramachandran also joined the party but after a confrontation with Karunanidhi in 1972, M.G.R. formed a separate Party called All India Anna Dravida Munnetra Kazhagam (AIADMK). Since then, the power of the state turn-by-turn remained between these two parties.

The Akali Dal is the second oldest Party in the country after the Congress. It was formed on December 14, 1920. The main objective of this party was to raise Sikhs as a political voice and play cult politics. After independence, in 1950, the party started the Punjabi Suba Movement under the leadership of Saint Fateh Singh. The party demanded that there should be a separate State for the Punjabi-speaking population. On November 1, 1966, the Punjab State came into existence for the Punjabi-speaking populace. It was only in the 1967 Assembly elections that the Akali Dal came to power. However, there was a clash among senior leaders of the party for supremacy which resulted in a breakup. The government could not complete its term. Later, Prakash Singh Badal carried forward the legacy of the Akali Dal by making it the Shiromani Akali Dal. Thus, the Akali Dal is a very successful example of cult politics. (Read about the party in detail in the next chapter.)

Whatever you say, the BJP is the most successful example of the politics of religion at the national front, with the resilience of secularism. For this, it has come a long way from the formation of the Jan Sangh to the formation of BJP via the Janata Party. Since the book focuses on the role of regional parties, so, we are not going into much detail here. In regional parties Shiv Sena's name can be prominently mentioned among the parties that have succeeded in the politics of religion. The Shiv Sena led by Bal Thackeray emerged as a major force in Maharashtra. The party strengthened its political base by making Hindu rights an issue.

Similarly, AIMIM's Asaduddin Owaisi emerged as a successful face of Muslim-society politics. However, AIMIM, the All India Majlis-e-Ittehadul Muslimeen, is a very old Party. Majlis-e-Ittehadul Muslimeen (MIM) was founded in 1927 by Nawab Mahmood Nawaz Khan, Qiledaar of Hyderabad State, on the advice of Nizam Usman Ali Khan of Hyderabad. The first meeting of the party was held on November 12, 1927. The party opposed Hyderabad's annexation into India and MIM was banned in 1948. Party leader Qasim Rizvi had gathered nearly 1.5 lakh razakars, or fighters, to protest against the merger of Hyderabad. Qasim Rizvi was arrested and jailed in 1948 and in 1957 he was released on the condition that he would go to Pakistan. Pakistan had assured him political asylum. Rizvi handed over the responsibility of MIM to Abdul Wahed Owaisi, a lawyer by profession, before leaving for Pakistan. Abdul Wahed Owaisi renamed it AIMIM, the All India Majlis-e-Ittehadul Muslimeen. Abdul Waheed was succeeded by his son Sultan Salahuddin Owaisi in 1975. He won the Assembly elections in Patharghati and Charminar, and later from Yakoutpura. From 1984 to 2004, he continued to win from the Hyderabad seat. In 2008, Sultan Salahuddin's son Asaduddin Owaisi took over the reins of the party. After that, the party also increased its mass base in Andhra Pradesh and Maharashtra. Candidates were also fielded in Bihar, Bengal and Uttar Pradesh Assembly elections. He also had good success in Bihar. In the second decade of the 21st century, the party rapidly increased its mass base among Muslims.

On the other hand many parties like the Hindu Mahasabha, Karpatri Maharaj's All India Ram Rajya Parishad, Baba Jayagurudev's Doordarshi Party, Hindu Swaraj Sangathan, Azad Hindu Fauj (State), All India Hindu Shakti Dal, Jai Ma Kali Nagarani Samiti, Satyuga Party, Sarva Dharma Party of Madhya Pradesh and the Hindu Praja Party jumped into the fray in the name of religion with no success.

The Indian Muslim League, which talks about Muslim rights politics, also did not succeed in India. The mafia also formed political parties under the guise of religion to portray themselves as political forces. Among them, Haji Mastan, the mafia chief alias the Don of Mumbai, can be named. Haji Mastan formed the Indian Minorities Security Federation in 1983, talking about Muslim rights. Haji Mastan was the party President till his death in 1994. This party did not succeed.

On the other hand, there are many successful examples in the political parties of caste and community. When the recommendations of the Mandal Commission were implemented, it polarised the castes considered backward classes and many political parties came forward in their support. Mulayam Singh Yadav in Uttar Pradesh and Lalu Prasad Yadav in Bihar emerged as strong leaders of Yadavs. Nitish Kumar became the leader of the Kurmis. The success story of Samajwadi Party, RJD and JD(U) is not hidden from anyone. What Chaudhary Charan Singh and Devi Lal were doing in the name of Farmers' politics in western Uttar Pradesh and Haryana, was actually Jat politics. Leader of Lok Dal Chaudhary Charan Singh became the Prime Minister of the country and later Devi Lal also rose to the post of Deputy Prime Minister. The Bahujan Samaj Party, founded by Kanshi Ram, became a major force of Dalit politics across North India. Not only the DMK and AIADMK in the south, but also the political land of Pattali Makkal Katchi (S Ramdas) of S. Ramadoss was created by connecting the Vanniyar community, considered to be the backward classes of the south.

In Tamil Nadu, the Vanniyar community is considered to have a population of about 10 percent. These include Chingalpat, North Arkot, South Arkot and Salem districts with a population of Vanniyars of up to 25 percent. Traditionally, most of the erstwhile forest labourers were agricultural labourers, but after political awakening, nearly half of the land is now owned. Among those who brought about a political awakening to the Vanniyar community, S.S. Ramasamy Padaichi and S. Ramadoss are prominent names. In 1951, Ramasamy Padayachi united the erstwhile forest workers of South Arkot and Salem and formed the Tamil Nadu Toilers' Party. At the same time, advocate M.A. Manikvelu Naiker formed a Common Wheel Party by associating the Vanniyar community of North Arkot and Chengalpattu with him. In the first Lok Sabha elections in 1952, the Toilers' Party won four seats. In the late 1970s, S. Ramadoss founded the Vanniyar Sangam and in 1987, the Sangam staged a demonstration in Tamil Nadu demanding reservations for Vanniyars. More than 1,400 houses of Dalits were torched. Subsequently, DMK's M. Karunanidhi, who became Chief Minister in 1989, made a provision for 20 percent reservations for the most backward community. Encouraged by this success, S. Ramadoss formed a new party called Pattali Makkal Katchi on July 16, 1989.

Like Vanniyar in Tamil Nadu, the Vokkaliga community in Karnataka is considered to be a major political force. Whether it is the Congress or the BJP, the rise in power cannot be assumed without the support of this community. H.D. Deve Gowda, Yediyurappa became the Chief Minister of the State on the strength of his community's political standing. Deve Gowda also adorned the chair of Prime Minister.

The ethnic politics looks equally strong in Punjab where Jat Sikhs have a complete hold over politics. Whether the government belongs to the Congress or any other Party, the Chief Minister has to be from the Jat Sikh community. Thus, in Haryana, the saying that the "Chief Minister has to be a Jat" is very famous. 'Three Lals' became famous in Haryana politics and two of them Devi Lal and Bansi Lal were from the Jat community while Bhajan Lal was a Bishnoi. It is another fact that Manohar 'Lal' Khattar has continued to be in power for the last two terms.

The dominance of religion and caste politics has increased manifold in states now, especially in north Bihar. In Uttar Pradesh, where earlier more parties were being formed regarding Muslims, leaders of even small castes have not hesitated to announce their parties. When the Peace Party became one such Party for minorities, a Nishad Party for Nishads, then O.P. Rajbhar formed a separate Party for Rajbhars. For Rajbhars, there were two parties in UP. Separate efforts were undertaken for Kurmi and Bhumihars. Though their individual role is not significant in the Uttar Pradesh elections, they are in a better position to garner alliances with major parties.

In Bihar, this trend began a long time ago. The Rashtriya Lok Samata Party leader Upendra Kushwaha demanded both posts and stature for the Kushwaha Samaj. He also became the Leader of the Opposition in the Bihar Assembly and graced the Ministerial post at the Centre. But later on after losing the 2020 elections badly, merged his party with Nitish Kumar's JD(U) and now he is

MLC at present. Mukesh Sahani after minting money from films, formed the Vikassheel Insaan Party (VIP). The VIP Party is the NDA's constituent Party and he himself is a Minister in the council of Nitish Kumar. Jiten Ram Manji, who formed the HAM Party, became a significant leader of the Dalits and by chance was made Chief Minister. Even if you do not consider Pappu Yadav, who on his own several times has become an MP, as the leader of the Yadav community, no one can deny his role as a regional leader. The amount of work he ensured in Bihar during the Covid period also broke the image of his being regional leader, but he still had to wait to enter Parliament and the Assembly. There has been the politics for minorities but nowadays focus is on their sub-groups. The leaders of the Pasmanda community have started demanding a different place for themselves.

Dalit politics also flourished in the country. Many small parties were also formed. These include parties like the Shoshit Samaj Dal and the Bharipa Bahujan Sangh, but they failed to make any mark. Those who assess the politics of the coming days are of the view that in almost every state, small groups of different castes and religions will exert more pressure and, if needed, new parties will emerge and intensify their demand.

(Well, it would be interesting to mention a survey here that the people of Madhya Pradesh appeared to be at the forefront when it comes to voting as per caste and religion. Two-thirds of the people talked about voting in their caste while the lowest figure was in Andhra Pradesh and Telangana.)

❑

3
Longing for a Separate State

After India gained independence, restructuring of the states was the foremost major task in hand. In many areas, organisations based on caste, language and culture began to struggle demanding separate statehood for their region. First, there were Sangharsh Samitiyaan demanding separate statehood and then many of them flourished as big parties and created a strong base for themselves in politics. Politics based on such issues, which started after Independence, still continues in various parts of the country and is bound to continue in future. Before independence, the British had a system of Princely States, that is, the status of the kingdom was mostly recognised as Princely States and landlords. After independence, efforts for reorganisation of states were initiated in 1948, discarding the pattern of the Princely States and deciding new parameters for reorganisation of states on the basis of language and regional characteristics. This was followed by another Commission for State Reorganisation. Then, there was a series of new states. The Bombay State was divided to form two erstwhile States of Gujarat and Maharashtra. Nagaland separated from Assam and the region separated from Punjab became the state of Haryana. From Uttarakhand, Jharkhand to Telangana, many such small states came into existence which were carved out from the big states. Still, there is a demand for further, more separate states in many areas.

The fact remains that if all the prevailing demands for a separate state are accepted in the country, there will be more than 50 states in India. As of now it is believed that the Union Home Ministry has more than 20 memorandums of demand from different states. The demand for a separate Kukuland from Manipur, Kongunadu from Tamil Nadu, Tulunadu from Karnataka, Kamtapur in North Bengal. Demand for the four states of Uttar Pradesh - Awadh Pradesh, Purvanchal, Bundelkhand and Paschimanchal or Green Pradesh - were raised aloud during Mayawati's government in 2010. There is also a demand to form Braj Pradesh, by merging the Agra Division of Uttar Pradesh, Bharatpur from Rajasthan and Gwalior in Madhya Pradesh. Similarly, the demand for the creation of Bhojpur state comprising the eastern part of Uttar Pradesh and parts of Bihar and Chhattisgarh has also reached the Union Home Ministry. The demand for a separate state of Vidarbha in Maharashtra is long pending. The agitation to separate Darjeeling and its surrounding areas from West Bengal to form Gorkhaland is also in existence. The Bodo movement also turned violent in western Assam with the demand for a separate Bodoland. In Assam itself, the Karbi community is also demanding a separate Karbi-Anglong region for itself. The Dimasa community is demanding a separate Dimarazi or Dimaland by merging a part of Assam and Nagaland. There is also a demand to merge the Terai parts of Nepal in Bihar and Jharkhand into separate Mithilanchal. There is another demand to create a separate Saurashtra region in Gujarat. There is a demand for a separate Coorg state in Karnataka. The demand for a separate Kosala state comprising a part of the existing Odisha, Jharkhand and Chhattisgarh started only after independence and has continued on so far. The Konkani-speaking areas of the Western Ghats in south India have demanded a separate Konkan region. There is a demand to merge Cooch-Behar and Jalpaiguri in West Bengal to Kamtapur. There is a demand for Garoland in the Garo area of Meghalaya.

By the time this book is being written, there are 29 states in the country, including Telangana. We must also delve into history to understand the reason for such demands and the politics behind it. When the British left in 1947, besides thousands of zamindari states and estates, there were 565 Princely States in the country. On January 26, 1950, when the Constitution came into force, there were 28 States and 9 Union Territories in the country, which were formed by merging different Princely States and feudal areas. At the same time, there was a demand for the merger of some states and simultaneously for a separate state in many places. The government had set up the State Reorganisation Commission in June 1948 to restructure the states, giving priority to linguistic and regional similarities. It is also known as the Linguistic Province Commission or the Akadhar Commission. Later, Prime Minister Jawaharlal Nehru established a separate States Reorganisation Commission in December 1953. It was built under the leadership of former Supreme Court Judge Fazal Ali. The Commission submitted its report on September 30, 1954. Based on his report, the State Reorganisation Act came into existence on August 31, 1956. Thereafter, many states were merged, leaving a total of 14 states and 6 Union Territories. Among the 14 new States that were formed, Andhra State and Hyderabad State were merged into Andhra Pradesh. There was no change in Assam, Jammu and Kashmir, Odisha and Uttar Pradesh. Bihar was slightly slashed and its Purulia region was given to West Bengal. Bombay State was further enlarged by giving Saurashtra state, Kutch, Berar and Nagpur districts and Marathwada area of Hyderabad State, while its southern area was given to Mysore State. The State of Kerala was made by merging the Kasaragod Taluk of Madras Presidency, Travancore-Cochin State and South Canara districts. The southern parts of Travancore-Cochin were given to the State of Madras. Punjab was further increased by the induction of Patiala and East Punjab State Union (PEPSU).

In this way, Pandit Jawaharlal Nehru had in a way reversed the existing geographical pattern and characteristic of the country by introducing a law to reconstitute the states. Many states were merged into one. At a time when people were coming together on linguistic and regional grounds on the issue of regional development, many small old states were merged together to form big states. After that, a new kind of politics gained momentum in the country and the movements for creation of different states increased. These movements became a very easy route to those wanting to enter politics and soon the demand for a separate state gained momentum in most states of the country.

According to Sadhana Sharma's book State Politics in India, the demand for a separate state on the basis of language is very old in the country. Such a demand was first raised in 1895 under British rule for a separate Oriya province. Social reformer and lawyer Madhusudan Das, also known as the father of Oriya nationalism, played an important role in the formation of a separate Odisha province during the British period.

Actually, Nehru blundered here in estimating regional nationalism. The first major agitation against Nehru's experiment of creating large states began in Bombay State immediately after it. When a separate Mahagujarat movement started in the Gujarati-speaking parts of the north, Marathi-speaking nationalists from the south started the United Maharashtra movement. As a result, on May 1, 1960, Bombay State was demolished and two new states, Gujarat and Maharashtra, came into existence. It was during Nehru's time itself that two separate new states were formed from the Bombay State.

The word Mahagujarat is said to have been coined by writer and politician Kanhaiyalal Maneklal Munshi. Nehru had suggested a formula to stop the protest and the movements of Gujarati and Marathi speaking population under which Bombay State was to be divided into three parts: Maharashtra, Gujarat and the Union Territory of Bombay. But the then Bombay State Chief Minister Morarji Desai denied it. The trifurcation of Bombay was not appreciated even by the people demanding a United Maharashtra.

Students protested outside the Congress office in Ahmedabad against Morarji Desai's stand. The demonstration turned violent and some students were killed. Indulal Yagnik, who was about to retire from politics, took the lead after the death of the students and gave a new edge to the movement by forming the Mahagujarat Janata Parishad. Though the movement led to two separate states, the political leadership remained in the hands of the Congress. Jeevraj Mehta of the Congress became the first Chief Minister of Gujarat and Yashwantrao Chavan became the first Chief Minister of Maharashtra. On the same day, a Joint Maharashtra Andolan Samiti was formed under the leadership of Left leader Shripad Amrit Dange. The movement led to the rise of several leaders in Maharashtra such as socialist Madhav Joshi, Narayan Ganesh Gore, Uddhavrao Patil and Madhu Dandavate to name a few.

Thus, once the formation of a separate state began, it progressed further rapidly. Nagaland was separated from Assam on December 1, 1963. For this, the Naga National Council led by Angami Japu Fijo launched an agitation. The movement also took a violent turn. Fijo had to leave the country. But soon Nagaland became a separate state and P. Shilu Ao became the first Chief Minister of Nagaland who was a prominent activist of the Naga movement. He started his political career from the Naga People's Convention in the 1960s. The Naga People's Convention created leaders who snatched political ground from the Congress in the North East.

Thus, the agitation expanded further with the demand for a separate state, which was considered an infallible measure of success against the Congress in every state at that time and the politics of an alternative governance began to emerge. After Nagaland, there was a demand in Punjab also to make Punjabi-speaking and Sikh-dominated areas a separate state and to make the Hindi-speaking region a separate state as Haryana. Akali leader Sant Fateh Singh and Chaudhary Devi Lal who was till then associated with the Congress strengthened themselves in the guise of such politics and created a strong image for themselves. As a result, two separate states emerged on November 1, 1966 in the form of Punjab and Haryana. Consequently, while the Congress lost its dominance in Punjab and the Akali government came to power in 1967, Chaudhary Devi Lal distanced himself from the Congress and strengthened himself as a stalwart in Haryana.

In 1972, three separate states of Manipur, Meghalaya and Tripura were formed in the North East. Manipur and Tripura were Union Territories earlier; they attained complete statehood. After Independence, two districts of Assam, named Meghalaya, were given some specific autonomy. But in the 60s, there was an agitation in these districts to separate them from Assam and form a hill state. The All Party Hill Leaders Conference (AHLC) led the movement. The movement was successful and Meghalaya emerged as a separate state. AHLC President Williamson Apang Sangma became the first Chief Minister of Meghalaya. He was the Chief Minister for a second term also till 1990. As far as the All Party Hill Leaders Conference is concerned, it emerged as a successful political party in the battle for a separate state. It governed Meghalaya for ten years and gave four Chief Ministers to the state.

In 1987, the Union Territories of Goa, Mizoram and Arunachal Pradesh got separate statehood. In 2000, Chhattisgarh, Jharkhand and Uttarakhand came into existence as three separate states. The long-drawn movement for creation of these 3 states can be a subject matter of an epic saga, so we are not focusing on it here. Chhattisgarh may have separated from Madhya Pradesh in 2000 and became a new state, but it was a very old demand going on since 1920 during the British period. At the Congress Annual Conference in 1924, the Raipur unit of the Congress had raised a demand to make Chhattisgarh a separate state. The demand was placed before the State Reorganisation Commission in 1954 but was not accepted. Chandulal Chandrakar established the Chhattisgarh Rajya Nirman Forum in the 1990s with the demand for a new state. The forum staged several agitations and strikes. In Madhya Pradesh, both the major parties, the Congress and BJP supported the demand for a separate state. Finally, on August 1, 2000, after the approval of the NDA Government, a separate State of Chhattisgarh was formed and Madhya Pradesh was divided into two states. As Congress and BJP leaders were associated with the agitation both these parties dominated in Chhattisgarh.

With the creation of Jharkhand, a regional Party, the Jharkhand Mukti Morcha emerged strong. The movement to create a separate Jharkhand state from Bihar is also more than six decades old, but the demand is even older. Jharkhand Mukti Morcha won six Lok Sabha seats in the 1991 general election. Shibu Soren became the first Chief Minister of the state when Jharkhand became a separate state in 2000. His son Hemant Soren also returned to power on December 29, 2019 and became the Chief Minister of the State for the second time. (You can read the details in the chapter on the Jharkhand Mukti Morcha.)

Like Jharkhand, there was a demand to make Uttarakhand a separate state even before independence. The demand was also raised at the two-day annual session of the Congress held in Srinagar from May 5-6, 1938. However, Pandit Hargovind Ballabh Pant and Badri Dutt Pandey had earlier constituted the Kumaon Council in September 1916. The objective of the Council was to solve the social and economic problems of the hilly region. In 1926, the Kumaon Council merged with the Indian National Congress. But the demand for a hill state separate from the United Provinces arose periodically. The demand was raised by Indra Singh Nile, a member of the Uttar Pradesh Legislative Council, in 1954 after independence. He also prepared a complete action plan of a separate state and handed it over to the then Chief Minister Govind Ballabh Pant. Subsequently, in 1955, the State Reorganisation Commission headed by Justice Fazal Ali had also recommended to the Nehru Government at the Centre to make the hilly region a separate state. But a separate state was not created then. On May 12, 1970, the then Prime Minister Indira Gandhi herself spoke of addressing the issue. On July 26, 1979, Bipin Chandra Tripathi, a renowned social activist and environmentalist of the mountains, along with Devi Dutt Pant, Indramani Badoni and Kashi Singh Eri, formed the Uttarakhand Kranti Dal in Nainital on the issue of a separate state due to continued apathy from the Uttar Pradesh government and the Centre.

The party fought a long battle for a separate State of Uttarakhand. In 1987, the Uttarakhand Kranti Dal passed a resolution to form a new state. In 1994, the agitation gained momentum and students and government employees under the Uttarakhand Sangharsh Samiti also came together in support of the demand for a separate state. The then Chief Minister Mulayam Singh Yadav refused to accede to the demand for a separate Uttarakhand. In protest, Uttarakhand Kranti Dal leaders started a fast unto death. Uttarakhand employees went on strike in the state government. The same slogan 'koda-jhangora khaenge-apna uttarakhand banenge' echoed all over the hilly region. On the call of the Uttarakhand Andolan Sangharsh Samiti, it was decided to reach Delhi on October 2, 1994 and hold a demonstration at Jantar Mantar. On the other hand, the Mulayam Singh government in Uttar Pradesh decided that the agitators would not be allowed to go ahead at any cost. Earlier, there was a blockade on the Narsan border. The administration was helpless ahead of the crowd of agitators in a convoy of hundreds of buses. As the convoy moved forward, the police administration arrived in full swing to stop it at Rampur Tiraha on the night of October 2, 1994. As the convoy moved forward, the police opened fire. Among the protesters were women who were abused and raped. It continued to wreak havoc all night. Then some locals came forward to help the protesters. Eight protesters were martyred in the incident. Mulayam Singh became the villain of the mountain forever. The Samajwadi Party was completely reduced to the mountain.

Uttarakhand finally came into existence as a separate state on November 9, 2000 after a long struggle. Even after the formation of a separate state, the Uttarakhand Kranti Dal, which was at the forefront of this struggle, could not become a major political force. There, the reins of power continued to swing between the Congress and the BJP. In the first Assembly elections held in 2002 after the formation of a separate state, the Uttarakhand Kranti Dal won only 4 out of 70 seats in the State. Bipin Chandra Tripathi became the party leader in the House. After that, in the 2007 Assembly elections, the party won 3 seats and in 2012, it won only one seat. In the 2017 Assembly elections, the party could not even manage to open its account.

After 2000, on June 2, 2014, a separate State of Telangana was formed by merging some districts of Andhra Pradesh. With this, there were 29 states in the country. After independence, Telangana (Hyderabad State) and Andhra Pradesh became separate states, but on February 20, 1956, the leaders of Andhra and Telangana entered into an agreement, after which the two states were merged into Andhra Pradesh. The merger agreement has been recorded in history as the Gentleman's Agreement of Andhra Pradesh. Although both were separate regions on linguistic grounds, one was a Kannada-speaking population and the other was Telugu-speaking. However, most of the ruling Congress MLAs at that time were not in favour of the merger. The leaders who signed the merger agreement included the then Chief Minister B. Gopal Reddy, Neelam Sanjeeva Reddy, Gauthu Latchanna, Aluri Satyanarayana Raju on behalf of Andhra State and the then Chief Ministers B Rama Krishna Rao, K.V. Rangareddy, M Chenna Reddy and J.V. Narsing Rao on behalf of Telangana. However, opposition to the Gentleman's Agreement also started shortly thereafter. In 1969, Jai Telangana in favour of Telangana and the Jai Andhra movement for a United Andhra started in the State. Students also jumped into the demonstrations and created law and order problems in several districts of the state. Student organisations were also divided into two groups, for and against a United Andhra Pradesh. On January 19, 1969, one such demonstration turned violent when a mob set fire to a sub-inspector's house. Police also opened retaliatory fire. Seventeen people were injured in the violence.

In 2000, when three separate states emerged in the form of Chhattisgarh, Jharkhand and Uttarakhand, K. Chandrashekar Rao formed his separate party Telangana Rashtra Samithi (TRS) in Andhra Pradesh on April 27, 2001. The TRS had a one-point agenda to create a separate Telangana state with Hyderabad as its capital. Before forming his own separate Party, K. Chandrashekar Rao was the leader of the Telugu Desam Party and resigned as Deputy Speaker to form a separate Party. The party was big just after creation. Within two months of its formation, it had captured two-thirds of the Mandal Parishad regional seats and one-fourth of the Zilla Parishads in the Telangana region. After that, there was a long struggle over the demand for a separate Telangana state. In 2013, when the Congress government was in power both at the Centre and in the state, a resolution was passed in the Congress Working Committee on July 30 to form a separate Telangana State by consensus. In the Andhra elections in 2004, TRS won 26 assembly and five Lok Sabha seats. In the 2009 elections, TRS contested 45 assembly and 9 Lok Sabha seats along with the Telugu Desam Party and BJP but won only 10 Assembly and 2 Lok Sabha seats. It was considered a major defeat for the TRS. Subsequently, in the 2014 elections, the TRS did not compromise with anyone. The party won 11 out of 17 Lok Sabha seats and 63 out of 119 assembly seats. After that Telangana also became a separate state in June. Thus, TRS emerged as a big Party from Telangana and K. Chandrashekar Rao emerged as a prominent leader. Then, in 2018, Chandrashekar Rao dissolved the Assembly and held the first Assembly elections after Telangana was formed. The party won 88 out of 119 seats. In the 2019 general elections also, the party contested the elections, distancing itself from the BJP and the Congress alike and won 9 seats.

In this way, we see that many parties have made their mark and identity by playing politics of a separate state. These include not only the North-Eastern parties, but also the easiest and most effective way to prepare the political ground for a separate state in the name of region and language from east to west and north to south. When Haryana separated from Punjab, for the first time, the Akalis succeeded in forming its government there. Devi Lal emerged as a senior leader in Haryana. Madhu Dandavate emerged in Maharashtra and later became the Railway Minister of the country. Jharkhand Mukti Morcha and Shibu Soren became a new strength in Jharkhand. T.R.S and K. Chandrashekar Rao are a great example in the south. However, there were some parties fighting for a separate state which could not build their own big political ground even after achieving the target. Uttarakhand Kranti Dal is an apt example of this.

❑

4
A Mixed Harvest of Fruits and Thorns

The history of splits and differences in the Congress is not new. Even before independence, in 1907, there was a historic split in the party between the Naram Dal and the Garam Dal. But in this book, we will talk about the parties formed from the Congress after independence. Many great and veteran leaders rebelled against the Congress and formed new parties, but even though some of them were successful initially, only a few remained in the race and the rest couldn't compete further.

Socialist Party

However, the organisation was formed as a Congress Socialist Party earlier in 1934. These were the leaders who were influenced by Communism in Russia and did not agree with Gandhiji's staunch non-violence. These Socialist leaders included Jayaprakash Narayan, Acharya Narendra Dev, Meenu Masani, Ram Manohar Lohia, Kamaladevi Chattopadhyay, Achyut Patwardhan, Yusuf Mehr Ali, Ashok Mehta, etc. In the freedom struggle, their association was like a united front with the Congress. Dr. Ram Manohar Lohia was considered a stringent critic of Prime Minister Jawaharlal Nehru. After independence, at the Nashik Conference in March 1948, the Socialist Party led by him decided to withdraw from the Congress. The main reason for this was the agitation in

Rewa on January 2, 1948, which demanded the holding of the elections and cancellation of Partition. Police opened fire on the demonstration and four agitators were killed. Lohia rejoined the Socialist Party only after it parted ways with the Congress. The second National Conference of the Socialist Party was held in 1949. It was at this Conference that Lohia presented the idea of Chaukhamba State. Hind Kisan Panchayat was also established during this period. Before the first Lok Sabha elections in the country, Lohia had coined a very interesting slogan against Nehru, "Rozi-Roti-Kapda do, Nahin to Gaddi Chhod Do"- (provide the masses with food, clothing and shelter, otherwise give up the chair). Later, the Socialist Party's subjects continued to merge and separate with the Socialist Party. Now the Uttar Pradesh Samajwadi Party describes itself as a Party carrying forward Lohia's legacy.

Bharatiya Jana Sangh

Shyama Prasad Mukherjee was the Commerce and Supply Minister in the first Interim Government formed after independence on August 15, 1947 under the leadership of Pandit Jawaharlal Nehru. According to Urmila Sharma and S.K. Sharma's book- Indian Political Thoughts, Mukherjee was the leader of the Hindu Mahasabha, but Shyama Prasad Mukherjee distanced himself from the General Assembly after Gandhiji's assassination. Sardar Patel had then accused the Hindu Mahasabha of killing Gandhiji as a result of the enmity created by it. Shyama Prasad Mukherjee then advised the Hindu Mahasabha to slow down its political activities. Angered by the Delhi Pact between Nehru and Pakistan's Prime Minister Liaquat Ali Khan regarding refugees from East Pakistan, on April 8, 1950, Shyama Prasad Mukherjee and Finance Minister K.C. Niyogi resigned from the Nehru cabinet. Then, on October 21, 1951, Shyama Prasad Mukherjee along with the RSS formed a separate Party called Bharatiya Jana Sangh. In 1977, the Bharatiya Jana Sangh merged with the Janata Party.

First major split after Independence: Congress breaks between Morarji Desai and Indira Gandhi

When Morarji Desai parted ways with the Congress in 1969, Dr. Shankar Dayal Sharma also separated for two or four weeks and went with Morarji. This was the first major division of the Congress since Independence. Dr. Shankar Dayal Sharma often pointed out that he parted ways with the Congress at Indiraji's behest. He was advised to find out with a separate group what the state of the documents of the organisation were. In those days, the Congress office used to be at Jantar Mantar. Shankar Dayal Sharma first captured it. It was he who took out all the necessary papers from the Headquarters and then Indira Gandhi formed her own Congress which was called Indira Congress i.e. Congress (I). Similarly, the other Congress which Nijalingappa formed was called the Congress (O) to which Morarji got associated with. The question is whether Morarji Desai formed a separate Congress or Indira Gandhi, the correct answer to which is that both formed their own Congress. Morarji Desai was at the forefront of the race to become Prime Minister after Lal Bahadur Shastri. But he lost the leadership battle to Indira Gandhi by a huge margin in the Congress. He was the Deputy Prime Minister and Finance Minister in Indira Gandhi's Council of Ministers. In July 1969, Indira Gandhi snatched the Finance Ministry from him. Morarji Desai resigned from the Council of Ministers describing the move as a blow to his self-respect. A reason for his removal was Indira Gandhi suggesting nationalisation of 14 big banks which Morarji Desai opposed. The Congress broke down in two due to differences between the two leaders. Brahmananda Reddy was then the President of the Indian National Congress. Reddy had announced the expulsion of Indira Gandhi from the Congress. On November 12, 1969, the Indian National Congress (Organisation) came into existence and Morarji Desai became a part of it. He was accompanied by many senior leaders of that era. Among them were K. Kamaraj, S. Nijalingappa, Neelam Sanjeeva Reddy, C.M. Poonacha, Atulya Ghosh, Tribhuvan Narayan Singh, etc.

In fact, it was a division of right-wing and left-wing ideologies in the Congress. Indira Gandhi was inclined towards the Soviet Union. The organisation that separated under Indira Gandhi was initially called the Indian National Congress (Requisition) which soon turned into Congress (I). These two groups were given another name at that time. One was called Syndicate and the Indira faction was called an Indicate. Most of the veteran Leaders of the Nehru-era Congress were initially in the Congress (O), but a few weeks later many of them joined Indira Gandhi. Jagjivan Ram, Kamalapati Tripathi and Hemvati Nandan Bahuguna were prominent among them.

When Indira Gandhi imposed the Emergency, the opposition parties came in unison against it. In the same process, the Congress (O) merged with the Janata Party in 1977.

Division of Indira Congress

Jagjivan Ram and Hemvati Nandan Bahuguna also parted ways with the Indira Congress when elections were due before the Emergency in 1977 and they formed the Congress for Democracy. However, till this point, Jagjivan Ram was considered loyal to Indira Gandhi. He was the Defence Minister of the country during the 1971 war with Pakistan. Even during the imposition of the Emergency in 1975, he supported Indira Gandhi. But when Indira's popularity fell sharply during the Emergency, Jagjivan Ram formed the Congress for Democracy on February 2, 1977. Jagjivan Ram became its President and former Uttar Pradesh Chief Minister Hemvati Nandan Bahuguna was the General Secretary. Among its other founding members was former Odisha Chief Minister Nandini Satpathy, Union Minister K.R. Ganesh and MP Dwarka Nath Tiwari. The party also merged with the Janata Party within a year of its formation. Similarly, in July 1977, Karnataka Chief Minister Devraj Urs (also known as ARS) separated in the south and formed a separate Indian National Congress (U). It had influence in Karnataka, Kerala, Maharashtra and Goa. (You can read about this party in detail in the next chapter.) The impact of the Congress (U) can be gauged from the fact that in the Lok Sabha elections held in 1980, the Indira Congress was successful in the South, including Karnataka, but the party lost the Karnataka Assembly elections. Indira Gandhi then made Kamalapati Tripathi the Working President of the Congress and assigned to him the task of strengthening the party in the south so that it should become stronger in the north. After 1980, Narasimha Rao was brought from Karnataka and given a major role at the Centre.

V.P. Singh's rebellion

After Indira Gandhi's martyrdom, Rajiv Gandhi became the Head of the Congress and the government. V.P. Singh and Arun Nehru were said to be his right and left hand. Rajiv Gandhi gave posts like Defence Minister and Finance Minister to V.P. Singh. He was a Congress leader in the Rajya Sabha from 1984 to 1987. But after the Bofors scandal, the two rebelled openly. V.P. Singh was the Defence Minister when the Bofors scandal came to light. Questioning the role of Prime Minister Rajiv Gandhi in it, V.P. Singh resigned from the Congress in 1988. Soon, on the birth anniversary of Jayaprakash Narayan, the Janata Dal was established on October 11, 1988. Five opposition parties merged with this Janata Dal. These included Lok Dal, Indian National Congress (Jagjivan), Janata Party, Janata Party (Secular) and Jan Morcha. V.P. Singh did not stop there and formed the National Front by merging the Telugu Desam Party, DMK and Asom Gana Parishad. The National Front defeated the Congress in the 1989 Lok Sabha elections to form the government with the outside support of the BJP. V.P. Singh was made Prime Minister and Chandrashekhar had no inkling of it . V.P. Singh was the President of the National Front and proposed Devi Lal's name for the post of Prime Minister. Devi Lal instead proposed V.P. Singh's name and it was passed. Chandrashekhar was left aghast. This government, which was created by deceiving each other, could not complete its term and lasted only 343 days, or less than a year. Chandrashekhar then became the Prime Minister with the outside support of the Congress which lasted for just over six months.

This was how a period of instability began in the country. For this, not only the politics of the country but also the foreign forces were said to be behind it. In Indira Gandhi's time, some opposition leaders were accused of being puppets in the hands of the CIA. Indira's confidants included many left-wing leaders, including Mohan Kumar Mangalam, and K.D. Malviya. Indira's inclination towards Moscow hit foreign powers like the United States. Therefore, in breaking the Congress not only did these leaders but foreign powers also played a role. Whether it was raising or running large-scale agitations/movements or bringing leaders into one fold, these tasks were not easy without massive assistance and funding. Indira Gandhi and Shankar Dayal Sharma openly accused the CIA of having a hand in all this. Even Morarji Desai was not spared from such allegations. It was also said that forces like the CIA supported a terrorist campaign like Khalistan.

When Rajiv Gandhi became the Prime Minister, he was accorded a grand welcome by President Ronald Reagan in the US. He hoped that since he was a young Prime Minister he would incline towards the US. To some extent, it happened too. Many young Congress Turks supporting liberal ideology were made Ministers.

V.P. Singh was also earlier considered to be the leader of socialist ideology. His son was given his first job by a multinational bank in the US. He was made Vice President directly. (Perhaps for a change of heart, ₹ 500 crores direct investment was also made through him) V.P. Singh was Finance Minister then. N.D. Tiwari was a frontline leader at that time. In order to weaken him he was removed from central politics and sent to UP. It was only in 1986 that the Ramswarup espionage scandal came to light in which two Ministers were made to leave Rajiv Gandhi's Cabinet. These included Chandulal Chandrakar and K.P. Singh Dev.

Ramswarup, who worked for the Intelligence Bureau and the Directorate of Military Intelligence (DMI) for nearly 20 years, was arrested for being a US spy. In the November 15, 1985 issue, India Today published an exclusive interview with Ramswarup. In it, he named some influential people of the Rajiv Gandhi Government. He went to Taiwan and enjoyed the hospitality of institutions that indulged in anti-Left activities during the Cold War. He was understood to have worked for the US intelligence Agency CIA. Ramswarup himself had told the media that he provided several important information to the DMI between 1962 and 1970 and was working for IB till August 1985. He was arrested in October 1985. Ramswarup claimed that whatever he had done with Israeli intelligence agencies was already with the knowledge of the government. He claimed that he was used by the government to hold a meeting between Israeli Defence Minister Moses Diane and Prime Minister Morarji Desai during the Janata Government in 1978. The IB, on the other hand, alleged that it was delivering confidential information of the country to the CIA through Israel.

Just a day before Ramswarup was scheduled to be produced before the Patiala House Court in Delhi in February 1986, two Union ministers, K.P. Singh Dev and Chandulal Chandrakar and Electronics Commission Chairman M.S. Sanjeevi Rao resigned. Their resignation was immediately accepted .

The Bofors case came to light shortly after the revelation of this case. There was a rift and discord in the Congress. Thus, there are many indications that foreign forces were active in weakening a strong government in the country. V.P. Singh's government was followed by Chandrashekhar's government. It fell too soon. During this time Rajiv Gandhi was assassinated. N.D. Tiwari's nomination was cancelled in the Lok Sabha elections that year. Narasimha Rao became the Prime Minister.

All India Indira Congress (Tiwari)

Narasimha Rao ran the Congress in his own way. He sidelined N.D. Tiwari. Tiwari was upset and once said to the media that if Rao became the Prime Minister, "should I now cycle around?" N.D. Tiwari received his education while residing at Anand Bhawan. He was considered loyal to the Gandhi family. In 1994, ND Tiwari resigned from the Congress and formed his own separate All India Indira Congress (Tiwari). In 1995, Arjun Singh also left the Congress and joined the party. Along with him, Natwar Singh and Rangarajan Kumar Mangalam also left the Congress and joined the Tiwari Congress. Sitaram Kesari was the Congress President, but the way Kesari was removed and Sonia Gandhi was made the President of Congress, was disrespectful for Keasri. In 1998, the Tiwari Congress merged with the Congress again.

Rebellion of top leaders

In 1996, when Sonia Gandhi was made the party's President after snatching the post of President from Sitaram Kesari, many senior leaders rebelled in the Congress. Madhav Rao Scindia split from Congress and formed a regional Party called Madhya Pradesh Vikas Congress. In Tamil Nadu, P. Chidambaram formed the Tamil Manila Congress (TMC). Bansilal formed the Haryana Vikas Party in Haryana. But later their parties merged back with the Congress. In 1997, Mamata Banerjee, another senior Congress leader, also rebelled against the Party High Command and formed a separate Party in Bengal called the All India Trinamool Congress. Among other senior leaders, Sharad Pawar had been associated with the Congress since 1978. He returned to the Congress in 1987 at the time of Rajiv Gandhi. After the assassination of Rajiv Gandhi, he was also a prime ministerial candidate against Narasimha Rao. But he was made Defence Minister instead. Ahead of the Lok Sabha elections in 1999, some Congress leaders like Sharad Pawar, P.A. Sangma and Tariq Anwar demanded that the Congress should declare only a person born in the country as the face of the Prime Minister's candidate. It was an indirect opposition to Sonia Gandhi. On this demand, the Congress Working Committee suspended the three leaders for six years. Then, in June 1999, Pawar and Sangma formed the Nationalist Congress Party.

In Gujarat, Shankersinh Vaghela joined the Congress in 1998 through the Janata Party and the BJP. In 2017, he quit the Congress in a controversy over the post of Gujarat Legislature Party leader and formed a new organisation, the Jan Vikalp Morcha. But this front also did not last long. Vaghela moved to the Nationalist Congress in 2019. He lasted only a year there. He also resigned from the NCP on June 22, 2020 after being removed as State President.

In this way, most of the Congressmen who separated and formed their parties could not succeed. Many of these parties merged with the Congress again or were gradually relegated to the margins. But two names remained exceptions. Mamata Banerjee and Sharad Pawar. Mamata Banerjee, with her combativeness, made a stronghold in West Bengal. Sharad Pawar was considered a Maratha Kshatrapa but could not create an image beyond Maharashtra due to his constant love for the Centre. It can also be said that like Mamata, he could never become an impactful force on his own in Maharashtra. His party has been swinging at number three position for a long time.

Actually, the very framework of the Congress paves the way for rebellion and it would not continue to remain so, can anyone guarantee that?

❑

PART -2

POLITICAL PARTIES IN STATES

5
Samajwadi Party: Flirting with National Politics

Whenever the history of regional parties is recorded in the country, those parties will find specific mentions which are indispensable not only today but for the future as well. Those are the parties which, with their ideology and deep penetration among the masses laid the foundation of their own political parties. The Samajwadi Party, which came into existence in Uttar Pradesh almost three decades ago, almost simultaneously with the Rashtriya Janata Dal in Bihar, is also one of these regional parties, which has not only made a strong presence in the State, but national politics also. The number of its seats in the Lok Sabha or the Legislative Assembly may fluctuate but its significance in national politics can never be undermined. Let us now focus on the Samajwadi Party. Mulayam Singh Yadav, a typical rustic and aggressive leader who belonged to the rural areas, not only became the Chief Minister of the state three times, but his son Akhilesh Yadav has also been the Chief Minister for a full term.

The history of the Samajwadi Party has been no less interesting. Born in November 1939 in Saifai village of Etawah district of Uttar Pradesh, at the age of just 15, Mulayam Singh Yadav came into contact with Dr. Ram Manohar Lohia, the great leader of social change in the country . It was during his mentorship that Mulayam Singh realised that political transformation alone would not bring much change in the country. Social change is very important. He was imprisoned several times for agitation over various issues for his people. He also faced imprisonment of 19 months during the Emergency. The tide of opposition to Congress was roaring high with each passing day in the country. All the leaders of the country were united in their role in the anti-Congress politics. Mulayam was also on the same path. So it was necessary for him to maintain a close rapport and harmony with many of them. During all that, Mulayam jumped into politics for the first time from the United Socialist Party in 1967 till 1989 as a member of parties like Bharatiya Kranti Dal, Lok Dal and Janata Dal, Janata Dal-Samajwadi, but for the first time in 1989 he became the Chief Minister of Uttar Pradesh. After forming the government, he came across some bitter experiences with the leaders of the Janata Dal. By then he had closely observed and understood many leaders including former Prime Minister V.P. Singh, Chaudhary Devi Lal, Chandrashekhar, CPI(M) and Harkishan Singh Surjit. The Ayodhya movement emerged as the biggest challenge for him only after he became the Chief Minister for the first time. Deep differences surfaced with V.P. Singh while he was the Prime Minister. There came a time when the Janata Dal was torn into two factions. V.P. Singh's government at the Centre fell. In UP, Mulayam continued the government with the Congress support. But it did not last. Then Mulayam finally laid the foundation of the Samajwadi Party by holding a Conference in Lucknow on November 4, 1992.

Beni Prasad Verma and Janeshwar Mishra, who had a stronghold in the Kurmi community in the State, were the second lead in the Samajwadi Party after Mulayam. Apart from the brief stay with the Congress for a few years, Beni Prasad Verma remained in politics with Mulayam continuously for 44 years at a time. There is one instance worth mentioning here. On the day of the party's Foundation on October 4, 1992, a crowd had gathered at Begum Hazrat Mahal Park. The party convention had begun. Beni

Prasad Verma was absent! It turned out that he was upset about something. Mulayam Singh left the Conference and approached him...and after some time, Vermaji was on the stage. After the formation of the party, Vermaji became the General Secretary of the organisation. The reason was that for the functioning of the organisation, he was to be given an ambassador car by the party, which was to be bought in the name of the party. Vermaji wanted it to be bought under his name. Eventually his word was accepted. Actually all the journalists who have covered Mulayam Singh Yadav or his party believe that the tact of keeping the supporters and all the people of the party connected together, Mulayam Singh has mastered, is rarely found in the leaders. Many leaders believe that one can learn from him how to meet the needs of one's leaders and Party workers.

Mulayam Singh is considered a shrewd player of politics. Obviously many gimmicks are tried. In the 1990s, Mulayam Singh, while sharing anecdotes from his wrestling era among some journalists in the capital, referred to a 'charkha daon'. After that, whenever Mulayam Singh made some unexpected political decisions, journalists would say with fun — "Mulayam ne 'charkha daon' chal diya".

Not only Beni Prasad Verma, many leaders of that period pinned high hopes on Mulayam Singh and his Samajwadi Party for non-Congress, non-BJP politics. Janeshwar Mishra, popularly known as Chhote Lohia, a seasoned and respected socialist leader, after the split in the Janata Dal, also chose the Samajwadi Party. Mulayam also kept many other socialists, including Bihar's socialist leader Raghu Thakur, associated with his Party. Ramsharan Das Gujar from Western Uttar Pradesh, Ramashankar Kaushik, Mohd. Azam Khan, Brij Bhushan Tiwari, Mohan Singh, Matashankar Pandey, Revathiraman Singh from eastern Uttar Pradesh, and many such leaders who once held prominent positions in the Janata Dal, all of them joined the Samajwadi Party. In fact, the kind of politics that Mulayam Singh was in favour of in the society, people got a glimpse of it only when he became the Chief Minister for the first time in the Janata Dal government in Uttar Pradesh. For example, as Chief Minister, he abolished the Octroi system on entering the limits of municipalities. In the 1990s, he advocated for the construction of toilets in villages. He argued that in villages women go to the roadside to defecate at night. They are embarrassed if the lights of the vehicles fall on them, so the focus of the government should be on improving the condition of the villages and the women there.

Post formation of the Samajwadi Party, in 1993 after becoming the Chief Minister again with the Bahujan Samaj Party (BSP) support, Mulayam gave the lease of land for farming to backward classes, poor upper castes, minorities, Dalits and ponds to fishermen. He furthered his Party's agenda by forming a Bhumi Sena to improve the condition of other lands lying vacant and make them cultivable. Thus the Samajwadi Party was successful in the coming years in filling the void created by the exit of the Congress in 1989.

With the implementation of the recommendations of the Mandal Commission, political consciousness and awakening among the backward classes and the stand taken by the Samajwadi Party on the Ayodhya issue in 1989, its status continued to rise. That was the period when he vigorously advocated constitutional and legal action in the Ayodhya case. This was the reason why the minorities, especially the Muslim community, accepted Mulayam Singh as their leader. This minority ditched the Congress in one stroke and sided with the Samajwadi Party. On the other hand, the backward classes also started seeing their future under the leadership of the Samajwadi Party and Mulayam. That is why as soon as the Bahujan Samaj Party and the Samajwadi Party came together in 1993, the graph of the BJP moving towards the heights of politics on the pretext of Hindutva and Ayodhya suffered a major setback. A loss which BJP could not amend till it brought the Backward Classes again in its fold in 2017.

In fact, since the formation of the Samajwadi Party, there have been two such turning points in its journey so far, where the party has derailed from its old ways, and for which the party had to pay a big price. First, a few years after the formation of the Samajwadi Party, there was the inclusion of Amar Singh, who had a great influence in the big corporate houses. A few days later, Mulayam Singh made him an MP (Rajya Sabha). From thereon Amar Singh's stature grew very fast in the party. By that time, the Samajwadi Party, which was known for the grassroots politics of the villages, poor, farmers, labourers and backward classes gradually began to be recognised as a pro-corporate political Party. Before Amar Singh's arrival in the party, the policy decisions that were taken after consultations with Janeshwar Mishra, Beni Prasad Verma, Azam Khan and other leaders, later Amar Singh alone was considered enough for them. It was absolutely so or not, but that was the message in the public and in the media. This trend continued and the rise of Amar Singh peaked when in 2003, Congress together with the other parties (though clandestinely) toppled the Mayawati-led Bahujan Samaj Party government running with the support of the BJP in Uttar Pradesh and Mulayam Singh Yadav once again became the Chief Minister of the State.

When Mulayam Singh became the Chief Minister for the third time in Uttar Pradesh, the functioning of the government proved to be different in many ways from the previous two governments of the Samajwadi Party. For example, the 'Uttar Pradesh Vikas Parishad' was formed in the name of development of Uttar Pradesh, Amar Singh being its whole-sole incharge. The Heads of well-known corporate houses of the country including industrialist Anil Ambani and film actor Amitabh Bachchan were its members. In the same government, Anil Ambani was given land taken away from farmers for the Reliance Power Project in Dadri, Noida. Opposition parties resisted it. The farmers were also not in favour of giving their land. Former Prime Minister V.P. Singh himself led the protests by reaching Dadri from Delhi several times. Later, due to controversies, matters came to a point that Anil Ambani had to withdraw from that project. On the other hand, film actor Raj Babbar, who came to the Samajwadi Party before Amar Singh, opened a front against Amar Singh. He was the first leader to raise his voice against Amar Singh in the party. He spoke to the media and questioned why Amar Singh was engaged in his own business through industrialists. He had no utility in the Samajwadi Party, yet why does Mulayam Singh assign so much importance to him, no one knows. In the years that followed, there were also leaders one after the other against the growing hegemony of Amar Singh in the party. It is another matter that the leaders who opposed Amar Singh were shown the way out of the party. In that episode, due to the exclusion or sidelining of leaders like Raj Babbar, Beni Prasad Verma, Azam Khan, a message was conveyed to the party that the only those would remain in the Samajwadi Party whom Amar Singh approved of. (Azam Khan was expelled from the party for 6 years in May 2009.)

Amar Singh also fully used his strong hold on the Samajwadi Party. He was a Rajya Sabha MP. The Samajwadi Party government was in Uttar Pradesh. Mulayam Singh was the Chief Minister. Various discussions (read criticism) were common regarding the functioning of government then. The top bureaucrats of the State were often seen entering Amar Singh's house in Delhi for some work. For the big officers of the districts of western Uttar Pradesh and important government bodies including Noida, Ghaziabad, this attendance had become a part of their job. It was the same period, when the Samajwadi Party was supporting the UPA government at the Centre led by Manmohan Singh on the one hand, and on the other, it had shown resentment against the same government and the Congress. Owing to this situation, a different message was going about the state government of the Samajwadi Party. It was also said that the Samajwadi Party, which had opened a front against the Congress, was taking a liberal stance towards the BJP. If this question was put to the Samajwadi Party, the answer would be that it had stopped the BJP in Uttar Pradesh. At that time (in 2004 the Samajwadi Party had contested 237 seats), there were three dozen Samajwadi MPs in the Lok Sabha. Well, the doubts of the people about the undeclared relationship between the Samajwadi Party and the BJP got stronger. In an election meeting in Uttar Pradesh, senior BJP leader Atal Bihari Vajpayee, while enumerating from the stage the shortcomings of the Congress, said that people should not vote for the Congress. However, if they wished, they could give it to the Samajwadi Party. After that, the situation of the party became so bad that in the 2007 State Assembly elections, the Samajwadi Party was thrown out of power ending the era of coalition governments that had been running in the State for almost 18 years, the Bahujan Samaj Party's full majority government came. Mayawati became the Chief Minister.

Since the formation of the Samajwadi Party, it has been the most important fact for it that in the last almost five decades, there has been no other leader in Uttar Pradesh like Mulayam Singh Yadav, who has truly remained with the masses, constantly struggling and fighting for them. Barring one or two occasions then, there were mostly the Congress Party governments at the Centre and in the State, and the leaders had nothing to struggle for. It is well known that if Mulayam Singh and his party were not in the government, they would be seen among the people and agitate on issues related to them. It was the effect of his belligerence and agitation among the people that in 2012 he got the Bahujan Samaj Party voted out which had made the government with an absolute majority in 2007 by winning 205 seats in the Uttar Pradesh Legislative Assembly, that is by winning 224 seats, even more than the Bahujan Samaj Party. At that time Amar Singh had also been expelled from the party. Even without him, this huge victory of the Samajwadi Party was considered very significant, because due to Amar Singh's exit from the party, it was assumed that the Samajwadi Party would not be able to get as much electoral donations from the corporate houses of the country, which it would have otherwise garnered. In a way, it was also a lesson for the party that if it has a strong foothold among the people, then money is not everything that matters in winning elections.

However, in 2012, the Samajwadi Party government was formed in Uttar Pradesh. At that time, Samajwadi Party Chief Mulayam Singh and the party's strong organisation had a leading role in the formation of the government, but there was also an important and different aspect of that victory. That was the politically unblemished face of Akhilesh Yadav, a strong advocate of clean politics on his part. The Samajwadi Party government in Uttar Pradesh in 2012 and Akhilesh Yadav becoming its Chief Minister can be called the second turning point of the party. Till then Akhilesh was a Party MP, but in 2012, when he took charge of the election campaign, there was hope among the people for a renewed Samajwadi Party. D.P. Yadav, the famous Bahubali of the State, had already been in the Samajwadi Party, yet in 2012, Akhilesh Yadav did not allow him a Party ticket for contesting elections. Despite being wanted by the leadership, he was adamant and finally he had his way. Just from there, a message went out to the people that whatever was already going on in the Samajwadi Party would not continue further. In fact, before that regarding the working style, the image of the Samajwadi Party was not very impressive. It was believed that the party also favoured people with criminal tendencies and background. The party provided them with political opportunities, so that they could be given a clean chit over time. In 2012, except for one or two big leaders, most of the party wished that Akhilesh Yadav should be the Chief Minister. Whereas, some big leaders were apprehensive and felt uncomfortable and insecure about working with Akhilesh when he became the Chief Minister. Nevertheless, keeping in mind the sentiments of most of the party's MLAs and leaders, Akhilesh Yadav was made the Chief Minister.

Akhilesh Yadav became the Chief Minister but all the decisions of the government were being taken by Mulayam Singh and his trusted ones. Also there were rumours that in those days Akhilesh was surrounded by an army of ministers and officers, who were creating difficulties rather than making the government's work smoother. Many ministers and bureaucrats also misused the opportunity of closeness with the then SP chief. Such leaders and officers functioned arbitrarily at some places, and the clean image of the government and Akhilesh Yadav was put at stake with their actions. During the tenure of the Akhilesh government, Amar Singh was not only brought back in the party, but indirectly he also became active on the old pattern. After that, problems were created for Akhilesh from within the family regarding the posting of favourite bureaucrats to special posts. Such activities were in a way damaging the organisation—namely Chief Minister and the political career of Akhilesh Yadav. At that time, Akhilesh Yadav, while being the Chief Minister, was also the State President of the Samajwadi Party.

But something unimaginable occurred in the party. What happened before the 2017 election is rarely seen in any major Party. The preparations for the election were on. Controversies arose regarding the selection of candidates. On behalf of Mulayam Singh Yadav, uncle Shivpal Yadav released the list of 325 candidates, forcing Akhilesh to release another list of 235 candidates. On December 30, 2016, in the course of the family feud for the struggle for supremacy and the strong intervention of Amar Singh, the party's National President Mulayam Singh Yadav expelled Akhilesh Yadav and Party General Secretary Prof. Ram Gopal Yadav from the party. Shivpal Yadav, who held a strong position in the state government, not only openly opposed Akhilesh, but people got to see the skirmish even on the public platform. It is another issue that later Akhilesh got his expulsion cancelled after the meeting. More than 200 MLAs of the party attended the meeting. On January 1, 2017, when the whole country celebrated the new year, Akhilesh called the National Convention of the party and removed his father Mulayam Singh Yadav from the post of Party President. In this Convention, he himself became the President and Naresh Chandra Uttam was made the President of the Uttar Pradesh unit. The first fortnight of January had been very strange for the party.

Shivpal Yadav later separated and formed his new party. Amidst the ever-increasing conflict within the Samajwadi Party, a new problem arose when the matter reached the Central Election Commission over the possession of its election symbol. However, by then it had become clear that more than 90 percent of the party's MPs, MLAs and office bearers of the Central and State organisations were supporting Akhilesh Yadav. Prof. Ram Gopal Yadav handled this in the party and the members on Akhilesh's side produced in writing to the Election Commission through an affidavit that they were all with the Samajwadi Party, which Akhilesh Yadav led. On January 16, 2017, the Election Commission's decision was made in favour of Akhilesh Yadav and since then he is the party's all-in-all. Soon Mulayam Singh Yadav was gracefully brought back to the party and he is now the Patron.

Well, in the family power struggle and Party organisation feud, Akhilesh Yadav won, but the 2017 Assembly elections stood as a tough challenge for him. In the last one-and-a-half years of his government, when he was supposed to reach the public and enumerate his achievements while preparing for the elections, he struggled with the troubles created by his family. It is also worth noting that the family feud was at its peak, some big and small bureaucrats were also fanning it indirectly. Even the officers of the Chief Minister's Secretariat themselves sometimes used to add fuel to those fights in such a way that Akhilesh Yadav's troubles would escalate. In fact, some bureaucrats and old Party leaders had created problems for Akhilesh Yadav within six months of his becoming the Chief Minister. The top leadership of the party, though it had the responsibility of keeping them all under control, was in a way ignoring them. At that time it was a common discussion that without the patronage from the High Command, no leader or officer could dare to hurt the pride of the Chief Minister. Between 2012 and 2017, this discord in the Samajwadi Party in Uttar Pradesh continued to bring trouble to the government, the organisation also weakened. As a result, the party lost the 2017 Assembly elections badly. The party, which won 224 seats in 2012, was reduced to around four dozen MLAs in 2017. This defeat was also an immense setback for Akhilesh Yadav because he had done much groundwork for the masses by moving away from the traditional working style of the Chief Ministers of the last several decades. Metro trains in many metros of Uttar Pradesh including Lucknow, Expressways from Agra to Lucknow and Lucknow to Ballia, Institute for Cancer Treatment in Lucknow, IT City, International Stadium, Medanta Hospital and land in Noida to the well-known IT Company Infosys, that Akhilesh could have profited out of these decisions but it did not happen. The party got so entangled in its own tussle that all these efforts proved to be futile in terms of electoral gains.

The Samajwadi Party, thus closely following its journey which fell from grace in three decades, is now once again struggling to gain a foothold. Its situation is comparatively better after the 2022 Assembly Election results. Akhilesh, the Chief, will have to reinvent its strategy. Analysts may claim that with 37.3 percent votes SP has strengthened its mass-base but its seat-share is a meagre 27.5 percent. BJP's seat-share is 63.3 percent which was 77.4 percent in the 2017 elections. Still the rule of 'First past the post' (the arrangement under which elections are held) a difference of a mere 2 percent translates into a great difference in the number of seats. There have been instances where parties having less vote percentage have been able to form a government. This is being considered as the Samajwadi Party's best show till date in general conditions. In 2012 when the Samajwadi Party formed the government it had only 29.15 percent votes. The number two Party was BSP with 25.91 percent votes. These two parties won 224 and 80 seats respectively. The election being a triangular one, the BJP had won 47 seats with 15 percent votes.

For the 2022 elections, Akhilesh had worked meticulously and formed an alliance with RLD, Om Prakash Rajbhar's party, Mahaan Dal et al. Simultaneously, he brought in many leaders including Swami Prasad Maurya, Dara Singh and Dharam Singh Saini to his fold, and had tried to prepare a huge canopy forging the Yadav-Muslim alliance. And because of this it was also 37.3 percent but the new vote bank of the beneficiaries shattered all the equations. It has been very clear that the vote percentage of BJP increases by five to six percent in the Lok Sabha elections. This happened in 2019 too. In the 2019 elections, the BJP alliance got 49.98 percent votes from UP, Mayawati's BSP had tied up with SP and BSP got 19.43 and SP got 18.11 percent votes. Congress got only one seat and 6.36 percent votes.

Now the question is what are the options Akhilesh is left with? Om Prakash Rajbhar's party is forced to leave Samajwadi khema and the same way Chacha Shiv Pal Yadav. They were literally asked to leave the alliance. The chances of joining hands with Mayawati are negligible and after getting hurt this badly, how far will the Congress compromise with its struggle to regain its ground? In the present situation, it is striving for this in all the states and its performance in the 2022 Assembly elections was abysmally poor and the vote percentage also dropped to 2.3. It has only a few options left. 1- Use its full might in all the states. 2- The states where it is in direct conflict with the BJP, mobilise all its resources and start working now on. This second situation leaves a few possibilities for Akhilesh. But it has been seen that the vote percentage of Congress stood at 19.5 percent at the national level. So will the Congress opt for a compromise? Leaving aside BSP, all fights will be against the sole enemy, i.e. BJP. Politics is a game of possibilities and probabilities. But it is certain that Akhilesh's

Samajwadi Party will have to be prepared to make a number of sacrifices, indulge in politics 24 x 7 and will have to start right now. (In the past Assembly elections he was accused of making a delayed start.)

The question remains whether Akhilesh is ready for this. He also has to see that his Muslim vote bank does not disintegrate. Nevertheless, it is undeniable that once Mulayam Singh Yadav, very diligently had raised the party to great heights; the party will have to work again from scratch to get it there once again. There is no dearth of people accusing the party leadership that it can reach the zenith only if it can keep all the party leaders together and does not confine itself to the family.

Will the party work in this direction? The answer ... again only the future can tell.

❑

6
BSP: Rise, Promises and Hopes

It is not uncommon in politics to announce the formation of a Party to represent and protect the interest of a section of society. But actually accomplishing it, with all possible machinations being used, is an entirely different game. There are not many examples in contemporary, post-independence Indian politics of this having happened.

This is the characteristic of the Bahujan Samaj Party (BSP) and if there was anyone behind this historic event in Indian politics, it was Kanshi Ram or Mayawati. (In fact, the story of BSP was initially associated with two stars - the first is Kanshi Ram and later Mayawati. That is why the names of these two stalwarts will repeatedly appear in this chapter.)

Kanshi Ram who later became famous as "Manyavar", was a Ramdasia Sikh from Ropar in Punjab who had a fire burning in him from his youth to fight the caste system that discriminated against people of his caste and many others. He worked in a government defence research laboratory in Pune where he faced discrimination based on caste and that made him an activist. He established a few organisations to fight against discrimination prevalent among government employees, among which BAMCEF, DS4 and BRC were prominent. This also marks the beginning of BSP.

Kanshi Ram very thoughtfully fought the battle of the Dalits. He knew that to sustainably fight a war, financial standing was a must. Also he was aware that a long war cannot be fought on an empty stomach. So he initiated his movement to strengthen the base among the government employees. In 1971, Kanshi Ram, D.K. Khaparde and Dinabhai founded the All India SC, ST, OBC and Minority Employees Association and in 1978 this became BAMCEF, or the All India Backward and Minority Communities Employees Federation. It pledged to fight the system of inequality that divides Indian society and to abolish the caste system. In his job, Kanshi Ram was able to influence lower-ranked staff and BAMCEF gave him the leverage to expand and strengthen his political activities.

The DS4 or Dalit Shoshit Samaj Sangharsh Samiti was also founded by Kanshi Ram in 1981 and starting from Punjab it spread to several states in north India including Haryana, Himachal Pradesh, and Uttar Pradesh. The Buddhist Research Centre, or BRC, was also established by Kanshi Ram in 1981, to propagate Buddhist teachings in order to present Buddhism as a viable alternative before Dalits.

Kanshi Ram dissolved the DS4 and BAMCEF when he founded the BSP in 1984. While the DS4 was kept alive as an independent organisation headed by Ishaan Singh Tomar, those remaining in BAMCEF registered it as an independent non-political organisation in 1987.

Separate identity

Kanshi Ram is known for Dalit power alone. He had formed the BSP to take forward what he called the ancient tradition of struggle against Brahmanism and the Brahmanical social order, broadly referred to as Manuvad. The ideals (and idols) of BSP were like Phuley, Shahu, Periyar and Ambedkar and many others who spent their lives fighting against the tyranny of the Brahmanical social order. The movement specifically told these communities to think about themselves as different and separate from Hindus.

It was in 1977 that Kanshi Ram spotted Mayawati, a fiery young woman from the family of the Dalit Jatav community of western Uttar Pradesh. She was born in a New Delhi hospital and her father Prabhu Das was an employee in a post office at Badalpur in present-day Gautam Buddha Nagar (Noida). She grew up studying in government schools and Kalindi College of Delhi University, completed her B.Ed. from a college in Ghaziabad and became a teacher in a school in Delhi. Her brother Anand Kumar worked as an assistant in the Noida authority office for a few years. She aspired to become an IAS officer, but she was destined for something bigger.

On the one hand, Kanshi Ram was strengthening his foothold among the employees and on the other hand, he was preparing to form the Bahujan Samajwadi Party. In 1984, though the country's electoral climate was quite different and almost one-sided after the assassination of Indira Gandhi, Kanshi Ram had already announced (April 14, 1984) his much-awaited political Party, the Bahujan Samaj Party, and gave Mayawati the chance of a lifetime and made her contest the election from the Kairana Lok Sabha seat of Western Uttar Pradesh. It was a warm-up election ... but victory was waiting for Mayawati. In 1989, she won the Lok Sabha seat from Bijnor in UP.

While Kanshi Ram was the ideological face of the BSP, it was Mayawati who went around the state, reminding the people of SCs, STs and OBCs that it was time they got a representative from amongst them to get "justice." She played strongly on the perceived feeling of injustice at the hands of the so-called upper castes, mainly targeting Brahmins and Kshatriyas, and coined colourful slogans like Tilak, Tarazu aur Talwar, inko maaro jootey chaar (Tilak, Tarazu, Talwar were indicative of Brahmins, Kshatriyas and Vaishya communities, and the people were exhorted to "beat them with shoes.")

She was also aggressive in criticising the religious practices of Hindus in general, and in public, she talked highly of Buddhism. She had said at the funeral of Kanshi Ram in 2006 that she and Kanshi Ram had been observing Buddhist traditions and customs. She has said on many occasions — as late as 2016 - that she would formally convert to Buddhism at the right time. Once she said she would do so "when the political conditions enable her to become the Prime Minister of India."

Kanshi Ram was undoubtedly the father of BSP, but the current form of today's BSP is undoubtedly Mayawati's contribution. The BSP's rise is in synchrony with that of Mayawati. She adopted a belligerent attitude towards the existing systems such as bureaucracy, legislature, executive, alleging that these were dominated by the upper castes, whom she referred to by a general umbrella term: Manuvadi. Her supporters often desecrated Hindu idols, raised anti-Hindu slogans and provoked Dalits against the Hindu community.

The misuse of the SC-ST Act (that aims to prevent and punish atrocities against the Dalits) was prevalent during the BSP rule in UP. It was common to come across cases when criminals were let off because they belonged to a particular caste, or people were prosecuted when they had a dispute with Dalits. Later, however, Mayawati did try to put a check on such misuse but by then the message had gone across that Dalits could not be treated with disdain any more. This strategy too paid her rich dividends as between the year 1995 and 2012, she remained the sole, undisputed leader of the SC and ST community, encompassing the Dalit castes.

Appealing belligerence

The belligerence appealed immensely to her constituents, who were simply and absolutely thrilled to see someone from among them, occupying the stage in full glory, unconcerned of her appearance, looks and language. She held out threats to everyone who had ever done wrong to this class, and warned of dire consequences to such acts of injustice once she assumed power.

The UP Assembly election was held in November 1993, a few months after the demolition of the disputed shrine in Ayodhya, the dismissal of the Kalyan Singh government and a bout of President's rule. The Samajwadi Party and BSP entered into a famous and unlikely alliance that most political observers of that time termed as path-breaking. It was for the first time that to stop the BJP from coming back to power, two parties claiming to represent the interests of the OBCs and Dalits, respectively, had come together in any major state. It was touted that it was going to be an unbeatable combination that would extinguish any chances of BJP's revival in UP. There were no clear winners. The BJP had won 177 seats, the SP-BSP alliance had won 176 (SP 109 and BSP 67), meaning that none had the numbers to form the government. Yet, thanks to Kanshi Ram's efforts, it was announced that the alliance would form the government with the arrangement that SP's Mulayam Singh Yadav would be the Chief Minister for the first two years and a half, followed by BSP's Mayawati for the second half of the five-year term. The political climate of UP was such at that time that no one doubted the sincerity of either Party in staying together against the BJP.

Mayawati kept up her belligerence at the BJP and the Congress alike, and maintained her part of the bargain with the SP. All this while, Kanshi Ram went around the state with his strident utterings against the upper castes, setting the tone for Dalit consolidation behind BSP. Mulayam, who had spurned an alliance with V.P. Singh's Janata Dal, sharpened his image as the sole well-wisher of the Muslim and Yadav communities. The SP-BSP combo had, thus, started acquiring an image of invincibility. It would have remained invincible if Mulayam and the Yadav community's inherent aggression especially against the SC community had not gained precedence over political expediency.

On the other hand, the politics at the Centre was on a different track. Mulayam Singh had rejected V.P. Singh's alliance with the Janata Dal, cementing his image as the sole well-wisher of the Muslim and Yadav communities. Thus the SP-BSP alliance began acquiring an image of invincibility. But the continuing aggression of the Yadav community, especially against the Scheduled Caste community, seemed overpowering and thus an 'seemingly invincible' alliance could not remain invincible.

The character of BSP has been full of unexpected twists and turns. It had been one and a half years since Mulayam Singh Yadav became the Chief Minister with the support of the BSP. Uttar Pradesh reeled under the heat spell of summer. On June 1, when Mulayam Singh held a meeting with his party office bearers in Lucknow just then a senior IAS officer P.L. Punia (today's Congress Rajya Sabha MP) suddenly appeared and gave a slip to Netaji (Mulayam Singh Yadav). Netaji's attitude changed instantly on reading the slip. He announced at the meeting that "you people should get ready for the elections." In the slip it was written that the BSP MLAs were about to withdraw support. Mulayam was surprised that Kanshi Ram had not given any such indication in the meeting held recently. Meanwhile, on the evening of June 2, Kanshi Ram and Party general secretary Mayawati were amidst a meeting at the VIP guest house, when some SP MLAs and Party workers, some of them with rifles, arrived there.

This rowdy group created a commotion and abducted them inside a room. The BSP leaders including Mayawati were abused, dragged and beaten up before they hid inside a room. This incident, known infamously as the 'Guest House case' changed the public perception of Mayawati and brought her close to the BJP. Incidentally, the leaders who came to Mayawati's rescue were Brahmins and other upper caste leaders of the BJP, such as Brahma Dutt Dwivedi and Lalji Tandon. On the night of June 2, 1995, the then Governor dismissed the SP-BSP government and invited Mayawati to take the oath as Chief Minister. She later proved her majority with the BJP support.

Proximity to BJP

The 'Guest House' incident led to an association between the BSP and BJP that helped Mayawati became Chief Minister thrice:

1. From June 3, 1995 to October 17, 1995 (BSP-BJP coalition)
2. From March 21, 1997 to September 21, 1997 (BSP-BJP coalition)
3. From May 3, 2002 to August 28, 2003 (BSP-BJP coalition)

Mayawati, and before that even Kanshi Ram, used to say famously that they did not want a strong government: "We want a majboor (helpless) government and not a majboot (strong) government until we form a government on our own" and this did happen when Mayawati formed a majority BSP government that lasted its full term from May 13, 2007 to March 14, 2012 - the first majority, single-party full-term government in several decades. The gambit of forming shaky governments with other parties, and letting them collapse after some time was a calculated gambit. The BSP was always the winner in the end. This happened repeatedly with the BJP and the 2007-2012 BSP government was actually made at the expense of the BJP.

Incidentally, Mayawati also never fulfilled her promise of converting to Buddhism as she did not want the Hindu Dalits to leave her fold.

Tough and aggressive

As Chief Minister, Mayawati always adopted a tough and aggressive stance in public and official situations. It is famously quoted that she never asked any officer or minister to sit when they visited her. It is also said, although not confirmed by anyone, that visitors were asked to remove their footwear outside the door and on occasions they were asked to sit on the floor. Her stance and demeanour were nearly regal, with matching gestures and speech.

After the Guest House incident, her attitude towards the SP, Mulayam Singh Yadav and his family members became hard and extremely tough. In public addresses she ridiculed Mulayam and referred to him as a gunda or hoodlum and worse. Her approach towards officers, especially those belonging to other castes, was especially noteworthy. She never referred to any one of them as aap. When visiting districts on her review meetings, she would give the officers a dressing down and suspend them on the spot. While this was resented by the bureaucracy, the assembled crowd of villagers, especially Dalits, were overjoyed. The one common feeling among such people was that there was at least someone from their midst (and caste) who had the guts to intimidate officers and show them their place.

Her aggressive attitude towards corporate houses, foreign companies and corporate political donations had led to many deadlocks in UP over the years. She famously banned the opening of stores of a nationwide chain of retail stores in Lucknow, leading to a walkout by this company. She also openly admitted that she urged all party members, leaders, supporters and admirers to donate money to the party since she did not accept any corporate donations. She flaunted the gifts of gold, precious stones etc. that were given to her by supporters, and also justified huge garlands made of currency notes and a multi-storeyed cake on her birthday on the same grounds.

The way Mayawati became conscious of her look later, has a different story behind it too. A Delhi-based sociologist believed that the more attractive her appearance was, the more likely there would be the expansion of the party. The women folk of her followers would love her all the more when she looked attractive. After coming to power for the first time, she became very cautious in this matter. Mayawati, who previously tied her hair back with a cotton scrunchie, very soon started wearing a diamond necklace around her neck. She had also cut her hair short citing the reason as this was more convenient and time saving. In the same way, she shared beauty secrets with female journalists too. She used to drink less water in public and often gave this advice - don't drink water, drink coconut water, the skin remains good. In general these things should not make any difference to the party and its performance, but her advisors believed that the more you appear elite and speak for the cause of the poor and downtrodden, the more popular you will be.

This also led to allegations that she accepted money for giving party tickets for all elections. While nothing has been heard officially on this, it is accepted in the party that those wishing to contest the election are supposed to manage their expenditure themselves as the party does not give any financial assistance for this purpose.

The BSP rule is often remembered for a tough stance against criminals and lawlessness. It is mainly because the party aimed more at the welfare and benefit of the Dalits rather than the persecution of others. In meeting this objective, action was taken against criminals who usually targeted Dalits and other weaker castes. Since this was more prevalent across the state, an environment of the BSP government being tough against criminals was created. Otherwise, there is also a history of criminals flourishing in the BSP regime.

Forays outside UP

All this while, officers, employees and police officers of the Dalit community continued to consolidate under BSP and Mayawati, making her hold stronger in the State.

The period between 2007 and 2012 was especially fruitful for the BSP. Not only did the party run a majority government in UP, it also strengthened itself elsewhere. In the 2004 Maharashtra Assembly elections, BSP had contested 272 of the 288 seats in Maharashtra, securing 4.18 percent vote share. In 2009 it contested 287 seats and managed to increase its vote share to 8 percent.

In 2009, it not only ruined the chances of some candidates, but also facilitated the victory of some Shiv Sena-BJP candidates by splitting the Dalit vote. However, BSP MLAs in Rajasthan and Madhya Pradesh did not show the same loyalty to Mayawati as they did in UP. This is the reason why defection between BSP MLAs has been common in these two states.

In the various monuments her government created in UP, statues of Maharashtra's Dalit icons like Jyotiba Phule and Shahuji Maharaj, besides Ambedkar, Kanshi Ram and herself figure prominently.

Another idea that emerged officially for the first time in her government was that of the division of Uttar Pradesh. Again in 2011, when the Mayawati government was nearing the end of its tenure, her government formally approved the move to divide the state into four units. It was a time when the government was beleaguered by anti-incumbency and sundry charges of corruption and misgovernance, and she stood to lose nothing by proposing the division. The Cabinet tabled a resolution in the Assembly session for the division of Uttar Pradesh into four small states of Harit Pradesh (western UP), Avadh Pradesh (central UP), Bundelkhand (south-western UP) and Purvanchal (eastern UP).

Operation clean-up

Another aspect for which the BSP is often remembered is the clean-up in the party that Mayawati undertook every time she formed the government. It was most remarkable in the 2007-2012 period which also saw the sensational scam and murders of three officers in the health department. By the end of 2011, Mayawati had shown the door to a dozen tainted party members, including an MP, MLAs, MLCs and office bearers. She also directed zonal coordinators, district Presidents, in-charge of Lok Sabha and Vidhan Sabha constituencies to identify members who had indulged in nefarious activities and prepare a report.

The politicians against whom action was taken included MPs and MLAs such as Dhananjay Singh - MP from Jaunpur, Ashok Kumar Chandel - MLA from Hamirpur Sadar constituency, who had criminal cases pending against them. Among other Thakur politicians who had been sidelined by the BSP are Jitendra Singh Babloo from Bikapur in Faizabad, Chandra Bhadra (Sonu) Singh from Isauli in Sultanpur, and Sher Bahadur Singh, BSP MLA from Jalalpur in Ambedkar Nagar.

Distrust of Thakurs

The BSP never put Thakurs close to its core, and its distrust of Thakurs goes back to 1997 when the party had split to save the Kalyan Singh government after the BSP pulled out of the coalition. At that time, of the 22 BSP MLAs who had walked out, 18 were Thakurs. Later in 2002, the two legislators who were arrested for plotting to topple the Mayawati government — Raja Bhaiyya and Dhananjay Singh — were also both Thakurs. It is also believed that by distancing her party from Thakurs, Mayawati always tried to mend fences with Brahmins who had been instrumental in bringing the community's electoral support to the BSP.

At the same time, the party went out of the way to keep Brahmins close. It was quite a contradiction since the party and Kanshi Ram in particular, always targeted Brahmins and the Brahmanical social order for the plight of Dalits. However, the formation of Dalit-Brahmin bhaichara (brotherhood) committees clearly indicated that Mayawati intended to create a wedge among the so-called upper caste monolith of the Hindu community and keep at least the Brahmins close in order to acquire power.

Satish Chandra Mishra, a noted lawyer and son of an illustrious judge T.S. Mishra, was among the earliest Brahmin leaders to have gravitated towards the BSP in the late 1990s. In a surprise move, he was made the party's General Secretary in 2004 and since then, he has remained probably the only confidante of Mayawati since the formative years of the BSP. He has been instrumental in voicing the BSP's views in the Rajya Sabha, as a lawyer in the Supreme Court, and as a spokesman and political strategist for BSP all these years. He can also be given credit for keeping at least one section of the Brahmin community close to the BSP.

No second line

Mayawati is known for her distrust of people in the party. No one in the party can claim to be close to her, and all office bearers enjoy their positions exclusively at Mayawati's discretion. Her distrust of senior leaders is also well known and that shows in the fact that none of the original leaders in the BSP dating back to 1993 are now with the party. Some of these are Raj Bahadur, R.K. Chaudhary, Swami Prasad Maurya, Naseemuddin Siddiqi, Brajesh Pathak, Haji Yakub Qureshi, Lalji Verma, Ram Achal Rajbhar and many more MLAs.

The UP unit of the party has also remained on tenterhooks since the beginning, and no state President has survived for more than a year. Apparently, as soon as any BSP leader strengthens himself or gets rooted, he is either shunted out or expelled on the charges of "anti-Party activities."

The absence of a second line of leadership has been a source of strength for Mayawati in that it enables her to make decisions as she pleases, without the need to consult any core group. For state-wide party organisations too, the zonal coordinators are changed frequently. One set of coordinators is put on the job of reporting on the activities of the other set and so on, and such reports form the basis of political and inner party decisions made by Mayawati.

Until recently, no one was authorised to represent the party before the media and her press conferences were always an occasion for her to read out a prepared statement and then walk away. Only for 2022 elections, she nominated a panel of spokespersons but this soon dissolved.

One-Upmanship

Whenever Mayawati has been out of power in Lucknow, she does not remain a member of the UP legislature. It is believed that she does not want to be a part of the House where she is not the leader. She has never accepted the role of the Leader of the Opposition in the State, and never been a member of the House as a mere legislator. She always got herself nominated to the Rajya Sabha when her Party lost in UP.

As Chief Minister, she never attended meetings of Chief Ministers called by the Prime Minister, whether it was Atal Behari Vajpayee or Manmohan Singh. She always used to send a Minister as her representative.

Such actions on her part have been largely welcomed by her core constituents, who feel a strong sense of pride that Behen Mayawati is never seen as subservient to anyone. She never went to airports to offer a traditional welcome to any Prime Minister. Her cosying up to the BJP in the past few years is also seen as a move to set her apart from other opposition leaders. It is understood that by getting herself photographed with other opposition leaders, she does not wish to lose her identity.. Her stand on Kashmir, Covid management and security matters have often coincided with that of the Centre. But this has been explained as a sign of her maturity as a national leader, rather than a clever ploy to keep all options open for the future.

What does the future hold?

There have also been allegations against Mayawati, sometimes for changing sides and sometimes not being able to handle her core voters. In the Lok Sabha elections in 2014, the BSP had fought it alone, while the SP and Congress had entered into a highly publicised alliance. In the 2017 Assembly election, the BSP went alone, while in the 2019 Lok Sabha election, the BSP and SP came together, putting aside all differences. The alliances did no good to either SP, BSP or Congress, as the BJP rode high on the crest of popularity fuelled by polarisation. The SP-BSP kept accusing each other of not being able to get their votes transferred to their candidates. The BJP has also apparently cooked up a formula of integration of upper castes along with the Most Backward Class and Dalits that has not been cracked by either party so far. In fact, the BJP gradually made a major dent in the vote bank of the Dalits and now it seems that apart from the Jatav vote bank of the Dalits, the BJP has also attracted a large group of other Dalits. But BSP's tryst with Brahmans did not work well in the 2022 elections. Rather, BJP improved upon its vote share of 2017.

BSP's recent proximity with BJP is known to all. Is this only proximity or pressure-politics can be a point of discussion. But the manner in which Mayawati in her electoral speeches during elections had avoided being harsh or aggressive towards the BJP such allegations are obvious. She has always portrayed SP as its adversary number one and also got a few votes transferred to the BJP on some seats but the fact remains that leaving the Jatav vote bank she could not keep votes of the Scheduled Castes with it. Similarly the Muslim vote bank did not pose any trust in her. It is said the backward class among Muslims has been supporting her but in these elections this class also chose SP over BSP. Mayawati's vote percentage in 2022 is reduced by at least 10 percent as compared to 2017. Does this mean Mayawati's Jatav vote Bank (around 14 percent) stands converted to the beneficiary bank? Mayawati's BSP has lost 17 seats this time compared to 2017, i.e. won only one seat. This is BSP's worst ever tally.

It is also true that the party's basic structure is shattered. Its original vote bank could not understand or digest its equation with the Brahmin caste. One must remember that this proximity with the Brahmin caste led to the party's victory in 2007 with 30 percent votes enabling it to form a government. After 15 years its vote percentage has reduced to a mere 12.9 percent. Mayawati's speeches might have damaged the chances of the SP but have surely benefited the BJP. One of her statements that 'If SP returns to power, Jungle Raj will again flourish in UP' affected the SP adversely but the BJP emerged the winner out of it.

There was a time in the early 2000s that Mayawati was named to be India's most promising politician, a true face of the Indian masses, a rags to riches story, and predicted to be India's Prime Minister one day. With her party's defeat in 2012 and subsequent electoral setbacks in 2014, 2017 , 2019 and the biggest in 2022, her image has taken a beating. At the same time, BSP is not seen in the race for power. In the BSP, not only have scores of leaders left the party, Mayawati herself was pushed into a corner over her failure to keep her flock of Dalit vote bank together.

❑

7
RLD: In the Throes of Political Mistakes

September 2012 was the month. The whole of western Uttar Pradesh witnessed the ongoing violent conflict between the Jats and Muslims. In West UP, a Muslim youth was killed in a case of molestation of a Jat girl in Kawal village of Jat-dominated District Muzaffarnagar and then two Jat youths were brutally killed in retaliation. After a fake video went viral on social media, there was a spurt of violence that created tension in Muzaffarnagar, Shamli, Baghpat and Meerut districts of West UP. As per official data more than 65 people lost their lives in Muzaffarnagar district alone in the conflict between the Jats and Muslims. However, if eyewitnesses are to be believed, the death toll was much higher. Muslims started migrating out of villages in Muzaffarnagar district and the district made headlines in the media across the country. A journalist was also killed in the riots in Muzaffarnagar and the then PM Manmohan Singh along with Congress President Sonia Gandhi visited the place. It was a rare moment. The developments, which began in the last week of August, continued to impact till September.

In the midst of all this, Chaudhary Ajit Singh, the then President of the Rashtriya Lok Dal, considered to be the main party of Jats and farmers in western Uttar Pradesh, was under tremendous pressure. Because only the Jats and Muslims were the casualties in this violent play of hatred. Ajit Singh faced a tremendous challenge as to what he should do. Akhilesh Yadav was in power in the State and was accused of lobbying with the Muslim side at the behest of his Cabinet Minister and veteran Muslim leader Azam Khan. And not only were all the youths from the Muslim side released but also the DM of Muzaffarnagar Surendra Singh and SSP Manzil Saini, who took proper action in the matter, were transferred overnight. This caused a furor among the Jats. The Jats were hopeful that Ajit Singh would definitely come to console them and to wipe away their tears. He was then the Civil Aviation Minister at the Centre. The Jats were positive about him raising his voice in their support and that he would certainly visit Kawal village to meet the victim Jat family. But Ajit Singh did not visit even once. His son and former Mathura MP Jayant Chaudhary made a formal attempt to go to Muzaffarnagar but was stopped by the police before he could reach Meerut. The incident broke the equation of Jat and Muslim votes of the Rashtriya Lok Dal in West UP, which ran since the times of the former Prime Minister and the father figure of RALOD Chaudhary Charan Singh. Ajit Singh could neither make the Jats nor Muslims his own during the Muzaffarnagar riots.

Two years later, in the 2014 Lok Sabha elections, Chaudhary Ajit Singh lost his traditional Lok Sabha seat, Baghpat, and his son Jayant Chaudhary lost his Mathura Lok Sabha seat. This time both had contested as UPA candidates. In the 2009 Lok Sabha elections, RALOD contested in alliance with BJP and won five Lok Sabha seats in West UP and had his best performance till date. Earlier, Ajit Singh used to be the only MP of his party. Ajit was defeated by former Mumbai Police Commissioner BJP candidate Dr Satyapal Singh in 2014 and Jayant's candidature could not withstand the aura of dream girl Hema Malini.

The Muzaffarnagar riots did not prove a setback only for the Rashtriya Lok Dal, but it changed the course of politics across the State. Politically, Muslims chose the Samajwadi Party and the

Jats voted on priority for BJP. In the 2017 ministerial elections, the Rashtriya Lok Dal got mitigated and the BJP ousted Akhilesh Yadav's government from power, claiming a huge majority to form the government in the State.

Two years later, the 2019 Lok Sabha elections were to be held. These elections were very challenging for RALOD. Earlier, Ajit Singh had never been out of the corridors of Parliament for five years. He lost in Baghpat for the first time in 1998 when he was defeated by BJP's Jat candidate Sompal Shastri. Sompal Shastri was also rewarded and given the Agriculture Ministry in Atal Bihari Vajpayee's government. Sompal Shastri's father the late Raghubir Singh Shastri was an MP from Baghpat in the fourth Lok Sabha and was close to Chaudhary Charan Singh. The 1998 defeat was the first blow to Ajit Singh. He had not faced defeat since he became active in politics in 1984. Ajit Singh's defeat was also going to hurt the Jats of Baghpat district. The Jats were dismayed that they defeated the only Jat leader in UP, but only a year later, the opportunity knocked when Atal Bihari Vajpayee's government fell and mid-term elections were held in 1999. Ajit Singh defeated Sompal Shastri by 1.5 lakh votes in this election. Then he continued to win all the Lok Sabha elections till 2014 and remained a celebrated leader of the Jats in UP.

In the 2002 ministerial elections also, RLD contested in alliance with BJP but when found opportune, he deserted the BJP and joined hands with Mulayam Singh Yadav. From August 2003 to May 2007, the Coalition Government of SP and RLD led by Mulayam Singh Yadav gave RALOD a chance to get six Ministers. In UP politics, the period from 2003 to 2009 can be termed as the golden period for RALOD. It had the highest number of MLAs and the highest number of Lok Sabha MPs during this period. Despite dodging the BJP in 2003, the saffron party once again extended a hand of friendship to Ajit Singh, considering him a powerful leader of the Jats in West UP. In 2009, RLD and BJP again contested the Lok Sabha elections in alliance. BJP gave him seven seats in UP out of which RALOD succeeded in winning five

(Baghpat, Mathura, Hathras, Bijnor, Amroha). These were good indications for RALOD. Ajit Singh also fielded his son Jayant Chaudhary for the first time in the same Lok Sabha elections and marched him to Parliament from the Mathura seat.

Ajit Singh made a similar mistake earlier after the 2009 general elections 2009 that he committed during the 2012 Muzaffarnagar riots . In 2009, the UPA-II government was formed at the Centre and Manmohan Singh became the Prime Minister again. The representation of western Uttar Pradesh in this government was absolutely zero. The West UP region, adjacent to the capital Delhi which Ajit Singh represented, has always been closely under the eyes of all central governments. Ajit Singh also got a chance to become Agriculture Minister in Atal Bihari Vajpayee's government from 2001 to 2003. About 8 years later, he was invited to join the Central Government again. Ajit Singh had been away from power at the centre for 8 long years and when he got a chance to join the UPA-2 government, he seized the opportunity with both hands. Manmohan Singh made him Civil Aviation Minister in December 2011. He held the post till May 2014. After winning the highest number of 5 Lok Sabha seats by contesting with BJP in 2009, Ajit Singh's change of mind proved to be his major political blunder. Three years later, during the 2012 Assembly elections, Ajit Singh once again tried to make amends with the BJP, but the BJP distanced itself from him in view of his previous track of fickle-mindedness. Ajit Singh had to face the loss. Since the break-up with the BJP in 2011, RALOD seems to be struggling for its survival in western Uttar Pradesh. In the 2017 State elections in UP, RALOD was pushed to zero. His only MLA from Baghpat district had also joined the BJP.

The Anuradha Chaudhary period

From 2002 to 2009, there was a time when Ajit Singh as well as Anuradha Chaudhary had a significant role in RALOD. Anuradha Chaudhary, the younger sister of Kiran Chaudhary, who was a

Minister in the Congress government in Haryana, joined the BJP in the late 90s and entered the politics of Muzaffarnagar. She could not stay in the party for long as that was the struggling period of the BJP. In 2002, on a RLD ticket, she was elected as MLA from Baghra Vidhan Sabha seat in Muzaffarnagar district and Ajit Singh managed for her an important department like PWD under Mulayam Singh Yadav's government. Before coming to RALOD, being the sister of Kiran Chaudhary, wife of Surendra, son of former Haryana CM Bansilal, was Anuradha Chaudhary's only introduction. But Anuradha Chaudhary, a very ambitious and electoral management expert, made a big mark in a small party like RALOD. Anuradha Chaudhary, who became MLA from Baghra, had been there for only two years. She expressed her desire to contest the Lok Sabha elections despite a meaty department like PWD in hand. By then, the Dostana of the RLD and the Samajwadi Party had become so strong that both had decided to contest the Lok Sabha elections in an alliance. Anuradha Chaudhary decided to contest from Kairana Lok Sabha seat. Ajit Singh cut off the ticket of sitting MP Amir Alam Khan of RALOD from Kairana and fielded Anuradha Chaudhary as the candidate. Angered by this, Amir Alam Khan also joined the Samajwadi Party. But it didn't matter then. Anuradha Chaudhary had a resounding victory over Kairana and was considered to be at number two position in RALOD only after Ajit Singh. In west UP's most talked about Lok Sabha seat, there was an equation of Muslim and Jat votes, which led to Amir Alam Khan and then Anuradha Chaudhary becoming MPs. Ajit Singh is said to have reaped benefits from the Jat-Muslim equation in Kairana and Muzaffarnagar seats for the Baghpat Lok Sabha seat bordering on these two districts.

Till 2009, there was a period in which it seemed that the reins of RALOD had slipped out of Ajit Singh's hand and went to Anuradha Chaudhary. When Anuradha Chaudhary became an MP, there was a by-election to the Baghra seat and Anuradha proved that she had no match in electoral management by getting her confidant Paramjit Malik elected. At that time, it was also said that Anuradha Chaudhary tutored RALOD in the art of winning elections. On her advice, tickets were also being finalised. Anuradha Chaudhary's growing stature can be gauged from the way she retained the status of Cabinet Minister in Mulayam Singh Yadav's government while she was an MP from Kairana. She continued to be the Chairperson of the Irrigation and Flood Control Commission and continued to run RALOD in her own way.

Before the 2009 Lok Sabha elections, Anuradha Chaudhary expressed her desire to contest from the Muzaffarnagar Lok Sabha seat instead of Kairana and Ajit Singh obviously acceded to it. RALOD, who was in alliance with the BJP and Anuradha were confident that they would register a landslide victory. She faced the BSP's candidate Qadir Rana. Anuradha Chaudhary also held a public meeting of the then Gujarat Chief Minister Narendra Modi at the SD Inter College ground in Muzaffarnagar a few days before the polls to make the election Hindu-Muslim and polarise the votes. Modi was considered to be the hardcore Hindutva face of the saffron party at that time. Anuradha felt that this would polarise the Hindu votes. But she forgot that Sangeet Som as Thakur representative on the Samajwadi Party ticket and veteran Jat leader Harendra Malik as Congress candidate were also contesting. Cent percent polarization of Muslim votes occurred in favour of Qadir Rana. Qadir got 275318 votes while Anuradha Chaudhary got 254720, Sangeet Som 106667 and Harendra Malik got 73848, thus Anuradha flopped. The 2009 election was the most spectacular election for RALOD. In seven Lok Sabha seats, it contested in alliance with the BJP and managed to make five MPs but a prominent leader like Anuradha Chaudhary lost. The huge split between Thakur and Jat votes put an end to Anuradha Chaudhary's desire to become an MP again. And this was the time when Anuradha Chaudhary's aura in RALOD began to fade.

Command returned to family

It is said that no woman can bear the interference of another woman in the family. In 2009, Ajit Singh's son Jayant Chaudhary contested for the first time from Mathura, he tasted victory and the situation in RALOD began to change. Jayant's wife Charu Chaudhary also kept an eye on the party's activities. A former RLD MLA says that after becoming a mother of two daughters, Charu also began to feel insecure. Ajit Singh was getting older and Jayant as well as Charu started indulging in the party matters. Jayant could not ignore Charu's choices. Charu was the daughter of a banker friend of Ajit Singh while Jayant and Charu were childhood friends when Ajit was working as an engineer in the US before entering politics. Close friends had grown up to become life partners. People close to Ajit's family say Anuradha Chaudhary and Charu also clashed over some issues a few months before the 2012 Assembly elections. Jayant made it clear to Ajit that this time he would himself finalise the tickets. Chhote Chaudhary was helpless before his son and daughter-in-law and Anuradha Chaudhary was left in a state of shock. A few months before the 2012 Assembly elections, Anuradha Chaudhary suddenly joined the Samajwadi Party and was made General Secretary of the party by Mulayam Singh Yadav. In 2012, the Samajwadi Party made a spectacular comeback and Akhilesh Yadav became the Chief Minister. Akhilesh also gave Anuradha Chaudhary the status of Minister of State a few months before the 2014 Lok Sabha elections. Anuradha Chaudhary also wanted to contest from Bijnor or Muzaffarnagar Lok Sabha seat but Amir Alam Khan, who had left RALOD and joined Samajwadi Party, pressured Akhilesh through Azam Khan and did not allow her ticket from anywhere. Alam thus, after ten years avenged his denial of the ticket from Kairana in 2004 that was handed to Anuradha. There was a Modi wave in the 2014 Lok Sabha elections and in UP no one but only the Yadav family in the Samajwadi Party succeeded. Angered by the defeat, Akhilesh also withdrew the status of Minister of

State from Anuradha Chaudhary. He felt that Anuradha among the Jats had not proved to be as useful to him as he was hoping for. Anuradha Chaudhary then joined the BJP during the Delhi Assembly Elections in 2015. Satyapal Malik (former Governor of Jammu and Kashmir) conspired against Anuradha Chaudhary in BJP in such a manner that she neither got any post in the party nor ticket from anywhere. Thus, the career of Anuradha Chaudhary, who became the biggest leader after Chaudhary Charan Singh and Chaudhary Ajit Singh in RALOD, faded.

Chaudhary Charan Singh's legacy

In fact, the Rashtriya Lok Dal, which we are currently referring to, was established in the 90s. Chaudhary Ajit Singh formed RALOD after parting ways with V.P. Singh's Janata Dal, just as Mulayam Singh Yadav formed the Samajwadi Party. As a matter of fact, the foundation of this political party of Jats and farmers of western Uttar Pradesh, which has waned several times, was laid way back in the 60s by Chaudhary Charan Singh, the fifth Prime Minister of the country. Chaudhary Charan Singh used to be a member of the Congress Party earlier. From April 3, 1967 to February 25, 1968 and then from February 18, 1970 to October 9, 1970, Chaudhary Charan Singh twice got a chance to become the Chief Minister of Uttar Pradesh. Charan Singh formed the BKD (Bharatiya Kranti Dal) in Lucknow in October 1967 which was later merged with the Janata Party during the first general election since the Emergency in 1977. In 1974, Chaudhary Charan Singh launched a campaign against Indira Gandhi in which he was joined by small parties like the Swatantra Party, Utkal Congress, Socialist Party, National Democratic Party and Kisan Mazdoor Party. All of them pooled together to form the Bharatiya Lok Dal, led by Chaudhary Charan Singh. Earlier, Charan Singh's BKD had staged a strong performance in the 1969 Vidhan Sabha Elections. BKD candidates had won all the Vidhan Sabha seats in the Jat dominated district of Muzaffarnagar, a record that no one could repeat. The Congress had formed the government by securing 211 seats in UP but BKD made its mark as the largest opposition party by winning 98 seats. It was because of this spectacular success in UP that Charan Singh's stature began to shine in the politics of the country. In the 1974 Vidhan Sabha Elections, the BKD raised this figure to 106. After this performance, Charan Singh's acceptance among non-Congress parties increased and he also became the leader of the Indian Lok Dal formed by merging smaller parties.

In fact, in the early 70s, Chaudhary Charan Singh played a pivotal role in the political equations against Indira Gandhi. It started with the Bharatiya Lok Dal. Chaudhary Charan Singh was the mastermind of the Janata Party when it was formed a few months before the general elections were held in 1977 after the Emergency. Since 1974 he had been engaged in an endeavour to unite the opposition against Indira Gandhi. Charan Singh was among the leaders who went to jail during the Emergency. Chaudhary Charan Singh was once the face of opposition parties for the post of PM and leaders like Rajnarayan were very close to him. But when the Janata Party won, Jayaprakash Narayan and Acharya Kripalani were entrusted with the responsibility of deciding the name for the post of PM. Both of them elected Morarji Desai as PM with Chaudhary Charan Singh as Home Minister. Within a year, differences surfaced, Charan Singh and Morarji Desai had to resign but within a year Charan Singh bounced back as Deputy Prime Minister. There was a revolt within the Janata Party against Morarji Desai and Chaudhary Charan Singh was sworn in as the Prime Minister on July 28, 1979. Indira Gandhi's Congress (I) promised outside support to Charan Singh. Yashwant Rao Chavan of the Congress (S) became Deputy PM but Indira Gandhi announced withdrawal of support just at the time of proving the majority of Charan Singh's government. Charan Singh's brief tenure as PM ended on August 20, 1979. But his name got etched in history as he got an opportunity to hoist the Tricolour at the coveted Red Fort.

Chaudhary Charan Singh is remembered for many major administrative reforms. Charan Singh was also associated with Mahatma Gandhi from the Movement of Independence. Charan Singh also played a major role in the Interim Governments formed before Independence and is remembered for a number of reformative measures. In 1934, he became an MLA from the Chhaprauli Vidhan Sabha seat in Meerut district (now part of Baghpat district of West UP) and from there his political legacy began in Baghpat district. He also went to jail several times during the British era. When Pandit Jawaharlal Nehru wanted to introduce a cooperative system in agriculture in India as in the Soviet-style economic reforms, Chaudhary Charan Singh strongly opposed it. He had argued that when the farmer of India is not able to manage his own sons, how would he handle cooperative farming? This enabled him to make a mark in national politics.

In the 50s, when Charan Singh was the Revenue Minister in Gobind Ballabh Pant's government in UP, he introduced many major agricultural reforms. Chaudhary Charan Singh will always be remembered for the abolition of the Zamindari system. PM Nehru did not support the idea of abolition of the Zamindari system. Charan Singh went to Delhi and explained the whole calculation behind it to Nehru to which he eventually agreed. This ensured the farmers' ownership rights over their lands. It is said that after the end of this practice, when the farmers got the lands registered in their names, the State got a huge amount in the shape of revenue. The money was spent in Uttar Pradesh mainly on construction of roads. Later, many states of the country adopted this model. Earlier, the condition of roads in UP was pathetic. Charan Singh is also credited for eliminating Patwari Raj. He made everyone an accountant (Lekhpal) and took many initiatives to eradicate corruption. Not only that, the police stations in the State did not have any provision of four wheelers. It is said that Chaudhary Charan Singh had bought the jeeps and given them to the police department. Charan Singh's great strength was his concerns about the well-being and upliftment of farmers all the time. It is said that once he was passing through Connaught Place in his car, his car stopped at a red light. He peered out of the window and told his driver that a village could be illuminated as much as the electricity being spent at a crossing here. Charan Singh in the shape of the Lok Dal handed over a golden legacy to the next generation which will always be remembered.

The struggle to save the glorious heritage

After the death of Ajit Singh from Corona on May 6, 2021, the Rashtriya Lok Dal faced a big challenge to save the golden legacy of Charan Singh. It is now dominated by Jayant Chaudhary, grandson of the former PM. Jayant is now the National President of RALOD. Though handing over the reins to Jayant was already doing the rounds within the party even before the 2019 Lok Sabha elections, Ajit Singh had something else in his mind. He was deeply disturbed by Jayant's and his own defeat during the 2014 elections. Ajit Singh wanted to revive the Jat-Muslim vote equation that was there since Chaudhary Charan Singh's time in West UP, which was shattered after the Muzaffarnagar riots. He also wanted an official transfer of heritage by handing over the traditional seat of Baghpat to his son. Jayant also believed that the second line had never been prepared in the party so he became the National Vice President of the party in 2019 while Ajit Singh remained the President. In 2019, Ajit Singh decided to contest the Lok Sabha elections from Muzaffarnagar to correct the equations worsened by the Muzaffarnagar riots and called his son from Mathura to Baghpat. He aspired to win both the seats. No other party has fielded its candidates in these two seats in this election. Ajit and Jayant, in a way, became joint candidates of RLD, SP, BSP and Congress. Despite this, both of them lost. In Muzaffarnagar, Ajit Singh lost by a narrow margin of 5,000 votes.

Jayant Chaudhary, who took over the reins of the party after his father's death, believes that the 2019 Lok Sabha elections were eye-openers and taught RALOD to prepare itself for a big struggle again. Joining the months-long farmers' movement on Delhi's borders, Jayant Chaudhary has launched a campaign to strengthen his roots in West UP.

The stance of joining hands with the Kisaan Andolan worked well for Chaudhary Jayant Singh. The 2022 election results proved to be an immense cheer for him. Though under the Alliance agreement he got only 33 seats to contest but managed to win 8. Out of these 33 seats, the party's candidates were at number 2 position and on 14 seats the party lost by less than 500 votes. The party's candidates were able to defeat contestants of the likes of Sangeet Singh Som and even Minister for Cane, Suresh Rana. The victory of controversial leader Nahid Hasan has dented the political career of Mriganka Singh, daughter of ex-minister Hukum Singh. But the big point was that RLD fought the elections with vigour and supported the Samajwadi Party till the end. It is remarkable that Jayant Singh did not succumb to temptations thrown to him.

But if RLD has to play a more prominent role in future and especially considering its history, it has to work very hard. Ever since the party was formed, it has not been able to get more than 4 percent votes. This time it got 2.85 percent votes (26..30 lakhs). It needs to be understood that Jat voters have a strong hold on 10 Lok Sabha and 40 assembly seats and it constitutes 12 percent of the people of the state. It is also true that due to Jayant's activism, the party got almost 11 lakh more votes than last time. But this is going to be a long fight. RLD will have to come out of the limits of being only the Jat Party, which will not be easy either. The party has to focus on stability and on the strategy of its alliance partner in future. Now when the 2024 Lok Sabha elections are not very far away, this is a bigger challenge.

❑

8
Small Parties of UP: Small But Potent

Till a decade, while discussing the political scenario in Uttar Pradesh, the largest arena of the country's politics, the name of four or more five big parties i.e. BJP, SP, BSP, Congress and Chaudhary Charan Singh's Party RLD used to be cited, but for the last few years parties confined to specific regions of the State also emerged and these so-called big parties were compelled to associate with them. There is one such party, Nirbal Shoshit Hamara Aam Dal, which we know under the name of the Nishad Party. Even though the party was formed only eight years ago, a heavy-weight party like the Bharatiya Janata Party has made the first alliance with this party for the 2022 Assembly elections in Uttar Pradesh and has registered a big victory. The Founder and National President of this party, Dr. Sanjay Nishad, did not mince words in saying that he had formed the party with the goal of ensuring representation in power by the Nishad community.

Prior to this, the BJP was forced to compromise with this party in the 2019 Lok Sabha elections and Praveen Nishad of the Nishad Party was elected Lok Sabha member from Sant Kabir Nagar. In its journey of eight years, before the BJP, the Nishad Party had an electoral alliance with the Peace Party. With each alliance, the party's Chief Dr. Sanjay has emerged stronger. In the

2017 elections, along with Apna Dal, Jan Adhikar Party and Peace Party, Nishad Party fielded 100 candidates but without much success. Only one MLA of Nishad Party could win. Sanjay Nishad stood third from the Gorakhpur Rural seat but he got 35,000 votes. This number of votes was enough to show strength. A year later, when elections were held for the Phulpur and Gorakhpur Lok Sabha seats, the Samajwadi Party caught hold of the Nishad Party and Sanjay Nishad nominated his son Praveen Nishad as the SP candidate from Gorakhpur, the seat vacated by Yogi Adityanath.

This was not only a setback for Yogi Adityanath, it was also a challenge for the BJP. Even though the ticket belonged to the Samajwadi Party, it turned out to be a miraculous win for the Nishad Party. The BJP had retained this seat by itself for almost thirty years. In 2019, in agreement with NDA, father Sanjay again made Praveen Nishad MP from Sant Kabirnagar seat. After making his son an MP for two consecutive terms, now by allying with the BJP he got himself nominated as MLC.

The rise of the Nishad Party is a hallmark of the growing significance of smaller parties in Uttar Pradesh. The politics of UP is full of such small parties and almost all of them have been formed with the goal of becoming a shareholder in power to give political representation to some caste, especially the backward class. It is interestingly remarkable to note that the area of influence of most of these parties is eastern Uttar Pradesh.

Till the last Assembly elections in Uttar Pradesh, the number of such registered small parties was 474, which has increased in numbers now. In the last elections, about 290 parties had entered the fray in UP, in which apart from the big parties like BJP, SP, BSP and Congress, except the Rashtriya Lok Dal, which is influential in western UP, all the other parties are identified as a small party.

These parties may be small in size but are capable of giving many sleepless nights to these so-called big political parties. The reason being that they themselves may not win any election but with their sphere of influence they have the ability to bring in enough votes that may cut the vote share of any major party and eventually it may face defeat.

Statistics reveal that in the 2017 UP Assembly elections, there were 32 such small parties whose candidates had secured between 5000 to 50,000 votes. There were also half a dozen parties whose candidates got more than 50,000 votes.

Realising the significance of smaller parties, the BJP entered into an alliance with Anupriya Patel-led Apna Dal (S) and Omprakash Rajbhar's Suheldev Bharatiya Samaj Party (SubhaSP) in the 2017 Assembly elections. The BJP gave 8 seats to the SubhaSP and 11 to the Apna Dal while it itself contested on 384 seats.

Subhaspa President Omprakash Rajbhar, who had once shared BSP founder Kanshi Ram's mission, left the BSP after a dispute with Mayawati to form Suheldev Bharatiya Samaj Party (SubhaSP) and has been contesting elections since 2004. Omprakash Rajbhar, who had a positive influence on the Rajbhar fraternity, tasted power only in 2017 when four of his MLAs entered into an alliance with the BJP, including Rajbhar himself who won from the Zahoorabad seat and became a Cabinet Minister in Yogi Adityanath's government. However, this did not last long as the confrontation between the BJP leadership and Rajbhar differed on various issues and eventually Rajbhar had to quit the Ministerial post, the alliance of both the parties was also broken-up. Before this, Rajbhar has been very vocal about his demands. At the time of the Rajya Sabha elections in June 2021, Rajbhar criticised the functioning of the state government. He alleged that the officers did not listen to him. He was not given the respect due to a Minister. He announced that his party would not support BJP candidates in the Rajya Sabha elections, whereas the central leadership of the BJP did not want any trouble or obstacle to come in the way of the victory of all the nine candidates. The matter went to the Union Home Minister Amit Shah. Rajbhar went to Delhi to meet Amit Shah. After the election, the BJP alleged that one out of four MLAs of Rajbhar's party did cross-voting. Therefore the agreement will be reviewed. Here BJP also engaged another minister Anil Rajbhar to counter O.P. Rajbhar. Within a year, his displeasure heightened to a level that he did not participate as a Minister in the government commemoration of the first year of Yogi rule. Om Prakash Rajbhar feared that the BJP was publicly celebrating his presiding deity Suheldev so that his original voter may swindle away from him. Meanwhile, the BJP went ahead with the unveiling of the idols of Suheldev. Before the 2022 elections, Samajwadi Party chief Akhilesh Yadav on first opportunity captured Om Prakash Rajbhar. Rajbhar did not make any concessions in cursing the BJP fiercely. Apart from Chaudhary Jayant Singh, the Samajwadi Party had a fresh partner in the form of Om Prakash Rajbhar. All was well till the election but the results were not as expected. Even though his party won 6 seats (in 2017 four seats were won together with BJP) as compared to 2017, his son Arvind Rajbhar also lost the election. However, Om Prakash Rajbhar claimed that the Rajbhar Samaj had a huge influence in 120 seats, especially in Purvanchal.

Another important name in the list of small parties of Uttar Pradesh is Apna Dal (S). It is headed by Anupriya Patel, daughter of Apna Dal founder the late Sonelal Patel. The alliance of this party with the BJP is old. The importance of this party, which has a good influence among Kurmi, a major caste of OBC, can be understood from the fact that Anupriya Patel became a Minister for the first time in the Narendra Modi-led NDA government at the centre and then again for a second term too, though after a short interval, she has been made a Minister again at the Centre. It is clear that at the time of elections, the BJP leadership wanted to keep this dominant party with influence in the Kurmi caste firmly associated with it. Apna Dal fought the 2017 election with the BJP and had nine MLAs in the House, next was the Congress with seven MLAs. It is noteworthy that Anupriya Patel's mother and sister led the other faction of Apna Dal. When Anupriya Patel became an MP from Mirzapur seat (another MP Pakodi Lal also won from Robertsganj), she wanted her husband Ashish Singh Patel to contest from Rohanian seat but Anupriya's mother and Apna Dal Governing Body President Krishna Singh wanted this seat for herself. She fought the election but Anupriya Patel did not support her mother. From here, the litigation started in the party and both the mother and daughter have taken the matter to the court.

Anupriya Patel's party put up a great show with the BJP in the 2022 elections. With this Apna Dal (Sonelal) is now reckoned as the third biggest force after the BJP and SP. The party chose three female candidates who won all 3 seats. It is remarkable that Apna Dal (Sonelal) has registered this victory within 10 years of its formation. It has 12 MLAs (11 in 2017) now with 2 MPs in the Lok Sabha.

Another small party in UP is Mahan Dal, which is headed by Keshav Dev Maurya. Remember not to confuse his name with a senior BJP leader Keshav Prasad Maurya. This party entered into an alliance with the Samajwadi Party in the 2022 Assembly elections. This was considered to be part of Akhilesh Yadav's strategy to bring non-Yadav OBC castes,especially Kushwaha, Shakya, etc. with the SP. The political base of this party in UP is among the most backward castes like Shakya, Saini, Kushwaha, Maurya, Kamboj of Bareilly, Badaun, Shahjahanpur, Pilibhit, Agra, Bijnor and Moradabad districts. In the 2017 Assembly elections, Mahan Dal had contested 14 Assembly seats, even though it could not win any seat, but the party got around one lakh votes. This time too it made tall claims but failed to win a single seat.

Another mentionable name is the Janwadi Party (Socialist) led by Sanjay Chauhan. Its political base is in the Nonia backward castes of the districts of Mau, Azamgarh, Ghazipur, Chandauli, Deoria, etc. of Purvanchal. In the 2019 Lok Sabha elections,

Akhilesh Yadav had fielded Sanjay Chauhan on an SP ticket from the Chandauli seat. Sanjay Chauhan gave a tough fight but lost in a close contest to Mahendra Nath Pandey of the BJP by 14,000 votes. Sanjay Chauhan's Party entered into an alliance with the SP in the 2022 Assembly elections but this time too failed to win a seat.

Peace Party and Ulema Council are popular small parties in UP, but these parties are no longer as effective as earlier. The Peace Party was founded in October 2008 by Dr. Ayub, a physician by profession. In the 2012 Assembly elections, four MLAs of the Peace Party were elected, including Dr. Ayub. However, the other three MLAs later parted ways with the party due to a dispute with the leadership. The National Ulema Council was also formed in the year 2008 itself.

Jansatta Party of Raghuraj Pratap Singh alias Raja Bhaiya also has 2 MLAs. The party runs on its own might and is considerably influential in Pratapgarh and neighbouring regions of the state.

❑

9
TMC: Time to March Alone

Simple white cotton saris, rubber slippers (Hawaai chappal) to wear and a house with clay-tiles to live in. This has been the lifestyle of a Chief Minister for three consecutive times. In her journey from Agnikanya to Didi and Banglar Mey (Bengal girl) Mamata Banerjee's identity has now moved far beyond West Bengal. A large section of the masses is eyeing her as an alternative to Narendra Modi. Mamata Banerjee registering tremendous victory in the face off with Bharatiya Janata Party that has used all its might in contesting recently held Assembly elections in 2021 is going to stay in everyone's memory for long. People often cite her name as the next face after Narendra Modi. Whether this aspiration turns into reality or not only time can tell. one thing is clear that because of its combative belligerence, the Trinamool Congress does not seem to be confined to West Bengal alone and has now started focusing strategically on small states.

Trinamool leader Mamata Banerjee's political career has not been less turbulent. It began at the age of 15 with her association with the students' union. More exciting and interesting than the origin of the Trinamool Congress has been its founder Mamata's own journey that has scores of struggles.

Her rise to fame is an incident that occurred when she was just 20. Jayaprakash Narayan (JP) was to attend a programme in Kolkata (then Calcutta) in April 1975 before the Emergency was imposed in the country. Prime Minister Indira Gandhi was also worried and annoyed by the ongoing JP movement in Bihar. It is said that the central leadership of the Congress may not have liked it if JP had returned undamaged from Indira's Advisor Siddharth Shankar Rai's state. But, during his visit to Calcutta on April 2, 1975, JP was manhandled by Congressmen while the police stood mute spectators. A girl had jumped high and low on top of the car in which JP was sitting. That girl was Mamata Banerjee. The vehicle in which the elderly Jayaprakash Narayan was sitting was not allowed inside the gate of the Institute where he was to make his address. The agitators rode on top of the vehicle and created a ruckus. JP also alleged he could have been killed there.

Mamata's activism was appreciated by the Congressmen and at the age of 21, in 1976, she was nominated General Secretary of the Mahila Congress. Even in the Lok Sabha elections held after the assassination of Indira Gandhi in 1984, she did not want to be pitted against any petty contestant. The seat was Jadhavpur and the contestant was CPI(M) veteran Somnath Chatterjee. He later became the Speaker of the Lok Sabha. Once, referring to him, LJP leader Ram Vilas Paswan had said, "When Mamata came to the Lok Sabha, she was interrupted by someone and guided, "The audience gallery is on the other side." Mamata smiled and showed her victory certificate. Even after becoming an MP, Mamata maintained the same demeanour as earlier. But she lost the Lok Sabha election in the anti-Congress tide of 1989. She may have lost the Lok Sabha elections, but she now centred all her activities and attention towards West Bengal politics. She was re-elected to the Lok Sabha in the 1991 elections. From here onwards her stature kept rising high and she never looked back. She didn't have to. After winning the election, she took over as the Minister of Youth Welfare and Sports in the P.V. Narasimha Rao Cabinet. This was her first tryst with becoming a Minister at the Centre. She had rebellion in her persona and she also believed that West Bengal was not receiving what it deserved. After being a Minister at the Centre for just two years, Mamata held a rally at the Brigade Parade Ground in Kolkata to protest against the policies of the Central Government and resigned from the Cabinet. She believed that in place of engaging in Delhi politics, she would rather deal with the left who was oppressing Congress workers in Kolkata.

In reality this struggle was a recrudescence for Di. Her struggle was getting intense and the ground was being laid for the Trinamool Congress. At the opportune moment, Mamata Di announced the formation of a new party Trinamool Congress on the first day of 1998, January 1, accusing the Congress of surrendering to the whims of the CPI(M). Mamata's political wisdom and adeptness can be gauged from the fact that her party Trinamool Congress soon fielded itself as an alternative to the Congress. In the 1998 Lok Sabha elections, she captured seven seats and won 60 seats in the 2001 Assembly elections in the state, capturing 30 percent votes. That too when her party contested on only 226 seats. As a result, the Congress lost the status of the main opposition party in the State and the Trinamool Congress captured that seat. The 2006 election proved to be a setback for her and the seats came down to 30. While her number of seats in the 2004 Lok Sabha was reduced to 2, what happened in Kolkata between 2006 and 2011 was surprising. The party bounced back and the political scenario was dominated by two leaves (party's election symbol). Mamata realised that the decline that occurred in 2006 could not be replenished by fighting independently. In the 2009 Lok Sabha elections, she ingeniously compromised with the Congress, which she had discarded ten years earlier, and contested 26 seats out of 42 seats in West Bengal. The vote transfer strategy worked for her and Mamata had won 19 seats. And with the doughty of these 19 seats, Mamata Di took the Trinamool Congress to the pinnacle of power in the 2011 Assembly elections in Bengal and won 184 of the 294 seats. She entered into an alliance with the Congress in this Assembly election again and, unconsciously Congress was set to be completely sidelined in West Bengal politics.

From the very beginning, Mamata aimed at ousting the Left from power in Bengal. She also changed her colleagues on several occasions as per her convenience and sweet will. Sometimes she sided with the NDA at the Centre and other times with the Congress-led UPA. She was with the NDA from 1998 to 2001. In October 2001, Mamata was assigned the Railway Ministry portfolio in the Atal Bihari Vajpayee-led NDA government at the Centre. Mamata was the first woman in the country to become Railway Minister. She has also served as Minister of State for Coal, Human Resource Development, Minister of State for Youth Affairs and Sports and Women and Child Development at the Centre. During her second term as Railway Minister, Mamata had showered upon Bengal a number of trains and other projects. She was a Minister at the Centre, but she spent most of her time in Bengal. That is why she was also mocked as Railway Minister of Bengal.

The Trinamool Congress' journey was sustained with Mamata's. She resigned from the Cabinet after just 17 months due to the Tehelka scandal and parted ways with the government. She then shook hands with the Congress. She became a Minister again under Atal Bihari's Government at the Centre for a few days in January 2004, but Mamata's innings did not last long as the NDA lost the Lok Sabha elections the same year. In 2006, she once again allied with the Congress.

The struggle

After the poor performance of the Trinamool Congress in the 2004 Lok Sabha elections, Mamata reincarnated her image as the Messiah of the poor in December 2006 through an anti-land acquisition struggle in favour of farmers in Singur and Nandigram and this would be considered a significant contribution to the rise of the Trinamool Congress in 2006. TMC had a mere 30 MLAs, not sufficient enough to bring down the government. The notice of Haldia Development Authority affected the people of 70,000 households. When an agitation was launched against the land acquisition, the Trinamool Congress led by Mamata Banerjee joined hands with the people to be affected by it. On March 14, 2007, police opened fire on the agitators, killing 14 villagers. Several people reportedly went missing during the firing. It is also said that along with the police CPM cadres also opened fire on the protesters. Bengali intellectuals also took to the streets to protest against the incident. The case of Tata's Nano factory in Singur along with Nandigram was also raised. This protest too was led by the Trinamool Congress. Tata finally decided to relocate the factory to Gujarat. The Trinamool Congress benefited directly from this and in the 2009 Lok Sabha elections, the Trinamool Congress won 19 seats in West Bengal. Moreover, the Trinamool Congress also won 97 of the 141 seats in the 2010 Kolkata Municipal Corporation elections. The Trinamool Congress also gained ground in the elections to other municipalities.

When Mamata achieved her goal by ending the 34-year-long Left rule in Bengal in 2011, she soon withdrew her support to the then UPA government at the Centre on September 18, 2012. The time of liberation from the clutches of the left had already come.

A striking characteristic of Mamata's persona is perseverance. In 1993, when Mamata was the President of the Youth Congress, she organised the State Secretariat Writers Building Campaign. The conflict with the Left was at its peak. Meanwhile, the police opened fire. Thirteen youth of the Youth Congress were killed. Since then, Mamata has celebrated Martyrs' Day on July 21 every year. After assuming office as Chief Minister, she also ensured jobs and financial assistance to one member each of the victims' families whose families were shot dead by the police. Mamata's sari was torn in a scuffle with policemen during the same operation. She had vowed on the same day that she would step into the Writers' Building only after ending the Left Front rule. She waited for about 18 years for it and finally entered the building only after she was sworn in as Chief Minister in 2011.

One noteworthy aspect in the history of the Trinamool Congress Assembly elections is that its vote percentage continued to rise from 2001 to 2021 (except 2006). In 2001, it was 30.66 percent and in 2021 it was 47.94 percent. With the formation of the Trinamool Congress, its first slogan was Maa (mother), Mati (the land), Manush (the People). The slogan struck chords with the people of West Bengal during the 2011 Assembly elections. Later, Mamata Banerjee named the same slogan the title of her book. According to a report published in June 2011, the Trinamool Congress slogan was one of the six most popular political slogans in India at that time. Mamata's political struggle also shows her vision. After coming to power in 2011, she focused the most on women and provided them with several beneficial schemes. Apart from giving books, shoes, uniforms and bicycles to the girls, she also focused on their nutrition. In Bengal, where the death-rate during pregnancy was very high, she made 12 waiting huts, that is, where pregnant women could stay in the last 12 weeks. This scheme worked very well and was much appreciated in tribal areas. The credit for improving policing through the Women's Security Centre also goes to the Trinamool Congress. And perhaps that was one of the reasons why besides Muslims Mamata bagged women as a major vote bank.

However, Mamata's stubbornness knows no bounds. (In the 2021 assembly elections, she contested (though lost) from the Shubhendu Adhikari's constituency just because she had sworn it before him. Her firm resolve in raising public issues, striving tooth and nail against the Left Front rule in Bengal made her a favourite with the people. Within 13 years, she succeeded in leading her party to power by uprooting the Left Front government in the state which they had ruled for nearly two and a half decades. Both Left and the Congress, which had been in power for years in Bengal politics have now totally lost their base in Bengal. Since both the parties got eliminated in the 2021 Assembly elections, Mamata Banerjee now owns the minority votes.

Simplicity has always been a part of Mamata Banerjee's life. The same simplicity seeps down to the Trinamool workers as well. She never gave up wearing white cotton saris and rubber-slippers, whether she has been a Minister at the Centre or just an MP. Even after becoming the Chief Minister, her attire and lifestyle remain unaltered. Not only that, the basic structure of her Tali Bari (Khaparel house) at Taliganj remained the same. She preferred to stay in her Tali Bari instead of shifting to the Chief Minister's residence. Her principal spokesperson Manav Jaiswal even claims that no leader in independent India has fought on foot as much as Mamata Di. Before Independence, Mahatma Gandhi often marched on foot. There may be an exaggeration in Manav's claim, but it is also true that Mamata never adopted the Rath yatra trend in politics though West Bengal is not a small state. Even leaders who call themselves socialists do not go ahead without their air conditioned rath yatra trail. No one ever saw her sitting in a car, and waving to the public like other leaders usually do. Mamata Banerjee is personally unblemished by any allegation of scam or corruption. Despite becoming a three-time Union minister and three time Chief Minister, her declared assets of less than ₹ fifteen lakhs only surprise people. The famous 'Time' magazine has twice placed her in the list of '100 most influential people in the world'.

It is not that after the overwhelming victory in West Bengal the Trinamool Congress did not participate in the electoral process in other states. But the results were not as expected. Apart from Bengali-dominated Tripura, the Trinamool Congress also made its foray in the states of Manipur, Jharkhand, Assam, etc. In Manipur's 2012 Assembly elections, the TMC had won 8 seats. The Trinamool Congress had become the only opposition party in the Manipur Assembly with 10 percent of the total votes.

But Mamata's journey after the BJP's growing presence in West Bengal, is not going to be easy. Struggles will surely hinder it. And perhaps that is why Mamata seems eager to contest even outside the State once again. Trinamool Congress is apparently serious about the Tripura elections. Womenfolk is her target group. That is why she has chosen states known for matriarchal culture. Goa and Tripura are such states. At the beginning of the 2022 election campaign, Mamata was being considered giving a tough fight. She had also brought many stalwarts into her party, but her party did not win even a single seat. In her endeavour to make her hold outside West Bengal, she has modified her strategy too. The slogan of 'Ekla Chalo Re' is appealing to the Trinamool Congress. It may also enhance their bargaining capacity at the national level. But it has to be kept in mind that it is feasible only when TMC has a unified rule over West Bengal. (The BJP is also not going to remain docile). A lot of the responsibility rests on Mamata's nephew Abhishek Banerjee in Trinamool. But Mamata's leadership is still the pivot of the Trinamool and hopefully will last for a long time. Age not being on her side, she needs to be watchful of her health.

❑

10
Shiv Sena: The Roar Hushed

In Indian politics there happens to be a regional party having influence over just one state, but wherever asked to comment upon, every politician thinks twice before reacting. The party is - Shiv Sena of Maharashtra. Its existence in power has never been for a long duration, cannot claim to have influence over the entire Maharashtra, have never even crossed the hundreds mark in the 288-member Maharashtra Assembly, but the fact remains that politics in Maharashtra can leave aside any other party, but not the Shiv Sena. The Shiv Sena is indispensable here.

The journey of the Shiv Sena, an organisation raised in the name of Marathi identity, has run through five decades. Shiv Sena is a party of Chhatrapati Shivaji and its apt symbol is Tiger.

It would be really interesting to study the journey of Bal Thackeray, from a lowly chawl to becoming a force to reckon with in a state like Maharashtra. Born on January 23, 1927 in Pune, Bal Thackeray's entire family moved to Bhiwandi, near Bombay (named Mumbai much later) a few years later. Father Keshav Sitaram Thackeray later changed his name to Prabodhankar. He was a truly talented and gifted person. The Thackeray title was also taken from the name of a British writer. Prabodhankar was a stage-artist, a screenplay-dialogue writer, a historian and also a social reformer with many other gifts to his credit. When Bal Thackeray was born 'after the birth of four daughters', it was only natural to receive much pampering, more so than his younger brothers. Meanwhile, the father also sent him to the RSS Shakha. But with his revolutionary attitude, his inclination was to become a cartoonist. His father helped by introducing him to good cartoonists of those times. Around 1950, he had earned a name for himself as a revolutionary cartoonist. He made cartoons of - from Churchill to Eisenhower—and his cartoons started appearing in the Sunday edition of The Times of India. There were also controversies over his cartoons so he had to leave the job thrice. He thought the newspaper he made cartoons for, imposed numerous restrictions regarding cartoons. In such a situation, later along with his brother Shrikant started running his own Marathi magazine Marmik.

Once he ran into a dispute with communist leaders in connection with making cartoons. The communists sent their goons to Thackeray's house. His father handled the situation and resolved the matter anyhow. But after this, perhaps Bal Thackeray's mind got stuck with the Communists. The communist leaders had no inkling what was going to happen next. In fact, Bombay was already dominated by three categories of people. Gujaratis and Parsis in trade, South Indians in jobs (they had settled here long ago) and ordinary working class labourers as business partners in the service sector who came from North India.

In the 1950s, when the reorganisation of the states was being considered by the government, the movement for reorganisation on the basis of language was gaining momentum. It was a very vigorous movement, to create sensitivity regarding regional identity. Then in Maharashtra also, the Marathis demanded a state for themselves on the basis of language, which was to be carved out mainly from parts of the surrounding states like Gujarat, Karnataka and Madras State. After a successful movement, Maharashtra was formed in 1960.

Now a different problem arose. The literacy rate of the Marathi people was lower than that of South Indians. Though Marathis also pursued higher education after 1950 but outsiders bagged most of the jobs. Bal Thackeray started raising this issue through his magazine by drawing cartoons and writing articles. First he taunted with sarcasm and then began fastidious attacking. At that time magazines were much in vogue. Popularity of Marmik was good. So people, mostly young, educated and unemployed, started approaching him. The whole of Bombay reeled under a strange discontent and this issue was getting worse. It was just not voiced loudly. Thackeray formed an organisation to raise this issue resonantly. Many happenings in Bombay in those days exasperated the local people. The local traders and industrialists were worried about the growing strength and interference of trade unions. Bal Thackeray viewed this as an opportunity and announced the formation of the Shiv Sena on June 19, 1966 and made it clear that Bombay was no longer going to be the same. He organised a meeting in Shivaji Park and the large crowd that gathered at the first meeting sent a clear message that a new force had emerged in Maharashtra. His plan of action of associating himself with the native Marathas started working and at one point of time Shiv Sena's call meant - full and final. In 1966, the first official rally of the Shiv Sena took place on the day of Dussehra, i.e. October 30. Not surprisingly, Thackeray's first target was the communists.

After a few days, the tension mounted to a level that the Shiv Sainiks attacked the Communist Party Headquarters in Dalvi building at Parel and ransacked it. The workers were badly beaten up. Later on June 6, 1970, the Communist Party MLA Krishna Desai was assassinated. This was the first political assassination after independence in Samyukta Maharashtra Bombay.

Bal Thackeray's power was increasing significantly. The organisation now aspired to be the torchbearer of Hindutva with focus on Maratha identity.

Elections to the Bombay Municipal Corporation were held in 1968. Out of 140 seats, Shiv Sena won 42 seats. In Mumbai, it is said that whoever owns BMC, owns Mumbai. This holds good even today and the main reason for this is its enormous budget (its budget in the year 2021-22 is ₹ 39,000 crores). Meanwhile, in 1969, the Shiv Sena raised the suppressed issue of the Maharashtra-Karnataka border. For the first and last time the state government of Maharashtra arrested Thackeray. As soon as Thackeray was arrested, riots broke out. Later the state government had to request the jailed Thackeray to restrain his people. After a week of bloody riots, Thackeray asked his people to stop.

In the 1960s, the firebrand socialist leader George Fernandes was hailed as the uncrowned king of Mumbai. He was the leader of all the small and big trade unions of the metropolis. At his behest, there were strikes in factories, chaos in the city. Then George was a great leader of the workers and trade unions there. In the 1967 Lok Sabha elections, 35-year-old George ended his political innings by defeating veteran Congress leader S.K. Patil in Mumbai. Socialist and leftist trade unions were very powerful in the industrialised state of Maharashtra. Therefore, the government had to constantly struggle with trade unions. With the founding of the Shiv Sena, Bal Thackeray linked up with Maharashtra Chief Minister Vasantrao Naik and Naik also used Thackeray extensively to break George's clout in Mumbai's working class. For this reason, many people jokingly started calling Shiv Sena 'Vasant Sena' during that period.

Businessmen started inviting Shiv Sena to stop the strike in their factory. At one point, the Shiv Sena even rejected George Fernandes's railway strike call in 1974. After the Emergency, when George became fully active in national politics, he diverted his attention from Mumbai. In the same period, Datta Samant emerged as a labour leader in Mumbai.

Initially, the Congress also encouraged Dutta Samant to cut down the dominance of the unions led by George, but when he too became a pain for the Congress government of Maharashtra through strikes and workers' demonstrations in the textile mills, the Chief Ministers of Congress also sought Bal Thackeray's help for 'treating' with them. Not only Vasantrao, but even after him, many Congress Chief Ministers blatantly used Bal Thackeray in the politics of Maharashtra and Mumbai periodically. But not for free, Bal Thackeray charged for his service the same political price as he wished to. Sometimes to strengthen the Shiv Sena and other times for the benefit of its candidates and other advantages. His friendship with Sharad Pawar was well known.

In the 70s and 80s itself, in many cities in Maharashtra, Congress and Shiv Sena constituted boards in Zilla Parishads, Municipalities and Municipal Corporations in coordination. After this the positions of branch head and department head were created. Shiv Sena is still working on this structure. Suketu Mehta writes in 'Maximum City'- "after establishing the organisation, Shiv Sena opened branches in every locality just on the pattern of the RSS."

Then began street politics, street movement ...... the Panchayati of the street, the 'Bombayia' colloquial language and tone in the speeches, fights over water-electricity, troubles between tenant-landlords, babus' corruption, household-family fights, every matter was being settled. This led to the rise of an army of Shiv Sena. These people were prepared to do anything for Bal Thackeray. Thackeray's oratory skills were amazing, aggression being its key element. The views expressed by Shiv Sena leaders were at times filled with vigour. Bal Thackeray tried to win the trust of the people by creating effective branches and efficient organisations. Shiv Sena first campaigned against South Indians. Then, North Indians were targeted. In 1991 and 1999, Shiv Sainiks dug out the pitch of the Feroz Shah Kotla ground, opposing the cricket match with Pakistan. Violent protests during the release of Deepa Mehta's film Fire, everyday skirmishes and protests against North Indians also tarnished Shiv Sena's image. By this time Shiv Sena began to realise that this stance was not going to take them very far. That is why Thackeray linked the

Hindutva concept with the Maratha identity, with which the North Indians also associated.

Along with Bal Thackeray, a few more people played a key role in establishing Shiv Sena of which Madhav Deshpande, an architect by profession, was the main one. It was his idea to create Shiv Sena as a regional power. The trio, along with three others, including Deshpande's partner Padmakar Adhikari and Shyam Deshmukh, who worked in a factory, played a crucial role in bringing Maratha workers to the Shiv Sena. Along with this, there was Vasant Pradhan, who worked in the railways, but later took up the cases of labourers by practising law.

According to Sujatha Anandan's book Hindu Hriday Samrat, the Shiv Sena did not record the name of any party executive in the documents to avoid government havoc during the Emergency. To avoid arrest, Thackeray decided to run the party without assuming any post.

By the 80s, it was clearly visible that Bombay was ruled by the Shiv Sena and Bal Thackeray. They had taken over the municipalities of Mumbai. He had won the trust of big industrialists. Bollywood was also seen standing with Thackeray. Big Bollywood stars, producers and directors all paid a visit to his house and registered their attendance.

However, with the passage of time, Bal Thackeray also took a U-turn. Surprisingly he supported the Congress in 1975 for the Emergency imposed by the Indira Gandhi government and again in the 1977 Lok Sabha elections. To express his support for the Emergency, Bal Thackeray himself had gone to the Raj Bhavan in Bombay to meet the then Prime Minister Indira Gandhi. He also congratulated Mrs. Gandhi, describing it as a bold move. Bal Thackeray also played an important role in the victory of Congress leader Murli Deora in the election of Mayor of Mumbai in 1977. However, there was collateral damage too. In 1978, the Shiv Sena suffered a severe loss in the elections to the Maharashtra

Legislative Assembly and the Bombay Municipal Corporation (BMC).

If we talk about the political journey, then Shiv Sena fought its first election in 1971. That too directly to the Lok Sabha. The candidates were fielded on five seats. Everyone lost. For the first time in the 1980 Lok Sabha elections, Shiv Sena succeeded in winning its first Lok Sabha seat. This was considered a great success. Meanwhile, Shiv Sena's relationship with the Bharatiya Janata Party started growing and its rapport with Pramod Mahajan was known to all. There was an alliance with the BJP, but after the assassination of Indira Gandhi in 1984, most of the parties took a plunge in the Congress wave. But again in 1985, Shiv Sena won the elections to the municipal corporations and its capture of BMC was as if no election had been held a year ago. It did not get any seat again in the 1989 Lok Sabha elections. In the 1991 Lok Sabha, it fought in alliance with the BJP, by contesting 22 seats and won 4 seats. But soon its number of MPs in the 1996 Lok Sabha also increased to 15 yet the expansion of power did not last long. Again it was reduced to (6) in 1998, and rose to (15) in 1999. After that, its number of seats in the Lok Sabha has always been more than 10 with maximum being 18.

The Shiv Sena contested its first Assembly elections in 1990 on 183 seats and won 52. After that its number of seats kept rising marginally each time. It won 73 seats in 1995 which is the maximum till date. The alliance with the Bharatiya Janata Party (BJP) benefits it immensely, and first for about four years, the humble natured Manohar Joshi became the Chief Minister and then the flamboyant Narayan Rane remained the Chief Minister for a year. For fifteen years both the parties remained unified but had to remain in opposition. Even in 2014, the alliance kept breaking down. Due to lack of consensus between the two parties, both contested the elections separately, but finally the government was formed under the leadership of Devendra Fadnavis. But in January 2018, before the 2019 elections, the Shiv Sena broke its ties with the BJP. But again there was an agreement to contest the 2019 Lok Sabha and Vidhan Sabha elections together. This time its share got 56 seats but irreconcilable differences emerged about forming the government. It broke up completely with the BJP and formed the government by partnering with the Congress and the Nationalist Congress Party, which were once considered to be its arch rivals. Uddhav Thackeray became the Chief Minister of this dramatically formed government. This was the first time that the Thackeray family accepted power.

Meanwhile, the party's vote share in the Assembly elections ranged between 16 and 24 percent. Sunil Gatade, who had been into journalism in Mumbai for several decades and closely watched the rise of the Shiv Sena, says that there has been a lot of change in the Shiv Sena, but the shakha pramukh is still its backbone, which works as a bridge with the public. Work like settling disputes between landlord-tenants to getting into and resolving small disputes, it is the main task for the workers.

Although it is politically believed that the Marathas, who had earlier stood firmly with the Congress in Maharashtra politics, have now joined the Shiv Sena, Hindutva has broadly associated them with other classes as well. 'Maratha' is its main calling. In 2007, the Shiv Sena supported the Congress candidate Pratibha Patil for the post of President even after being under alliance with the BJP. Bhairon Singh Shekhawat, the then Vice President and senior BJP leader in that election, was the candidate of the BJP-led NDA. Again despite being in alliance with the BJP, it preferred Pranab Mukherjee of the Congress.

Shiv Sena gained both real political strength and power in the 90s. In 1989, it started publishing his mouthpiece Saamana, in Hindi as well as Marathi. It also became its effective platform to connect with the common man. The Shiv Sena first formed the government in the State in 1995 in collaboration with the BJP. Manohar Joshi of the Shiv Sena became the Chief Minister. After being Chief Minister for four years, Narayan Rane was again made CM by the Shiv Sena. At the Centre, first in the government of Atal Bihari Vajpayee and then in the government of Narendra Modi, the leaders of Shiv Sena also got the portfolio of Union Ministers. Manohar Joshi was also the Speaker of the Lok Sabha. However, after being in power for five years in 1995, the Shiv Sena and BJP alliance had to face defeat in the next election in 1999. Then they sat in the opposition in the House for a long time. The Congress has woven such a fabric with the Nationalist Congress Party, SP, RPI that the leaders of BJP and Shiv Sena remained yearning for power. Although once upon a time Shiv Sena leaders were afraid to leave the party fearing the wrath of Bal Thackeray. But this also happened from the late 90s. Leaders like Chhagan Bhujbal, Narayan Rane and Sanjay Nirupam left the party. His own nephew Raj Thackeray parted company.

It is true that Shiv Sena has no charismatic leaders beyond father Uddhav Thackeray and son Aditya Thackeray duo. Aditya is the Head of the youth wing. At the same time Uddhav is by nature antithetical to Bal Thackeray. He is gentle and taciturn, unlike his father. And this is the one of the reasons for the losing power within the span of two and half years.

But in May-June 2022, after the operation of Eknath Shinde, no matter how strong the Shiv Sena looks externally, it may have formed the government, but its internal information system is not only weak but their leaders are not dependable. After the formation of the government of Eknath Shinde and Devendra Fadnavis in Maharashtra, Shinde is telling his part of the party as the real Shiv Sena so that his government can survive. But in Maharashtra, the real Shiv Sena is considered to be of Uddhav Thackeray, even if the Supreme Court or the Election Commission decides anything in this matter.

Even if Shinde's Shiv Sena is recognised, its stability will always be questioned. But after this fact, it is also true that Uddhav Thackeray will have to struggle a lot to keep his party alive and maintain his influence.

At the end, one more question will also arise why the Shiv Sena could not make an impact on the public at the national level even after being a party older than the BJP. Although the Shiv Sena contested elections in many places in UP, MP and Goa, nothing much could be achieved. If a party wants to hold ground in any state, then the prominent leaders of the party need to visit there to address meetings, hold rallies, raise local issues strongly and yes, big known faces of the state have to be associated with the party.

Did Shiv Sena do all this? No. Secondly, its controversial and intimidating face prevents it from associating with people from other states.

On the other hand, Uddhav's cousin Raj Thackeray separated and formed the Maharashtra Navnirman Sena. But the public seemingly rejected him. Journalist Sunil Gatade says that mere oratory doesn't work in politics. Raj's behaviour alienates his own people from him. The road ahead for MNS is very difficult. Even in the BMC elections in Mumbai itself, he has faced a severe setback since his initial days.

❑

11
NCP - Under the Guiding Light of a Maratha Satrap

There are only a few people in Indian politics who have no enemies yet have innumerable friends. At the same time, there will be very few parties which are run by a single family, but with an immaculate division of labour to look like a splendid jigsaw puzzle. The party has a father-daughter-nephew's trio, so has Patel, Patil, Anwar and Nawab. The party's name is Nationalist Congress Party, i.e. NCP. If you have to speak about NCP, you have to speak less of the party and more of Sharad Pawar and his style. The same reflects in this article.

It was the last year of the last century. In May, just before the Lok Sabha elections, three senior Congress leaders Sharad Pawar, P.A. Sangma and Tariq Anwar rebelled against Sonia Gandhi. They objected to Sonia Gandhi being handed over the reins of the party calling her a woman of foreign origin, thus she cannot be the destiny of India. The trio separated from the Congress and announced the formation of the Nationalist Congress Party (NCP) on June 10, 1999. Time elapsed, P.A. Sangma passed away on March 4, 2016 and Tariq Anwar returned to the Congress after gaining from NCP, but Sharad Pawar-led NCP is still moving ahead.

Sharad Pawar is not named Maratha Kshatrapa just like that. His role in all-India politics of the last three to four decades cannot be viewed independently of him. He has also played a special role in the politics at the Centre based on his stronghold in Maharashtra's politics. He has been a stalwart of the political pitch of cricket. He continued as Chairman of the Mumbai Cricket Council for more than ten years. He also headed the Board of Control for Cricket in India (BCCI) from 2005 to 2008 and the International Cricket Council from 2010 to 2012 which makes him the first politician to make his mark in the ICC. Apart from this, Sharad Pawar has a good name in the industry as well. Sharad Pawar owns several media houses and sugar mills in Maharashtra.

Born on December 12, 1940 in Baramati village of Pune, Govind Rao Pawar, father of Sarat Chandra Govindarao Pawar, worked in the Baramati Kisan Cooperative Bank and his mother tended the fields in Baramati. One can now gauge his economic background in his childhood days. Sharad Pawar completed his high school education in a government school in Baramati, after which he moved to Pune for further studies. Pawar also became the general secretary of the college as a student leader while studying commerce at BMCC College in Pune. He was married to Pratibha Pawar, daughter of former cricketer Sadu Shinde, on August 1, 1967. Sharad and Pratibha Pawar's only child is Supriya Sule. Supriya is an MP from Baramati. In view of her activities, it can be said that Supriya has also distinguished herself by entering politics under the guidance of her father. Pawar's nephew Ajit Anantrao Pawar is active in Maharashtra politics and is Deputy Chief Minister. Younger brother Pratap Pawar runs a famous Marathi newspaper and his grandson Rohit Rajendra Pawar also is an MLA now. Sharad Pawar's brother Vasant Pawar was associated with the Shetkari Kaamgaar Party for a long time and was murdered in a land dispute. Pawar got a chance to witness politics and engage in social service from an early age.

Yashwantrao Chavan, the first Chief Minister of Maharashtra and the architect of modern Maharashtra, is considered to be the political guru of Sharad Pawar. It was only in the 60s that he succeeded in getting attention by the then Chief Minister of Maharashtra - Yashwantrao Chavan. It was under his guidance that Sharad Pawar joined the Youth Congress first and then remained active in the Congress Party. Sharad Pawar was identified as a youth Congress leader for his work for the advancement of the Congress in Maharashtra. Sharad Pawar became an MLA from Baramati for the first time at the age of 26 in 1967. Since then, Sharad Pawar has seen many ups and downs in politics, but has never looked back. In 1974, the Congress appointed him the State Secretary of Maharashtra. Vasant Dada Patil was among Sharad Pawar's lighting guides. When Vasantdada Patil became Chief Minister in 1978, Pawar became a Member of his Cabinet. Sharad was friends with Shiv Sena Chief Bal Thackeray despite having different political leanings. By that time, the Janata Party had come to power at the Centre. The Janata Party was commanded by Sharad Pawar's friend Chandrashekhar. In Maharashtra, no party had won a majority of 145 in the 288-member Assembly. Janata Party got 99 seats, Congress 69 and Congress (I) of Indira Gandhi or say, INCA- 62. The remaining seats went to other smaller parties and independents. In such a situation, the fragmented Congress (Devraj Urs) and Indira Gandhi's Congress (INCA) joined hands and formed the government to deny the possibility of a Janata Party government. Under the agreement, Vasantdada Patil of Congress became Chief Minister while Shivraj Patil became the Speaker of the Assembly. Sharad Pawar was made Minister of Industries in Vasantdada's government. But the Janata Party was not going to rest and relax! Janata Party President Chandrashekhar and Janata Legislature Party leader Uttamrao Patil ventured on exploring opportunities to destabilise Vasantdada's government. Soon they got the opportunity. In July 1978, Sharad Pawar, who was close to Chandrashekhar and a member of Vasant Dada's cabinet, broke 40 of the 69 Congress MLAs and then the broken faction got the support of Janata Party, Pageant Workers Party, Republican Party etc. and the 4-month-old Vasantdada Patil government collapsed.

Vasantdada Patil then termed Sharad Pawar's move as a stab in the back. The disciple fared better than the mentor. Disciple Sharad Pawar owned several sugar mills by now.

Maharashtra Assembly Speaker and INCA leader Shivraj Patil was also removed from the post as soon as the new government came in and was replaced by Janta Party's Pranlal Vora as the Assembly Speaker. With Pawar as Chief Minister, the cooperative's politics and sugar politics in Maharashtra roared very high. But at the same time, a lot of constructive work was accomplished in the field of roads, education and health in rural Maharashtra and these made Sharad Pawar very popular in rural Maharashtra. But in the 1980 mid-term elections, Congress (I) alias INCA got a huge majority at the Centre and Indira Gandhi became Prime Minister again. Indira dismissed nine non-Congress state governments as soon as she came to power. Sharad Pawar's government was among those 9 state governments to be dismissed. This was followed by new Assembly elections and a major surprise incident in this Assembly election. In fact, Sharad Pawar's friend and Shiv Sena Chief Bal Thackeray was also a friend of Indira Congress leader Abdul Rahman Antulay at that time. But in this election, Bal Thackeray preferred his friendship with Antulay and separated the Shiv Sena from the Assembly elections. INCA also benefited from Shiv Sena's not contesting elections and won a two-thirds majority. Thackeray's friend Abdul Rahman Antulay became the Chief Minister. Sharad's party did not succeed but managed to save its Baramati Assembly seat.

Sharad Pawar was elected National President of the Congress (Samajwadi) in 1983 and won his first Lok Sabha election from Baramati in 1984 from the same party. But he did not like being in Delhi and returned to State politics through the 1985 Assembly elections. In the 1985 Assembly elections, the Congress (Samajwadi) got 54 seats and Sharad Pawar became the Leader of the Opposition in the Assembly. But in the meantime, Shiv Sena's influence in the State began to rise and INCA also started losing ground. Indira Gandhi's period was now over and INCA was under command of Rajiv Gandhi. All the influential leaders of Maharashtra INCA like Shankar Rao Chavan, Shivraj Patil, N.K.P Salve were all busy in Delhi's politics or Rajiv wanted to keep them in Delhi. But for this Rajiv needed a strong kshatrapa in Bombay (now Mumbai) and with this in mind, Rajiv extended a hand of friendship to Sharad Pawar.

Sharad Pawar also found the political bargain profitable and joined INCA in 1987. A few months later, in 1988, Rajiv brought Chief Minister Shankar Rao Chavan to Delhi as Finance Minister and a place was vacant for Sharad Pawar in Maharashtra. Rajiv Gandhi made Sharad Pawar Chief Minister with the intention of curbing INCA's deteriorating organisational structure, internal factionalism and Shiv Sena's growing influence. Pawar fared well. In the March 1990 Assembly elections, the Congress was pushed to nearly 141 seats with a majority in the 288-member Assembly. Pawar managed to become the Chief Minister for the third time with the help of independents. At the end of 1990, helped by Rajiv, Pawar's friend Chandrashekhar had become the Prime Minister. During Chandrashekhar's time, Sharad Pawar frequently shuffled between Mumbai and Delhi. In almost every matter, he appeared like Chandrashekhar's undeclared advisor. Whether it was the economic situation or the Ayodhya case, or allowing the American fighter planes to refuel in Bombay to attack Iraq - Sharad Pawar always stood aside Chandrashekhar and this started hitting Rajiv Gandhi. Rajiv Gandhi, realising Pawar's ambition, tried to snipe at him and was inclined to remove him as Chief Minister. Sharad Pawar has also elaborated on many instances of that period in his book On My Terms. At one point, Sharad Pawar also writes that during the Chandrashekhar government, the Ayodhya issue was nearing settlement, but it was then that Prime Minister Chandrashekhar announced his resignation over a very small dispute and the settlement matter went into the background. But it is also a fact that when Chandrashekhar resigned, the same Sharad Pawar was sent by stunned Rajiv Gandhi to persuade Chandrashekhar to withdraw his resignation. And then Chandrashekhar replied to him:

"Go and tell your leader that Chandrashekhar does not change his decisions thrice a day". Chandrashekhar refused to withdraw his resignation and the country moved towards mid-term elections.

In May 1991, there were only two phases of Lok Sabha elections (and two remaining) when Rajiv Gandhi was assassinated at Sriperumbudur in Tamil Nadu during the election campaign. In the remaining two phases of elections after the assassination, the Congress got overwhelming sympathy votes and the Congress emerged as the largest party with 232 seats. Then, in Rajiv's absence, there was a lineup of Prime Ministerial contenders in INCA. Apart from contenders like Narayan Dutt Tiwari, Arjun Singh, Sharad Pawar, Narasimha Rao, a camp in INCA tried to make Sonia Gandhi's choice and Vice President Shankar Dayal Sharma as Prime Minister. But the main contest was reduced to a Sharad Pawar versus strong South Indian lobby of newly elected Congress MPs. The Arjun Singh faction also extended its support to senior leader Narasimha Rao after his name came up from the South Indian lobby. Even Sonia Gandhi agreed to Narasimha Rao's name. In such a situation, Sharad Pawar considered stepping back. He also wrote in his book Life on My Terms - From Grassroots and Corridors of Power. "In 1991, the 'self-claimed loyalists' of 10 Janpath agreed to Sonia Gandhi to replace him (Pawar) with Narasimha Rao as PM, because the Gandhi family did not prefer a person, having a mind of his own, as PM."

Sharad Pawar was appointed Defence Minister in Narasimha Rao's Cabinet. However, he also held power in Maharashtra in a 'proxy avatar' by making his close aide Sudhakar Rao Naik as Chief Minister. But Prime Minister Narasimha Rao had also given a lot of priority to the anti-Pawar lobby of Maharashtra in his government. Shankar Rao Chavan was made Home Minister while Shivraj Patil was the Speaker, Lok Sabha. Even this could not diminish Sharad Pawar's political clout. A joke popular in the media of that time was that 'if Pakistan made a mistake as of 1965, this time by the time an agreement like Tashkent was reached, India would have erected a Pakistan View apartment on the occupied land.' It was a light satire on Pawar's prowess as a builder. But soon Sharad Pawar had to go back to Malabar Hill (the Centre of Maharashtra's politics also called Lutyens of Mumbai). When the serial bomb blasts took place in Mumbai in early 1993, Sharad Pawar was sent to Bombay as Chief Minister for the fourth time in a hurry and miraculously Sharad Pawar controlled the situation quickly. There were newspaper headlines at that time - Salaam Bombay, Salaam Sharad Pawar. He was highly praised for handling the situation in Mumbai. But the biggest achievement of his tenure as Chief Minister was to revive the cooperative movement, the backbone of Maharashtra's rural economy. But it is also true that the Congress lost in 1995 when he was Chief Minister and for the first time the Shiv Sena-BJP (remotely run by Bal Thackeray) government was formed. The Congress suffered a crushing defeat in the 1996 Lok Sabha elections. Congress got 140 seats and BJP got 160 seats. Another round of coalition and unstable governments was in sight. The Congressmen looked ahead of Narasimha Rao. Rao also faced allegations of corruption and his trials in the Court had already begun. Sharad Pawar had reached the Lok Sabha from Baramati for the second time in 1996. But Narasimha Rao, who was embroiled in the court case, instead of selecting any fire-brand leader, chose senior Bihar Congress leader Sitaram Kesari as the Congress President. As soon as he took over the Chair, Kesari tried to show down Narasimha Rao and forced Rao to step down as leader of the Parliamentary Party. In 1997, Sitaram Kesari himself became the leader of the Congress Parliamentary Party. But he was a Rajya Sabha member and hence made Sharad Pawar the Leader of the Congress in the Lok Sabha. Both Sharad Pawar and Rajesh Pilot stood up to contest the Congress President's election against Sitaram Kesari in 1997 in the organisational elections within the party. But the

Congressman being a Congressman never dares to go against the leadership, no matter how the party leadership is. Even in 1997, most Congressmen expressed their faith in Sitaram Kesari, who had already seen 80 springs. Both Sharad Pawar and Rajesh Pilot lost badly.

In the 1998 mid-term elections, the Congress won 33 of the 48 seats in Maharashtra and 4 seats were won by the RPI of Congress ally Ramdas Athawale. The Congress won a total of 141 seats and BJP rested at 182. The results were being announced and in a dramatic development on the night of March 14, Sitaram Kesari was removed as Congress President and replaced by Sonia Gandhi. President K.R. Narayanan initiated the process of forming the government. According to Sharad Pawar's supporters, Sharad Pawar had told Sonia Gandhi candidly: – 'Most of the regional parties are ready to form a government under my leadership. The United Front people also want this and even leaders who have contested elections with BJP like Jayalalithaa and Mamata Banerjee are willing to support me. Even Chandrababu Naidu and Chautala's party (which had fought against the Congress in their respective States) do not object to my leadership and as of today I have the support of 281 MPs. So, if the party permits, shall I stake a claim to form the government?' But Sonia Gandhi did not respond to Pawar and on March 17, 1998, informed President Narayanan that 'the Congress is not in a position to form a government'. Later that evening, Narayanan invited Atal Bihari Vajpayee to form the government. Sharad Pawar had missed out on a very close distance to the Prime Minister's post. Atal Bihari Vajpayee became the Prime Minister while Congress leader Sharad Pawar was made the Leader of the Opposition in the Lok Sabha. Pawar remained the Leader of the Opposition in the Lok Sabha for the next 13 months. The next day, when the Vajpayee government fell by one vote on April 17, 1999, 13 months later, Sonia Gandhi claimed the support of 272 MPs before President Narayanan. When Narayanan asked for proof in support of the claim, Sonia

Gandhi asked for some time. But despite getting 3 days, she failed to garner support. It is believed that at the behest of Sharad Pawar, the Samajwadi Party (20) and two Parties of Left Front - RSP (4), Forward Bloc (3) refused to support the Congress on behalf of 27 MPs of their party and the country moved towards mid-term elections.

On the evening of May 15, 1999, Sharad Pawar, P.K. Sangma and Tariq Anwar together issued a letter that created political turmoil across the country. The issue of foreign origin of Congress President Sonia Gandhi was raised in that note. The note was signed by Sharad Pawar, P.A. Sangma and Tariq Anwar. After the leakage of the letter, a big political controversy erupted and protests by Congressmen started all around. Sonia Gandhi left the party and confined herself to 10 Janpath. Congressmen continued to request Sonia Gandhi to return but she was not willing to step out. The political drama lasted for 3 days and then the Congress Working Committee met on May 19, 1999, which was presided over by Pranab Mukherjee in the absence of Sonia Gandhi. The three leaders who wrote the letter were expelled from the Congress and it was then that Sonia Gandhi took over as the party leader. Now, even though the Congress may have become friends with the NCP in Maharashtra, the distrust of the two leaders is the same as it was twenty years ago.

Sharad Pawar's political tenure has been much discussed as compared to other leaders, during his tenure as Chief Minister, he used to visit Maharashtra five days a week. As Chief Minister, he took several important decisions. The promotion of the cooperative sector in Maharashtra was also done during his tenure. Important decisions like reservation for women, setting up of Women Self-Help Groups, police in Maharashtra, etc. has also been allowed to wear full pants instead of half pants during his tenure.

It is no less surprising that a party whose leader has been four times Chief Minister and sometimes as a Minister at the Centre and once Prime Minister candidate has never had even ten

MPs in the Lok Sabha. He had a maximum of nine MPs in the ninth and tenth Lok Sabhas. The same can be said about NCP's performance in Maharashtra. NCP never got more than 25 percent seats in the 288-member Assembly. After the formation of NCP, it contested 223 seats and won only 58 seats and in 2004 the number increased to 71, 62 in 2009, 41 in 2014 and 54 again in the 2019 Assembly. Political analysts see Pawar's strategy in this. Pawar either becomes king himself or king maker. He has been focusing on his and his family's participation in power, but he continues to influence the party, connects the workers and does not refrain from sharing the cream with them. It is also believed that he did not take much interest in going far beyond his sphere of influence which is considered to be western Maharashtra, Marathwada and Konkan.

According to senior political analyst Professor Suhas Palshikar, "Pawar had high expectations from himself when this party was formed in 1999. It had been nearly a decade since the Congress was in a bad phase at that time and all three hoped that many others in the Congress would support them. There was also a perception that when no party gets a clear majority, it can play a more important role. Today, when the party is completing 20 years of its history, it is necessary for this party to evaluate itself. "

Opposing the Congress and remaining associated with it led to the NCP not being very effective at the national level. Otherwise, in the rest of the states like Mamata Banerjee's TMC in West Bengal and Jagan Mohan Reddy's YSR Congress in Andhra were formed by former Congress leaders and Congress is finished from those states. But Sharad Pawar and NCP failed to do anything like that. In fact, Sharad has not been able to isolate the NCP from the Congress and that is the reason why he has not been able to do much in other states.

Sharad Pawar's political and practical conduct has always led to cordial relations with the ruling party in the opposition. In politics and in the party also, he has been able to divide and assign the work brilliantly which few politicians can match. If daughter Supriya Sule in the family looks after the politics of Delhi and the Centre, nephew Ajit Pawar is the politician of the state. Son-in-law Sadanand Sule handles the family business. The responsibility of all the senior functionaries of the party is fixed and they work in tandem. But now the question arises as to what after Sharad. Ajit Pawar has a strong hold among party organisations and workers in Maharashtra. He, like Sharad Pawar, wakes up early in the morning and becomes active. His political understanding and experience of running the government is very developed. But Ajit is a nephew and Supriya is a daughter. Supriya Sule has also been in parliamentary politics for more than 15 years. Her role in the party's actions and decision-making process is becoming very effective. So, she can also claim to be the NCP's supreme leader after Sharad Pawar. The party could be on the verge of collapse if Supriya Sule and Ajit Pawar lock horns for supremacy. Because in that case, even if the voters of the people and the party are divided into Ajit and Supriya, most of the leaders and the second row of the organisation would support Supriya Sule.

Sharad Pawar's political astuteness has been his characteristic and strength since his early days. Constantly being watchful of the political nerves and vibes and strengthening his ground are two qualities he masters in. It was with this wisdom and confidence that he rebelled against Indira Gandhi after the Emergency and left the Congress. But, he has shown amazing practicality in maintaining political relations. Not only is he adept at making concrete political relations, he is also very skilled in wrapping up relationships. Maintaining a separate pressure group within a party and even when fallen apart saving a brief space to reconnect is his speciality.

In the 2019 Maharashtra Assembly elections to 288 seats, BJP got 105 seats and Shiv Sena 56. NCP and Congress finished third and fourth respectively with 54 and 44 seats. After such confusing results, Pawar met Prime Minister Modi at Parliament

House before forming the government with Uddhav Thackeray along with the Shiv Sena and Congress. Sharad Pawar's meeting surprised both the Congress and the Shiv Sena, but eventually the government was formed by the Congress, Shiv Sena and NCP. Pawar formed the government with the Shiv Sena, which also gave the BJP veterans a taste of crushing defeat. Though BJP leaders tried to bring his nephew Ajit Pawar into their fold, Sharad Pawar managed to cut it off well. BJP's concerted efforts to form the government in Maharashtra came to a halt. Sharad Pawar has emerged as a strong leader of the opposition and an ally of the Congress in the country's politics for some time now. But even then, every political activity of Pawar raises questions. He meets Modi, Amit Shah and other leaders of the ruling coalition and there is a lot of speculation about it, but it is usually not easy to understand what he's up to next.

There was a time when Sharad Pawar was diagnosed with cancer while being in-charge of the Ministry of Agriculture and the Board of Control for Cricket in India (BCCI). But his life and its struggles were praised even by his opponents. Undergoing chemotherapy as well as holding two responsibilities alongside, it was not an easy feat. But Pawar accomplished both well and eventually managed to conquer cancer. He was awarded the Padma Vibhushan in 2017, which is considered to be the second highest honoured civilian award in the country.

❑

12
JDU: All Roads Lead to ...... Nitish

Even after becoming the Chief Minister for the eighth time, is there a need to tell the history of a party leader or his party? Neither happens but you must know the roots. Therefore, before becoming the Chief Minister for the eighth time in Bihar, must see what turn Nitish Kumar's party has gone through.

In 1990, along with the Janata Dal rule in Bihar, in the stream of social justice, conflict began to erupt between different ethnic groups for participation in power. This struggle was mainly against the Yadav influence in power. First of all, the economically and educationally prosperous Kurmi caste leaders in the districts of Patna, Nalanda, etc. of Central Bihar, started opposing it seeking their share in power and governance. But Lalu Prasad by declaring Muslim-Yadav (M-Y) formula tried his best to deprive other castes of power. Due to Lalu's (M-Y) equation, a rift emerged between the social justice caste groups. Non-Yadav and non-Muslim castes started protesting at various levels for participation in governance and socio-political mobilization began.

This protest was initiated by the Samata Party, formed in 1994 by George Fernandes and Nitish Kumar. George, along with a total of 14 MPs, including Nitish Kumar, broke ties with the Janata Dal and formed the Janata Dal (George), which was then named the Samata Party in October 1994. The Samata Party later became the Janata Dal (United). For the first time in 1995, the Samata Party fought against Lalu Prasad Yadav in the Bihar Legislative Assembly election and contested over 310 seats out of 324 Legislative Assembly seats. But the party could not beat Lalu Prasad Yadav in the electoral fray and managed to win only seven seats.

But both George and Nitish had sensed the fragility of time. They tied with BJP. In the general elections of 1996, an alliance was formed between the Samata Party and the Bharatiya Janata Party (BJP) and the Samata Party contested over a total of 81 seats in several states. The Samata Party made its presence felt by winning a total of 8 Lok Sabha seats, i.e. six seats in Bihar and one each in Uttar Pradesh and Odisha. After that the government of Atal Bihari Vajpayee was formed at the Centre and all the Allies were made part of the government. Vajpayee then made George the Defence Minister. Nearly two years later, in the 1998 Lok Sabha elections, the Samata Party contested over 57 seats and won 12. Of these, 10 seats were from Bihar and two from Uttar Pradesh.

In the 2000 Bihar Legislative Assembly election, the Samata Party contested over 120 seats and won 34 seats while the BJP won 67. The National Democratic Alliance (NDA) led by the BJP claimed a total of 151 MLAs and the alliance led by Lalu Prasad Yadav had the support of a total of 159 MLAs. Nitish Kumar was sworn in, by the then Governor, as the Chief Minister, under the pressure of Atal Bihari Vajpayee's government at the Centre. For the first time, Nitish Kumar became the Chief Minister of Bihar for just seven days. But soon he resigned from the post of Chief Minister as the magical number was not in his favour.

On the other hand, the Samata Party tried to expand its base in other parts of the country as well. In 2001, Radhabinod Koijam of the Samata Party became the second Chief Minister in Manipur. But after about three months, he had to resign due to the lack of a majority.

Later, George Fernandes and Nitish Kumar merged the Samata Party with the Sharad Yadav-led Janata Dal (United) in 2003. JDU was formed on October 30, 2003 with the merger of Sharad Yadav's Janata Dal, Lokshakti Party and Samata Party. The election symbol of this party was an arrow and the flag was registered in green-white colour. But with Brahmanand Mandal opposing the same, the official merger of the Samata Party could not take place and the Election Commission maintained the existence of the Samata Party. After this Brahmanand Mandal became the National President of the Samata Party. Senior Party leader Raghunath Jha joined Lalu Prasad Yadav's Rashtriya Janata Dal. In 2005 the Samta Party contested on 10 seats under the leadership of Uday Mandal but the party could not register any success.

In fact, the foundation of the split in the Janata Dal was laid before the 1999 Lok Sabha elections. The then Chief Minister of Karnataka J.H. Patel -faction extended support to the National Democratic Alliance. Infuriated H.D. Deve Gowda formed the Janata Dal (Secular) and Janata Dal (United) was formed under the leadership of Sharad Yadav.

In the 2004 Lok Sabha elections, JD(U) contested over 24 and 16 seats respectively in alliance with the Bharatiya Janata Party (BJP). JD(U) won six seats. In the February 2005 Bihar Assembly elections, in absence of a clear majority, President's rule was imposed in Bihar. But with victory in the October-November 2005 election, JD(U) formed the government with the BJP and Nitish Kumar was chosen as the Chief Minister. In the 2009 Lok Sabha elections, JD(U) succeeded in winning 20 seats and in the 2010 Assembly elections, by winning 115 seats, again successfully formed the government in Bihar.

In 2006, a situation arose when Nitish Kumar removed George Fernandes from the post of Party President and made Sharad Yadav the President. It was from this point onwards when George began to be sidelined in politics. In the same party that George had formed, he lost the election of the President to Sharad Yadav in April 2006. The situation worsened when Nitish did not even give a ticket to George in the 2009 Lok Sabha elections. George contested as an independent candidate from Muzaffarpur in 2009. He lost miserably. However, later Nitish made him an MP from the Rajya Sabha. Later, George Fernandes shunned public life due to his ill-health and he died on January 29, 2019 after a prolonged illness.

The Janata Dal (United) had an alliance with the BJP since the time of the Samata Party. But before the 2014 Lok Sabha elections, JD(U) broke its 17-year-old alliance with the BJP. Actually JD(U) leader Nitish Kumar was upset with Narendra Modi, the then Chief Minister of Gujarat, being nominated the Chairman of the BJP Election Campaign Committee.

Sharad Yadav, declaring the break-up with NDA said that the Alliance had side-tracked from its national agenda and JD(U) was unable to carry on with the BJP now. Nitish, the Chief Minister of Bihar, said that it had become essential to end the confusion prevailing in Bihar. The situation worsened and despite all efforts, the alliance could not be saved. Nitish had blamed Narendra Modi for the break-up of the alliance. He alleged that some people were envious of his achievements and creating problems at the behest of an outsider (Narendra Modi). Nitish also relieved 11 Ministers from the BJP Quota. But Narendra Modi was declared the Prime Ministerial candidate. Sharad Yadav resigned as the convener of the National Democratic Alliance soon after the alliance broke up.

After the breakup with the BJP, JD(U) contested the 2014 Lok Sabha elections with the Communist Party of India but could win only two seats while BJP - Lok Janshakti Party and Kushwaha's Party RLSP alliance won 31 seats. Nitish Kumar resigned from the post of Chief Minister after a crushing defeat in the Lok Sabha elections and administered the oath of Chief Minister to Jitan Ram Manjhi. With the support of Rashtriya Janata Dal of Lalu Yadav, Jitan Ram Manjhi proved his majority. Here, after the historic victory of Narendra Modi and BJP in the 2014 Lok Sabha elections, there was a sort of rebellion in JD(U). About two dozen MLAs and several senior party members accused Nitish Kumar of dictatorship. A delegation of the aggrieved leaders met then Party President Sharad Yadav and shared their concerns with him. These MLAs were Anil Kumar, Gyanendra Singh Gyanu, Poonam Devi, Madan Sahni, Ravindra Rai and Raju Singh. They accused Nitish and said Nitish's 'arrogance' was the reason for the shameful defeat of JD(U) in the Lok Sabha elections. He did not consult anyone before breaking up with BJP so the public taught him a lesson and left them in the lurch.

In the Assembly elections held in October-November 2015, Nitish Kumar contested the elections by joining hands with Lalu Prasad Yadav. The voting was held in five stages. In these elections, the ruling Janata Dal United (JDU), Rashtriya Janata Dal (RJD), Congress, Janata Dal, Samajwadi Party, Nationalist Congress Party, Indian National Lok Dal and Samajwadi Janata Party (National) contested the elections by forming a Mahagathbandhan. In contrast, the Bharatiya Janata Party entered the electoral fray along with the Lok Janshakti Party, the Rashtriya Lok Samta Party and the Hindustani Awam Morcha.

In these elections, Lalu Prasad Yadav's RJD and Nitish Kumar-led JDU won 101-101 seats each. The Congress had fielded candidates on 41 seats and BJP on 157 seats. RJD emerged as the single largest party with 80 seats, JD(U) got 71 seats and BJP got 53 seats. In these elections, the government of Mahagathbandhan was formed and the Big-Bro Lalu Yadav kept his promise and made Nitish Kumar the Chief Minister.

In April 2016, Nitish Kumar also became the National President of Janata Dal (United). Sharad Yadav proposed Nitish Kumar's name for National President at the meeting of the JD(U) National Council, which was unanimously accepted. Sharad Yadav has held this post since 2006. After completing three terms, citing the party Constitution, Sharad Yadav had said that he would not file the nomination for Presidentship for the fourth time.

After about a year, in 2017 the tussle between JD(U) and RJD started. Nitish Kumar broke ties with RJD on the allegation that Lalu Prasad Yadav and his children had acquired disproportionate assets and illegal assets in the name of a fake company. In the year 2017, JD(U) broke away from the Mahagathbandhan and Nitish Kumar again formed the government with the BJP support.

Senior JD(U) leader Sharad Yadav on the party's National President Nitish Kumar's decision to join hands with the BJP adopted a rebellious attitude and revolted against Nitish by attending a rally of Rashtriya Janata Dal in Patna. JD(U) General Secretary K.C. Tyagi had written a letter asking Sharad Yadav not to attend the RJD rally. Tyagi had also said that if Yadav joined it, it would be construed as an act against the principles of the party.

During the Bihar tour, Sharad Yadav had said that JD(U) was part of the Mahagathbandhan with RJD and Congress. JD(U) was not Nitish Kumar's party alone but his party too. Yadav had also claimed that the real JD(U) is with him while the government JD(U) is with Nitish.

Nevertheless, the Janata Dal (U) removed Sharad Yadav as the Leader of the party in the Upper House and was replaced by Ramchandra Prasad Singh (RCP Singh). RCP Singh had been a confidant of Nitish Kumar. At that time JDU had 10 members in the Rajya Sabha. JD(U) had earlier suspended its Rajya Sabha member Ali Anwar Ansari from the Parliamentary Party for attending a meeting of opposition parties called by Congress President Sonia Gandhi.

Subsequently, the Sharad Yadav-led JD(U) claimed before the Election Commission that he represented the original party and that most party workers, members of the National Council and State Presidents were with them. The Yadav faction also claimed the JDU's election symbol, the Arrow and the offices allotted to the party. But barring only three, all party MLAs and all MPs had expressed their faith in Nitish Kumar's leadership.

The Innuendo over Sharad Yadav's termination of Rajya Sabha membership owing to sharing of stage at RJD rally had intensified. In the year 2017, the Rajya Sabha membership of Sharad Yadav was cancelled with immediate effect. The membership of another rebel JD(U) leader, Anwar Ali, was also terminated. In May 2018, Sharad formed his new party, Loktantrik Janata Dal. Sharad Yadav also contested from Madhepura on the RJD ticket in the 2019 Lok Sabha elections but lost to Dinesh Yadav of JDU by nearly one lakh votes. In order to revamp the organisation, Janata Dal (United) President Nitish Kumar on October 16, 2018 appointed Prashant Kishor as the National Vice President of the party. With this appointment, Kishor in a way occupied the second highest position in the party and thus became a powerful leader. Kishor, who had worked for several parties as an election strategist, had joined JD(U) on September 16, 2018. It was common knowledge that Kishor was close to Nitish. Senior party leaders believed that Kishor's appointment would help the party to expand its base.

Earlier, after the success of JD(U), RJD and Congress grand alliance in the 2015 assembly elections, Nitish Kumar had made Prashant Kishor his Advisor for the implementation of government plans and programmes. Kishore held the rank of a Cabinet Minister at that time. Prashant Kishor had campaigned for the BJP during the 2014 Lok Sabha elections, during the Bihar Assembly elections in 2015 for RJD, JD(U) and Congress Mahagathbandhan and for Congress during the 2017 Uttar Pradesh Assembly elections.

In October 2019, the Janata Dal (United) National Council meeting unanimously re-elected Nitish Kumar as the party's National President for a term of the next three years. According to the party Constitution, his tenure was till the year 2022. Due to the Assembly elections in Bihar in 2020, Nitish Kumar assumed the charge of handling the party. Assembly elections in Delhi were also imminent. Since the Bharatiya Janata Party and JDU did not even have an alliance in Delhi, Nitish Kumar tried his best to get the support of the voters of Bihar. Earlier, Janata Dal (United) had contested alone in Jharkhand. Under the leadership of Nitish, JD(U) could not achieve the expected success in the 2020 Vidhan Sabha elections. JD(U) could win only 43 Assembly seats due to opposition from the Lok Janshakti Party leader Chirag Paswan and other political reasons.

In December 2020, Nitish Kumar relinquished Party Presidentship in favour of his confidant associate and then Rajya Sabha MP Ramchandra Prasad Singh (R.C.P. Singh). R.C.P. Singh was earlier an Indian Administrative Service officer of Uttar Pradesh cadre and had been the Principal Secretary in the Nitish government. Nitish Kumar made him a member of the Rajya Sabha and General Secretary of JDU. R.C.P. Singh became a Rajya Sabha MP for the first time in 2010. After this, he was again sent to the Rajya Sabha in 2016. Meanwhile, just before the National Executive meeting, six out of seven JD(U) MLAs in Arunachal Pradesh joined the BJP. In the 2019 assembly elections, JD(U) contested on 15 seats and became the second largest party in Arunachal by winning 7 seats.

In March 2021, Nitish Kumar inducted RLSP Chief and former Union minister Upendra Kushwaha, to the JD(U) as part of an effort to increase the support base in Bihar. The Rashtriya Lok Samata Party (RLSP) led by Upendra Kushwaha merged with JD(U). Upendra Kushwaha unconditionally joined JD(U). But Nitish Kumar made Upendra Kushwaha the Chairman of the Parliamentary Board. Later he was made a Member of the Bihar Legislative Council. Coming from Koiri (Kushwaha) society, Kushwaha has been active in politics for a long time. He had also held the post of Leader of Opposition in the Bihar Legislative Assembly. After JD(U) got fewer seats in the Bihar Assembly Elections in 2020, Nitish Kumar started strengthening the political equation. Nitish Kumar is from the Kurmi community. The population of the Kurmi and Kushwaha community in Bihar is said to be about two percent and six percent respectively. The move is an attempt to forge a powerful political partnership with the Kurmi and Kushwaha (Luv-Kush) castes.

In 2013, Kushwaha, who was a Rajya Sabha member of JD(U) adopting a rebellious attitude, broke ties to form the Rashtriya Lok Samata Party and became a part of the BJP-led NDA before the 2014 Lok Sabha elections. After this election, Kushwaha was made Minister of State for Education in the Narendra Modi government. The return of JD(U) to the NDA in July 2017 changed the equations once again and the RLSP broke away from the NDA and became part of the RJD-led Mahagathbandhan.

In the 2019 Lok Sabha elections, Kushwaha had contested from Karakat and Ujiarpur Lok Sabha seats but had to face defeat. Before the Bihar Assembly Elections 2020, Kushwaha contested this election by breaking ties with the Mahagathbandhan and forming a new alliance with Mayawati's BSP and AIMIM. In the Assembly elections, Upendra Kushwaha was projected as the Chief Ministerial candidate by his Alliance, but his alliance partner Hyderabad MP Asaduddin Owaisi's Party AIMIM while it won five seats in the Muslim-dominated Seemanchal region, RLSP could not win even a single seat.

R.C.P. Singh got a place in the expansion of the Modi government in July 2021. But senior JD(U) leader Rajiv Ranjan Singh alias Lalan Singh could not make it to the Union Cabinet. In the year 2019 also, the Narendra Modi government had proposed a Union minister to ally JD(U). Even then R.C.P. Singh was the first choice of the BJP. But there was no talk about Rajiv Ranjan Singh alias Lalan Singh, one close to Nitish Kumar. JD(U) wanted two ministerial posts. Nitish Kumar decided not to join the Union Cabinet so that there was no confrontation between the two leaders.

No one had an inkling what would be the outcome of the turmoil that started in the party from July 21. R.C.P. Singh became a cabinet minister in the centre but was uneasy in the party. Nitish Kumar was also not as comfortable with him as before. There was a clear lack of mutual warmth in behaviour even in public places.

Here R.C.P. was also getting close with the top brass of BJP. From here on he began to grow apart from Nitish.

R.C.P.'s Rajya Sabha term was about to end and as per Nitish's wish, Lallan Singh laid such a siege for R.C.P. that his re-nomination became impossible. Eventually his term was not renewed. R.C.P. was left alone. Absolutely alone. All by himself, in a lurch. The BJP also considered maintaining a safe distance and did not embrace him. But the matter did not end there. There were allegations of corruption on R.C.P. This was happening for the first time that preparations were being made to expel a former national president from the party on charges of corruption.

The party has also decided that now there will be no nomination from his party in the Union Council of Ministers. Chief Minister Nitish deliberately started avoiding the meetings of the Center and also did not hesitate in expressing his displeasure. He neither went to the meeting of NITI Aayog, nor to the meeting of Chief Ministers nor to the banquet in honour of President Draupadi Murmu. One the other hand, party president Lallan Singh alleged that plans are being made to use R.C.P. in the Chirag model. On August 8, The city of Patna became the centre of the meetings of Lalu Prasad Yadav's RJD and Nitish Kumar's JD(U) and on 9th again came the announcement of severing ties with the NDA. On the 10th, Nitish became the Chief Minister for the eighth time. A record in itself. Along with this, came great relief to JD(U) with a stronger zeal to fight further. Nitish Kumar knows how to awaken a weakening party. In all this scenario he kept his aspirations high and planned his moves ardently.

Now it has to be seen how far Nitish Kumar can go with RJD leader Tejashwi Yadav. Is Nitish mighty enough to become an epicentre of challenge to Narendra Modi in 2024 or will continue to establish new records in Bihar only.

❑

13
RJD - Story of One Struggle to Another

Bihar happens to be the earliest of the states from where the Congress rule began to shake. It started in 1967 when the Socialists defeated the Congress and formed the government. The coming together of socialist parties as an alternative to Congress and then disintegrating again is an important phase of Indian politics. But a few days later, a successful movement commenced in 1974 led by Jayaprakash Narayan. When Congress again lost in 1977 after the Emergency, a Socialist government was formed under the leadership of Karpuri Thakur. Due to differences amongst the Socialists, the government fell again and the Congress came back to power. But even before that, the youth had started mobilising in Bihar politics. Lalu Yadav was also one of them. Students in Patna University started their political journey from there itself. Lalu Prasad Yadav was active in the Jayaprakash movement but came in contact with prominent Janata Party leaders during the Emergency. The youth from Phulwaria village in Gopalganj district won the 1977 general election on an Indian Lok Dal ticket. But what is to happen would happen for sure.. Neither the State Government nor the Janata Government at the Centre lasted long. But Lalu now focused his attention on regional politics. Success came to him soon. In the Bihar Legislative Assembly in 1985 he became the Leader of the Opposition.

V.P. Singh arrived on the central stage and the Congress faced defeat in 1989. V.P. became Prime Minister. A year later, in 1990, after the Janata Dal's victory in the Bihar Assembly elections, the process of formation of government began, but came to a standstill on the matter of the post of Chief Minister. The then Prime Minister Vishwanath Pratap Singh wanted a senior Bihar Leader and former Chief Minister Ram Sundar Das as Chief Minister while Chandrashekhar was supporting his disciple Raghunath Jha for the same. Amidst the controversy, Deputy Prime Minister Devi Lal proposed Lalu Prasad Yadav's name. Sharad Yadav, Mulayam Singh Yadav and Nitish Kumar belonged to the Devi Lal camp and Lalu Yadav was his favourite too. In the 1990 elections Sharad Yadav and Mulayam Singh Yadav played a major role in ticket-distribution.

Being the former Chief Minister, Ramsundar Das was considered a natural contender. He was also an MLA . That was the era of true democracy in the parties. In a triangular power-struggle, out of 122 JD(U) MLA, Lalu Yadav got 55 votes, Ramsundar Das 51 and Raghunath Jha got 16 votes. Lalu Prasad Yadav became Chief Minister on March 10, 1990. From here on a new caste-based politics began in Bihar in which elections went caste-centric..The caste mobilisation became stronger after the announcement of reservation for backward and most backward castes by the Central Government on the basis of the recommendations made by the Mandal Commission. Along with this, the battle for supremacy for power-sharing among the backward and most backward castes also started. Due to the dominance of Yadavs in power under the leadership of Lalu Prasad Yadav, the Kurmis first raised their voice in Bihar and in 1994, the Samata Party was formed under the leadership of Nitish Kumar. But now Lalu Yadav's stars were shining and he again became the Chief Minister by winning the 1995 elections. But by 1997, the star began to waver and in 1997, when Lalu Prasad Yadav had to go to jail due to his involvement in the fodder scam, he refused to leave the chair. There were voices rising against him in the Janata Dal. Inder Kumar Gujral was the Prime Minister in the United Front government at that time.

The period between 1996 and 1998 is considered most unstable in Indian politics at the Centre because of the involvement of S.R. Bommais' name in the Hawala scandal who had to resign from the post of National President of the Janta Dal. Lalu Yadav was made the National President in his place. Lalu used to laugh and say — Hawala ne Janta Dal mere hawale kar diya. The CBI probe into the involvement of Lalu Prasad in the fodder scam was initiated during the 13 days of Atal Bihari Vajpayee's government, but was carried forward during the H.D. Deve Gowda government. Circumstances had made H.D. Deve Gowda the Prime Minister but he felt threatened by popular leaders. That is why first he got Ramkrishna Hegde removed and thereafter he clipped the wings of Lalu Prasad Yadav.

Inder Kumar Gujral has written in his autobiography Matters of Discretion that one day in 1997, when Lalu Prasad Yadav, troubled by the clutches of CBI on the fodder scam, went to the Prime Minister's residence to meet him. Deve Gowda kept him waiting for two and a half hours till the CBI director arrived there. The Janata Dal President Lalu Yadav felt bad and on the same day he made up his mind to oust Deve Gowda with the help of Sharad Yadav and Congress Chief Sitaram Kesari. Now it was Inder Kumar Gujral's turn at the Centre. Gujral was considered Lalu Prasad Yadav's choice. But even under his rule, the CBI's grip on Lalu Prasad Yadav kept tightening. On the basis of evidence CBI Chief Joginder Singh announced the filing of a chargesheet against Bihar Chief Minister Lalu Prasad Yadav and Bihar Governor A.R. Kidwai also permitted it. His close aides like Ram Vilas Paswan, Nitish Kumar and others deserted him and Janata Dal President Lalu Yadav was now feeling lonely. Under these circumstances he agreed to resign as Chief Minister but refused to leave the post of

National President of the Janata Dal. But senior leaders of Janata Dal did not agree to this. The matter remained unresolved.

As a result, on July 5, Lalu Prasad Yadav announced the formation of the Rashtriya Janata Dal. The very next day, along with seventeen Lok Sabha members and eight Rajya Sabha members, he broke away from the Janata Dal on July 5, 1997 and established the Rashtriya Janata Dal. Lalu Prasad Yadav was elected the President of the party.

Before going to jail, on July 25, 1997, Lalu Yadav made his wife Rabri Devi the Chief Minister of Bihar. Bihar got its first woman Chief Minister with this, but Lalu's political decision received a lot of criticism. The command of the government remained in the hands of Lalu Prasad Yadav. On July 30, 1997, he surrendered in the fodder scam case and since then legal proceedings are going on against him. In 2000, Rabri Devi managed to return to power with a reduced majority.

On the other hand, a different drama was going on at the Centre. Lalu Prasad Yadav had announced a separate party - the Rashtriya Janata Dal which was not a part of the United Front government, but three Ministers from his party, Raghuvansh Prasad Singh, Kanti Singh and Jai Narayan Nishad, remained in the central government led by the then Prime Minister Inder Kumar Gujral.

Lalu Prasad Yadav began his social mobilisation after becoming the Chief Minister. He started mobilising the Yadavs and Muslims. Yadavs are 12 percent and Muslims 18 percent by population in Bihar and thus he aimed for around 30 percent of the votes. Keeping this equation in mind, Lalu stopped Lal Krishna Advani's famous Rath Yatra in Samastipur on September 23, 1990 and arrested him. On Lalu's action the BJP withdrew support to the Janata Dal government at the centre and Bihar. Vishwanath Pratap Singh's government at the centre collapsed but Lalu Prasad Yadav's government survived.

After Lalu's imprisonment, Rabri Devi remained the Chief Minister till February 1999. Thereafter, President's rule was imposed in the state for about a month and Rabri Devi again became the Chief Minister on March 9, 1999 and remained in office till March 2, 2000. In the Lok Sabha elections held in 1998, a year after its formation, the Rashtriya Janata Dal registered its presence by winning 17 out of 54 Lok Sabha seats in Bihar (at that time Jharkhand was not separated). However, it did not register any success in other parts of the country. In the year 1999, the Rashtriya Janata Dal entered into an agreement with Mulayam Singh Yadav's Samajwadi Party, but Lalu Prasad did not benefit from this alliance. In the general election of October 1999, the Rashtriya Janata Dal entered into an electoral pact with the Indian National Congress but won only seven seats.

In the Assembly elections held in Bihar in 2000, the Rashtriya Janata Dal won a maximum of 124 seats in the then 324-member Bihar Legislative Assembly. Jharkhand was still part of Bihar. BJP was reduced to 67, Congress 23, Janata Dal 21 and Samata Party 34 seats only. There was no majority with RJD. This situation led to a political upheaval in Bihar. The NDA government was headed by Atal Bihari Vajpayee at the Centre. In Bihar, Nitish Kumar supported by some other parties including BJP took the oath as Chief Minister, but could not prove a majority in the Assembly and resigned from the Chief Minister's post after only seven days. Lalu Prasad exhibited efficient political management and formed the government along with other allies including Congress. Rabri Devi again became the Chief Minister and remained in the Chair for five years till 2005.

In November of the same year, Bihar was divided and Jharkhand was formed. Rashtriya Janata Dal in the year 2004 maintained the lead by winning 22 out of 40 seats in the Lok Sabha elections. It remained an integral part of the United Progressive Alliance of UPA and Lalu Prasad was the Railway Minister in the Manmohan Singh Ministry at the Centre.

The political crisis over the Rashtriya Janata Dal (RJD) deepened after the February 2005 Assembly elections. RJD contested on 215 seats but could win only 75 seats. However, this number was more than the seats won by other parties. But no party had a majority. Ram Bilas Paswan's Lok Janshakti Party had 29 MLAs and thus possessed the key to form the government. Whichever coalition they supported could have formed the government. But LJP refused to support any party or alliance. As a result, President's Rule was imposed in the State from March 2005 to November 2005.

In October elections were held in the State again and the RJD was reduced to 54 seats. The National Democratic Alliance (NDA) of the Bharatiya Janata Party and the Janata Dal (U) got a majority and Nitish Kumar became the Chief Minister. In the year 2009 in the Lok Sabha elections, the RJD broke ties with the UPA in a dispute over distribution of seats. Lalu made an agreement with Ram Bilas Paswan's Lok Janshakti Party and Mulayam Singh Yadav's Samajwadi Party and the so-called Fourth Front contested elections in many states. But Lalu's Party got only four seats in Bihar.

The RJD's situation deteriorated in the November 2010 Assembly elections and could win only 22 Assembly seats. Before the elections, Lalu broke the pact with the Samajwadi Party led by Mulayam Singh. The RJD's period of electoral failures continued and in the 2014 Lok Sabha elections, it could win only four seats. Lalu's wife Rabri Devi and older daughter Misa Bharti also lost the election.

Wherever there was a non-NDA Government at the centre, RJD had many of its members as Ministers, Jayaprakash Narayan Yadav, Tasleemuddin, Kanti Singh, Raghuvansh Prasad Singh, Raghnath Jha and Ali Ashraf Hashmi to name a few.

Because of the punishment in the fodder scam case, Lalu Prasad Yadav lost his membership of Parliament in 2013 and could not take part in active politics. Lalu Prasad Yadav has been accused of familialism (Parivarvaad) for first bringing his wife and then children into politics.

A total of 64 cases were registered in the fodder scam and Lalu Prasad was also made an accused in six. In one of the cases, Lalu was convicted for the withdrawal and rigging of Rs 37.7 crore in Chaibasa. He was sentenced to five years and due to this punishment, he was banned from participating in electoral activities.

But the politics of Bihar has seen numerous ups and downs. One who has always been considered an enemy, can also become an ally or friend. In 2015, Lalu made a pact with Nitish Kumar, who broke away from the BJP, and in the Assembly elections, the RJD once again made a strong comeback by winning 80 seats and became the single largest party. Nitish's party bagged 71 seats. As promised, Lalu made Nitish the Chief Minister, while Lalu's younger son Tejashwi Prasad Yadav was made the Deputy Chief Minister of Bihar and elder son Tej Pratap Yadav was made the Health Minister. But this alliance did not last long and after 20 months, in 2017, Nitish broke away from RJD on the issue of corruption and again joined hands with BJP and formed the government. The RJD once again became part of the Opposition in the Bihar Assembly.

The performance of the Rashtriya Janata Dal in the 2019 Lok Sabha elections was very poor and the party could not win a single Lok Sabha seat. But a year later, in the 2020 Legislative Assembly elections, Lalu Prasad's younger son Tejashwi Prasad Yadav gave the party a big success. RJD emerged as the single largest party in the State by winning a total of 75 Vidhan Sabha seats.

Lalu Prasad is out on bail in the fodder scam case and his health is also deteriorating. But his sons Tejashwi Yadav and Tej Pratap Yadav are challenging the combined power of Nitish Kumar and BJP. The sword keeps hanging over the Bihar government formed with a very small margin. Lalu is again trying his best to strengthen his party even under the trials of the fodder scam while his younger son Tejashwi Yadav is handling affairs of the party .

The Rashtriya Janata Dal which was initially supported in other states now has practically no existence in other parts of the country except Bihar. The party had established its units in many north eastern states and Hindi-speaking regions including Jharkhand and also contested elections in many states. The RJD had contested the 2021 Assembly elections in Assam in alliance with 'like-minded' parties but did not get the expected success anywhere. The party's Jharkhand Chief Gautam Sagar Rana broke ties with the party and formed a separate Party along with other members. Now Rana has named this party Rashtriya Janata Dal Democratic.

The fodder scam case is considered to have an important role in the formation of the Rashtriya Janata Dal. The politics of Bihar cannot be understood without RJD and it is unlikely to change in future also. Now in Bihar caste politics has made class struggle irrelevant or a thing of the past. Class struggle was also the basic premise of Left parties. Thus Lalu Prasad also weakened the Left as well.

Now the Rashtriya Janata Dal is indirectly under command of Lalu Prasad Yadav's son Tejashwi Yadav. But it is still widely seen as the party of Lalu Prasad Yadav. Challenged by a sudden crisis, Lalu Prasad Yadav had formed this party during his heydays in his political journey. The crisis still looms large on him till date. Tejashwi Yadav has so far shown political maturity but the real challenge before him is to mend and reinvent the image of the party and widen the social sphere balancing the caste equations. The future of the Rashtriya Janata Dal also largely depends on how successfully he keeps the flock together. However despite all this manoeuvring Lalu Yadav has carved a place for himself in history. Whenever the rise of the backward classes, specially Yadavs will be discussed, Lalu's name will be supreme.

❑

14

LJP - Dare to Enjoy the Fruits of Power

The story of the third largest political force— the Lok Janshakti Party- revolves around its founder Ram Vilas Paswan only. Ram Vilas Paswan was not called a political meteorologist in vain. He knew the people's mind and also the very nerves of power, that is why for more than fifty years he was either 'in' power or 'circumvented' the power. Personally he was so tactful and well behaved, whether he was in or out of power, he could change the lives of many for good. In the early years of his political career, Ram Vilas Paswan, influenced by the ideas of socialism and Ambedkar, became a member of the United Socialist Party and won the 1969 Bihar Legislative election from the Alauli Assembly constituency and became a follower of Jayaprakash Narayan and Raj Narayan. He spent the entire Emergency period in jail. After the Emergency was lifted, in 1977, he became a member of the Janata Party, he has a record in his name by winning the Hajipur Lok Sabha constituency with the highest number of votes. After the split of the Janata Party in the year 1979, he joined Charan Singh's Janata Party (Samajwadi) and again won the 1980 Lok Sabha elections from Hajipur.

In later years a trend of assigning importance to individuals over ideology developed in the parties following the socialist line of thinking, and many leaders started forming their own party. Ram Vilas Paswan also formed the Dalit Sena in 1983. The Dalit Sena as a political and social organization worked for the welfare of Dalits at the political, administrative and social level on issues related to them. Later, Ramvilas renamed it the Scheduled Caste Sena (Scheduled Caste Army) along the lines of Bhimrao Ambedkar's Scheduled Caste Federation.

Ram Vilas Paswan lost the 1984 election. Meanwhile, public opinion against the Congress began to build up across the country. Various parties of the socialist stream attempted to unite. The Janata Dal was formed by the efforts of leaders like Devi Lal and Vishwanath Pratap Singh and Ram Vilas Paswan was also its senior member. He again won from Hajipur constituency in the 1989 Lok Sabha elections.

He became the Minister of Labour and Welfare in Vishwanath Pratap Singh's Cabinet. Vishwanath Pratap Singh's government crumbled in 1991. The Lok Sabha elections were held again but this time Ram Vilas Paswan was elected from the Rosda area. In 1996, he again won from Hajipur. Meanwhile, the age of political instability continued and the government of the then I.K. Gujral fell in November 1997. Elections to the Lok Sabha were held again in 1998 but again no party got a mandate for majority. The National Democratic Alliance (NDA) government was formed under the leadership of Bharatiya Janata Party (BJP) leader Atal Bihari Vajpayee. But this government also collapsed in April 1999 and again the Lok Sabha elections were held. This time the NDA got an absolute majority and Atal Bihari Vajpayee became the Prime Minister. Ram Vilas Paswan also became a Union Minister.

(Meanwhile Bihar leaders Nitish Kumar and George Fernandes formed the Samata Party which later changed to Janata Dal (United). Lalu Prasad Yadav formed the Rashtriya Janata Dal (RJD) after his name in the fodder scam and made his wife Rabri Devi the Chief Minister. Caste equations in the politics of Bihar gave a chance to these two parties who were beginning to make an impact. Lalu Yadav had mobilised Muslims and Yadavs in his favour, while Nitish Kumar involved himself in mobilisation of Kurmi, Koiri, extremely backward and upper caste people. The vote of Dalits was divided between the two parties.

Ram Vilas Paswan was part of the Janata Dal and then the NDA through the Janata Party, but when the political situation in Bihar changed, he founded the Lok Janshakti Party (LJP) in 2000. In Bihar, this party started deepening its influence among the lower castes and Dalit community. Paswan had formed this party with a very few people and its aim was to connect together the lower strata of the state. Ideologically the party was formed to attain social justice and raise the voice of the suppressed Dalit class but it was a political weapon for Ram Vilas Paswan.

In 2004, LJP did well in Bihar in alliance with Congress and Lalu Prasad Yadav's Rashtriya Janata Dal when in the Lok Sabha elections, the LJP won four seats. A year later, in the February 2005 Assembly elections, the LJP won 29 seats. Ram Vilas remained a part of the Congress-led government at the Centre as part of strategy and contested elections in Bihar in alliance with the Congress. Both the factions of Nitish Kumar and Lalu Prasad Yadav kept trying to get support from Ram Vilas but Paswan placed the demand of a Muslim Chief Minister. Neither of the two leaders agreed to this. Ultimately the government could not be formed and President's Rule had to be imposed. This was followed by re-elections in October-November 2005. But in this election, LJP was reduced to just 10 seats. RJD also lost heavily and Nitish Kumar and BJP got together to form the government.

In the 2009 Lok Sabha elections, Ram Vilas Paswan formed the Fourth Front, forming a historic alliance with Samajwadi Party President Mulayam Singh Yadav and RJD President Lalu Prasad Yadav. At the time of elections, this alliance had 64 MPs in the Lok Sabha. The three parties together contested all the 120 Lok Sabha seats in Uttar Pradesh and Bihar. Under this alliance,

SP fielded candidates on all 80 seats in Uttar Pradesh, RJD on 28 out of 40 seats in Bihar and LJP on the remaining 12 seats. But this front failed to perform as expected and could win only 28 out of 120. The Lok Janshakti Party could not win even a single seat, while RJD was reduced to just four seats. The LJP again contested the 2010 Assembly elections with the RJD but won only three seats. LJP got only 6.75 percent votes. But the matter does not rest here. On the other hand, Nitish Kumar had also left no stone unturned to demolish Paswan's well guarded fort. In his efforts to win the Dalit's hearts he declared 21 out of the 22 castes of the Dalit community as Mahadalits, in which he succeeded. (After this, in 2018, the then Chief Minister Jitan Ram Manjhi included the Paswan caste and thus included everyone in the Mahadalit. It is believed that Dalits constitute 17 percent of the population in Bihar and of these Dusadh (Paswan) is 6 percent.)

On February 27, 2014, the LJP again announced an alliance with the BJP-led NDA after 12 years. In the 2014 Lok Sabha elections, LJP contested 7 seats, Upendra Kushwaha led RLSP 3 and BJP 30 seats. LJP won six out of seven seats in its account and the entire alliance won 31 out of 40 seats in Bihar. Ram Vilas Paswan's son Chirag Paswan also contested for the first time and won from the Jamui seat. Ram Vilas Paswan was made a Minister at the Centre.

As an NDA constituent, the LJP contested the 2015 Bihar Assembly elections on 40 seats, but won only 2 seats. The NDA also included RLSP and Jitan Ram Manjhi-led Hindustani Awam Morcha (HAM) in this election. BJP contested over 160 seats, LJP 40, RLSP 23 and HAM 20 seats. BJP got 53, LJP 2, RLSP 2 and HAM got one seat. The alliance of Lalu Prasad Yadav and Nitish Kumar could not last more than two years. In 2017, Nitish Kumar joined the 53-seat BJP and returned to the NDA and formed the government in Bihar. Senior LJP leader and Ram Vilas Paswan's brother Pashupati Kumar Paras was made the Minister of Animal and Fisheries Resources in the Nitish cabinet.

The LJP once again participated in the Lok Sabha Elections in 2019 with the BJP-led NDA. Out of 40 seats in Bihar, BJP got 17, JDU 17 and LJP got six seats. LJP was also given a Rajya Sabha seat under the seat-sharing formula. LJP won all the six seats. Party President Ram Vilas Paswan did not participate in these elections owing to health problems and became an MP through the Rajya Sabha and a Minister at the Centre. His younger brother Pashupati Kumar Paras contested from Hajipur, the traditional seat of Ram Vilas Paswan, and won.

Meanwhile, keeping in mind his deteriorating health, LJP President Ram Vilas Paswan handed over his political legacy to his son Chirag Paswan and the command of LJP completely went into the hands of the young brigade. Ram Vilas also advised his son that two of his contemporaries Lalu Prasad Yadav and Nitish Kumar never let Paswan become the Chief Minister even though he was a leader of bigger stature than both of them. Ram Vilas asked Chirag to make a political settlement with Lalu Prasad Yadav and Nitish Kumar only on equal terms or seek his due share as both kept trying to uproot him from Bihar.

(Prince Raj, newly elected MP and son of former MP Ramchandra Paswan, was given the command by the State Unit of Bihar. Before nominating as President, Chirag Paswan was made the Chairman of the Parliamentary Board of LJP. Chirag Paswan's dominance was visible in all the decisions of the party. To make the Bihar State President Pashupati Kumar Paras as the National President of the Dalit army was also Chirag Paswan's decision.)

Bearing in mind the lesson from his father, Chirag Paswan demanded 40 seats for LJP for the 2020 Legislative Assembly elections. But JDU President and Chief Minister Nitish Kumar was not prepared to assign more than 25 seats to LJP. Tension escalated between the two parties on this issue and Chirag Paswan sharply and openly criticised the functioning of the Nitish government on the issue of mishandling of the Corona epidemic, alleged disturbances in law and order and alleged misappropriation in flood relief. He refused to accept the 'Saat Nischay' scheme run by the Bihar government. Chirag claimed that all the works of 'Saat Nischay' were still incomplete and this scheme is nothing but a box of corruption.

The troubles of the BJP leadership grew as the distance between the two parties, both its allies, continued to grow. With the intention of weakening the LJP and separating it from the BJP, Nitish Kumar made the Hindustani Awam Morcha led by Jitan Ram Manjhi a part of the NDA. The BJP also tied up with the Vikassheel Insaan Party led by Mukesh Sahni.

Ultimately, LJP President Chirag Paswan announced to contest the elections on his own sans any alliance. Chirag Paswan announced that the next government would implement the 'Bihar First, Bihari First' Vision Document. The party contested on 143 seats across the state. The LJP fielded candidates on all the seats from the JDU's share. Chirag Paswan declared to support the formation of the NDA government under the leadership of BJP after the elections. Chirag called himself the Hanuman of Narendra Modi and despite contesting a separate election, he continued to support the BJP but fired openly against Nitish.

Meanwhile on October 8, 2020, the party's founder Ram Vilas Paswan succumbed to a prolonged illness. But Chirag could not cash in on it in the elections. LJP won only one seat. Raj Kumar Singh of LJP won the lone Matihani Assembly seat in Begusarai district by a small margin and he too later joined Nitish's party. LJP got a total of 23,83,457 votes in the entire state which was 5.66 percent of the total valid votes. But Chirag succeeded in defeating JD(U) candidates. JD(U) could win only 43 seats while BJP won 74 seats. According to a survey, JD(U) suffered a loss in 35 seats due to LJP's opposition.

On the other hand, at the time of Cabinet expansion at the Centre, the Lok Janshakti Party began to disintegrate. Five LJP MPs revolted against Chirag and elected Pashupati Paras as the

Leader of the Parliamentary Party. Later, Pashupati Kumar Paras was also included in the Union Cabinet.

The battle for leadership in the Lok Janshakti Party reached a cross-cutting situation. The faction led by Pashupati Kumar Paras removed Chirag Paswan as the Parliamentary Party Leader. The Paras faction removed Chirag Paswan from the post of National President. Soon after this, the Chirag Paswan faction expelled the five rebel MPs from the party for anti-party activities and today Chirag Paswan is struggling for his existence and it is believed that Paswan's own vote bank is still with Chirag. But Paras is also trying his best to remain pivotal. There is a possibility of seeing the uncle-nephew duo on the same page, but when? Only time can tell. Right now LJP's future is rather uncertain. The tree which Ram Vilas Paswan planted and nurtured, grew big and fructified. Paswan consumed it and shared it generously with others but what the future holds cannot be predicted. It is a rare phenomenon in Indian politics when the Leader of a small regional party remains an effective Minister for more than two decades, regardless of the government at the Centre. … and this record is in the name of Ram Vilas Paswan.

Bihar has a unique record of small parties. Former Chief Minister Jitan Ram Manjhi's Hindustani Awam Morcha have been doing good work in their respective sections but could not handle their vote bank efficiently. Neither did they form a second line of leadership, nor could they inculcate any hunger for power in the party.

Mukesh Sahani's Vikassheel Insaan Party (VIP) has also had an influence of its own. The lack of awareness among its voters situated on the banks of the Ganges did not convert into a big vote bank. This is the reason why the achievement of these parties in general elections is not very important. Mostly only the party Chiefs or their kins are able to reach the House and one or two manage to become a Minister.

❑

15
DMK-AIADMK - Shared Legacy, Straight Fights

Tamil Nadu is the largest state in South India. Since the time of the Madras Presidency, there has been a strong opposition to North Indian supremacy in this region of the country's south coast. Its basic call is the opposition of the Brahmanical system and the Hindi language. The policy adopted by Dravida Munnetra Kazhagam, formed in 1944 for cultural identity, by uniting people on the basis of language and regionalism, proved to be very effective. However, over time the politics of linguistic identity split into two streams, the DMK and the AIADMK, but the politics of Tamil Nadu continued to grow along the same path. The battle for power in the state has been confined between these two parties for almost five decades. After winning the first election post- independence, the famous English scholar Chakravarti Raj Gopalachari was made the Chief Minister of Madras Province (now Tamil Nadu). In 1954, Kumaraswamy Kamaraj of Congress became the Chief Minister. Later in the election of 1957 also, he continued to be the Chief Minister. For the first time in India, the policy of compulsory education for children in any state was initiated during his tenure. Kamaraj is considered the Father of the children's mid-day meal scheme in the country. He was followed by Minjur Bhaktavatsalam in October 1963. During this time, the DMK leadership engaged itself with providing Tamil identity on a linguistic basis. On January 26, 1962, when Hindi was adopted as the official language, two days before it DMK Munnetra Kazhagam observed a day of mourning in the entire Madras province. In the year 1967, the Congress tasted defeat in the Assembly elections and DMK leader Kanjeevaram Natarajan Annadurai was made the Chief Minister. After this defeat, the Congress could never return to power here even after six decades. DMK and AIADMK, both the parties derive from the same political heritage. Their modus operandi is also almost the same, but in the struggle for power, the effort to be a notch ahead of each other has created differences between them. In 1968, the state was rechristened as Tamil Nadu. The very next year, at the age of sixty, Annadurai died and Muttuvel Karunanidhi became the Chief Minister. He has a record of becoming Chief Minister five times in six decades and has left an indelible mark on Tamil Nadu politics.

Karunanidhi was born in 1924 in the village of Thirukkuvalai in the then Madras Province. Now the house where Karunanidhi was born has been converted into a museum. There are pictures of him from the Pope to Indira Gandhi alongside. Karunanidhi's family was financially poor, but he was an enthusiastic child willing to read and move on. The community in which he was born traditionally practised playing the musical instrument 'Nadaswaram'. There is an anecdote of childhood, when Karunanidhi used to go to the village temple to learn music, he did not learn anything special to play there, but he read the first lesson of caste discrimination there. Karunanidhi, a so-called lower caste boy, was not allowed to enter the temple wearing any cloth above his waist. Only certain melodies were taught to him. The caste-based distinction was also prevalent in the music, which left him disinterested in music. But, this opened the door to the politics of retaliation. At a young age, Karunanidhi was greatly influenced by the ideas of thinker E.V. Ramasamy 'Periyar' and got involved in the 'Aatm Gouravam' movement founded by him. This movement was infused with non-Brahmanical sentiments. Dravid people were agitating to rise against 'Aryan Brahmanism'. Karunanidhi entered the world of political movements at the tender age of 14. It started with the 'Remove-Hindi Movement', when in 1937 Hindi language was introduced as a compulsory language in schools. Influenced by Periyar's ideology, young youth took to the streets in protest. Karunanidhi was also one of them. He made the pen his weapon and started penning his thoughts. Dramas, pamphlets, newspapers and speeches became his munitions. He was working in Coimbatore to write scripts for commercial plays. This art of writing worked when Periyar and Annadurai caught sight of him. Seeing his eloquent oratory and writing style, he was made the editor of the party magazine Kudiyarasu.

When the country attained independence in 1947, differences arose between Periyar and his aide Annadurai. With the independence of the country, Periyar and Annadurai parted ways. Annadurai joined mainstream politics and in 1949 the new party 'Dravida Munnetra Kazhagam' was founded. Karunanidhi joined Annadurai and became his chief associate in the new party. By becoming the party's first cashier, he single-handedly undertook the responsibility of raising funds for the new party. But in the meantime he also got inclined towards cinema. Now he was rearing the ideology on the 35mm screen (there was no 70mm then). In 1952, he wrote Parsakshi, a blockbuster full of melodrama. The poor Tamil hero who has to endure the tortures of tyrannical North-Indian moneylenders, Brahmin leaders and an insensitive government, the film aptly voices the Dravidian identity, the premise on which the foundation of his party was laid.

In the 1960s, he was becoming very popular for Tamil films by writing historical and social stories advocating social change. Sivaji Ganesan made his on-screen debut through the Tamil film Parasakthi written by him which turned into a blockbuster. A scene in this film hit the right chord with the masses in which he challenged the superstition prevailing in society. Parashakti proved to be a turning point not only in Tamil cinema but also in

Karunanidhi's life. This film gave a new height to the ideology of the Dravidian movement by taking it to the masses. It was through Parashakti that two prominent actors of Tamil cinema, Sivaji Ganesan and S.S. Rajendran emerged in the film world. M.G. Ramachandran also acted in several films written by Karunanidhi. Both of them used to work in films together. Along with this, both these stalwarts of Tamil films continued to carry forward DMK politics under the patronage of Annadurai.

Karunanidhi provided an ideological base to DMK politics with his eloquent speeches, while silver screen hero M.G. Ramachandran took the fight for Tamil identity to the masses through his popularity. The party contested its first Assembly election in 1957, and Karunanidhi was among 13 elected MLAs. It took only 10 years to overturn Tamil Nadu's political power. In 1967, the same party with thirteen MLAs won an absolute majority and Annadurai became the first non-Congress Chief Minister of the State. The raging linguistic controversy in South India and the 'anti-Hindi sentiment' had worked. Congress's position in Tamil Nadu is that till date it has remained an 'ally' of other Dravidian parties. Just two years after assuming power, at 69 Annadurai died of cancer. Now, Karunanidhi was the new Chief Minister.

In 1971, Karunanidhi was successful in winning an election on his own. After assuming charge, Karunanidhi wanted to introduce his son Muthu from his first wife Padmavati into films, though his film was unsuccessful at the box office. But, this led to a widening of the gap between Karunanidhi and MGR. MGR had helped a lot in making him the Chief Minister, but over time some differences arose between the two, which only grew with time. When the political tension between the two escalated, MGR accused Karunanidhi of corruption and raised many other questions, which annoyed Karunanidhi and in 1975, MGR was expelled from the party.

Now it was MGR's turn. MGR got himself involved in the formation of AIADMK as soon as he left the DMK. In this task, his heroine of the silver screen, Jayalalithaa, supported him. That was the period when, as an actor, MGR had become the most popular face of Tamil cinema. He was giving tough competition to his partner in reel and real life. In 1977, both MGR and Karunanidhi came face to face for the first time. It was like a cinematic contest which had the writer on one side, the hero on the other. The Hero was assured and proud of his popularity. The writer had the illusion that his mighty pen had created the hero, but on the screen the public viewed only the hero. In 1977, MGR defeated Karunanidhi and his party in the elections so that it could not resurface again until MGR died. It continued like this for the next ten years.

Then in 1987, after MGR's death, a dispute broke out in the AIADMK over the party leadership. It had MGR's wife Janaki Ramachandran on one side and MGR's heroine on the silver screen and party's youth leader Jayaram Jayalalithaa on the other. Jayaram Jayalalithaa was born on February 24, 1948 in an Iyer Brahmin family in Melurkot village of Pandavapura taluk in Mandya district of Mysore state. She lost her father Jayaram at the tender age of two years, her mother took her to Bangalore, where her parents lived. Later she started working in Tamil cinema and changed her film name to 'Sandhya'. Her early education took place first in Bangalore and later in Chennai. Instead of studying at Stella Maris College in Chennai, she studied further with a government stipend. When she was still in school, her mother convinced her to work in films. At the age of 15, she started as a lead actress in Kannada films. She was the first actress to wear a skirt on screen. Apart from Tamil, she worked in about 300 films in Telugu, Kannada, English and Hindi. She began her political career with M.G. Ramachandran in 1982, after getting membership of the All India Anna Dravida Munnetra Kazhagam (AIADMK). As soon as she joined, she started working as a publicity secretary. MGR now started liking the heroine of reel life in real life too. Later, seeing her English speaking prowess, party Chief MGR sent her to the Rajya Sabha in 1984. But the concoction of beauty with power was not pleasing to some in the party and those people also successfully displayed their discomfort. The rift between such leaders and MGR also manifested occasionally. In those days, she used to write a column about her personal life in a Tamil magazine but MGR prevented her from doing so at the behest of other leaders. With her becoming a member of the Rajya Sabha, in 1984, when MGR became incapacitated due to a brain stroke, Jaya wanted to take over as the Chief Minister, but then Ramachandran even removed her from the post of Deputy Leader of the party. MGR died in 1987. Those who had been waiting for the disintegration of the AIADMK, their dream was now becoming a reality .... and the happiest was DMK Chief Karunanidhi. Now the leader of one faction of AIADMK supported MGR's widow Janaki Ramachandran and the other was with Jayalalithaa. But Jayalalithaa declared herself the heir to Ramachandran's legacy. This internal battle of the AIADMK gave Karunanidhi an opportunity to reclaim the political power he had lost. While Jayalalithaa tightened her grip on her rival party, Karunanidhi was claiming how a Brahmin leader could challenge her in 'Dravida Nadu'.

When Indira Gandhi was trying to establish Rajiv Gandhi as her successor in politics at the Centre, she met P. Chirambaram at the airport during the first quarter of 1984. In that meeting before the 1984 Lok Sabha elections, Rajiv Gandhi was greatly impressed by Chidambaram, who had turned 40 and was a senior advocate in the High Court. Experts recall when Rajiv became the Prime Minister, he proposed to give the Ministry of Textiles to Chidambaram, but Chidambaram requested that since his family was in the cloth business so he should be given some other Ministry. He was an MP for 6 consecutive terms. Meanwhile, when Prime Minister Narasimha Rao took over, he tried to reverse the ongoing alliance between the Congress and the DMK and appointed Buta Singh to speak to AIADMK Chief Jayalalithaa. This annoyed the Congressmen in the State.

Now as the Congress high command decided to tie-up with AIADMK Munnetra Kazhagam in Tamil Nadu, then opposing it P. Chidambaram and G.K. Moopanar with their supporters formed a new party on March 29, 1996. Later on, the Congressmen loyal to G.K. Moopanar formed a new regional political Party, the Tamil Nadu Makkal Congress. There were many occasions when G.K. Moopanar was offered the top leadership, yet he suggested the name of some other leader for this and chose to focus on the task of strengthening the party. G.K. Moopanar was a supporter of Kumaraswamy Kamaraj from the very beginning and K. Kamaraj too looked upon him as his political successor. In 1999, Moopanar refused to support the BJP-led government's trust vote in the Lok Sabha, which ultimately led to the downfall of the Vajpayee government, short of only one vote.

Chidambaram was again made the Finance Minister when the Congress government was formed in 2004. During this time the left parties supporting the government disagreed with him over disinvestment and other issues. In November 2008, he was given the Home Ministry when the Congress government was again formed in 2009 at the Centre. On May 15, 2017, the CBI registered an FIR against the media company INX. It was alleged there were various irregularities in the approval of the Foreign Investment Promotion Board (FIPB) to INX Media Group for receiving foreign funds of ₹ 305 crores. P. Chidambaram was the Finance Minister when the Company was granted the approval in 2007. Chidambaram came under the radar of probe agencies when INX Media promoter Indrani Mukerjea and her husband Peter Mukerjea were questioned by the ED. The ED had also registered a case of money laundering in this regard in 2018. Indrani Mukerjea told the investigating officers that in exchange for FIPB approval Chidambaram had sought help for his son Karti Chidambaram in the foreign money case. The CBI had also arrested P Chidambaram's son Karti Chidambaram from Chennai airport in February 2018. Later Karti Chidambaram got bail from the court. Allegations were levelled against him that he had demanded $1 million to stall a possible investigation against INX Media. Chidambaram was the Finance Minister in the first UPA government at the time of this deal in 2006. In a matter related to 2G spectrum also, a case was registered against Chidambaram and his family in the hawala case. It was alleged that the Finance Minister's financial authority for allowing foreign investment is limited to ₹ 600 crores, yet the Aircel-Maxis deal worth ₹ 3,500 crores was passed without the approval of the Cabinet Committee on Economic Affairs. But, P Chidambaram has always denied all the charges levelled against him and his son alleging they were motivated by a political vendetta. He said that they have not run away but have taken refuge in law to protect their interests.

Although Karunanidhi came to power in the 1989 elections, the Jayalalithaa-led AIADMK got 27 seats in the Assembly and became Tamil Nadu's first elected Leader of the Opposition. Despite strong opposition from MGR's wife Janaki, Jayalalithaa had become supreme in the AIADMK. It was perhaps Karunanidhi's biggest political mistake to consider Jayalalithaa as a weak opponent. On March 25 the same year, an incident took place which completely turned the tide of Tamil politics. The occasion was the budget session in the Tamil Nadu Legislative Assembly. Jayalalithaa was the Leader of the Opposition in the State Assembly. When Karunanidhi presented the budget, Jayalalithaa demanded his resignation. An altercation between members of the ruling party and the opposition side began. During the skirmish, someone inside the house threw slippers at Jayalalithaa, another one tried to pull the pallu of her sari. As pointed out by party members and several members present in the Assembly at that time, there was a brawl inside the House between the members of the ruling DMK Party and the Opposition. Jayalalithaa was attacked by members of the ruling party at the behest of the then Chief Minister Karunanidhi. Jayalalithaa appeared before the media in the ripped sari and compared the incident with Draupadi's cheer haran from the

Mahabharata period and said that she was treated like Draupadi in the House. She publicly swore that she would not step foot in the House until the woman's honour was restored. Her announcement was termed as a drama by some sections of the media but it helped her gain ample media coverage and earn public sympathy. During the 1989 general elections, the AIADMK formed an alliance with the Congress Party and was successful. Under her leadership, the AIADMK also won by-elections in Marungapuri, Madurai East and Pernamallur Assembly constituencies. But her anger over DMK leader Karunanidhi never waned. Jayalalithaa always considered Karunanidhi as her enemy. One can recall the VIP guest house incident between Mayawati-Mulayam Singh Yadav's Party in Uttar Pradesh. Mulayam-Maya entered a truce once but here there was no scope.

In 1991, after the assassination of Rajiv Gandhi, Jayalalithaa's party contested the elections along with the Congress and formed the government in the state. She was the first elected woman Chief Minister of the State and the youngest Chief Minister of the State from June 24, 1991 to May 12, 1996. In the year 1992, his government initiated the 'Cradle Baby Scheme' to protect the girl child so that orphaned and destitute girl children could have a happy life. In the same year, police stations with only women personnel were opened. In 1996, her party and Jayalalithaa lost in the elections. After this defeat, many cases of corruption against his ministers were exposed which led to public sentiment going against the government. As Chief Minister for the first time, many serious allegations were made against her. She never married but extravagantly spent money on the lavish wedding arrangements of her adopted son V.N. Sudhakaran.

Although she had to go through a very difficult period due to serious allegations, in 2001 she once again managed to become the Chief Minister of Tamil Nadu. After coming to power again, she banned the sale of lottery tickets, fired two lakh employees simultaneously for going on strike, stopped free electricity to farmers, increased the price of rice in ration shops, cancelled the ration cards of those earning more than ₹ 5,000 per month, increased bus fares and banned animal sacrifice in temples. Meanwhile, in the corruption case, the Supreme Court declared her appointment illegal and she handed over the Chair to her trusted Minister Panneerselvam. When she was relieved of some charges by the Madras High Court, she again took over as the Chief Minister in March 2002. However, after losing badly in the 2004 Lok Sabha elections, she allowed animal sacrifice and the farmers got free electricity. In April 2011, when a coalition of 11 parties won a majority in the 14th State Assembly, she became the Chief Minister for the third time. She took the oath as Chief Minister on May 16, 2011 and remained Chief Minister till her death, i.e. December 5, 2016. She was always involved in some controversy or the other since the beginning of her political career, but then she managed to establish a large community of fans. She could not never forget her bitterness towards Karunanidhi. In the month of January 2015, Karunanidhi was often dragged and arrested at midnight on corruption charges amidst the glare of the flash lights of the cameras.

It is no less than a contradiction in itself that the AIADMK, which resulted from Brahmin opposition, was led by the Brahmin leader Jayalalithaa and as a universal leader, she gained such popularity that people themselves began to respectfully call her Amma. She died on December 5, 2016 at 11.30 pm at Apollo Hospital, Chennai. She was admitted to the ICU after suffering a heart attack. She was buried because of her association with the Dravidian movement, which does not believe in any tradition and ritual of Hinduism. Leaders associated with the Dravidian movement were against the general Hindu tradition and did not even use caste titles with their names. Nevertheless, seeing Jayalalithaa's biography and faith, a Brahmin Pandit performed the last ritual and buried her. Her political mentor MGR was also buried after his death. Adjacent to his grave is the grave of

Annadurai, a prominent leader of the Dravidian movement and founder of the DMK. The reason for the burial was also said to be political. Jayalalithaa's Party AIADMK wanted to save her political legacy in the same way as MGR's. It was also reportedly said that the rituals followed in this case were in accordance with the Sri Vaishnava tradition.

In the politics of the state, there was turmoil between the regional parties, but Karunanidhi also kept moving forward. It was Karunanidhi who made a regional party like the DMK a part of an alliance with both the Congress and the BJP in the governments at the Centre. When V.P. Singh's coalition government was formed at the centre, the weightage of regional parties got enhanced in national politics. During the coalition governments, Karunanidhi's role in national politics automatically gained prominence. There are few such personalities among Indian politicians who possess multifaceted talent like Karunanidhi. He was an able administrator. But promoting the family in politics also weakened his party. He was an influential and flamboyant leader. His attitude towards the media was also very cordial. He was a voracious reader and scribed for his magazine every day. Political analysts cannot ignore the fact that he has led the most extended family of politicians. In fact, no other family enjoyed power in the central government for 15 consecutive years as much as the DMK. Karunanidhi had tied up with the BJP-led NDA in 1999 and later did not hesitate to become a part of the Congress-led UPA government either.

There was a time when Karunanidhi supported Periyar's social reform movement, flagged anti-Hindi sentiment and took forward the cause of Sri Lankan Tamils. He tried to forge links with separatist groups in Tamil Nadu but Prabhakaran, who was influenced by MGR, was not willing to befriend him. This angered Karunanidhi but he was helpless. There came a time when Prabhakaran destroyed all other Tamil factions, including those close to Karunanidhi. But even then Karunanidhi never spoke openly against this bloodbath. After MGR's death, a battle broke out in Sri Lanka between the LTTE and India's peace-keeping forces. Circumstances came to a point when Karunanidhi got inclined towards Prabhakaran.That was the period when the Indian public sentiment had turned against Prabhakaran. This was a huge difference between MGR and Karunanidhi. For this reason, Karunanidhi's government was also dismissed in January 1991. It was argued that under the DMK government LTTE people had become very active in Tamil Nadu. This later proved to be true to a great extent, because during this time on May 21, former Prime Minister Rajiv Gandhi was assassinated in Perumbudur, Tamil Nadu. After the assassination of Rajiv Gandhi in Perumbudur, Tamil Nadu, fingures were openly pointed towards Karunanidhi's Tamil love for supporting the extremist organization Liberation Tiger of Tamil Elum 'LTTE'. Later Rajiv Gandhi's killers were arrested from Tamil Nadu itself. Karunanidhi once again came into the limelight in 2009 when in an interview to NDTV he called LTTE Chief Prabhakaran his friend. However he later explained that his statement was not viewed in the right perspective.

Karunanidhi had three wives. His first wife Padmavati Ammal died in 1948 after four years of marriage and thereafter he married Dayalu Ammal. While keeping this marital alliance intact, he also married Rajti in 1966. His sons from his second marriage, K. Alagiri and M.K. Stalin became well-known names in politics. Karunanidhi's daughter Selvi is married to his sister's son Murasoli Selvam, who oversees the Kannada operations of Sun TV, owned by Kalanidhi Maran. Karunanidhi's nephew Murasoli Maran has been an MP for 36 years and been involved in central politics alongside four Prime Ministers as a Minister. Finally, under Vajpayee, he was also the Minister of Commerce and Industry. The internal equation of DMK Munnetra Kazhagam was completely shaken by the death of Murasoli Maran in 2003. Murasoli has represented the DMK at the Centre for almost three and a half decades, balancing it very efficiently. After his death, the eldest son Kalanidhi continued to manage the Sun TV business, but the second son, Dayanidhi, took over the father's political legacy. But Dayanidhi Maran, like his father, could not balance the internal power centres of the party. It so happened that he came to be called a supporter of Karunanidhi's third son Stalin in DMK politics. When Dayanidhi Maran was forced to resign following the Aircel-Maxis row, Karunanidhi's daughter Kanimozhi was made the key negotiator with the alliance partners. She took upon herself to make A. Raja a Minister which culminated in his resignation and eventual arrest in the 2G spectrum scam. Kanimozhi was also arrested in that connection. Karunanidhi, wept bitterly when he visited his daughter in Delhi's Tihar Jail. He was so angry with the leadership of the then Congress government that he did not consider it appropriate to even meet Sonia Gandhi and returned to Chennai. It was a rare instance as Karunanidhi never left Delhi without meeting Congress President Sonia Gandhi.

After 2000, when Stalin's supporters clenched the organisational elections of the DMK, Alagiri was furious. He stopped his supporters from attending Stalin's programmes. On January 29, 2001, on the orders of the then Chief Minister Jayalalithaa, Karunanidhi's residence in Gopalapuram, Chennai was raided. That was the case of rigging in the contract for the flyover to be built in Chennai. Seventy-eight-year-old Karunanidhi was dragged out of the house by the police. He kept screaming but the policemen did not show any mercy and arrested him forcibly amidst all the media glare. DMK leader Murasoli Maran was arrested in the same case after being pulled from the car. Stalin was also arrested. On receiving this news, Alagiri along with his half-sister Kanimozhi visited him in jail. Karunanidhi was released five days after his arrest but he could not forget this humiliation for life. The immediate effect of this action of the Jayalalithaa government on the DMK was that it unified all the members of the Karunanidhi family once again. But, it was only a brief spell of good fortune. A few days later, the struggle for power between the two brothers, Alagiri and Stalin, resumed and reached a climax when Stalin barred DMK workers from participating in Alagiri's programs. This enraged the supporters of Alagiri. There were also violent protests and incidents of arson in Madurai. Angered by the DMK leadership, Alagiri fielded 15 of his candidates in the Assembly elections. As a result, leaders like P.T.R. Palanivel from Madurai and Kirutinnan from Sivaganga were defeated. Jayalalithaa's party AIADMK made hay while the sun shone. She once again came to power as the Chief Minister. DMK M.P. Kirutinnan was assassinated on May 20, 2003. At that time the party's organisational elections were being held and M.P. Kirutinnan was demanding election of office bearers through voting in three districts including Shiganga. The very next day, Alagiri was arrested on charges of conspiracy to murder. Then at that time not only DMK but Stalin also came out openly in his brother's defence. He accused Jayalalithaa of politics of vendetta and misuse of power. Alagiri was later released on bail. Stalin was made the party's General Secretary the same year.

In 2005, there was a dispute between Karunanidhi and the Maran family over Sun TV shares. The Maran family bought 5.75 percent shares of Karunanidhi's wife Dayaluammal in Sun TV at a reduced price. A year and a half later in April 2006, when SunTV owner Kalanidhi turned his company into a public limited company, Karunanidhi came to know then that Kalanidhi had deliberately reduced the price of his company's shares to take advantage. Karunanidhi was distraught that his family had cheated him. Angered by this and realising the need to make his way in the media industry, Karunanidhi started his own personal TV channel. In the elections held in May 2006, the DMK won again and Karunanidhi became the Chief Minister for the fifth time. Despite this success, the conflict between Alagiri and Stalin grew in the party. On May 9, 2007, a survey report was published in Kalanidhi's newspaper Dinakaran, stating the choice of the people of the State as Karunanidhi's successor. According to that survey, Alagiri and Kanimozhi were at 2 percent each but Stalin was said to be the choice of 70 percent of the people. Only 26 percent supported others. It is said that before publishing this survey, Kalanidhi did not talk to Karunanidhi about this. As this survey got published, Alagiri and his supporters were furious. Alagar's supporters raided the office of Dinakar newspaper and set it on fire. In this violence, three people were killed and many were injured and the gap between Stalin and Alagiri widened. In fact, be it the case of films or media or airlines (SpiceJet) or other companies, this family has become the owner of multi-billions of dollars. Karunanidhi's third wife Rajathi Ammal is Kanimozhi's mother. Even after withdrawing support to the UPA, he got Kanimozhi made a member of the Rajya Sabha. The Maran brothers played very smart from the beginning. But, politics and business together make a deadly concoction, the byproduct of which this political family had to face many times.

In September 2007, Karunanidhi sparked a huge controversy when he questioned the existence of Lord Rama by saying — "people say 17 lakh years ago there was a man, Ram. Do not touch the bridge (Ram Setu) built by him. Who was this Ram? From which engineering college did you graduate? Where is the proof of this?" His expression is very useful to understand the politics of one of the most stalwart leaders of South India, M. Karunanidhi and the DMK, and the politics of the state of Tamil Nadu. The anti-Brahmin politics that Karunanidhi represented for the past half a century was based on this aggression, which he inherited from his political mentor C.N. Annadurai and the ideological ideal 'Periyar'. Karunanidhi is one such name in the politics of Tamil Nadu, without whom political discourse here is incomplete. The political scene in Tamil Nadu has seen several changes since the death of Karunanidhi on August 7, 2018.

It was an immense burden for any leader to replace Karunanidhi or take over the reins of the party after his death. For M Karunanidhi's third son, M.K. Stalin (Muthuvel Karunanidhi Stalin), this responsibility became even more challenging because his party had been out of power for the past eight years.

It is also true that Stalin neither has Jayalalithaa's charisma nor oratory skills like his father Karunanidhi possessed, but he has his own unique style of working. His style of functioning was evident soon after Karunanidhi's death. When the state government did not provide space for Karunanidhi's last rites at Marina Beach, the DMK cadre supporters went on a rampage. DMK took the matter to court. The Chennai High Court ruled that Karunanidhi's last rites could be performed at Marina Beach. When this decision was delivered, people paid homage to their leader in Rajaji Hall. There was a surge of happiness among the supporters as soon as the High Court's decision came. But then people saw that Karunanidhi's son and Party Working President M.K. Stalin, with folded hands, appealed to his cadres to maintain peace. During Karunanidhi's funeral, he was seen to be completely composed, keeping his emotions well under control. The biggest milestone in Stalin's political career came on August 28, 2018 when he was elected unopposed as the party President at the DMK Council meeting. Now he had replaced the man who was not only his father but also a leader who had led his party for 50 years amidst all the ups and downs.

Stalin made his debut in the party in the early 1970s but then his only identity was as the son of Chief Minister Karunanidhi. During the Emergency, the youth leader Stalin was arrested during the MISA movement. It is said that he suffered brutality in jail. But, when he got out of jail, this young leader, still known only after his father, became known by his own name throughout the State. Now he had become that hero of the youth. This earned respect for him in the party cadre, and people's sentiments also got attached to him. After this Stalin did not look back. He became the party President in August 2018, but the journey to this point had not been easy. He had to encounter all kinds of challenges. In January 2017, he was made the first Working President of the party. Stalin contested the Assembly elections for the first time in 1984, although he lost to a senior ADMK leader from the

'Thousand Lights' constituency. However, he later won from the same Assembly constituency in 1989. He had to face defeat in the 1991 elections but later he won the seat in 1996. Before this, he was also the Mayor of Chennai from 1996 to 2000 and during this time he earned accolades for his good work. He not only improved the condition of roads in the city but also improved the infrastructure, for which the party cadre and common people remember him even today. When the DMK came to power in 2006, Stalin was made the State's Local Administrative Affairs Minister. Stalin managed to win the 2001 and 2006 elections from the 'Thousand Lights' region. In 2001, Stalin, Karunanidhi and a few others had to be arrested for rigging the construction of an overbridge in Chennai, but later the government could not file a chargesheet. In 2011 and 2016 he contested from Kolathur Assembly and managed to win both times. Alagiri is only three years older than Stalin. From the very beginning, he accused his father of being biassed and promoting Stalin. When the disputes between the two brothers increased, Karunanidhi decided to send the eldest son Alagiri to Madurai. Alagiri happily went to Madurai and began to expand his influence by making the whole of South Tamil Nadu his work area.

M.K. Stalin was also criticised for promoting his son Udayaniti Stalin in the party. His differences with his brother M.K. Alagiri continued to grow. But in 2013, Karunanidhi chose Stalin as his successor and announced that M.K. Stalin would take over the reins of the party after him. After this M.K. Muthu and M.K. Alagiri both were expelled from the party and Stalin monopolistically started running the affairs of the party. M.K. Stalin is the only leader in the history of Tamil Nadu who has held the post of Deputy Chief Minister. In 2010. The International Tamil Meet was organised by M. Karunanidhi. Alagiri boycotted the meet citing the reason for not getting respect in the party and his supporters raised slogans at the meeting. Matter between the two brothers worsened in 2013 due to political tussle.

Many experts in Tamil politics believe that Stalin was the chief strategist for the 2014 Lok Sabha elections and the 2016 state Assembly elections. From the selection of candidates to the decision on allies, he also played an important role. In January, ahead of the 2019 Lok Sabha elections, Stalin launched the 'Oratchi Sabai' programme to reach out to people across the State, a similar program he had organised in 2015 as 'Namakuname'. During that programme, Stalin has been seen talking to the common people while sitting under a bunch of coconut trees or in improvised tents. His visit was taken seriously by the people and Stalin was highly praised. Stalin is usually compared to his own father. Karunanidhi was not only a prolific writer but he also had an amazing ability to deliver speeches. Stalin is also mastering the same art. In 2015, Stalin went on a campaign tour across the state called Namakuname, under which he was meeting people from all sections of the society. His 'Namakuname' campaign was both praised and criticised. The way Stalin was stopping by the roadside chaiwalas, riding a motorcycle with his party supporters, all this was termed as a stunt show by his detractors and critics. But there are many politicians engaged in such political stunts in Indian politics. But Tamil Nadu has no parallel in the politics of charisma. There is currently no illustrious leader in the AIADMK after Jayalalithaa's departure and Palanisamy and Panneerselvam lack the charm that is essential in Tamil Nadu politics. They have been fighting like anything .

After Stalin's bumper victory and rounded with many troubles AIADMK district secretaries spoke out to shun the "dual leadership" system and came out publicly in favour of a strong unitary leader. On 11 July 2022, The Party General Council abolished the dual leadership model and empowered E K Palanisamy to be the Party Supremo. O. Panneerselvam was expelled as Party treasurer and primary member of the party for "anti-party" activities by the AIADMK General Council.

Therefore, Stalin doesn't face any danger at the moment, if he will ever be in trouble then it will emanate from his own people. Now that there appear no more miracles, it will be interesting to observe if any one Party will still be able to get bulk seats in the elections. Initially, after the three Chief Ministership periods of the Congress, till today the Congress has not been able to hold the reins again. Governments kept changing between AIADMK and DMK. Be it in the Lok Sabha or Assembly, whichever party got majority, had won seats in bulk.

❑

16
What's in a Name? Shakespeare was Wrong!

Karnataka is the largest state in South India. During the British, it was known as Mysore State which changed to Karnataka in 1973. It got its new name from the fine black soil that is best for cotton cultivation. Karnataka is made up of two words Karu and Nadu. Karu means black and Nadu means land. In the regional language, people called this area south of the Krishna river as Karunadu and the British used to pronounce it as Carnatic.

In 1950, Maharaja Jayachamarajendra Wadiyar of Mysore State accepted the accession to India and retained the title of Rajpramukh till 1975. But with independence, the integration movement started in Mysore State. People demanded merger of neighbouring states of Madras State, Hyderabad State and Kodagu and Kannada speaking areas of Bombay with Mysore State and the new state should be named Karnataka. After 17 years of this movement, their demand was accepted on November 1, 1973 and the State came into existence by the name of Karnataka.

The struggle for power in Karnataka has long been between the Congress and national parties such as the Janata Dal and the BJP, but from time to time regional parties also flourished here and some of them got to play a major role in the State. Among the parties which made their mark, the name of Janata Dal Secular Party stands prominent. Actually Janata Dal has an interesting story of making and breaking several times.

Janata Dal (Secular)

Though this party was formed after breaking away from a national party, its leader H.D. Deve Gowda had become the Prime Minister of the country, but its support base remained confined to only some parts of Karnataka (northern part). However, the party keeps fielding its candidates in Kerala and Arunachal Pradesh and in the rest of the country. The Election Commission has given it the status of a regional Party in Karnataka, Kerala and Arunachal Pradesh.

The history of the party as recorded on the official website of Janata Dal (Secular) traces its roots to Jayaprakash Narayan. Its leaders come through the Janata Party - Janata Dal via Janata Dal (Secular). H.D. Deve Gowda started his political career with Congress in 1953 and remained a member of Congress till 1962. In 1962, he contested the election as an independent candidate from Holenarasipura Assembly seat and won the seat. He continued winning this seat for six consecutive terms till 1989. When the Congress split in 1972, he joined the Congress (O) and was the Leader of the Opposition in the Legislative Assembly from March 1972 to 1976. When Emergency was imposed in the country in 1975, Deve Gowda also became a follower of Jayaprakash Narayan. Deve Gowda was also arrested during the Emergency and was lodged in Bangalore Central Jail from 1975 to 1977. When the Janata Party was formed in 1977, H.D. Deve Gowda was made the President of the Karnataka unit of the party. After that, between 1983 and 1988, the Janata Party government was formed in Karnataka under the leadership of Ramakrishna Hegde, then Deve Gowda was made a Minister in it. In 1989, when the Janata Dal was formed under the leadership of V.P. Singh, a large part of the Janata Party joined the Janata Dal, but Subramanian Swamy formed the Janata Party (Jayaprakash). Deve Gowda became the President of its Karnataka unit. But he lost from the Holenarsipura Assembly seat to Janata Party (JP). He was defeated after winning for 26 consecutive years. Soon after that he left the Janata Party(JP) and joined the Janata Dal. He was made the President of the Karnataka unit of the Janata Dal and in 1994, under his leadership, the Janata Dal registered a major victory in the Karnataka Assembly elections. After that he became the Chief Minister of Karnataka. Deve Gowda's Raja Yoga was on the cards. In the year 1996, the Congress under the leadership of Narasimha Rao was defeated. The non-Congress and non-BJP parties formed a united front to form the new government to which Congress provided outside support. Deve Gowda was surprisingly chosen for the Prime Minister of this government. He was the Prime Minister of the country from June 1, 1996 to April 21, 1997.

In the year 1999, some leaders of the Janata Dal joined hands with the Bharatiya Janata Party under the leadership of George Fernandes and joined the National Democratic Alliance. After this the Janata Dal broke into two parts. Many leaders including Madhu Dandawate and Siddaramaiah formed the Janata Dal (Secular) under the leadership of H.D. Deve Gowda. Deve Gowda was made the President of this new party. Although Deve Gowda lost in the 1999 Lok Sabha elections, he won in the 2002 elections. In 2004, the Janata Dal (Secular) made a comeback in Karnataka. In 2004, the party came to power in the State in alliance with the Congress. But this had occurred under the leadership of Siddaramaiah. The party had won 58 Assembly seats. The party manoeuvred again. In 2006, Janata Dal Secular formed the government in alliance with the BJP. H.D. Deve Gowda's son Kumaraswamy was the Chief Minister of this coalition government for about 20 months. But the year 2008 witnessed a major decline in the performance of Janata Dal (Secular). The party could win only 28 seats. Deve Gowda expelled Siddaramaiah and C.M. Ibrahim from the party.

Siddaramaiah initiated a movement called 'Ahinda' to unite the backward classes and minorities. Later both Siddaramaiah and Ibrahim switched to Congress. Siddaramaiah was made the Chief Minister and stayed for five years. Very few people have been fortunate enough to achieve this remarkable feat in Karnataka.

(Deve Gowda belongs to the Vokkaliga community and it is his political strength that gives him a good hold on his community. The keys to power in Karnataka remain with Vokkaligas and Lingayats. Once upon a time, in Vizianagaram state, this caste held the reins of administration. So much so that Vokkaliga is more keen on putting impediments for Lingayats, rather than enriching itself; and vice versa. Yediyurappa, the former Chief Minister of Karnataka, belongs to the Lingayat community. The number of Lingayats in Karnataka is considered to be more than Vokkaliga. Yediyurappa belongs to the prominent Lingayat community in the State.)

The snake-and-ladder game continued with the Janata Dal (S). Its popularity kept on rising but Deve Gowda's dominance in his region remained intact. In the 2009 Lok Sabha elections, Deve Gowda defeated the BJP candidate from his home district Hassan seat by a record 2,91,113 votes. For the first time in Karnataka, a leader had won a Lok Sabha seat by such a huge margin. The BJP had fielded Hanuma Gowda against him. Even in 2014, under the Modi wave in the country, Deve Gowda won the Hassan seat by taking 509841 votes. Although Deve Gowda's Party won from Hassan in the 2019 elections as well, Deve Gowda contested that election from Tumkur instead of Hassan and defeated BJP candidate G.C. Basavaraj by about 13,000 votes in a close contest.

In 2018, once again with a twist of fate the Janata Dal (Secular) returned to power in Karnataka. The Congress staked claim to form the Janata Dal Secular government under the leadership of Kumaraswamy by giving unconditional support. However, the Janata Dal Secular had only 37 MLAs. The Governor did not accept the claim and got Yediyurappa sworn in without a majority.

He was given a considerably long time to prove a majority. This was considered biassed. The matter went to the Supreme Court. The Supreme Court asked Yediyurappa to prove his majority immediately. But Yediyurappa could not garner a majority even in two weeks and had to resign. After this, the Janata Dal Secular and Congress government was formed under the leadership of Kumaraswamy. Before the formation of the government, we all remember that path-breaking picture in which the leaders of all the opposition parties of the country (including Sonia Gandhi, Mamata Banerjee, Akhilesh Yadav) attended and displayed the unity of the opposition in the country as if in full swing. But it actually did not happen. The coercion from the Congress increased and at one occasion, Kumaraswamy even burst into tears in full glare of the public. The Congress MLAs revolted and after running for almost a year and two months, this government was toppled midway.

There has been another problem with the Janata Dal (S). That is his vote bank. Its vote bank always remained stable. Especially when it is considered a Party of a certain class, the Vokkaliga. The party was never able to grab a major share from the other sections. Wherever it got support from, apart from Vokkaliga, it could not go beyond that. The figures also testify that barring the initial 1999 Assembly elections (10.4 percent), its vote bank remained at 19-20 percent. ..and perhaps this is also one of the reasons why the Janata Dal (Secular) could not get a bigger share in the power of the State. Yes, it can boast of giving a Prime Minister to the country in the form of H.D. Deve Gowda.

Badavara Shramikara Raitara Congress

Badavara Shramikara Raitara Congress was founded in the year 2011 by BJP leader B. Srimalu who parted ways with the BJP. In the 2013 elections, the party contested 150 seats in the State and won four seats. This party lasted a total of three years. B.Srimalu again joined the BJP in 2014.

Karnatak Janata Paksh

In 2012, when Karnataka Chief Minister B.S. Yediyurappa had a dispute over the Chief Ministership, he formed his own Party named Karnataka Janata Paksha. Yediyurappa resigned from the BJP membership on 30 November and formed the party on 9 December 2012 along with his supporters. The party contested the Karnataka Legislative Assembly elections in 2013. But the party could win only 8 out of the total 203 seats in the State. However, the party got more than 10 percent of the total votes in that election. BJP, on the other hand, also suffered a major loss in the elections and came down from 110 seats to 40 in the state. Although Yediyurappa formed the party after breaking away from the BJP, the character of the party was kept secular.

Karnataka Pragyanyavanta Janata Party

This party from Karnataka was founded by PMD Mahesh Gowda on January 19, 2016. However its expansion in public began in 2016. After that Mahesh Gowda started a public campaign in Karnataka. Upendra Rai, senior artist of Kannada films also joined in. But he soon left the party after a difference of opinion with Mahesh Gowda. In the 2018 Karnataka Assembly elections, the party won two seats. This party supported the alliance of Congress and Janata Dal Secular in the elections. However, when this alliance came to power, Mahesh Gowda also joined the NDA.

Maharashtra Ekikaran Samiti

Even though the name of this party was Maharashtra Ekikaran Samiti, it functioned in the region of present day Karnataka. This party also contested the 1962 election on 6 seats and also won all the 6 seats. This party was founded in 1946 as a Sangharsh Samiti and had only one demand that the Belgaum district of Mysore State should be merged with Bombay State to form a

Maharashtra State. It was registered in the Election Commission as a political party only in 1962. However, when the country became independent in 1947, Belgaum district was made a part of Bombay State. In 1948, the Belgaum Urban Council passed a resolution demanding that the district be included in Samyukta Maharashtra, claiming that the district is Maratha dominated. But the States Reorganisation Commission rejected their demand and recommended Belgaum district to be made a part of Mysore State. In the year 1956, when the State Reorganisation Act was passed in the Parliament, this district was included in the Mysore State. The party continued to dominate the Belagavi and Khanpur seats. The party broke into two before the Karnataka elections in 2018. Under the leadership of Kiran Thakur, a separate party was formed under the name City Integration Committee, while another party under the name of Intermediate Integration Committee was formed under the leadership of Deepak Dalvi. In 2018, both the parties fought against each other and lost even the three seats they had won for a long time. Both the parties could not win a single seat.

Other parties

Other regional parties in Karnataka that merit some attention were the Kannada Nadu Party formed in the early twenty-first century. It was founded by Vijay Shankeshwar but in 2004 this party joined Janata Dal Secular. Bengaluru Navnirman Party was founded on September 22, 2019. The party, however, has kept its support base confined to Bengaluru and its surroundings. It dreams of a bigger Bangalore and is trying to confine itself to the Bengaluru Municipal Corporation elections for the time being. Most of the party members are local social workers. Another such regional party is the National Development Party (India). It was founded in 2008 by Maulvi Jamiruddin. Karnataka businessman Hari L. Khodi had founded the Urs Samyuktha Paksha Party on January 16, 2004. The party eyes were on the Dalit vote bank of the State.

Most of the party members are local social workers. Filmmaker Upendra also formed the Uttam Prajakiya party on September 18, 2018. The name of All India Hindustan Congress can also be taken in such parties of Karnataka, it was founded by Budh Prakash Sharma on November 15, 2015. Although the headquarters of the party is in Rajasthan.

❑

17
Ping-Pong Politics

In Rajasthan politics is characterised with little to no tremors. The reason is amply clear. In the 200-seat Assembly, there are only two parties facing each other, both are the National Parties-Congress and the BJP. Voters too seem to be content by assigning power once to Congress, next time to BJP. Yes, there is no such calculation in the Lok Sabha elections, where votes are cast purely on national issues. But as in Indian politics, many parties were formed out of Congress and some even formed governments, but such sabotage was rarely seen in the Bharatiya Janata Party. Only a few examples will be found. And those who tried to do so came back to the roots (including Yediyurappa in Karnataka). There is a similar example in Rajasthan too. The leader is Hanuman Prasad Beniwal and his party is the National Democratic Party.

Generally, the politics of the State BJP in Rajasthan ran on the strength of Bhairon Singh Shekhawat and later Vasundhara Raje Scindia showed the same capability. It was clearly said about Bhairon Singh that he never wanted more than 90-95 of his party to win in the State Assembly. He kept the remaining five-six or ten MLAs to him separately from the party. The strategy was-that Bhairon Singh Shekhawat owed the responsibility of their fighting the election and winning as an independent candidate.

Hanuman Prasad Beniwal, the former President of Rajasthan University, had rebellion in his nature. As a Jat leader, he is well recognized in Nagaur and the nearby region. After leaving the university, he worked for the party in the BJP for a few years and became an MLA from Nagaur's Khinvsar Assembly in 2008 and managed successfully for the second time in 2013. But a few days after becoming an MLA for the first time, he entered into a rift with Chief Minister Vasundhara Raje. Though he aspired to contest the Lok Sabha elections in 2014 itself but it didn't materialise in BJP. In 2013 itself, he was allegedly in association with the Congress. When he did not get a ticket from the Bharatiya Janata Party in the 2013 elections, he contested as an independent and defeated the candidate of the Bharatiya Janata Party by more than 23,000 votes, while in the 2008 election also he got more than 24,000 votes this time beating the BSP candidate.

Beniwal has always been a rebel. In 2013 also, he had a dispute with Minister Yunus Khan. After this, there was a furore in Rajasthan University in 2015 and many youths and policemen were injured in stone pelting and skirmishes. His attitude was reflected in the Assembly also. In 2017, once he came to the Well and tore the papers etc. just because the Speaker did not allow him to ask questions.

He held a Hunkar rally in Jat-dominated areas just before the Assembly elections in 2018 and announced the formation of the Rashtriya Loktantrik Party, contested the election and three MLAs of the party were also elected. These include Narayan Beniwal from Khinvsar, Pukhraj Garg from Bhopalgarh and Indira Devi Bawri from Medda.

With the 2019 elections approaching, Beniwal's desire to go to the Lok Sabha resurfaced and the Bharatiya Janata Party also realised when a seat could be ensured with his support, why not form an alliance with him. Despite the opposition of Vasundhara Raje, the BJP dedicated the Nagaur seat to him and in return got support in all the seats. The BJP did not want any dent in the Jat votes. It was alleged that Vasundhara Raje defended Chief Minister Ashok Gehlot and ignored the corruption of the Gehlot government. Gehlot also returns the favour and does not get the corruption charges against her investigated during his tenure.

Beniwal's rebellion is still seen spurring occasionally. On one hand he seems to be supporting the farmers and on the other Congress is the enemy number one to him. He once held the Sonia Gandhi family responsible for the Corona expansion. It is alleged that BJP 'uses' him in its own way. Beniwal himself says - whatever the BJP cannot say, I say it. What Beniwal would do next is uncertain, but in the coming elections also, with the intent of keeping the Jats on its side, the BJP will definitely try to keep him in its close quarters. By the way, Beniwal has been insisting that he has to become the Chief Minister somehow.

Another prominent leader unhappy with Vasundhara Raje in Rajasthan formed a new party by shunning the BJP. Once a member of the Council of Ministers of Bhairon Singh Shekhawat and Vasundhara Raje, Ghanshyam Das Tiwari, a popular leader once known for strengthening BJP roots, left the BJP in 2018 after being MLA for six consecutive terms and formed his Bharat Vahini Party. In April 2018, he wrote a letter to the then Party President Amit Shah, demanding the dismissal of Vasundhara Raje's government. Forming his own Party did not go down well with his supporters too. His journey lasted for only two years and he returned to the BJP again in December 2020.

❑

Delhi

18
Aam Aadmi Party - A New Epicentre of Opposition Politics

The historic and amazing 2022 Punjab Assembly results may sooner or later put the Aam Aadmi Party into the category of National Parties but such meteoric rise of a Regional Party is the reason for featuring it here. The Aam Aadmi Party is the single regional party that has formed governments in two states now. Such tremendous success has brought the Aam Aadmi Party into one of the top most spots where it has endless opportunities. A party that grew out of a movement and finally got established on December 26, 2012 is very likely to soon take centre stage in Indian Politics and governance. The strategy of keeping an equal distance with all adversaries quietly is characteristic of Party Chief Arvind Kejriwal and thus he is interested in keeping his cards close to his heart.

It is hard to believe this is a party that grew out of a movement. A movement which had shown a new ray of hope to the country and its architect was Anna Hazare, a hardcore Gandhivadi. The movement for Jan Lokpal Bill (Citizen's Lokpal Bill) was started on April 5, 2011 at Jantar Mantar by social worker Anna Hazare and his associates. Magsaysay Award winner Arvind Kejriwal,

India's first woman IPS Kiran Bedi, renowned philanthropist Advocate Prashant Bhushan, founder of Patanjali Yogpeeth Baba Ramdev, eminent poet Kumar Vishwas were involved in this movement. The movement had created an atmosphere like V.P. Singh had done about Bofors during the tenure of Rajiv Gandhi. Due to many reasons including the resentment created against the Congress rule, the effect of the fast was visible all over the country and supporting it, people took to the streets in the capitals of many states including Delhi. The agitators were demanding the government to make a strong anti-corruption Lokpal Bill and also gave a draft of the Lokpal bill to the government. The then Congress-led government led by Manmohan Singh did not pay any heed to it. Even towards Anna Hazare's fast, the attitude of the government and his allies in the Congress rule remained neglectful. But as this fast turned into a movement, the Government hurriedly formed a Committee to avoid any possible danger and accepted the passage of Lokpal Bill in Parliament by August 16.

The bill introduced by the government in the monsoon session held in August was described as weak and in stark contrast to the Jan Lokpal. The government put many obstacles in its way and on August 16, Anna Hazare and his associates were arrested which flared up the movement all over the country. A large number of dharnas, demonstrations and fasts were organised across the country for the next 12 consecutive days. Finally, on August 28, Anna announced the suspension of his fast after Parliament passed a resolution agreeing to three of Anna's conditions. Meanwhile, news of Arvind Kejriwal forming a political party started pouring in from Anna Hazare's platform.

Although Anna Hazare wanted to keep politics out of the anti-corruption Jan Lokpal movement, Arvind Kejriwal was in favour of contesting the elections by forming a separate Party to achieve the goal of the movement citing ' if you wish to change the System you have to be the System'. He believed that efforts to get the Jan Lokpal Bill through discussions only had gone futile. India

Against Corruption also conducted a survey on social engagement services and the idea of joining politics gained wide support in this survey. But Anna differed from this view and so they parted ways.

There was also a large section of those who supported Arvind Kejriwal's idea. Manish Sisodia was closest to Arvind. The story of Arvind and Manish Sisodia's friendship today is also interesting. Manish had his own NGO "Parivartan" and later he formed the NGO ``Kabir" with Arvind Kejriwal and worked against the ration mafia in Delhi. Both the NGO's offices were placed nearby in East Delhi. Renowned lawyer Prashant Bhushan was engaged in "Campaign for Judicial Accountability". The centre of Arvind's meetings was now Sunder Nagari and sometimes his meetings were held in a church near Gole Market. This is where the foundation of India Against Corruption was laid. India Against Corruption had some rallies followed by the Anna movement. In Ramlila Maidan, many people including Kumar Vishwas, Sanjay Singh, Arvind Gaur, Swami Agnivesh to name a few joined the movement and after the formation of the party, the role of everyone including Yogendra Yadav expanded. Prashant Bhushan has also been Arvind Kejriwal's lawyer. In his opinion the party should be expanded all over the country. On one hand, the number of supporters of the party was increasing who agreed with Arvind Kejriwal, while many people including Kiran Bedi, Santosh Hegde agreed to Anna Hazare's idea of not forming a political party and parted ways. Arvind Kejriwal announced the formation of a political party on October 2012 2, and then the Aam Aadmi Party was formally launched on November 26, 2012, the anniversary of the Indian Constitution. Now many youths including Durgesh Pathak, Dilip Pandey associated with the Anna movement came together who had once reached Delhi to prepare for the civil service examination here.

After becoming a political party, Delhi Assembly elections were imminent and Arvind Kejriwal was pitched against Sheila

Dikshit, the head of the 15-year-old Congress government of Delhi, a popular Chief Minister. As part of the strategy, the party started Bijli-Pani Satyagraha. People were fed up with the rising electricity bills. In October 2012, Arvind Kejriwal grabbed headlines by visiting Banaram's house in Tigri by connecting the electricity supply that was earlier disconnected for non-payment of his ₹ 15,000 bill. Kejriwal met Cheena Maharaj of Valmiki Temple on Mandir Marg, Mahatma Gandhi's favourite place During independence movement and sought his opinion on three possible election symbols options (broom, tap and candle) from the Election Commission. The broom became the first choice. In this way, Kejriwal was successful in breaking into the Congress stronghold by worshipping at the Valmiki temple.

There is a famous story here. Once Cheena Maharaj met Sheila Dikshit, who was the Chief Minister of Delhi and said that the people of Valmiki Samaj do not have a house, to which Sheela's response stunned him. She said - should I give a house in Rashtrapati Bhavan .... It was from here that Cheena Maharaj distanced himself from the Congress and got close to the Aam Aadmi Party, as a result more than five supporters of Cheena Maharaj, including Rakhi Birlan, Ajay Dutt, contested the elections. Arvind Kejriwal and the entire Aam Aadmi Party started attacking Congress leaders aggressively. After the Nirbhaya accident in December 2012, the opposition came out in the public in the form of agitation, dharna, demonstration against the Congress government and the Aam Aadmi Party also took advantage of this opportunity. Arvind Kejriwal not only 'gheraoed' Sheila Dikshit and then Home Minister P. Chidambaram, AAP workers even staged a guerrilla protest at the homes of many politicians.

The Aam Aadmi Party showed to the people a dream of relief struggling everyday with its Bijli-Pani Satyagraha, women's safety and succeeded in establishing an instant connect with them. AAP activists went to the poor colonies, got the people to sign and create public opinion against the government regarding electricity and water. In Sunder Nagari of North East Delhi, where he gathered experience of working against the ration mafia, from the house of Santosh Koli, in March 2013 Arvind Kejriwal fasted against the increased electricity and water bills claiming that more than one million people signed the petition. The Aam Aadmi Party said that these people believed that the government has failed in the field of electricity, water and ensuring women's security. This campaign was especially effective among JJ colonies, lower class families living in unauthorised colonies. Now Arvind started canvassing that he has come into politics to change the system. Arvind Kejriwal said from several forums, "We are common man. If we find our solutions in the Left ideology, we will borrow ideas from there and if we find our solutions in the right wing ideology, we are happy to borrow ideas from there as well. "

The political attack intensified after the 'broom' AAP's election symbol came to the fore. Songs like 'paanch saal Kejriwal'... were hummed. On the other hand, people from the film industry were also joining in. A campaign was launched to connect people through Facebook, and Twitter. The campaign of calling the 15-year-old Congress government dishonest and Arvind Kejriwal as an honest choice was gaining momentum.

The new initiative of Mohalla Sabhas took place in May 2013. Arvind Kejriwal and Manish Sisodia also started visiting these Mohalla meetings and assured that now the government will pay heed to their problems, and would work from grassroots. Whoever visited there---from Congress, BJP, Left parties et al.---were offered the Aam Aadmi Party cap to wear with the slogan printed on it-'I want Swaraj'. Elections were held in December 2013 and the Aam Aadmi Party proved itself different in the public view by announcing 11 candidates in June itself. It was informed that the average age of these 11 candidates is 37 years, a total of 97 applications were received for these seats; most of the applicants have been instrumental in Anna's Jan Lokpal movement. It was widely publicised that right from the election, the Aam Aadmi

Party had challenged the BJP-Congress that there is a scope to send persons with a clean image, patriotic in nature and believer in politics of sacrifice in the Assembly against sending criminal, corrupt and characterless people to the House. On the other hand, the tradition of selling tickets at the preference of the High Command by paying crores of rupees has also been challenged by the Aam Aadmi Party. There was no family---Parivasrvaad---in the Aam Aadmi Party, so the party did not even consider the names of two members of the same family for the ticket. Along with preparing the election manifesto for the whole of Delhi, the party prepared a separate manifesto for each constituency.

In the results declared on December 6, the party won 28 seats in the 70-member Delhi Assembly. With this, it emerged as the second largest Party after the Bharatiya Janata Party, which won 32 Assembly constituencies. Arvind Kejriwal defeated Chief Minister Sheila Dikshit of the ruling Congress Party by nearly 25,000 votes. Congress was reduced to only eight seats but it found it appropriate to support Arvind only. As soon as the government was formed, the party started fulfilling the promises made in its manifesto, like refusing to take vehicles with special protection and 'Lal Batti'. On December 31, Arvind Kejriwal announced 50 percent discount in electricity prices till April, directed to conduct CAG audit of Power Companies. It was announced that 20 kilo litres of water would be given free of cost. As soon as the government was formed, the confrontation with the central government and the Delhi Police also began.

In February 2013, Arvind Kejriwal ordered his monitoring department to register an FIR against several influential people, including Mukesh Ambani and M. Veerappa Moily, for irregularly increasing the price of natural gas. Now the dispute with the Centre has reached its peak. Kejriwal started demanding full status to Delhi and at the same time he alleged that the Delhi Police was not following his and his ministers' instructions.

It was alleged that even after the order of Delhi Law Minister Somnath Bharti, the police did not take action against a criminal dealing in drugs and sex. Similarly, another SHO was accused of not taking action against those accused of raping a foreign woman. It is common knowledge that from the time Delhi got statehood, the Central Government has control over the police. Kejriwal put the blame of such crimes on the absence of police control under the Delhi government. In protest, Kejriwal and his ministers and supporters marched in a procession to meet the Home Minister. When the police stopped them at Rail Bhawan near the Home Ministry and Parliament House, Kejriwal and his supporters started a dharna there. This protest lasted for about 30 hours. The matter got resolved after the announcement of action against two junior police officers, but Kejriwal was successful in conveying the message to the people of Delhi that the Lieutenant Governor and the Central Government together are not allowing the Delhi government to function.

The Arvind Kejriwal government called the Assembly session from February 13 and announced the passing of the Jan Lokpal and Swaraj Bill. He had a tussle with the Home Ministry and the Lieutenant Governor over the introduction of the Jan Lokpal Bill and Lieutenant Governor Najeeb Jung said that the Kejriwal government could not pass the bill from the Assembly, and that the approval of the Central Government was necessary for it. But the Kejriwal government stood firm on passing it. Along with the Congress, which was supporting the government from outside on this issue, the BJP and two other MLAs opposed the bill. As 42 out of 70 MLAs were in protest, Kejriwal could not introduce the bill in the Vidhan Sabha. Making it an issue, Kejriwal resigned on February 14, 2014 and recommended the dissolution of the Assembly.

After the fall of the Government, AAP started preparations for the 2014 Lok Sabha elections by becoming aggressive against the Congress and the BJP. Kejriwal said he would not contest but later contested from Varanasi against Bharatiya Janata Party's Prime ministerial candidate Narendra Modi. Candidates were fielded on 432 seats across the country, Arvind Kejriwal himself lost by 3.70 lakh votes. In Punjab, the party got success in four seats but had to face defeat in the whole Country including Delhi.

Unilateral victory in the 2015 election ...

But in Delhi, the Aam Aadmi Party continued its aggression and in the 2015 elections gave a message that what it did in its 49-day government, will continue." The BJP, buoyed by the victory at the Centre, also tried a new experiment and contested naming Kiran Bedi as its Chief Minister face, the first woman police officer who had once shared the stage with Arvind Kejriwal during the movement, but the Bharatiya Janata Party lost poorly. Arvind Kejriwal became a shining star in politics by winning 67 Assembly seats in 70. After winning he again announced a waiver of electricity, water bills and now slowly started carrying forward the government's vision on education, health, water, electricity. Yet, during the election, his estrangement with his associates increased on the allegations of the selection process of candidates and fielding candidates of criminal nature.

Some conflicts also...

The first National Council of the party was of 320 people and after that the National Executive of 23 people was formed. The former Law Minister Shanti Bhushan donated rupees one crore to the party. But in the meantime controversies started over the removal of the facts of the funding from the party's website. Yogendra Yadav was expelled from the party over the allegations of anti-party activities. Prashant Bhushan also quit the party and together with many others, including Anand Kumar, Ajit Jha, formed a political party called Swaraj Abhiyan.

On the other hand, the Aam Aadmi Party started spreading its hold in Punjab due to the four seats it won in the Lok Sabha. The party announced its intention to contest the Assembly elections in December 2015. The general atmosphere was also in his favour but the party could win only 20 seats out of his 112 candidates in the 117-member Assembly. The party was now the main Opposition Party and the SAD stooped to the third position. The MPs also separated amidst some controversies and in the 2019 Lok Sabha elections, the party's candidates could not repeat the performance in Punjab and none other than Bhagwant Mann could win.

After winning the Delhi Assembly elections, Sanjay Singh got the distinction of becoming a Rajya Sabha MP from Delhi on January 28, 2018. Narayan Das Gupta and Sushil Kumar Gupta got placed among other party leaders in the remaining two Rajya Sabha seats from Delhi. But now Arvind Kejriwal's distance from Kumar Vishwas and Ashutosh, who were his partners during the struggle, increased.

The party made major preparations for the 2020 Assembly elections. He brought his achievements to the public on a large scale through public platform, claimed to have curbed corruption and that corruption in all departments was reduced by about 80 percent and also informed that 50 corrupt officials were sent to jail, electricity charges up to 200 units were waived while water was made free up to 20,000 litres per month. Schemes like education, improvement in hospitals, free medicine, free testing- treatment, free travelling in buses, free pilgrimage were also mentioned in its campaigns. The network of CCTV cameras was also installed and this action was brought to public knowledge. Arvind Kejriwal blatantly asked the public to confirm his ten guarantees and if the Aam Aadmi Party government has worked on them, then vote in its favour ... the public was so impressed by this candidness that in 2020, once again by winning 62 seats, Congress was decimated.

Punjab election revolution

What the Aam Aadmi Party has done in the 2022 election results in Punjab is like 'neither ago nor in future' thing. Never before in the electoral history of Punjab's 117-member assembly has a party won 92 seats in any assembly election. Congress won 87 seats in 1992 and 77 seats in 2017. Shiromani Akali Dal got 75 seats in 1997 and 73 in 1985. Getting 45.2 percent votes in a multi-angular contest was a remarkable feat. The Aam Aadmi Party whose strike rate was only 17.9 percent in 2017 had risen to 76.9 percent this time. The Congress and the Akali Dal were in shock. The amazing work it did in the Malwa region was amazing. The party won 90 percent of the seats here and winning from this area alone was enough to invite him to form the government. The figures confirm that till 2017 the vote bank of the Akalis was mostly rural, but in 2022 its influence increased significantly in urban areas. Bhagwant Mann became Chief Minister.

Party's victory in Punjab has various meanings. This victory of the Aam Aadmi Party would be considered as a sign of sea-change in the politics of the states. After the governments in two states and getting decent vote percentage in Uttarakhand and Goa, the party will be eyeing the upcoming assembly elections,especially in the neighbouring Himachal Pradesh and Gujarat of Punjab. The party can win a lot of seats in these elections because of its beneficial promises. especially in Gujarat. In Gujarat, elections have mostly been held face to face between the two major parties, but now this scenario is likely to change. Aap has a strong influence in Surat Municipality and has also increased the base of workers in the state. Even after not being able to do much in Uttarakhand, AAP will try to make use of the freebees-strategy of electricity and water in Himachal.

But the real strategy will now have to be seen in the 2024 general elections.So far, apart from the above, sometimes TMC's Mamata Banerjee tries to become centre of the opposition's strategy and sometimes TRS's K. Chandrashekhar Rao sees possibilities for himself. Now after a new game in Bihar, Nitish Kumar is a new face in this league. It will be interesting to watch the Congress party unwillingly being compelled to make place for the Aam Aadmi Party in the politics of the opposition. There are many reasons for Kejriwal to get more respect than Mamata Di and KCR. But the faster route to the Lok Sabha elections passes through Uttar Pradesh, Bihar, Maharashtra, Madhya Pradesh, apart from Tamil Nadu, Aam Aadmi Party will have to really toil itself there. Arvind Kejriwal is also playing much at Patriotic field to counter BJP.

From Arvind Kejriwal's politics around youth, employment, religious facts, what is most alluring is the schemes to give freebies, be it electricity or water. Party's efforts to improve the quality of education in schools, a lot that has been done free of cost in hospitals, were also appreciated even at the international levels. The concept of Mohalla clinic was also a new experiment. But people of Delhi chant 'Dil Maange more' because Delhi is after all Delhi and people from all over the country come here and aspire to have more than what they get.

It is true that "freebees" are gaining popularity these days. Parties are alluring people and thus making and running governments on this promise. Not only confined to AAP, all other parties would also certainly make use of this tool. Then what would AAP's strategy be? This will be interesting to observe.

❑

Andhra Pradesh

19
YSR Congress: Jagan and the Fruits of Power

The story of The YRS Congress is no less charismatic. A story where the hero is first a famous leader of a Party, decimates the original party, launches his own and also becomes the Head of the State. This is truly rare in the politics of Andhra Pradesh and rarest of rare in the politics of the country. In Andhra Pradesh Assembly elections 2019, YSR Congress created a stir by winning 151 out of 175 seats i.e. 86 percent seats and Jagan Mohan Reddy became the Chief Minister of the State like his father. The 85 percent vote-charisma is not novel in electoral politics, but it has happened only in small states. However, the YSR Congress did not come to power for the first time, but the charisma performed by Y.S. Jagan Mohan Reddy after the death of his father Y.S. Rajasekhara Reddy made TDP that had parted ways with NDA including Jansena Party, floored altogether. After this election, the name of YSR Congress Party became a popular name across the country.

Jagan Mohan Reddy was born on December 21, 1972 in the house of Y.S. Rajasekhara Reddy in Pulivendula village in Kadapa district of Andhra Pradesh who later became the Chief Minister of Andhra Pradesh. Jagan was educated at Hyderabad Public School. He completed his graduation from Nizam College. He has done

B.Com and MBA. He got married to Bharati on August 28, 1996 who is the daughter of Dr. E.C. Gangi Reddy, a local from her village. Jagan and Bharati are parents to two girls.

But more interesting than Jagan's story is to know the story of his father Rajasekhara Reddy. What Rajasekhara Reddy did is no less mesmerizing. As soon as Rajasekhar a became a doctor, he was bent upon building a hospital for the poor. Even before entering into politics, he wanted to do something so he could earn a name for himself. His intentions were good and luck being on his side, in 1978 he became an MLA from Pulivendula and also a Minister. His level of popularity can be gauged from the fact that he continued to be elected even when NT Ramarao's popularity was at its zenith. Later, when he went to the Lok Sabha, he was elected as MP four times from the 9th to the 12th Lok Sabha. Then he returned to State politics and was leader of the Opposition from 1999-2004. But in the last year, when he felt that Chief Minister Chandrababu Naidu's popularity was fluctuating mercurially, Jagan travelled through the State and toppled Chandrababu's government. He first became Chief Minister in 2004 and implemented various public welfare programmes. He was charged with allegations over corruption and several others, including his son Jagan Mohan Reddy, faced CBI probe. But in the midst of controversies he again became Chief Minister. That too when the TDP-led opposition was united. He was the first to become Chief Minister of the State two terms consecutively. But destiny had planned something else. On September 2, 2009, he and four officers were killed along with him during a helicopter accident in the dense forests of Nalamala. Bad weather had caused this air-crash, it was informed.

Meanwhile, Jagan Mohan busied himself with handling the vast legacy of his father's politics along with his business. He paid much attention to his father Rajasekhara's Lok Sabha constituency. And in 2009, he was also elected as an MP from Kadapa on behalf of the Congress. But the death of his father had shattered him. After

Rajasekhara's death, the atmosphere was different in the State. There was a deep melancholy and reports of suicides flooded the State as soon as the news of Rajasekhar broke. After Rajasekhara's death, all the MLAs seemed eager to make Jagan the Chief Minister, but the Congress High Command did not seal his name. Finance Minister K. Rosaiah was instead made the Chief Minister. Jagan realised that his father's traditions were being blown up. He continued raising voice for six months, but then in March 2010, he marched on his journey - Udarpoo Yatra - the Shok Yatra - in memory of his father. He went to the house of all the supporters who committed suicide in love for Rajasekhara. Later, he even went to the houses of those who got burnt in suicide attempts. There were about 150 such people. Jagan's popularity was rising and this irked the Congress High Command. He was pressured to discontinue the journey immediately. On September 29, 2010, he and his mother Vijayamma resigned from the Congress and announced the following week that they would form a new party. And the day came on March 12, 2011 when Jagan announced the formation of YSR Congress. Bye-elections were held and both of them won from Kadapa and Pulivendula Assembly respectively. But this euphoria was short-lived. On May 27, 2012, the CBI arrested Jagan Mohan Reddy on charges of embezzlement. The CBI alleged that Jagan illegally acquired large properties using his office when Y.S. Rajasekhara Reddy was Chief Minister. Apart from Reddy, CBI accused 58 companies of investing in Reddy's business. These companies were given mining and leases as allotment of projects by Reddy. His judicial custody continued to be extended.

Meanwhile, Jagan Mohan started a hunger strike while in jail against the Congress or the UPA's consent to the dissolution of Andhra. Mother Vijayamma also started a hunger strike. After his release in 2013, Reddy called for a 72-hour Bandh to protest against the formation of Telangana and Jagan and his mother resigned from their Assembly seats also. Then came 2014 Assembly elections. In Andhra Pradesh, the Telugu Desam Party overtook YSR Congress in a nail-biting contest. The YSR Congress won 67 of the total 175 seats by securing 45 percent votes in this election. But the Telugu Desam Party captured 102 seats with 47 percent votes and formed the government.

But Jagan had no intention to lose. He was performing well as leader of the Opposition waiting for the opportune time. On November 6, 2017, YSR Congress Party President Jagan Mohan announced Praja Sankalp Padyatra from Kadapa district covering 3000 long kilometres. In it, the party gave the slogan of Rawli Jagan, Kavli Jagan (Jagan should be back, we want Jagan back to power). During the Padyatra, Jagan Mohan visited 125 Assembly constituencies in 430 days and felt the nerves of the people inquiring about their plight. He benefited immensely from the Padyatra in the 2019 Assembly elections. Jagan's government was formed with 49.95 percent votes and more than 85 percent seats.

Now it was Jagan's turn. He cancelled the TDP government's plan to make Amravati the capital and set up three separate capitals for judicial, administrative and legislative branches in Kurnool, Amravati and Visakhapatnam. The YSR Congress was very much against making Telangana State, so the possibility of the party getting hold in Telangana is low. TDP is trying to regain power but Chandrababu Naidu is yet to perform in a manner which can make him hopeful for 2024. In Andhra Pradesh, the YSRC Party's bumper victory in local body elections (victory in 547 zilla parishad seats) shows its continuing strong hold.

Though there is still a long time to go, the BJP is also working hard and fast. Jagan has sometimes suffered because of the BJP government at the Centre. But the biggest problem baffling the BJP is its vote share. The BJP will have to find a partner but it has a problem with the TDP that has parted ways with it and Chandrashekhar Rao's party in Andhra doesn't seem in a mood to indirectly support BJP. So this is how Jagan stays in power for the time being.

To counter BJP's ongoing efforts and reinventing his image, Jagan sought resignation from all his ministers and reconstituted the Cabinet in April 2022. Jagan wants to limit himself to state only. He is not willing to play at national ground but wants to secure his state's position on a larger level.

❑

Andhra Pradesh

20
Telugu Desam: The Onset of Charisma Politics

The foundation for the Telugu Desam Party was laid by Nandamuri Taraka Rama Rao, one of the most famous film stars of undivided Andhra Pradesh. Popularly known as NTR the actor assiduously built the party on just one issue – Aaatma Gauvaram (Self-Respect and Telugu Pride).

Having strode the Telugu cinema like a colossus for close to four decades, the superstar was an icon who acquired fame for portraying roles of a pantheon of gods and mythological characters. Sometime in the 1980s a thought crossed the mind of this actor to give back to the society in general and Telugu people in particular who showered love and affection in making him a superstar, a space he shared with another hero of that generation Akkineni Nageswara Rao.

While mulling over the idea and discussing the issue with friends, the "high command" attitude of the Indian National Congress under Indira Gandhi provided the much needed spark to launch the party on March 29, 1982. The selection of date is significant since NTR held a firm belief that the 29th day in the calendar brought him good luck since his early days on the silver screen.

In the run up to the formation of the party, Rama Rao was influenced by politics in neighbouring state of Tamil Nadu or Madras, as the State was called before being rechristened.. The city was home to all major producers of South India and those associated with Telugu film industry. Many film stars also stayed put in the city for long durations, and shuttled between Hyderabad or other cities depending on work schedules and other engagements.

For nearly 50 years, politics in Tamil Nadu had a strong connection with the film industry starting from the likes of C.N. Annadurai, M. Karunanidhi, M.G. Ramachandran and J. Jayalalithaa besides others who continue to straddle between politics and the industry.

While the seeds of the move into politics were sown in the early 1980s with Rama Rao expressing desire to perform 'Prajaseva', it took some time to germinate a green shoot. There were a series of events happening in the then Andhra Pradesh. The Congress Party under Indira Gandhi was seeking to re-establish its hold in national politics in the post-Janata party phase with Sanjay Gandhi playing an important role. After the premature death of his younger brother in an aircraft accident, Rajiv Gandhi stepped in to fill the void and help his mother tide over the personal and political crisis.

In those days, the Congress Party effected a change of Chief Minister in quick succession, leading to resentment among people, the party and its leaders against the 'High Command' imposing its will over the State. The choice of T. Anjaiah, who rose from the ranks of daily wage earner to a union leader and Labour Minister at the Centre, to replace M. Chenna Reddy created a situation during the visit of Rajiv Gandhi to Hyderabad.

Anjaiah, known for his politics of accommodation and having sworn-in with a jumbo Cabinet, came to the airport with the Council of Ministers, party workers complete with a band in attendance. Having been used to such a reception to Sanjay Gandhi, the Chief Minister did what he thought appropriate but managed to earn the wrath of the pilot-turned-politician in Rajiv Gandhi.

The dressing down Rajiv Gandhi gave to the Chief Minister for descending on to the tarmac with an enthusiastic band of supporters and visuals of a hapless Anjaiah triggered a sympathy for the latter. That one incident literally changed the face of politics in Andhra Pradesh. Aatma Gauvram became the catchword and turned into a slogan around which people of all hues rallied around. A new political party was born. In a way, the formation of this regional party was also the result of the externalisation of the internal power tussle between two dominant communities – Reddys and Kammas, NTR hailed from.

Early days

Once he decided it was time to launch a regional party to serve the state, NTR started work and was assisted in the task by a former Congress leader Nadendala Bhaskar Rao, who was disenchanted with the Grand Old Party for ignoring his claims to be appointed a Chief Minister amid a string of changes effected in the state. The decision to go ahead with the formation of the party came about in a dramatic fashion. NTR came to Hyderabad from Chennai to a tumultuous welcome from people who thronged the airport to have a glimpse of the star amid the buzz of his entry into politics. Reaching the residence of Bhaskar Rao straight from the airport, a meeting of the yet to be named party's steering committee was held where NTR was chosen as its President. From here the assembled moved to MLA quarters where a meeting was scheduled at the Club Hall. Soon the accommodation proved to be inadequate as people kept pouring. The meeting was shifted to the lawns and in the midst of the noises, NTR delivered a speech at the end of which he christened the party—Telugu Desam. Then he put himself on the task of drawing up the party flag, with a yellow background considered good with symbols of a hut, a plough and a wheel in different colours to represent the working and toiling classes.

In order to gauge the public sentiments and build upon the euphoria created by the announcement, NTR embarked upon twin strategies hold party conventions or Mahanadu in three separate regions of erstwhile Andhra – Rayalseema, Coastal areas and Telangana and the cities selected for the public outreach were Tirupati, Visakhapatnam and Hyderabad.

The Founder also came up with a unique idea to enrol people into the party. He issued advertisements in a popular Telugu Daily, Eenadu. Those desirous of joining the TDP could fill in the form given in the advertisement and mail it to the party office. Eenadu, founded by Cherukuri Ramoji Rao in 1974 became the vehicle through which the TDP and NTR reached households every day. The unprecedented coverage over the next few months as the leader atop the Chaitanyam Ratham crisscrossed the length and breadth of the state.

Rath Yatra mode of campaign

Aware that his popularity as a cinema star needed to be sustained as people thronged both the venues and road NTR used to travel, the TDP founder decided to make himself visible by travelling in an open jeep and soon came upon the idea of a permanent vehicle that could carry him through the state while providing the bare minimum comforts on the road.

The filmstar possessed a Chevrolet convertible that lay in the dump at a studio in Madras (Chennai). Disagreeing with traditional mode of making local arrangement to travel by road in cities and towns after reaching major destinations by air or rail, NTR put his trusted people to make the vehicle roadworthy complete with an open hatch, a ladder to reach the top of the vehicle, fitted with loudspeakers and floodlights. Inside came a cot, a revolving chair and a bench to accommodate a few people with space for storing water and party material.

If one looks back, the concept of hitting the road on a vehicle fitted with some facilities for comfort was revolutionary back then. Since then it has been replicated by different political parties and their leaders across the country. In a way, NTR introduced a novel concept in Indian politics that remains relevant till date. Of course, as time progressed the interiors and comfort kept pace with emerging technology.

Even though the idea to convert the old ramshackle vehicle into an election jalopy was visualised in early April, it took more time to make it ready to withstand the rigours of journeys on roads some of which can add to the woes of both men and machines.

Another spin-off of NTR legacy was the concept of roadshows. Once it was decided to hold a public meeting in every district, there was little time to lose. The new party working to put its structures in place could rely on the huge network of NTR Fan Clubs numbering into hundreds. The enthusiastic fans turning out in numbers in the run-up to the formation of the party were now eager to lend a helping hand in setting up the party across the state, in districts, towns and villages. And when the Ratham got ready to roll, NTR hit the road with vigour accompanied by catchy signature tunes selected with care and blaring from the loudspeakers as the vehicle carried the founder from village to village, town to town and city to city across various districts.

The crowds kept increasing from thousands to lakhs even as political parties led by the Congress continued to hope the popularity of the film star would wane over time. Nothing of that sort happened as the Ratham kept moving ahead. On spotting people alongside, the van would pull to a side and NTR would climb atop the vehicle waving, accepting garlands showered on him by ecstatic crowds. Backed by powerful oratory honed by years in the film industry, the booming voice could be heard and recognised miles away and its pitch would reach a crescendo depending on the chord NTR hit with the crowds. The onward journey of the Ratham continued.

The daily grind itself became a talking point. NTR connected to the people through simple gestures, staying at makeshift accommodation, bathing by a tube well, washing his pair of Khaki dress and drying them in the open before restarting the journey. These gestures, witnessed never before in modern day politics created a buzz around the founder as one who was like any one of the ordinary people. His connection with the common people continued to grow even as leaders of the Congress Party discounted his ability to make a major electoral dent. On her part, Indira Gandhi described NTR as a 'political joke' while state leaders continued to maintain the party would do well when elections were due in March 1983.

"Between June 14, when Rama Rao set out on the first phase of campaign tours, and January 3 when he arrived in Tirupati to make the last speech of his campaign, he had travelled for a total of 70 days, reaching every nook and corner of the state and covering a total distance of 35,000 kilometres. He was seen and heard by an estimated 3 crore people–a record for the history books. No man had travelled in the state so extensively in living memory; no man had spoken so eloquently, articulating the frustrations and aspirations of his people; no man was received with so much warmth, love and affection; and no man had so electrified so many people with orator and swayed the emotions of his people so much that they could do anything for him. Not since Mahatma Gandhi, anyway", wrote senior journalist S Venkata Narayan, in his biographical book on NTR.

Rice for ₹ 2 and welfare promises

It was during the first round of his public meetings that NTR made an announcement which is now an essential part of every political party promise. In one of those early sojourns that took him to Kadapa, an important city in Rayalseema region, he declared to provide subsidised rice at ₹ 2 per kilogram. The idea was not new. Its origin can be traced to Tamil Nadu when the DMK under C. Annadurai promised to provide rice at Rupee One per Padi (approximately 1.5 kg). The announcement by the TDP president kindled hope among the poor and the marginalised sections of the society.

While the Congress criticised the scheme ridiculing it as a grand plan that cannot be implemented considering resources required for it, the party soon became nervous. Its Chief Minister came up with a scheme to provide rice at ₹ 1.90 per kg and when it was rolled on, the measure sought to reinforce the TDP offer was viable while the Congress realised the welfare measure resonated with ordinary people. It was TDP and NTR who got the credit either way.

The TDP president did not stop at rice. He promised to make available inexpensive clothes for common people and permanent houses for the poor and needy. After all, the film actor ridiculed the government questioning its use if it could not provide food, clothes and shelter to the poor and those in need of these. The basic issue of 'Roti Kapada and Makan', proved to be the game changer like never before.

Now when one looks back into history a few such schemes which were dismissed as populist and sops are now standard entries of most governments. The ₹ 2 per kg rice is now expanded in many states to Atta just as the Mid-day meal scheme envisaged by K. Kamaraj in Tamil Nadu and given a boost by the successor DMK government was adopted by the Centre as a national programme with the objective of providing nutritious food to the children of poor when they come to school, which in turn increased enrolment and raised the level of literacy in India.Even today people may think that this scheme is ten - twenty years old, while the reality is that it is almost sixty five years old.

The first electoral test

With reports from the ground suggesting a groundswell of support for NTR at the roadshows and Eenadu devoting reams of newsprint reporting the movement of the TDP president, political parties began to take note of it. The elections were due in March but suddenly the dates of the poll schedule were made for the month of January. There was not much time to lose and NTR had to halt his campaign midway to make preparations for his biggest and first test – assembly elections.

While some state leaders of the Left parties sought alliance and a greater share of seats, NTR was unwilling to concede much. Eventually, the TDP fielded 289 of the then 294 seats in undivided Andhra Pradesh Legislative Assembly leaving the rest five to Maneka Gandhi's Sanjay Vihar Manch. The outfit was floated by the widow of Sanjay Gandhi as she fell out with Indira Gandhi. The TDP agreed to accommodate as she promised to campaign in the state. The move suited the party as her support meant Indira Gandhi's Bahu campaigning against the party led by her Saas and her 'Jeth' Rajiv Gandhi, on whom his mother began to rely after the death of Sanjay Gandhi. The family battle and its popularity were now to be contested in the electoral field. The process of selecting candidates was elaborate with NTR taking in inputs from some independent observers as also the lists drawn by Eenadu whose reporters covered the rallies and road shows throughout. The list contained the educated youth, professionals and members representing a cross section of communities. Telugu Pride and the Call of Mother Telugu (Telugu Talli Pilistondi -Maa Telugu Bula Rahi Hai) remained the central theme while NTR was the prime face on all posters with each candidate taking a picture with the President and putting them on campaign materials.

Despite widespread support and voluntary donations from Telugu speaking people in the State and other parts of India, the party was low on funds. As for candidates, the party gave a limited amount of money for those from Scheduled Castes/Tribes and Women along with publicity material, posters, pamphlets, audio-cassettes of party songs and speeches of NTR. NTR heading a party which had minimal experience on how to organise as a political outfit was also unconventional in his campaign as the Ratham yatra proved. Crowds drew to him like bees to a flower and he endeared those who assembled by igniting the Telugu pride and promising to bring a change in the lives of the ordinary who otherwise lived on the margins. His voice generated hope.

While one opinion poll by a popular publication gave the Congress a comfortable victory, just days ahead of the voting Eenadu predicted a landslide win for TDP and Congress reduced to double digits. Both parties remained confident after the voting. Counting commenced on January 6 and when the process was complete history was made. The nascent TDP Party was voted to office with a massive 201 seats decimating Congress that could win just 60 seats, CPI (6), CPI-M 5) Janata Dal (1) and others (20).

A party that was formed barely nine months ago defeated the mighty Congress led by Indira Gandhi, who was revered in Andhra Pradesh as Indiramma so much so that it gave her the majority of seats in 1977 when the Janata wave swept other parts of the country. On January 9, 1983 NTR took the oath as the Chief Minister, the first non-Congress person to assume office. The ceremony at the Lal Bahadur Stadium was witnessed by over 2.5 lakh people who wanted to personally witness history in the making.

While heading the government and laying down a code of conduct for the party members in public life, NTR also began to dabble in national politics. He was very much part of the opposition conclaves held in various parts of the country between 1983 and 1984. The moves did cause concern in the Congress camp as also Indira Gandhi who was in the midst of a major problem at hand in the form of the crisis in Punjab. The conclaves focused on legitimate regional aspirations with nationalistic commitment. TDP's stupendous victory underscored the importance of how people of various regions viewed the polity of overdependence on the Centre as opposition parties began forging unity.

Political setback

It is in this backdrop these developments the Congress government at the Centre became wary of NTR while within the TDP his differences with Bhaskar Rao grew over time. Rao who fashioned himself as the brain behind TDP and the rise of NTR was irked over being ignored, gradually re-established his ties with Congress leaders and struck when the opportunity came.

Bhaskar Rao who was part of NTR from the beginning felt slighted as the TDP Supremo gradually distanced him and went alone on the Ratham. The chasm grew and there were disagreements on issues including the Opposition conclaves. Even though he was a Minister in the Cabinet, Rao felt slighted at the treatment being meted out to him and struck when an opportunity came. During 1984, NTR had to travel to the United States on more than one occasion. First, to attend to his wife who was undergoing treatment there and later, for his own heart surgery in July that year. A law and order situation in Hyderabad and series of events led to Rao working up the numbers claiming support from a sizeable number of legislators including some from the TDP while Rama Rao cut short his visit to arrive in India complete with bandages on surgical wounds.

Despite the numbers still with Rama Rao, who was then ably assisted by his second son-in-law Nara Chandrababu Naidu who crossed over to join the TDP earlier. Yet, on August 16, the Governor Ram Lal swore-in Bhaskar Rao as the Chief Minister and the whole situation changed suddenly. Rama Rao and his party legislators were taken into custody for trying to stay put inside the Raj Bhavan unleashing a sympathy wave. Rao was given a month to prove his majority but events over the next few weeks undid the plans. Most leaders in the Opposition rallied round NTR. The bonding over Opposition Conclaves and dismissal of two non-Congress governments, Farooq Abdullah's National Conference regime earlier and now TDP stood out like a sore thumb. Pictures of NTR in a wheelchair accompanied by leaders of the opposition travelling up the Raisina Hill to meet President Zail Singh remain etched in memories just as these visuals created a new template in Indian politics.

Meanwhile, as public opinion began to add to the pressure against the Central government, the Congress leaders moved in to ring fence attacks against Indira Gandhi. Governor Ram Lal was asked to step down and Shankar Dayal Sharma brought in. With Rao unable to prove his majority by the end of the period granted by his predecessor, Sharma directed Rao to step down and swore NTR in again.

The power of the people, charisma of NTR and extraordinary support by leaders of the Opposition turned the tables on Congress leadership. NTR was back at the helm as the Chief Minister after a gap of one month.

The second stint at governance

The TDP's popularity remained intact and soon after the assassination of Indira Gandhi, when the country was preparing for Lok Sabha elections, NTR convinced Rajiv Gandhi who was also the Congress President to agree for early dissolution of the State assembly amid plans to hold it along with general elections. Yet, some political moves on the part of NTR resulted in the State polls to be held in January 1985. Though the Congress swept the Lok Sabha polls on the back of sympathy wave, Andhra Pradesh remained a bastion of TDP with the party winning 30 of the 42 seats in the Lok Sabha polls. With the opposition numbers reduced drastically in the new House, TDP member P. Upendra became the Leader of the Opposition.

In the Assembly elections of January 1985, TDP continued to flourish winning 202 of the 294 seats while the Congress dropped 10 seats for the previous election to bag 50. NTR began his second term that continued uninterrupted for a full five years. His son-in-law Chandrababu Naidu meanwhile gradually began to build a network within the party apparatus.

Losing power, regaining it and change of leadership

While there was criticism of the lack of governance of NTR during his first two years, post-coup and public sympathy allowed the party to come back. Yet, towards the end of the second term anti-incumbency set in. NTR was aware that he was losing grip over the party and unable to keep his legislators and Party leaders in check. The Telugu Desam Party lost the 1989 elections. The Congress under redoubtable Marri Chenna Reddy swept to power winning 181 seats and the TDP down to 74. The party attempted to remain politically relevant with NTR seeking to play a role outside the State as the National Front Government under Vishwanath Pratap Singh came into being at the Centre. NTR became its Chairman.

The ground situation in the state continued to change and by the end of 1990, Congress replaced Chenna Reddy with N Janardhana Reddy. In the ensuing assembly elections, the TDP was returned to power with NTR assuming office once again in December 1994. The party was no longer the one he created in 1982, after years in power and outside, the outfit acquired its own share of ills even as NTR came close to a biographer turned partner Lakshmi Parvati. She entered his life much after the death of his wife in 1984 and during the period when loss of power and loneliness played on his mind. NTR family, friends and supporters were experiencing discomfort over the development and the growing clout of Lakshmi Parvathy, who did not conceal her political ambition as a physically less agile Chief Minister and TDP president increasingly depending on her.

In less than nine months into the new government, Chandrababu Naidu effected a change by removing NTR and becoming the Chief Minister in September 1995 and continued in office for 10 years till May 2004. Naidu moved in riding on the wave of unpopularity of Lakshmi Parvathy and resentment against her interference in both the party and the government. The impression was that the Chief Minister was being influenced by her. While there was a group who went with her, Naidu proved to be a better strategist as he garnered support of the legislators and more importantly of the family including Daggubati Venkateswara Rao, who like him was married to one of NTR's daughters. It is another matter that Venakteswara Rao, husband of D. Purandeswari, who served as a Minister in the Manmohan Singh Council of Ministers, found no place in the Naidu team later.

The party under Naidu

Since 1995 Chandrababu Naidu remains its President. Having cut his political teeth in Congress, and serving as a Minister in the Andhra Government in the 1980s, Naidu crossed over to the TDP later and slowly built his support base. Just as the regional party under NTR sought to carve a role for itself in national politics, Naidu made most of the opportunity in 1996 during the United Front coalition government first under H.D. Deve Gowda and later under Inder Kumar Gujral. He became the Convener of the Front and would shuttle between Hyderabad and Delhi sorting out issues that cropped up ever-so-often among the coalition partners and with the Congress, supporting it from the outside. Later in 1999, Naidu jumped ship extending support to the Vajpayee government from the outside. In the bargain TDP got the post of Speaker with the party nominating Ganti Mohan Chandra Balayogi to the post.

By 2004, the TDP found itself in the political wilderness. The party lost power to Congress under Y.S. Rajasekhara Reddy, a diehard Congressman. Naidu and Reddy were once youth

Congress leaders of their districts in the mid-1970s and knew each other well but took different political paths.

Between 1999-2004 the TDP government under Naidu sought to build Andhra Pradesh and Hyderabad as India's answer to Silicon Valley of the United States. Naidu preferred to call himself as the Chief Executive Officer of the State. He promoted IT in a big way, undertook major infrastructure projects to usher in development. In the process, the farmers and other sections felt ignored. It appeared that the Shining India campaign at the Centre was reverberating itself as Shining Hyderabad in Andhra.

Sensing an opportunity, his political opponent Rajasekhara Reddy undertook a Padayatra across the State and eventually walked away with the votes when elections were held in 2004. Naidu lost both power and political friends. For the next decade, TDP remained in the opposition. The unfortunate death of Rajasekhara Reddy in a helicopter crash, internal struggle within the party with the Chief Minister's son Y.S. Jagan Mohan Reddy with party central leadership created fertile ground for Naidu to bounce back in 2014. By then the Manmohan Singh Government had split Andhra Pradesh carving out a separate Telangana , a demand that was first raised by M Chenna Reddy in 1970s and then by K. Chandrasekhara Rao who was once in the TDP but parted ways in 2001 to form the Telangana Rashtra Samiti.

In 2014, backed by the pro-unification sentiment and belief of the people that TDP under Naidu could re-build the residual Andhra Pradesh, the party rode to power in divided Andhra Pradesh winning 117 of the 237 seats it contested. The TDP government promised to build a new capital at Amravati on the lines of Singapore. Despite five years in office, the project did not gather much pace. Riddled by charges of corruption and inefficiency, the TDP faced a rout in the 2019 assembly elections as Jagan Mohan Reddy and his YSR Congress got overwhelming support from the people. Jagan Reddy, like his father undertook a padayatra that earned him both affection of the voters.

The decision of the party to have an electoral alliance with the Congress in 2019 also shocked many of its supporters. For the party founded on the basis of its anti-Congress stance shook hands with it. Today, the party is seeking to recapture the lost glory and remain relevant in the two Telugu speaking states of Andhra Pradesh and Telangana. But it doesn't look easy. The party base is weakening in Telangana and Jagan Reddy is riding the popularity chariot in Andhra Pradesh.

❑

21
AIMIM: New Sensation

Wherever elections are held nowadays, one question is often asked, is Owaisi's party also contesting? Even after 35 years of formation Owaisi's Party is still a state recognised party, i.e. the regional party. But the way this party has made a dent in the vote bank of the minorities, it is not surprising if it gets the status of a national party in the coming few months. Originally from Andhra Pradesh or rather Hyderabad, this party is slowly expanding and has entered Maharashtra, Bihar, Telangana. The next target is the Uttar Pradesh elections.

Although the parent party of All India Majlis-e-Ittehadul Muslimeen (AIMIM) is also included, it was a party before independence, but the real identity of this party is from Sultan Salahuddin Owaisi becoming the Lok Sabha member from Hyderabad in 1984. Sultan remained MP for six consecutive terms till 2004. And after this he got his son Asaduddin Owaisi to contest the Hyderabad seat. Thus, the year when Barrister Owaisi turned 25, he became an MLA from Charminar Assembly constituency in the same year, but he became the talk of the nation only after becoming an MP. He talks of Muslims but at the same time opposes Jinnah's two-nation theory. When Mumbai was attacked in 2008, his party called for the arrest of terrorists, including Zakir Rehman Lakhvi and Hafiz Saeed. Similarly, he has been an advocate of backward classes in government jobs and he has also raised his voice for this. But he has also been expressing concern that leaders of secular parties are not able to transfer their votes in favour of Muslim candidates. He believed that Muslims should become their own political force like the backward classes, Dalits and Yadavs had. Similarly, their demand was instead of Haj subsidy to Muslims, that money should be used for the education of Muslim women. His open condemnation of ISIS was also widely praised.

The advantage of such discussions was that the party's support base grew even in a liberal community of minorities. On the other hand the fanatical speeches of his brother and MLA Akbaruddin Owaisi continued to create a different kind of sensation in the party. By the way, the roots of the party are very old. According to the party's official website, All India Majlis-e-Ittehadul Muslimeen, also known as Itehad Bainal Muslimeen, has its roots dating back to 93 years. It was established on November 12, 1927 at a meeting held in Hyderabad hosted by Nawab Mahmud Khan Qiladar. The meeting was attended by prominent people of the Muslim community, including the Ulema-e-Mashkin. The objective of the establishment of the party was stated to be the social, economic and educational upliftment of the Muslims. Nawab Bahadur Yar Jung was elected its first President in 1938. Nawab Bahadur Yar Jung is also known for the Khaksar movement led by him in Hyderabad. This movement was started by Inayatullah Khan Mashqiri in 1931 in Lahore. The aim of this movement was to free India from the British Empire and establish a Hindu-Muslim government in the country. (History of Khaksar Movement in India 1931–1947, Amalendu De). It is said to have been founded in 1927 as Majlis-e-Ittehadul Muslimeen (MIM) by Nawab Mahmud Nawaz Khan, the Qiledaar of the Hyderabad State, on the advice of Osman Ali Khan, the Nizam of Hyderabad. In 1944, Syed Qasim Rizvi took over the leadership of the party. Vakil Qasim's intentions were quite aggressive and he also formed a militia organisation of Razakars. These Razakars were given special training in fighting.

The purpose of this organisation was to oppose the merger of Hyderabad State in India. It is also said that Qasim had raised an army of about one and a half lakh Razakars. In 1948, the MIM was banned in view of Qasim's anti-India stand. Qasim Rizvi was arrested and put in jail.

The article 'Holding them captive?' The grip of the Majlis-e-Ittehadul Muslimeen on the community remains strong, despite minor dents appeared in The Hindu on April 27, 2003. Qasim Rizvi remained in jail from 1948 to 1957. He was released on the condition that he would go to Pakistan, where he was being offered asylum.

Qasim Rizvi is said to have handed over the responsibility of the party (MIM) to a lawyer, Abdul Wahid Owaisi, before going to Pakistan. Abdul Wahid Owaisi changed its name to AIMIM, i.e. All India Majlis-e-Ittehadul Muslimeen. However, there is no specific mention in the party's own website about the status of the party between 1948 and 1960. The website directly talks about the Hyderabad Municipal Corporation elections of 1960 after 1948. In this election, the party was victorious in 24 blocks of the municipal corporation and became the main opposition. Abdul Wahid Owaisi's son Salar-e-Millat Sultan Salahuddin Owaisi also won from Mallepally Division in Hyderabad in this election. (1960 - Contests the polls to the Municipal Corporation of Hyderabad, aimim.org/our-history/)

In this way the party's winning streak in Hyderabad began with the Sultan. The reason for the party's success with the Sultan was a controversial speech by the Sultan, in which he called on Muslims that the Indian government had left Muslims to their fate. So Muslims have to stand up and strengthen their own ground. Sultan was the President of the party for more than 33 years till 2008. In Andhra Pradesh, the Sultan was considered to be the main key to the Muslim vote bank. All the Muslim votes of the State were considered to be mobilised with him. It was said about Sultan that in Andhra Pradesh whichever Party he supported would get Muslim votes. It was during Sultan's tenure that the Election Commission registered AIMIM as a political party in 1992. In 2001, the election commission also gave the party the status of regional Party in Andhra Pradesh. In 1984, Sultan entered the Parliament by winning the Lok Sabha elections from the Hyderabad seat and continued to win from this seat till 2004.

Sultan Salahuddin refused to contest from Hyderabad in 2004 owing to his ill health and got Asaduddin contested and also handed over the reins of the party to him. He died in 2008. After the new generation came to power, new methodology was also adopted in the party. Due to the controversial statements of Asaduddin Owaisi and his younger brother Akbaruddin Owaisi, the party remained in news constantly in the media and this helped it considerably in increasing its base. Akbaruddin was arrested on January 8, 2013 for his hate speech. One of his speeches had gone viral on social media, in which he was shown saying that If the police is removed for 15 minutes, then 25 crore Muslims will see 100 crore Hindus. The speech uploaded on YouTube was claimed to have been delivered by Akbaruddin at a public meeting in Adilabad on December 24, 2012. Earlier in 2007, Tehelka magazine had published a report of Owaisi's threat to Bangladeshi feminist writer Taslima Nasreen, in which Owaisi threatened to behead if the writer stepped in Hyderabad. In January 2015, Asaduddin Owaisi also made a controversial statement.

Criticizing the ghar wapsi program of Hindu organisations in Hyderabad on the occasion of Eid-ul-Nabi, Owaisi had said that every person is a Muslim by birth. His parents and society change his religion. ('Every child is born a Muslim', says AIMIM's Asaduddin Owaisi, hits out at Hindu outfits—January 7, 2015, PTI).

A special type of social polarisation was taking place in Andhra because of the Owaisi brothers. The popularity of AIMIM started increasing among the people of a particular community. Taking advantage of this, the party also competed in the 2012

Maharashtra Civic elections wherein the party won 11 seats in Nanded Municipal Council. In the same year, the State Election Commission gave it the status of a regional Party in Maharashtra as well. In 2014 and 2019 each, two MLAs were elected from Maharashtra. Apart from Asaduddin Owaisi's victory from Hyderabad in the 2019 Lok Sabha elections, Imtiaz Jaleel's victory from Aurangabad in Maharashtra surprised everyone. In March 2013, the party won three seats each from Bidar and Basavakalyan in the Civic elections in Karnataka. In 2014, the party got regional Party status in Telangana State as well. The party contested five Lok Sabha seats and 35 Assembly seats that year. It won one Lok Sabha and seven Assembly seats. In November 2020, the results of the Bihar Assembly elections brought great news for Asaduddin Owaisi. In this election, AIMIM surprised everyone by winning five seats in Seemanchal area of Bihar. This was perceived as the growing influence of Owaisi among the Muslims. The party contested 20 seats in the State. Political analysts began to believe that more such shocking results could come. But when the results of the Bengal elections were announced on May 2, 2021, Owaisi did not get any success there. The party had contested seven seats in Bengal and was hoping to repeat the same miracle in these Muslim-majority seats as in the neighbouring state. But it didn't happen.

Looking at the rising graph of the party, Asaduddin Owaisi also started trying to change his image. To further increase acceptance, he tried to create a new group of nationalist Muslims. After Pakistan's victory over India in a T20 World Cup match in October 2021, when Pakistan Home Minister Sheikh Rashid called it a victory for Muslims and Islam of India and Bangladesh, Owaisi responded to Sheikh in his speech in Muzaffarnagar. He slammed Sheikh by saying, 'There is a minister in our neighbouring country—pagal hai poora. He has described the Pak victory over India in cricket as the victory of Islam. Thank Allah our people did not go there, otherwise they would have to bear with these lunatics. What does Islam have to do with cricket? These people have no shame. You mortgage your country to China and talk about Islam. That China has imprisoned two million Muslims. They are being forcibly fed pigs. You cannot even make medicine for malaria. Can't make motorcycle tyres. India is far ahead so don't mess with us.'

In this way, AIMIM is looking for an opportunity to become the representative Party of Muslims across the country. Muslims do not have any separate Party of their own in North India. The community there associates themselves with national or regional parties only. In such a situation, Owaisi's endeavours are slowly moving forward to fill this gap in the north. But even now the relatively larger parties consider AIMIM to be a vote-katua party and some even describe it as the 'B' team of the Bharatiya Janata Party because Muslim votes get divided due to the entry of AIMIM into the field.

However Owaisi's party could not put up a decent show in the 2022 UP Assembly elections. Its candidates got even fewer than NOTA.

Whatever one may say, AIMIM is creating new ripples in Indian politics.

❑

Odisha

22
A Peculiar Tradition, Repeat Unlikely

Patnaiks have been ruling in the State of Odisha, the principal region of eastern India, for the last four decades. The power story of the Patnaiks began with Janaki Ballabh Patnaik who became the Chief Minister for two consecutive terms from 1980-1989 and then from 1995-1999. JB, a longtime Congressman and close to former Prime Minister Indira Gandhi, became the Chief Minister of Odisha for two consecutive terms but, when the new Patnaik father-son duo arrived in this story it created such a stronghold here that till now other politicians are unable to grasp this magic. Janaki Ballabh Patnaik was highly educated and after completing his graduation in Sanskrit at the time of Independence, he obtained a master's degree in Political Science in 1949. The second Patnaik, i.e. Biju Patnaik, a true leader of the people, entered the politics of Odisha, who they remember as Biju Babu, i.e. the hero and Founder of Biju Janata Dal. The story of Biju Janata Dal is step-to-step analogous with the story of Biju Babu. It was Biju Babu who devoted his entire life in protecting the cultural traditions of Odisha. From a courageous pilot to a freedom fighter who became an industrialist and he later turned into a politician after independence. Adventure was his passion. During his school days, he cycled from Cuttack to Peshawar with some of his friends and after that at the age of just 18, he trained in aviation at Delhi's Flying Club as a commercial pilot. During the training itself, he met Gyan Devi, a fellow trainee. Gyan Devi belonged to a Punjabi family and was originally from Rawalpindi. They fell in love and tied the nuptial knot .

Biju Babu performed the first challenging task as a pilot during the Second World War when he was assigned the task of safely evacuating the Indians trapped in Rangoon. On one side there was the army of Britain and the Allies and on the other side, the fighters of Japan and the Azad Hind Fauj were with it. Pilot Biju accepted this challenge and flew the plane himself several times and went to Rangoon and evacuated thousands of Indians safely from there to different parts of the country. During this he was also attacked many times but Biju turned out to be lucky and every time he had a narrow escape. Immediately after independence, when Pakistan attacked Kashmir, the Maharaja of Kashmir, Hari Singh, terrified of the attack, appealed to the Prime Minister of India, Jawaharlal Nehru, for help and at the same time expressed his desire to merge with India. Nehru also did not disappoint Hari Singh and decided to send an army to help the Kashmiris, but the million dollar question remained—who would fly first with the Army contingent? During that crisis, pilot Biju Patnaik took upon himself and justified this leap of faith in him. He accepted this challenge also and landed at Srinagar airport with the first consignment of the Indian Army. Other aeroplanes full of soldiers also landed next to him and then Kashmir could be saved. A similar situation was created on the international stage when Indonesia was liberated from Dutch occupation in the last months of 1946, but by 1948, the Dutch once again attacked Indonesia. Then Sukarno, the supreme leader of Indonesia, sought immediate help from his friend Nehru seeking asylum in India. Then again the same question arose. Who will go to Indonesia flanked by Dutch soldiers from all sides and who will bring the leaders there safely to India? Then Nehru remembered Biju Patnaik, the pilot who successfully completed the Rangoon and Srinagar operations. Here also Biju was successful in accomplishing this task as well. Later Sukarno became the first President of Indonesia. For this act of bravery, Biju Babu was conferred an honorary citizenship of Indonesia and was also awarded as 'Bhoomi Putra' of Indonesia. When Sukarno's daughter was born, she was named Meghavati by Biju Babu. It is said that it was raining heavily when she was born, so Biju Babu named her as Meghavati Sukarnoputri. Commemorating the contributions of Biju Babu, Indonesia has now named a room of its embassy in Delhi after him. Meghavati Sukarnoputri became the President of Indonesia in 2001. (The same Meghavati Sukarnoputri has recently converted to Hinduism in Muslim-majority Indonesia.)

After Independence, Biju Patnaik got involved with Congress in the 1950s. In the late 1950s, he was made the State Congress President and finally in 1961 he was made the Chief Minister. In 1977, he was made the Minister of Steel and Mines in the government of Morarji Desai. In the 1990 elections, when the people of the State expelled Janaki Ballabh Patnaik from power, Biju Patnaik was elected. He once again became the Chief Minister of Odisha from the Janata Dal and remained the Chief Minister for the entire term.

Only a few politicians could handle Biju Babu's plainspoken nature which was often abrupt at times. His critics often called him an autocratic dictator. He came to be called Utkal's Bull. In 1967, when Indira Gandhi became the Prime Minister, only a year had passed, speaking at a gathering of students in Cuttack, Biju Babu said—If I want, I can make Indira Gandhi dance in front of you people on this platform'. There was a huge uproar on this statement and eventually his political path parted ways with that of Indira Gandhi. After this he formed his own regional party under the name of Utkal Congress. Later in the days of Emergency, like other opposition leaders, he was also imprisoned. After his release from jail, he merged his party with the Janata Party and was made

Minister of Steel and Mines in Morarji Desai's government. Biju Babu had a penchant for building big industries, undertakings, ports, airports, etc. The Paradip Port of Odisha is considered as the gift of Biju Patnaik.

During the year 1989-90, there were Janata Dal governments both at the Centre and in Odisha. V.P. Singh was the Prime Minister and Biju Patnaik the Chief Minister of Odisha. In fact, Biju Babu had a big role in making V.P. Singh the Prime Minister. In December 1989, sitting with Arun Nehru and Kuldeep Nayar in Odisha Bhavan itself, Biju Babu had made a complete plan for V.P. Singh's coronation, placing Devi Lal as the pawn and betting on Chandrashekhar. But, in August 1990, as soon as V.P. Singh ignited the issue of the Mandal Commission, Biju Babu confronted it and started criticising him vehemently. At that time, Biju Babu criticised V.P. Singh and said- 'V.P. Singh is no different from Rajiv Gandhi in playing dirty tricks to divide the society.' Biju Patnaik died on April 17, 1997. His body was wrapped in the national flags of three countries (India, Indonesia and Russia) on April 19, 1997 on his last journey.

After the death of Biju Patnaik, his associates formed a new party on December 26, 1997- 'Biju Janata Dal'. Then the question who would be the President came up. By then Naveen Patnaik, son of Biju Babu, had earned a good reputation as a writer in English. From the very beginning, Naveen Babu believed in -no favours -no enmities. He only aimed at the development of Odisha and its people. He became an MP in the 1999 general election, but immediately returned to State politics and concentrated here. He came to power by winning the 2000 Assembly elections and since then it is only Naveen Patnaik's era that is going on in Odisha. He has completed four terms as Chief Minister and this is his fifth term. Yes, the fifth term of a man who neither possesses great oratory skills nor is able to deliver lengthy speeches in Oriya fluently, despite being in power for twenty years.

In the 2000 Assembly elections, the Biju Janata Dal contested alongside the BJP. In Odisha's 147-seat House, the BJD was successful in winning a total of 68 seats while the alliance partner BJP got 38 seats. The Congress Party, which had been in power for a considerable time, was relegated to the opposition. Naveen Patnaik was made the Chief Minister of the coalition government. In the 2004 Assembly elections, both the allies put up another good show and won 93 seats in total and Naveen Patnaik returned as Chief Minister. Kandhamal came into limelight in the last week of August 2008 when mass riots broke out after the killing of Swami Lakshmanananda Saraswati at Janmashtami celebrations. Those incidents completely changed the mood of the State. In the changed scenario, Naveen Patnaik distanced himself from the BJP. The BJD had severed ties with the BJP before the 2009 Assembly elections. Fighting the 2009 elections independently, the BJD won 103 seats. It increased its representation in the 2014 elections to 117. In 2014, when the Modi wave was going on across the country, Odisha remained completely untouched by its impact and BJD MPs won 20 out of 21 parliamentary seats in the State. In the 2019 Lok Sabha elections, the BJD could win only 12 out of 21 seats but in the Assembly elections it won 112 out of 146 seats. In 2019, Patnaik began his fifth consecutive term as Chief Minister. One wonders how Naveen Patnaik has accomplished all of this. Until a few years ago, he could not speak Oriya in public. His Oriya speeches were written in Roman. Although, now he has overcome this hurdle to a certain extent, he is still not a very good orator. Whether he is speaking in Naupada, in Kalahandi or Rourkela, his speeches are stereotyped. He begins by saying how pleased he is to be at the place, recalls the sacrifices of local leaders (like Birsa Munda in Rourkela) to Bijubhai's contribution to the region, and then delivers his message. Good governance and leader Naveen Patnaik's Mr Clean image is considered to be the working for BJD's repeated electoral successes in Odisha. Organisational disruptions within the BJP, Congress and other rival parties in the State also helped retain the BJD's popular support base. For many years, the BJD has been demanding that Odisha be given 'Special Status'. The party always took a firm and clear stand against the communal forces. BJD has always been in the forefront to fight against corruption in public life and wilful neglect of the State by the governments at the Centre. The party has always supported the matters pertaining to women, youth, farmers, labourers, trade unions, religious minorities and weaker and backward sections of the society.

Naveen Patnaik's public image clearly manifests his detachment from power, money and family. Despite a considerable long tenure as a Chief Minister, there is no corruption charge against him or any person claiming closeness to him. As soon as Patnaik gets any such signal, he immediately discards such people and banishes them forever. There are many such examples of leaders and bureaucrats of Odisha. Within an hour of becoming the Chief Minister, Naveen Patnaik sacked three of his Ministers as they were accused of corruption. Since then, he has tried to maintain the 'Mr Clean' image. However, at times his government and the party had to face serious allegations in mining matters and chit fund scams. He refused tickets to two MLAs and an MP because they were arrested by the CBI, but he offered tickets to the sons of these two MLAs. If politicians are caught for corruption, the police can rest assured not to be intimidated by any call from the Chief Minister's Office. Secondly, Odisha also has a welfare scheme for the low income group which is quite effective. NITI Aayog CEO Amitabh Kant congratulated Naveen Patnaik instead of any BJP Chief Minister as Bhubaneswar became the first city to get 100 percent immunisation and Puri became the city with 24-hour water supply. The credit for including eggs for nutrition in the mid-day meals of school children also goes to Naveen Patnaik.

In 2019 Chief Minister Naveen Patnaik also inaugurated a Haj House in Bhubaneswar. Sometimes the Chief Minister himself, his officials or top officials call up the common people to enquire whether they are getting all government services properly. Police stations in the State are being rendered people-friendly. In order to promote anti-corruption measures, the government also took steps like stopping the pension of tainted officers, and seeking their resignations. A former MLA from the ruling BJD's Kalahandi area was also arrested in a disproportionate assets case.

In 2019 itself, Naveen implemented the Kalia scheme for the farmers of Odisha and gave the first instalment of ₹ 5,000 to every farmer, it made a great impact. His active supervision during the Fanny storm increased people's trust in him. Odisha is considered a backward State, but Chief Minister Naveen Patnaik has made and implemented all the schemes for every section. This stopped migration out of the State, instead attracting big industrialists. Along with increasing industrial development and employment, rice was given at Re 1 per kg for the poor. Recently, his work is also being praised during the storms of Amphan and Corona. Political experts in Odisha say that the BJD has got the maximum number of women's votes due to the initiative of promoting the Self-Help groups. The Chief Minister announced the creation of a new department 'Mission Shakti' for Self-Help Groups. Providing pucca houses to the rural poor is one of the priorities of the state government.

Opponents also believe that Naveen Patnaik is a serious man and a person of simple living who believes in politics of principles. He does not spoil relations with anyone, nor has any other political ambitions. He changed the picture of Odisha and inculcated self-respect in the people there. Odisha's ever-growing economy has led to a record reduction in poverty and the credit for increasing farmers' income also goes to Naveen Patnaik. The State has carved a niche for itself in the field of sports and tourism. Naveen Patnaik has probably introduced more social welfare measures than his predecessors. During the last seven years, the average growth of Odisha has been around 8 percent as compared to the national average of around 6.9 percent. A separate budget is presented for agriculture in Odisha. The state government has decided to convert the State's SCB Medical College at Cuttack into AIIMS plus an institute of integrative medicine by making substantial investments to provide it in a State-of-the-art medical facility. His government has set up four new medical colleges, and seven more are in the pipeline. Although Naveen Patnaik did not show much interest in sports in his initial years as Chief Minister, he managed to place Odisha on the sports map of the world after successfully hosting the Hockey World Cup 2018 at the Kalinga Stadium in Bhubaneswar. Odisha has hosted many national and international sporting events especially in the last two years. The State is creating world class sports infrastructure by setting up several centres. During the last Olympics (2021), when India's women's and men's hockey teams were leading the winning campaign, Odisha's name was also well recognised as the sponsor of these teams.

At times it seems that the Bharatiya Janata Party has also laid down its arms here and is only interested in performing the role of the opposition in a limited way. Union Education Minister Dharmendra Pradhan also now lacks the attitude as the Leader of the Opposition he once demonstrated before Naveen Babu's fifth term. Biju Janata Dal is the only big party among the regional parties, which cannot be written off soon..

Right now it seems that the word Anti-Incumbency has no meaning for Biju Janata Dal. The rest is with the future.

❑

23
For We Fight Till Death and Then Some More

The political scenario in Kerala is very unpretentious and divided into two clear components. All the major political parties have been divided into two alliances since 1970, one is the Left Democratic Front (LDF) of the Left-inclined ones and the other is the United Democratic Front (UDF) of the middle-path followers. According to A. Sridhar Menon's book - A Survey of Kerala History, Kerala is the first such state in the country, where the coalition government came into existence in the early 1960s of the last century. However, the LDF was founded in 1979 by Communist Party of India (CPI) leader E.M.S. Namboodiripad and P.K. Vasudevan Nair, whom everyone fondly called PKV.

For a long time since 1980 in Kerala the LDF government and UDF government have been ruling alternatively, yet, forty years later the UDF returned to power for the first time in a row in the 2021 elections. The constituent parties of LDF include CPI(M), CPI, Kerala Congress (M), NCP, Janata Dal (S), Loktantrik Janata Dal, Indian National League, Congress Secular, Kerala Congress (Sikera Thomas), Janadhipatya Kerala Congress etc. From the LDF side Chief Ministers have been like this - between 1980 and 2001 E.K. Nayanar thrice, between 2006-2011 Achuthanandan once and Pinarayi Vijayan twice in a row in 2016 and 2021.

As far as the political scenario in Kerala is concerned, there is a long story of instability between 1957 and 1980, a game of alliances being concocted and new parties being formed and merged. In the second election to the State Assembly, coalition politics emerged here. In the 1967 Assembly elections, the CPI(M) came to power in alliance with seven parties. By the 1970s, all the major parties in the State were divided into two alliances. One was led by the CPI(M) and the other was led by the Congress.

There was a lot of uproar in Kerala in 1963 after a sex scandal came to light. On February 20, 1964, Home Minister P.T. Chacko was thrown out of the Cabinet by the then Congress Chief Minister R. Shankar. A few months later, on August 1, 1964, Chacko passed away. Annoyed by this, 15 political supporters of Chacko, who were Congress MLAs, moved a no-confidence motion, led by K.M. George, against Shankar's government. Then, on October 9, 1964, George and R. Balakrishna Pillai formed a separate Kerala Congress. Its other prominent leaders included M. Kurovinkunal, M.P. Pillai. The party also contested the Lok Sabha elections in 1967 but failed to win a single seat. But soon young leaders like K.M. Mani and P.J. Joseph strengthened the party among the youth. After the demise of K.M. George in 1976, the two young leaders K.M. Mani and P.J. Joseph and senior leader R. Balakrishna Pillai were against each other over supremacy in the party. Pillai believed that he was now the senior most leader of the party, so he should be accepted as the party leader, but Mani and Joseph had more supporters in the party. Pillai was left isolated and just before the 1977 Kerala Assembly elections, Pillai formed a separate Party, the Kerala Congress (Balakrishna Pillai). But soon, Mani and Joseph fell apart and within two years another major break-up took place at the party. In 1979, K.M. Mani parted ways and formed his own party, the Kerala Congress (Mani). The media then started calling the Joseph-led Kerala Congress the Kerala Congress (Joseph). In 1985, both Mani and Pillai merged their parties with the Kerala Congress.

Even this friendship did not last long and in 1987 K.M. Mani then rebelled in the party and staked his claim on the party's name and symbol. A major legal battle broke out between Mani and Joseph for this and the court eventually ruled in Joseph's favour. In 1989, R. Balakrishna Pillai once again quit the Kerala Congress. P.T. Chacko's son P.C. Thomas was also a big face of the Kerala Congress. However, Joseph had no good terms with him as well. So he stayed in the Kerala Congress Mani. In 2004, he rebelled against the party with the support of the BJP and contested the Lok Sabha elections by forming the Indian Federal Democratic Party and also won one seat. He was part of the BJP-led NDA in this election and this was the NDA's first victory in Kerala. However, it was only in 2005 that the Indian Federal Democratic Party merged with the Kerala Congress. In 2014, the battle for predominance in the Kerala Congress resumed. Two groups were formed. P.C. Thomas became President of the Kerala Congress (anti-merger) faction but in 2015 Thomas also parted ways with the group to form the Kerala Congress (Thomas). The Left Democratic Front did not accept Thomas. Then, in August 2015, Thomas joined the BJP with his faction and became a part of the NDA alliance. Then, in 2016, when the party name and symbol court's decision came in Thomas's favour, he again renamed his party Kerala Congress (Thomas) as Kerala Congress.

In the early 2000s, in the Kerala Congress (Joseph) there was a revolt led by P.C. George, T.C. John and an MLA P.C. Jeprage teamed up to form the Kerala Congress Secular. The party became a constituent of the Left Front. However, in 2010, the party merged with the Kerala Congress (Mani). Kerala Congress (Mani) was formed in 1979 by a split in Kerala Congress.

In 1979 when the Left parties formed the Left Democratic Front, the State's leading Congress leader and former Chief Minister K Karunakaran formed the United Democratic Front (UDF). In UDF, besides Congress there were Kerala Congress, Kerala Congress (Jacob), Indian Union Muslim League,

Revolutionary Marxist Party (John), All India Forward Bloc, Bharatiya RJD. The UDF alliance formed a government in Kerala in 1982 and K Karunakaran became Chief Minister again. After Karunakaran, A.K. Antony and Oommen Chandy were also the chief ministers of the UDF. In the 2019 Lok Sabha elections, the UDF had won 19 of the 20 seats in the State, but in the 2021 Assembly elections, the alliance could win only 40 of the 140 seats in the State.

Apart from LDF and UDF, BJP is also trying to stage a third front by forming the National Democratic Alliance (NDA) with its southern sects in Kerala politics. The NDA constituents in Kerala include Bharat Dharma Jana Sena (BDJS), All India Dravida Munnetra Kadgham, Kerala Kamaraj Congress (KKC), Democratic Social Justice Party (DSJP) and Janadhipathya Rashtriya Sabha (JRS) besides BJP.

The political awareness in Kerala is so high that the formation and breakdown of parties has also taken place on a large scale. There are more than seventy such parties and if we go into details, a separate book will be required. Nevertheless, we will try to tell you as many parties as possible, even if briefly.

Travancore State Congress and Kochi State Praja Mandalam can be mentioned as pre-independence parties. The Kochi State Prajamandal Party was founded on February 9, 1941 in Thrissur by an organisation of youth who wanted to launch a political movement in the State of Kochi. Among these youngsters, E.I. Warrior, V.R. Krishna Ezuthaken, S. Neelkanda Iyer, K.N. Namboodiripad, etc. were involved. S. Neelkanda Iyer was elected as its first Chairman. The party's first objective was to uphold the sovereignty of the King of Cochin and to uphold equal political rights for the people. In the same year, the party leaders went ahead and helped the people due to the floods in the State and made their acceptance among the people. The party also constituted the Cochin Kisan Sabha to connect with the farmers. In 1945, when the Cochin Legislative Council elections were held, Prajamandal won a majority. However, after independence, the party merged with the Congress.

On September 21, 1947, just after independence, Mathai Manzooran founded the Kerala Socialist Party in Kozhikode. It was a small Party to say, but within two decades it played a pivotal role in Kerala politics. It also played a role in forming the first Communist government in the State. However, within two years of its formation, the party also had to see a split in 1949. Party leaders N. Srikanth Nair, K Balakrishnan and Baby John parted ways to form the Revolutionary Socialist Party.

Travancore, which had the status of a princely State, had Malayali-speaking as majority and Tamilians as minority. The Tamil community felt that they were being discriminated against and formed several organisations to represent themselves. One of them was the Travancore Tamil Nadu Congress. In the Travancore State elections in 1948, the party won 14 of the 120 seats. The party's performance was quite good in areas with Tamil influence. The party eventually merged with the ruling Congress in 1957.

Immediately after independence, the Cochin Party formed in Kerala in 1949 was only aimed at not mixing Cochin with Travancore and making it a unified State. S.N. Sadasivan's book—Political and Administrative Integration of Princely States—states the party had given the slogan that 'Cochin was for the Cochinans'. It also demanded a separate Cochin State. (pp. 61-62).

According to Election Commission data, the Cochin Party fielded 12 candidates in the 1951 Travancore-Cochin Assembly elections, out of which only one candidate could win. However, by 1954, the party had disappeared from Kerala politics. Rich plantation owners of Travancore and Cochin formed a political party called Travancore Cochin Republican Praja Party in 1951. A.V. George was made its General Secretary and A.C.M. Anthraper was its Chairman. In the 1951 Assembly elections, the party fielded seven candidates and spent a lot of money but even a single candidate could not win . A.V. George was second to Kottayam. However, the party also disappeared from the scene the following year. Similarly, Tamil-land People's Front, Tamil Nadu Toilers' Party can be named among the Parties seen in the 1951 State elections.

Before the 1967 elections, Christian social activists and priests Father Joseph Vadakkan and B. Wellington formed the Karshak Tozilali Party. With this, the party formed the government in the State along with the Communist Party of India. E.M.S. Namboodiripad was the Chief Minister of this government and B. Wellington of the Krashak Party became Health Minister.

Around 1970, a Workers' Revolutionary Party (India) was also formed. A. Achuthan's Party was a Left Party but could not make much of a mark as a separate Party. Kerala became the Joint Socialist Party in 1968 after a revolt in the United Socialist Party. In fact, then there were two ministers of the United Socialist Party in the Kerala government, P.K. Kunju and P.R. Ugly. After differences with the government, the party High Command asked the two ministers to resign to which both of them disobeyed and formed a separate Party in the name of the Kerala Joint Socialist Party. The following year, in 1969, the party was renamed as the Indian Socialist Party. As a result of revolt in the Revolutionary Socialist Party several small parties were formed. The Revolutionary Socialist Party (Srikanandan Nair), the National Revolutionary Socialist Party can be named among them. The National Revolutionary Socialist Party was formed in 1977 and contested the 1977 Assembly elections as an ally of the CPI(M). In 1982, the party left the Left Front and joined the Congress-led United Democratic Front, but the party did not succeed in both the elections.

After the death of Indian Muslim League leader Abdurrahiman Bafakhi Thangal in January 1973, its Kerala unit got divided and a new party called the Muslim League (Opposition) emerged. The party became part of the CPI(M) led Left Democratic Front And later in 1985 it merged again with the Indian Union Muslim League.

In 1974, K.G. Gopalkrishna Pillai and R Ramachandran Nair formed the National Democratic Party (Kerala). In fact, the party was the political wing of Nair Service Society, a social organisation of Nair society. It was formed demanding reservation for the Nair community. The party contested its first election in 1982 as a constituent of the UDF as an ally of the Congress and won four seats. After that, however, the party's performance continued to decline and the party ended in 1996. However, in 2019, the Nair community leaders re-established their political organisation by name of the Democratic Social Justice Party. K.S.R. Menon was made its Chairman.

In 1980, Congress leader A.K. Antony had formed a separate party called Congress (A). Antony was earlier a student leader who moved well ahead in politics. He was the President of Kerala Students Union in 1966. When he was made the Chairman of the Kerala Pradesh Congress Committee in 1972, he was the youngest leader to adorn the post. When Devraj Ars rebelled against Indira Gandhi and formed a new Congress in the south in 1979, Antony joined it, but he did not continue with Ars and formed his own regional party, The Congress (A), in Kerala. However, the party did not last even two years and the Congress (A) merged with the Congress (I) in 1982.

In 2005, K. Karunakaran, a prominent party leader in the State, rebelled and formed the National Congress (Indira) in the Kerala unit of the Congress. But soon it was renamed as the Democratic Indira Congress (Karunakaran). Karunakaran's son K Muralitharan became the party president. The party contested the elections along with the Left Front but could not make much of an impact. Later, some Party leaders joined Sharad Pawar's NCP and Karunakaran and Muralitharan returned to the Indian National

Congress. This is how the party went into oblivion.

Former Prime Minister H.D. Deve Gowda's Party Janata Dal (Secular) also broke down several times in the State. Jayakumar Ezutupally, Surendra Mohan and M.P. Virendra Kumar parted ways and formed the Janata Dal (Left). However, he later returned to JD(U) Secular. Similarly, on August 7, 2010, M.P. Virendra Kumar split the party and formed the Socialist Janata (Democratic) Party. But the party also merged with Nitish Kumar's Party JD(U) on December 29, 2014. Virendra did not stay in the JD(U) for long and joined the Democratic Janata Dal in 2018 along with his supporters.

Kerala's present has been under the shadow of two alliances and the same is expected to continue in future as well.

❑

24
A Story of Twists, Turns and Returns

After independence, the power of Assam remained with the Congress for almost three decades. During this time people began to raise their voice for rights of their community and also regional rights in the State. Many parties were formed and then broke up soon. New States were also formed. When the first Assam Assembly elections were held in 1952, from there to 1962, the Socialist Party and the Praja Socialist Party were the main opposition in the State for ten years. Meanwhile, the movement for a separate Meghalaya started and the All Party Hill Leaders Conference emerged fast in that region, which is now the new State of Meghalaya. After the 1962 elections in the State, this party was the main opposition in the House for the next ten years. Meghalaya became a separate State in 1972 carved out of Assam. Next there was a tremendous political change in Assam from 1978 and the period of instability also began. Between 1978 and 1985, at times the Janata Party, the Plains Tribals' Council of Assam and the Communist parties formed the government, and sometimes the Congress remained in power with the support of communists and independents. The President's Rule had to be imposed several times in between. Assam remained the only State from which many States were carved out. Right now, even though a national party like the BJP is in power in Assam, it is not easy to carry out development work in the State without the support of regional parties. But the stature of the Asom Gana Parishad in the regional politics in Assam is truly unmatchable. Despite the fact that no regional party has broken up as many times as the Asom Gana Parishad .

Asom Gana Parishad

Prafulla Kumar Mohanta and Bhrigu Kumar Phukan, who emerged from the student politics of Assam, founded the Asom Gana Parishad in 1985 along with Biraj Kumar Sarma of All Asom Gana Sangram Parishad. During 1971-72, when there was unrest in East Pakistan and it was emerging as a new country to be known as Bangladesh, a large number of Bangladeshis migrated and settled in Bengal and Assam. In 1979 Praful Kumar Mohanta became the President of the All Assam Student Union (AASU) and Bhrigu Kumar Phukan was elected General Secretary. In the same year AASU launched a movement against illegal infiltrators from Bangladesh. Their demand was that the names of the infiltrators or illegal migrants should be removed from the voter list. This movement went on for years. Even the 1983 Assembly elections were held in a turbulent atmosphere of demonstrations in the State. During that time Biraj Kumar Sarma's All Asom Gana Sangram Parishad and Asom Sahitya Sabha also joined this movement along with AASU. The movement gained momentum and soon regional parties like the Assam Jetiyabari Dal and Purbanchalaya Lok Parishad and Sadau Asom Karmachari Parishad, Assam Jetiyabari, Yuva Chatra Parishad, Asom Yuvak Samaj and many organisations of government employees joined the movement.

When the movement gained momentum, on August 15, 1985, the Rajiv Gandhi government at the Centre and the state government signed the famous Assam Accord with the agitators. It was signed on behalf of the agitators by Prafulla Kumar Mohanta, Bhrigu Kumar Phukan and Biraj Kumar Sarma. After this agreement, Hiteshwar Saikia's government headed by Hiteshwar Saikia was dissolved and elections were announced in the State.

The agitators organised the National Convention on October 13-14, 1985 at Golaghat. In this Convention, on October 14, 1985, a new political party, Asom Gana Parishad, was announced by the agitators. Prafulla Kumar Mohanta was elected the President of this new party. The All Assam Students Union was dissolved. Parties such as Assam Jetiyabari and Purbanchalaya Lok Parishad were merged into the Asom Gana Parishad.

Assembly elections were held in Assam in December 1985 and the Asom Gana Parishad formed the government by winning a total of 67 seats out of 126. Although the Congress formed the government with the Left and other parties after defeating the Asom Gana Parishad after five years, in the 1996 elections, the Asom Gana Parishad again formed the government with the National Front and Mohanta again became the Chief Minister. However, during this time the party kept breaking and mending again. In March 1991, Party General Secretary Bhrigu Kumar Phukan revolted and established a separate Natun Asom Gana Parishad along with several party leaders including MP Dinesh Goswami, former Minister Brindaban Goswami, Assembly Speaker Pulkesh Barua and other leaders.

In 2000, there was another split in the Asom Gana Parishad. Senior Party leader Atul Bora along with Pulkesh Barua founded the Trinamool Gana Parishad. In 2001, the Trinamool Gana Parishad allied with the BJP. From then onwards, troubles began for Mohanta in the party. He was accused of corruption and murder of his opponents. Prafulla Kumar Mohanta was finally thrown out of the Asom Gana Parishad on July 3, 2005 after allegations of involvement in anti-Party activities. Thereafter, Mohanta formed his own Asom Gana Parishad (Progressive) Party.

During this, after being out of power, the leaders of the Asom Gana Parishad and other leaders who had formed separate parties began to realise that staying fragmented is not going to help them with the politics of the State. Finally, on October 14, 2008, everyone again held a conference in Golaghat. In this conference Prafulla Kumar Mohanta, Atul Bora and Pulkesh Barua re-merged their parties into Asom Gana Parishad. But the battle for supremacy in power is unending. Continual breakdowns keep happening in the parties. In 2011, young student leader Sarbananda Sonowal, who was considered a firebrand of the Asom Gana Parishad, resigned from all posts and joined the Bharatiya Janata Party. Two years later, on July 3, 2013, Atul Bora also joined the BJP. In 2016, when the BJP formed its North-East Democratic Alliance for the North-East States, the Asom Gana Parishad also became a part of it. But in January 2019, expressing displeasure over the Citizenship Amendment Bill, the Asom Gana Parishad distanced itself from the BJP-led North-East Democratic Alliance. Soon, after the passage of just two months, it went back to the Democratic Alliance. BJP gave 3 seats to the party to contest but it could win none.

All Party Hills Leaders' Conference

The All Party Hills Leaders' Conference, founded by William A. Sangma is considered to be a party of Meghalaya, but it fought a long battle to carve out Meghalaya from Assam and create a new State. Captain Williamson Apang Sangma was considered an elite leader of the Garo tribe. His home region which was then part of Assam was actually the combined habitat area of the three tribes. The Garo are said to have had their ancestors from the Toras of Tibet and settled in this part of India, while the Khasi and Jaintia tribes are believed to have had Mongolian ancestors. Captain Sangma had also served in the Army. In 1952 he joined the Autonomous District Council of Garo Hills. More Councils were formed to demand autonomy in these different hilly parts of Assam. These include Khasi Hills Autonomous District Council,

Jaintia Hills Autonomous District Council, Lushai Mizo Hills, North Cachar Hills District Council etc.

On June 16, 1954, all these Councils convened a meeting at Shillong and demanded a separate hill State under the Sixth Schedule of the Constitution. It was decided at the meeting that a status of Eastern Hill State to this hilly part of Assam will be demanded. Even before the meeting, Thog Wilson Reade of Khasi National Durba had demanded a separate hill State, but Sangma led the movement successfully in favour of this demand. In the meeting at Shillong, it was decided that the leaders of all the councils should sign the MoU together. Thus the All Party Hill Leaders Conference came into existence. The hard work of these leaders paid off and on January 21, 1972, a new State was formed in the form of Meghalaya, the eastern hill region of Assam.

Plains Tribals' Council of Assam (PTCA)

The PTCA was a political party from Assam, which spoke for the rights of native Indian Scheduled Castes and Tribes as opposed to the Garo-Khasi and Jaintia communities, but in 1966 it started an armed movement demanding a separate State, known as the Bodo Movement. A separate Udayachal was demanded under the leadership of Samar Brahma Chaudhuri and Charan Narjari. In 1966, the PTCA boycotted the elections demanding separate demarcation of seats for tribals and people of Indian origin. A large meeting was called in Bhatamari village. Considering this a violation of Section 144, the police opened fire, in which hundreds of people were injured or sent to jail. Soon the mutual conflict in PTCA escalated. Most of the leaders were in favour of fighting their battle democratically but a faction of it started an armed wing led by Binay Brahma. At the same time the All Bodo Student Union started a movement for a separate Bodoland. It rejected the PTCA's demand for a separate State. The extremist faction of the Bodo Students Union killed the PTCA President and some other leaders. In this way the young Bodos ended the movement of

PTCA and started the movement in the name of the Autonomous Council of Bodoland.

"PTCA in Bodo Politics"- a research paper in Political Science of Bodoland University Kokrajhar, states that PTCA was the first tribal party in the plains of Assam. In this paper Samarjit Baro and Jyotiraj Pathak, write that this party worked to create political consciousness among the common and Bodo tribes of the north bank of the Brahmaputra river. This party fought for their rights, demanded for the development of the region and to give it the status of a Union Territory. However, the internal differences within the party escalated to a level that it could not sustain itself for long. When there was a clash between the government and the Bodo people it could not decide which side to pair with. Though the party lost its support base, it sowed the seeds of autonomy.

The Bodos are the major tribe of Assam that is of Indian and Indo-Mongolian origin. The Indian Statutory Commission or also known as the Simon Commission, formed in 1928, records that the Bodos who call themselves Assamese and are part of the Assamese society have opposed the inclusion of Goalpara district in Bengal.

On February 13, 1967, when Prime Minister Indira Gandhi announced among the All Party Hill leaders that Assam would be reorganised according to the federal structure, some Bodo youth and scholars also convened a meeting in Kokrajhar district and formed a political party for themselves. The result of this discussion held at the meeting came into existence in the form of the Plains Tribal Council of Assam (PTCA). Biruchan Dole was made its President. Samar Brahma Choudhary became the Vice-President and Charan Narjare the General Secretary.

United Minorities Front (UMFA)

Like the Asom Gana Parishad, the United Minorities Front, Assam was also established in 1985. A student organisation was also behind. This regional Party was founded by the All Assam Minority Students Union in collaboration with the Civil Defence Rights Committee (CRPC) and other minority religious and linguistic organisations of Assam. In fact, this party was formed by the All Assam Student Union against the migrants from Bangladesh and to oppose the Assam Accord and for the rights and support of Bengali Hindus and Muslims. The first President of UMFA was Kalipada Sen. In the year 2005, this party merged with All India United Minorities Front.

Bodoland People's Front

Bodoland People's Front is also a regional Party of Assam which was earlier part of the BJP-led National Democratic Alliance which later joined the Congress-led UPA. The party was formed in 2005 and Hagrama Mohilari was its first President. This party contested the Assam Legislative Assembly elections for the first time in 2011 and surprised everyone by winning 12 seats. With this the party emerged as the third largest party in the State after Congress and All India United Democratic Front. The party contested over only 29 seats. Before the 2016 elections, the Bodoland People's Front had tied up with the NDA. The party got 16 seats and won 12 of them again. But in the 2021 Assembly elections, the party left the NDA and tied up with the UPA and won only 4 seats. After this, the party also ended its alliance with the UPA.

All India United Democratic Front (AIUDF)

It is also known as Sarv Bharatiya Sanyukt Gantantrik Morcha. It is a regional Party of Assam, which has made a great impression on the political scenario of the State. It was established on October 3, 2005 by Maulana Badruddin Ajmal, the country's leading perfume trader. By the way, it was relaunched in Delhi in February 2009 as a National Party. In the 2011 elections, the party won 18 out of 126 seats in the State, but in 2016 the seats were reduced to 13. After this the AIUDF contested the 2021 election against the BJP and became the main opposition winning 16 seats. Badruddin is considered a very controversial leader and is also the State President of Jamiat Ulema-e-Hind, Assam. There was also a period when his party had three MPs but today he is the sole MP from his party. ..but he is also the only MP having a maximum of seven children. During the 2021 Assembly elections fought along with the Congress, on January 22, he claimed in a meeting that if the BJP comes to power, it will destroy three and a half thousand mosques and ban Muslim women from wearing burkhas and Muslim men to wear their skull caps. Badruddin's statements proved fatal for the Congress, which was dreaming of returning to power in the 2021 Assembly elections, and the BJP returned to power in the elections. .. and because of this the Congress has also severed its ties with Badruddin's party.

❑

25
Worthwhile Labour Pains and TRS

The political background of Telangana, a state with 33 districts surrounded by Maharashtra, Chhattisgarh, Karnataka and Andhra Pradesh, has not been easy. After decades of struggle, the bill for the bifurcation of Andhra Pradesh was passed in the Lok Sabha on February 18, 2014. All those political parties which were demanding the creation of a separate state of Telangana, were gathered to celebrate in Delhi. But even at such times, one person who seemed somewhat worried was the current Chief Minister of Telangana and President of Telangana Rashtra Samithi, K. Chandrashekar Rao, also known as KCR. He was apprehensive that the Bharatiya Janata Party would play a trick in the Rajya Sabha on the issue of Telangana's separation. But as soon as the Telangana bifurcation bill was passed in the Upper House, KCR heaved a sigh of relief. Actually KCR had given a slogan 5 years ago 'Ek aur dhakkaa Telangana pakka'. The matter progressed slowly. But after this the people took to social media to tarnish KCR's image. It was alleged that till a few years ago he was addicted to alcohol. On this issue, YSR Congress leader Roja even blamed the TRS chief - "Raat men bar, din me darbar". But KCR remained undeterred.

KCR is a poet of the Telugu language. That is why he named his daughter Kavita. KCR, who once carried forward the Youth

Congress, soon joined the TDP. He began his political career by joining the Youth Congress Party from Medak district. He won four consecutive Assembly elections from Siddipet. He was made the Drought Relief Minister in the N.T. Rama Rao government of Andhra Pradesh in 1990. KCR also assisted Chandrababu Naidu during the TDP coup in 1995. After becoming the Transport Minister in the Naidu cabinet in 1996, he also served as the Deputy Speaker in the Andhra Pradesh Legislative Assembly from 2000 to 2001. But Chandrababu Naidu was never on the same page with KCR regarding Telangana. KCR resigned from the post of Deputy Speaker and also TDP to raise his voice for a separate Telangana state and formed his own party TRS.

KCR did whatever he could regarding Telangana. KCR sided with the Congress in 2004 and also became Labour Minister in the Manmohan Singh government formed after the defeat of Atal Bihari Vajpayee. Later, the Left parties also persuaded Naidu to form an alliance with TRS for the 2009 Assembly elections. But the votes of TDP did not shift to the TRS candidate, and TRS had to be content with only 10 Assembly and 2 Lok Sabha seats.

After the death of Y.S. Rajasekhara Reddy in September 2009, the commotion in Andhra politics changed the complete scenario. It felt clear to KCR it is now a matter of 'now or never'. He went on an indefinite fast in November 2009. His deteriorating health promulgated the issue of creating a separate state of Telangana. On the night of December 9, 2009, the Central Government accepted the demand of KCR by announcing the commencement of the formation of the 29th State of India. But this happiness did not last long for KCR as the people of Andhra Pradesh were not happy. The political cadre there revolted and forced the Central Government to reconsider within 15 days the issue of the separate state formation of Telangana. The Srikrishna Committee sought a period of one year with an appeal to the political parties to maintain peace till then. But KCR did not remain idle. He was constantly vocal on this issue. He managed to garner full spirited support in Telangana. In 2012-13, as the Lok Sabha elections began to unfold, the Congress purported that it was losing hold in Andhra Pradesh now. KCR also started pressing harder on UPA Chairperson Sonia Gandhi. On July 30, 2013, the proposal for a separate state of Telangana was passed in the Congress Working Committee. The Andhra Pradesh Reorganisation Bill 2014 was approved by the Lok Sabha on February 18, 2014 and by the Rajya Sabha on February 20, 2014. With the approval of the President, Telangana became a State on June 2, 2014. With the elections, KCR also became the Chief Minister. It was the biggest win of KCR's life. Even before KCR, for 5-6 decades, different leaders had raised the issue of Telangana, but in vain. People started calling KCR 'Father of Telangana'. But the problems were far more in numbers. The biggest issue was the capital of the new state. Andhra Pradesh did not want to leave Hyderabad. But eventually it was decided that the capital of both the states would remain Hyderabad for ten years and by then Andhra Pradesh would have to make a new capital.

On the electoral front, TRS was able to claim success. Meanwhile, KCR took steps for the benefit of Telangana people for which he would be always remembered. At a cost of ₹ 20,000 crores, he got 46,700 water sources prepared in Telangana to raise the groundwater level of the drought-prone state. Apart from this, the Telangana government started a water grid project to connect every household and industry with water connections and by spending ₹ 35,000 crore, pipelines to the length of 126,000 kilometres were laid in villages and cities. KCR also launched a scheme to provide two-room houses to the poor, enhanced pension allowance of the elderly in the state, introduced 6 kg of rice in a month for each member of the family which benefitted 28.6 lakh people. His US-educated son K.T. Rama Rao also functioned well for KCR. He not only sought votes in the urban assemblies, but also made agreements with the industrialists for the industries in the state. Apart from this, KCR's nephew T. Harish Rao, who was an old party worker having good recognition in the rural areas of Telangana. Both of them were made Ministers by the party. KCR's daughter K. Kavita also became MLA from Nizamabad Legislative Assembly. She has played an important role in preserving the cultural heritage of the state. All these circumstances benefited the TRS in the second Assembly election of Telangana as a state. TRS formed the government with an overwhelming majority in the 2018 Assembly elections, winning 88 seats. Chief Minister K. Chandrashekar Rao again took oath as the Chief Minister of the state on 13 December 2018. Because in the first Assembly election, where TRS got 63 seats out of 119, in the 2018 Assembly elections, TRS added 25 more seats to its previous tally and 70 percent of the seats in the state.

Now Assembly elections are to be held in Telangana before December 2023. Electoral strategists foresee BJP's entry in the electoral frame of Telangana State. BJP has consistently tried to build cadres at the grassroots level in Telangana since 2018. At the same time, the BJP has been accusing the TRS of not fulfilling the promises waiver for farmers' loans and others made to the voters. The BJP leadership is now following the pattern which earlier Chandrababu Naidu and later KCR did to win power in the state. Now BJP State President Bandi Sanjay Kumar is completely focused on travelling across the State spreading this message.

Here the BJP has raised another issue that due to the merger of Hyderabad with the Indian Union on September 17, 1948, September 17 should be celebrated as Telangana Liberation Day. In this regard, Union Home Minister Amit Shah has also addressed a public meeting in Nirmal city on September 17, 2021. The BJP has accused that KCR had demanded an official festival on September 17 during his agitation for demanding a separate Telangana. But after coming to power, he backtracked from his stand. While the districts of Maharashtra and Karnataka which were part of the erstwhile Hyderabad state have been celebrating it officially. Then why not only TRS? In fact, in this case, KCR is afraid its Muslim vote bank may scuttle by this.

In the ongoing efforts of other parties against TRS in Telangana, an incident in June 2021 created ruckus. The former Health Minister and MLA of the state E. Rajendra resigned from the post. After he switched to the BJP, many TRS leaders also approached and joined the BJP. It remains to be seen, what new strategy TRS adopts in the coming months.Talking about the Assembly elections in Telangana, K. Chandrashekar Rao, who has become the Chief Minister twice, now looks a bit weak in the third election of the state, but he is still far ahead of his opposition. Local Party All India Majlis-e-Ittehadul Muslimeen (AIMIM) is certainly helping him to stay strong. But if we look at the results of Greater Hyderabad Municipal Corporation, in the upcoming Assembly elections, BJP is sure to put up a strong fight. It is believed that Hyderabad will be the gateway for the BJP in Telangana. Apart from this, Y.S. Sharmila, younger sister of Andhra Pradesh Chief Minister Jagan Mohan Reddy, is also bent upon improving the image of the party in Telangana. She is making rigorous efforts to create a place for the YSR Congress in Telangana.

Chandrashekar Rao has stepped into politics of the centre but this is not going to be a cakewalk for him. BJP's major victories and AAP's tremendous show in Punjab in the 2022 elections will surely place him in a tight corner. We shall witness some interesting combinations again.

❑

Punjab

26
Akali Dal: Guarding Against Vote Bank Poachers

Punjab, the most sensitive state in the country after Jammu and Kashmir, is always remembered as much for fun and gaiety (once upon a time) as much for political stability despite numerous contradictions. The crisis of political stability has mostly been a characteristic of smaller states in general, but the history of Punjab is different. This State has two poles of power, one is Congress and Shiromani Akali Dal is the other. The Akalis may or may not be ruling but they have always been at the helm of affairs.

Having completed a century in 2020, the Shiromani Akali Dal has the distinction of being the oldest regional and the second oldest political party in the Indian sub-continent with a glorious history of struggles both pre and post-Independence. The party has the record of one of the most peaceful struggles both during colonial rule and in free India. So owing to this glorious past, this party deserves an elaborate and gracious space in this book.

Though this is true that the party that was created to articulate ambitions and aspirations of the Sikh community, the second largest minority in the country, has played a proportionately much larger role than its demographic status in the political dynamics of the country, including the struggle for freedom. The party at one stage was a nursery for Sikh political leaders contributing to not only the Congress but also the Communist Party of India and this included Minister of Foreign Affairs Swaran Singh and Chief Minister Partap Singh Kairon. Another salient feature of the party was its democratic character and content where every decision used to be taken after thorough discussion in the Working Committee.

The Shiromani Akali Dal is the party whose volunteers suffered extreme brutalities during various agitations and thousands went to jail for the cause of the Panth and the people, many of whom sacrificed their lives. Even Pt. Jawaharlal Nehru had been arrested under the Jaito Morcha launched by the Akalis. Mahatma Gandhi described one of the Akali agitations as India's First War of Independence, such was the national focus the struggles in Punjab invited during that period. It is because of the struggles and sacrifices that the history of the party is characterised as glorious. You may presently look at it as a family-centric party (read Badal family) but the past is entirely different.

The Akali Dal remained a political organisation but its roots remained attached to Sikhism. This was also one of the reasons for its rise. The role of this bond between the Sect and the Akali Dal has been played by the Shiromani Gurdwara Prabandhak Committee. Remember that the Shiromani Gurdwara Prabandhak Committee was set up primarily for the independence and later management of Sikh pilgrimage sites.

Set up on December 14, 1920, the role of the Shiromani Akali Dal that has crossed a century has also to be seen in the context of the geo-political dynamics of this region. This is the party that was born in Sikh struggles for the liberation of the gurdwaras including the Golden Temple (Darbar Sahib) from under the control of the priestly class belonging to the Udasi and Nirmala sects who had introduced non-Sikh practices in the shrines.

The creation

The watershed moment in the Sikh religio-political discourse during colonial period was the setting up of the SGPC to carry on the gurdwara liberation and reforms struggle on November 15, 1920 at Akal Takht, the temporal seat just opposite Darbar Sahib (Golden Temple) created by Sixth Guru, Guru Hargobind symbolising state power. This body finally acquired statutory status under the Sikh Gurdwara Act, 1925 marking the end of the gurdwara liberation struggle, one of the most peaceful in history. The Akali Dal was originally created at Akal Takht by this body on December 14, 1920 to mobilise volunteers for this liberation struggle. One of the founders of this Sikh Party was Kartar Singh Jhabbar who had returned from Cellular Jail, Andaman known as the Kalapani. He was sentenced to transportation during agitation against the Rowlatt Act, of which the Jallianwala Bagh tragedy was a part. Sarmukh Singh Jhabal was nominated as the first President of the party. The prefix Shiromani was added to the Akali Dal on March 29, 1922.

The twin objectives of the Akali Dal was "to serve the Panth by carrying along all Akali Jathas and to implement the directive from the SGPC for managing the gurdwaras." (Jagtar Singh, Rivers on Fire : Khalistan Struggle, Aakar, Delhi, 2020, p 315). Its role kept evolving over the years. Both the Akali Dal and the SGPC were banned by the Punjab government for the first time on October 12, 1923.

The first major political action of the Shiromani Akali Dal in history was the decision by its Working Committee on January 16, 1928 to boycott the Simon Commission. (Akali Te Pardesi, January 18, 22, 1928). As the dominant player in the Sikh religio-political matrix, the Akali Dal under Master Tara Singh arrived at an understanding with the Congress for the 1937 Assembly elections to contest from 24 seats. This was the first foray of the Akali Dal in legislative politics. The Akali candidates thus elected were to be part of the Congress Legislature Party technically. The Shiromani Akali Dal won in 11 seats, the Congress from six Sikh seats besides 10 Hindu and two Muslim seats, the Khalsa

National Party 13 seats with the Unionist Party capturing 98 seats. Significantly, the Hindu Mahasabha was victorious from 12 seats while 2 seats went to Ahrar, 2 to Muslim League, 2 seats to Itihad-i-Millat, 1 to Congress Nationalist Party and 16 to Independents. (Sukhmani Bal Riar, The Politics of the Sikhs 1940-47, Unistar, Chandigarh, p. 18, cit K. C. Yadav, Elections in Punjab 1920-47).

Continuing the cooperation with the Congress even outside the Assembly, the Shiromani Akali Dal at a meeting in 1937 decided to join hands with the Congress in the freedom struggle too. The Sikh political discourse entered another phase with the demand for Pakistan formally raised by the Muslim League in 1940. The SGPC and the Akali Dal were the first outfits to oppose this resolution. The Akali Dal controlled SGPC called for a separate Sikh Homeland in case the demand for Pakistan was to be conceded.

Akalis for Azad Punjab

As the Sikh state issue entered the Sikh discourse, the Akali Dal came up with the Azad Punjab Resolution on June 5, 1943. The party stated: "The Shiromani Akali Dal hereby declares that in the Azad Punjab the boundaries shall be fixed after taking into consideration the population, property, land revenue and historical tradition of the communities .... if the new demarcations are effected on the above mentioned principles then the Azad Punjab shall comprise Ambala, Jullundur, from the Lahore Divisions and out of Multan Division, Lyallpur district, and some portions of Montgomery and Multan districts. The Shiromani Akali Dal shall make this demand and shall fight for the same." (Ibid., pp 44-45).

Under changed circumstances now, the interim government headed by Pt. Nehru, was finally constituted on August 24, 1946 in which Baldev Singh was inducted as representative of the Sikhs.

Post-Independence scenario

After the initial confrontation after 1947, the Akali Dal under the presidency of Giani Kartar Singh aligned with the Congress with the directive to its MLAs to join that party with effect from March 18, 1948. This decision to extend total cooperation to the Congress was on the surface, unconditional although it was implied that the Congress would take all steps for the protection of the Sikhs and their rights which had not been clearly defined at that time. Giani Kartar Singh himself joined the Congress. Three of the Akali MLAs Swaran Singh, Ishar Singh Majhail and Udham Singh Nagoke had already shifted to the Congress. This arrangement did not last long and the Akali Dal broke away from the Congress on July 30, 1950 but it was now pitted against fresh struggles. The decision to join the Congress was dictated by the notion that it might facilitate in getting the promises fulfilled through the Constituent Assembly given by the Congress from time to time.

The Akali narrative henceforth started evolving under new dimensions focussed on what was defined as the dignified space in new India evoking strong reaction from the Hindu strata in the state. This confrontation triggered high level tension in the Punjabi society beginning with the Punjabi Suba agitation for the creation of a Punjabi speaking state in accordance with reorganisation of other states on a linguistic basis. The Sikh legislators signed a 13-point demand charter on November 15, 1948 demanding adequate protection for the rights of the community. The main issues that were perceived to ensure dignified space included 5 percent representation in the central cabinet with one cabinet minister and a deputy minister being a Sikh, the office of Governor and Chief Minister in Punjab should alternate between a Hindu and a Sikh, Sikhs should get 50 percent reservation in the State cabinet with 40 percent reservation in the government jobs. Gurgaon district and Loharu tehsil should be taken out of the state.

The alternative suggested to these demands was to carve out a new state of Punjab which should include the districts of

Hoshiarpur, Jalandhar, Ludhiana, Ferozepur, Amritsar, Gurdaspur and Ambala. The princely states had not been merged with Punjab by that time. It is this demand for a new Punjab which was perceived by a section of the Hindu leadership as 'Sikhistan'. The only Sikh member who did not sign it was Partap Singh Kairon who later became the Chief Minister. (Ajit Singh Sarhadi : Punjabi Suba, U.C. Kapur and Sons, Delhi, 1970, p. 167).

The Congress government at the Centre set up the State Reorganisation Commission on December 22, 1953 to bring cultural and linguistic contiguous areas in the regions under one unit as far as possible but Punjab was kept out. This Commission submitted its report in 1955 but Punjab was excluded.

The demand for Punjabi Suba (Punjabi linguistic state) was earlier adopted at a Sikh convention held at Amritsar on April 4, 1949. (Ajit Singh Sarhadi, Punjabi Suba, p. 179). Akali Dal senior leader Master Tara Singh emphasised the need for autonomy at a press conference in Delhi in 1949 saying, "Not only do we want an area with a majority of the Sikhs but also complete internal autonomy". (Dr. Ajit Singh : Shiromani Akali Dal, Arman Publications, Kapurthala, 2005, p. 95). Later, however, the emphasis shifted to Punjabi speaking areas.

The articulation of the demand for a Punjabi speaking state found expression in the Akali Dal manifesto for the 1952 general elections. The party stated: "The true test of democracy, in the opinion of the Shiromani Akali Dal, is that the minorities should feel that they are really free and partners in the destiny of their community… The Shiromani Akali Dal is in favour of formation of provinces on a linguistic and cultural basis throughout India, but it holds, it is a question of life and death for the Sikhs for a new Punjab to be created immediately. The Shiromani Akali Dal has reasons to believe that a Punjabi speaking province may give Sikhs the necessary security. It believes in a Punjabi-speaking province as an autonomous unit of India ''. (Dr. Ajit Singh : Shiromani

Akali Dal, Arman Publications, Kapurthala, 2005, pp. 96-97, cit. Election Manifesto of Shiromani Akali Dal 1952).

Master Tara Singh logically explained this demand at the 10th All India Akali Conference at Amritsar on February 11, 1956 stating: "If Punjabi Suba is formed, not only our culture and language are protected, but also our religion will be ensured proper protection and security". For him, the issue at stake was not just political but that of the very existence itself of the Sikhs in the backdrop of repeated attacks on their separate and exclusive identity and the perception of being subsumed in the broader Hindu stream.

First Punjabi Suba agitation

The immediate provocation for launching the first Punjabi Suba agitation was provided by an order promulgated by the Amritsar district magistrate on April 6, 1955 banning raising of Punjabi Suba slogans under Section 144 IPC. The Akali Dal at its Working Committee meeting on April 24, 1955 at Amritsar warned of agitation in case the ban was not lifted by May 10. Master Tara Singh courted arrest along with 10 others on May 10 marking the start of the agitation that ended on July 12, 1955 during which 12,000 men, women and children including Akal Takht Jathedar and the Golden Temple Head Priest courted arrest. This was the first major agitation launched by the party post-partition. This perhaps was the first such agitation of this magnitude in free India. This also was the first mass agitation associated with the Akali Dal since 1947 in which virtually the entire Sikh religio-political leadership was arrested. The parleys between the Centre and the Akalis finally led to what is known as the language-based Regional formula.

The relationship between the Akali Dal and the Congress entered a new phase after the implementation of the regional formula. The Akali Dal renounced active politics on September

30, 1956. Under the new arrangement, the Akali Dal was to restrict itself to religious, social and cultural concerns while the Akali leaders were to contest election on Congress ticket. The Congress had allocated the Akalis 22 seats for the Assembly and 3 seats for Parliament. This arrangement fell subsequently after the election. Master Tara Singh too got disenchanted with the regional formula and came out against it on June 14, 1958.

Second Punjabi Suba Morcha

The second Punjab Suba Morcha (agitation) started with the arrest of Master Tara Singh on May 24, 1960. The agitation gained momentum and 17,821 Akalis were arrested by July 25, 1960, at Amritsar alone.

The Prime Minister in his speech on August 15 opposed the Punjabi Suba demand as threat to the country's unity, thereby implying it was secessionist. About 25,000 Akali volunteers had courted arrest by that time. He ruled out creation of a Punjabi-speaking state and said: "Tamasha (drama) is going on in Delhi and Punjab about the Punjabi Suba," and asserted, "This demand might be good or bad but there were many wrong things in the movement and there is danger to the freedom of the country". Going a step ahead, Nehru at a news conference on October 21 banged his table and declared, "We will not accept the demand for Punjabi Suba. It is a communal demand and will be crushed at every cost". (Sarhadi, Ajit Singh: Punjabi Suba, UC Kapur and Sons, Delhi, 1970, pp. 330-31).

In an effort to mobilise support from the opposition parties at the national level, Sant Fateh Singh made it clear on October 28, 1960, that, "We do not seek a Sikh majority area. We are not bothered by percentages. We want the Punjabi Suba to comprise an area, where the Punjabi language is spoken regardless of the fact whether the Sikhs are in the majority or in the minority." Sant Fateh Singh announced his decision to go on an indefinite fast from December 18, 1960 as part of the intensification of the agitation.

Sant Fateh Singh decided to break his 22-day old fast on January 9 at 9 am following an appeal from the Prime Minister accompanied by some sort of assurance. However, he ended his fast half an hour earlier fearing adverse reactions to his decision as this was in violation of the pledge that was administered to him by Darbar Sahib Head Granthi Giani Chet Singh. It stated, "Sant Fateh Singh, you are taking a pledge to fast unto death and till the Prime Minister hears you and concedes this constitutional demand, your fast will continue". (Kapur, Prithipal Singh: Master Tara Singh and his Reminiscences, Singh Brothers, Amritsar, 2015, p. 87, Quoted from Jaswant Singh (ed): Master Tara Singh, Jiwan Sangharash-te-Udesh).

After this, the government released all the detained Akalis. According to one estimate, about 30,000 Akalis had courted arrest from the time the agitation (morcha) was launched on May 24, 1960. Pt. Nehru later conveyed to Sant Fateh Singh at a meeting on May 12, 1961 that the creation of the Punjabi Suba was neither in the interest of Punjab nor in India.

The next such fast was undertaken by Master Tara Singh from August 15, 1961 till the acceptance of the Punjabi Suba demand. Master Tara Singh started his fast on August 15 after taking a pledge at Akal Takht and performing Ardas (prayer) at the Golden Temple (Darbar Sahib). He was to take only lemon water.

The Prime Minister reiterated his earlier position that it would provoke communal polarisation while speaking in the Rajya Sabha the next day. Perhaps he too had in mind the strategic location of Punjab when he extended the logic that the consequences of agreeing to the demand were far graver, far more far-reaching, and would affect the whole future of Punjab and India. He went a step further saying, "It will be resisted—I do not say there is going to be a civil war or anything like that. It will not be resisted by the outsiders, but by the people in that Suba". (Sarhadi, Ajit Singh: Punjabi Suba, U.C. Kapur and Sons, Delhi, 1970, p. 357).

Maharaja Yadvindra Singh and former Indian Foreign Service officer Hardit Singh Malik met Home Minister Lal Bahadur Shastri on September 30 who agreed to the setting up of a committee. Both of them rushed to Amritsar with this assurance. The Akali Dal working committee deliberated upon the offer. Master Tara Singh finally agreed to end his 48-day fast on October 1, 1961 at 7 pm.

Congress MLA Lala Jagat Narain and Inder Sen, Secretary, Punjab Hindi Raksha Samiti, on October 6, 1961, warned the government against any political settlement with the Akalis, declaring, "The Hindus of Punjab would not accept it."

Akali Dal Splits with Qualitative Shift from Urban to Rural Leadership

With the factional fight between Sant Fateh Singh and Master Tara Singh escalating, the party entered a new phase in its history with shift from urban to rural leadership that in the long run had multiplier effect down the line, including at the level of concerns of the new leadership that now focused more on rural areas. Both the factions decided to stage their respective show of strength at the General Body meeting of the Akali Dal convened at Amritsar on August 18. The Sant Fateh Singh faction claimed that about 200 delegates, 72 circle jathedars (presidents) and nine MLAs attended its general body meeting in front of Akal Takht. This faction elected Sant Fateh Singh as the President. The Master Tara Singh faction claimed the participation of 230 delegates and several MLAs.

The real test, however, was to be the SGPC. A notice was given by SGPC members supporting Sant Fateh Singh to the requisition meeting of the general house that was duly convened on October 2. Master Tara Singh faction lost by 76 to 72 votes. Sant Chanan Singh was elected as the SGPC President on September 18.

Akalis and autonomy

Although the Akali Dal contested the 1967 Assembly election on the demand for Sikhstan with autonomy on the Jammu and Kashmir pattern, the autonomy issue entered the party's political discourse mainly with the resolution adopted at its Conference at Batala held on September 28-29-30, 1968. This issue was to reverberate in the Akali domain in the coming years but mainly when the party was not in power.

This Resolution was taken ahead by the Anandpur Sahib Resolution adopted by the party working committee meeting on October 16-17, 1973 at Anandpur Sahib and ratified by the party's general house on August 28, 1977 though widely opposed at the national level.

Meanwhile, Akali Dal Chief Parkash Singh Badal first became Agriculture Minister (March 28, 1977–June 19, 1977) in the Janata government at the Centre and later Chief Minister of Punjab for the second time from June 20, 1977 to February 17, 1980. Parkash Singh Badal's first term was brief. For the first time, he remained Chief Minister for a little more than a year from March 27, 1970–June 14, 1971. During the second term, it materialised gradually.

The same proposal was carried forward and when the Akali Dal under the leadership of Harcharan Singh Longowal started the Dharma Yudh Morcha on 4 August 1982, it was also one of the main demands. This is when the Akali politics of Janrail Singh Bhindranwale surfaced on the horizon and the roots of terrorism started getting firmer. The assassination of Prime Minister Indira Gandhi on October 30, 1984 also took place and amidst all this Rajiv Gandhi became the Prime Minister with a large majority and marathon round of talks went on. An agreement was reached between Sant Harcharan Singh Longowal and Rajiv Gandhi on July 23, 1982 and the entire matter was handed over to the Sarkaria Commission. But the accord was not appreciated by the fundamentalists and on August 20, 1982, within a month from the date of the agreement, he was murdered near a gurdwara in Sherpur village, some distance from Patiala.

It is certain that in the meantime there was considerable political instability in Punjab. Four decades after Independence, for about ten years, the President's rule was imposed in eight different phases in Punjab. Due to terrorism also, Punjab was under President's rule in two phases from October 10, 1983 to September 29, 1985 and again from May 11, 1987 to February 25, 1992. Punjab returned to its normal political discourse with the Assembly election in February 1997. The Akali Dal under the leadership of Badal distanced itself from the Panthic outlook with this election.

Parkash Singh Badal emerged as the most dominant leader beginning with 1994 and he consolidated his grip on the Moga Conference. Of course, it was not for the first time that the concept of Punjabiat had entered the Akali discourse as this was the theme of the party on which it contested the 1969 Assembly election. This manifesto stated, "The Shiromani Akali Dal is committed to the unity of Punjabis, strengthening the bonds between different communities and to provide equal opportunities to all Punjabis." In his Presidential address in the Moga Conference, Badal emphasised Punjab, Punjabi and the spirit of Punjabi.

The year 1997 marked another phase of the party and this was characterised by its long association with the Bharatiya Janata Party whose mother-organisation the Rashtriya Swayamsewak Sangh advocates Hindu Rashtra. This association with the sectarian BJP impacted the ideological positioning of the Akali Dal Party on issues like Article 370 over the years that the party at one stage had included in its agenda. The Akali Dal supported the scrapping of Article 370.

In an unprecedented experiment, the party gave eleven tickets to the Hindus in the 2012 Assembly election out of whom nine won but the Akali Dal in the process continued to dilute its core content and concerns.

The Akali Dal started getting alienated from its core Sikh base and the lowest ebb was observed in the 2017 Assembly election when the Akali Dal was reduced to a mere 15 seats in a House of 117. Its vote percentage was 25.2 only and it was 9.4 short of the percentage of 2012.

Still the fact remains, Shiromani Akali Dal is the oldest regional party representing an ethnic minority in the country that has survived many ups and downs over the years depending upon the contemporary political conversation. This is the party that has also impacted the national political discourse at times. The party underwent a historic shift towards Punjabiat from Panthic in 1996 after Parkash Singh Badal took over as its first non-Panthic President as he was even non-Amritdhari (non-baptised) unlike all of his predecessors. This shift at the 75th anniversary Conference at Moga on February 25, 1996 far off from the traditional agenda was to play a pivotal role in shaping the politics in coming years. This shift came to be known as the Punjab, Punjabi and Punjabiat agenda although no resolution was specifically adopted for this purpose. This discourse had dominated the speeches of the leaders, mainly Badal. This shift can best be understood in the context of the earlier religio-political framework concretised in the 1974 Constitution of the Shiromani Akali Dal whose first two objectives were "1- Propagation of Sikh religion and its code of conduct, denunciation of atheism and apostasy to take steps for the management of gurdwaras and reforms therein. 2- To reinforce the exclusive Sikh identity and strive for the creation of a geo-political environment in which national sentiments and aspirations of the Sikh Panth are fully manifested and flourish." (Translated from the Shiromani Akali Dal Constitution, 1974).

Badal created a record by becoming the Punjab Chief Minister five times beginning from 1970. For the first time, the Akali Dal government completed a full term of five years under his Chief Ministership beginning in 1997. The party again remained in power under his command for two successive terms from 2007-

2017, a record. The party faced humiliating defeat after these two terms in 2017 Assembly elections held under the shadow of the sacrilege of Guru Granth Sahib at Bargari. This is the blot that the party now carries...and it is not as if the party did not get wide recognition at the national level. Parkash Singh Badal was the Agriculture Minister at the Centre and his daughter-in-law Harsimrat Kaur Badal was the Cabinet Minister at the Centre for a long time. Apart from this, many leaders of the party, including Surjit Singh Barnala had held ministerials, and other constitutional posts at the Centre and States.

But after the farmers' agitation in the last months, the Akali Dal severed the 24-year-old ties with the NDA. Sukhbir Singh Badal, who took charge of the party after the elderly Parkash Singh Badal, is now under pressure to lead the party towards new dimensions. It is said that the Akali Dal had conducted a survey regarding its alliance with the NDA, in which the party was concerned about the declining index of popularity of Prime Minister Narendra Modi in rural Punjab and Amarinder Singh's popularity being higher than Sukhbir Badal even after the alliance with the NDA in the cities. The party did not see much benefit in keeping the ties with the BJP intact. This was a crucial decision for Sukhbir Badal in view of the 2022 Assembly elections. Although Sukhbir is considered an expert in electoral juglary. He shunned the BJP and joined hands with the BSP but AAP's tsunami in the 2022 elections shattered his plans. Akali won mere 03 seats. It got 18.4 percent votes only compared to 33.2 percent of 2017.

One of the main reasons for this party having survived all the vicissitudes of time is the institutional support. Being the voice of the party, the Sikh institutions like the SGPC, the Akal Takht and the gurdwaras at the local level provided unstinted support to the party. For years, the meetings of the party at the local level normally used to be held in gurdwaras and the party headquarters was in the Darbar Sahib (Golden Temple) complex that used to be the venue of historic party conferences. The delegate session is still held in the Darbar Sahib complex. After all, the Akali Dal was created by the Shiromani Gurdwara Parbandhak Committee.

This party has gone through several phases, got bruised but survived and going by its support base and institutional support, it would continue to be one of the political choices for the people in Punjab. But 2024 would observe a sea-change in the party. To be or not to be with the BJP would be a crucial and interesting decision.

❑

27
A Tale of Entries and Exits

Several political parties showed their mettle in the Chhattisgarh elections. But even before they could run they vanished barring Ajit Yogi's Party who had served as the Chief Minister of the State. By launching the Janata Congress he tried to create a difference but his dream did not go down well with the people of Chhattisgarh in 2018 and in alliance with BSP his party was reduced to only seven seats. The public voted in favour of Bhupesh Baghel (Congress) and a record number of MLAs were elected in the new Chhattisgarh which reduced the BJP to 14 seats.

Chhattisgarh was carved out of Madhya Pradesh and came into existence on 1st November, 2000 as the 28th state of the country. Though Atalji had no direct connection with Chhattisgarh, the common Chhattisgarh people consider him to be the architect of the State which is an interesting story to tell and goes like this.. Addressing an election rally at Sapreshala ground in Raipur in the 1998 Lok Sabha elections, he had said that if all the 11 Lok Sabha seats are given to the BJP, a separate Chhattisgarh State will be created. However, after the election results were declared, the BJP won 7 out of 11, while on the remaining 4 seats, Congress Ajit Jogi (Raigad), Pt. Shyamacharan Shukla (Mahasamund), Dr. Charandas Mahant (Janjgir), and Khelsai Singh (Sarguja) emerged victorious. In the same Loksabha election, Dr. Raman Singh defeated Motilal Vora from Rajnandgaon. Not only that, after becoming the Prime Minister, Atalji inducted Dr. Raman Singh, Ramesh Bais and Dilip Singh Judev of Chhattisgarh into his Cabinet. Nevertheless, Atalji kept his promise and gave the Chhattisgarh people a separate State. He has also played a key role in the development of Chhattisgarh. His love for Chhattisgarh was somewhat different. Owing to this love his friendship with the first Chief Minister Ajit Jogi was at another level. Ajit Jogi himself reiterated several times that Atalji often rose above the party line and took crucial decisions. He recalled that representatives of 200 nations had attended the 50th anniversary of the United Nations. 'Atalji, Sharad Pawar and I (Ajit Jogi) had the opportunity to attend that ceremony. The then Prime Minister Narasimha Rao had requested Atalji to lead the delegation but Atalji assigned Jogi for the leadership.'

But even though Ajit Jogi was the first Chief Minister, there was considerable tension and pressure within the Congress. During 2014, a bye-election was to be held at Antagarh in Chhattisgarh. Manturam Panwar was the Congress candidate. He filed his nomination. On the last date for withdrawal, Manturam withdrew his name without informing the party. At the end of 2015, an audio tape surfaced containing discussion regarding buying and selling. It was alleged that the tape contained the voice of Ajit Jogi, his son Amit Jogi and Puneet Gupta, son-in-law of the then Chief Minister Dr Raman Singh. The talks were about Manturam Pawar withdrawing his name. After the tape scandal came to light Chhattisgarh's State Congress Committee expelled son Amit Jogi from the party for six years. At the same time, it was recommended to expel Ajit Jogi from the party. In fact, Jogi did everything in his power to maintain his dominance in the party, but Motilal Bora being in Delhi, Jogi's voice was not heard.

But Jogi was not weak. The number of MLAs supporting Ajit Jogi was around 10-12. At the same time, about 10 to 15 former MLAs were also seen with him. A distraught Jogi announced the split of the Congress in the afternoon of June 6, 2016. This was the second partition by the Congress after the formation of Chhattisgarh state. Earlier in 2003, senior Congress leader Vidyacharan Shukla left the Congress and went to the NCP.

In Chhattisgarh, 29 out of 90 seats are reserved for tribals. In such a situation, there was no other big leader in the tribal and Satnami community as compared to the popularity of Ajit Jogi. In the 2013 elections also, the BJP government was formed under the leadership of Raman Singh by getting only 0.76 percent more votes. Obviously in the next election (2018) due to Ajit Jogi and his supporters, there was speculation of loss to the BJP like the Congress.The results of the Assembly elections could have led to a hung Assembly and Ajit Jogi could have been the 'kingmaker' in such a situation. But nothing of this sort happened and due to anti-incumbency towards the Raman Singh government, Congress got an absolute majority and more than one-third of seats 68 (currently 70). Jogi caused a huge dent to BJP and BJP was reduced to 15 seats (currently 14). The alliance of Janata Congress Chhattisgarh and BSP had to be content with 7 seats (6 seats after the death of Ajit Jogi). It got 7 percent vote share.

Ajit Jogi's entry into politics is also very interesting. It was in 1985 when Indore collector Ajit Jogi was asleep in his bungalow. The phone in his bungalow rang. One of his employees picked up the phone and mentioned that the Collector saheb was sleeping. There was a heavy voice that ordered him to wake up the Collector and get him to talk. Ajit Jogi hurriedly woke up and came to the phone line. As soon as Ajit Jogi said hello on the phone, a voice from the phone roared - You have two and a half hours, do you want to join politics or remain a Collector? Digvijay Singh will come to pick you up, tell him about your decision. In fact, the caller was none other than former Prime Minister Rajiv Gandhi's PA V. George. Two and a half hours later, when Digvijay Singh reached Ajit Jogi's bungalow, Collector Ajit Jogi was Congress leader Ajit Jogi. It is said that Ajit Jogi came in contact with Rajiv Gandhi when he was Collector in Raipur. After his entry into the

Congress Party he was made Rajya Sabha MP where he completed two terms. He frequented the Lok Sabha though.

Controversies never spared Jogi. The biggest one associated with Ajit Jogi was his being a tribal or not. However in September 2018, the Supreme Court later ruled in his favour as a tribal. In 2003, Ajit Jogi was also accused of trying to buy BJP MLAs, a sting operation also surfaced citing this. In 2004, Ajit Jogi's car met with a near fatal accident in which though his life was saved, he was permanently paralysed leaving him incapacitated. However, despite his condition he managed to achieve positions for himself but could not contribute much for the party.

After the death of Ajit Jogi, all was not well with the Janata Congress in Chhattisgarh. Out of the four Party MLAs, Devvrat Singh and Pramod Sharma have aligned with the Congress. However, due to the hurdles of the Defection Law, it had not been possible for them to join the Congress. Ajit Jogi's wife and Kota MLA Renu Jogi and Lormi MLA Dharamjit Singh are a few big names with Janata Congress Chhattisgarh. Several senior leaders associated with the party since its formation have gone back to the Congress.

Though Jogi's Party appeared in the 2018 elections, before that many parties emerged and vanished in Chhattisgarh. Many candidates of the Gondwana Republic Party (Gompa), Chhattisgarh Mukti Morcha (Chhamumo) and Chhattisgarh Samaj Party (Chhap) contested elections but most of them could not even save their zamanat. The Gondwana Republic Party, Chhattisgarh Mukti Morcha, Chhattisgarh Samaj Party, Chhattisgarh Vikas Party, Jai Chhattisgarh Party etc. are few other small regional parties. Moreover, the Samajwadi Party has been active here for a very long time, yet it has never been able to show its strength in the electoral fray, except during the Janata Party's regime.

Former Lok Sabha Speaker P.A. Sangma had formed a new party—The National People's Party, and appointed Chhattisgarh tribal leader and former Union minister Arvind Netam as its Executive Chairman. But The National People's Party remained on paper and Arvind Netam returned to the Congress. At the time of the last election, the Chhattisgarh Swabhiman Manch raised a hue and cry but it could not succeed.

The Chhattisgarh Swabhiman Manch now remains only a name. The late Tarachand Sahu, who was a four-time MP from Durg Lok Sabha, founded the Swabhiman Manch in 2008. Tara Babu became the first State President in the Chhattisgarh state and was an MP from Durg Lok Sabha seat for four consecutive terms. But he could never become a Union Minister and who regretted it till the last days. After constant neglect in the party, he finally revolted against the BJP. After his death, the Swabhiman Manch merged with the BJP.

❑

28
Piecemeal Politics

Haryana was carved out of Punjab in 1966. From then till the end of the twentieth century, the politics here revolved around the three Lals. These three Lals were Chaudhary Devi Lal (better known as Tau Devi Lal), Chaudhary Bansi Lal (known as Vikas Purush of Haryana and also known for his arrogant nature) and the third Bhajan Lal, who became the new leader of manipulative politics. Talking about regional politics in Haryana, Chaudhary Devi Lal appears to be the greatest name of all. Although all these three leaders, at some point of time, formed their own regional parties, they could not make it successful. During the 1970s-1980s in Haryana, Devi Lal emerged as a big challenge to the Congress. Chaudhary Devi Lal belonged to a big landlord family of village Chautala in Sirsa district of Haryana. He actively participated in the freedom movement. In 1930, he was arrested by the police from outside the Congress office while demonstrating in support of Lala Lajpat Rai. He was then only a Class X student at Dev Samaj Public High School, Moga. After independence, he carved for himself an image of a big farmer leader. In 1952 he was elected MLA to the Punjab Legislative Assembly on a Congress ticket. He also played a vital role in the creation of Haryana State carved out of Punjab. While being a Congress MLA from 1962 to 1967, he raised the voice of a separate Hindi-speaking State from Punjab. This effort by him and the Akali leaders for a separate Punjabi speaking area paid off and on November 1, 1966, Haryana became a separate State.

In the 1970s, when Indira's supremacy in the Congress Party was on a high, many prominent leaders of the Congress were not able to digest it and started leaving the party. Devi Lal was also one of them. He left the Congress in 1971 and contested the 1972 Assembly elections against two Congress veterans. He stood against Bansi Lal from Tosham and against Bhajan Lal in Adampur. Although he lost in both the seats, later in 1974 he won the election from Rodi.

In 1975, when Indira Gandhi declared Emergency in the country, Devi Lal was also arrested. He remained in jail for 19 months. After that in the 1977 elections he won from Bhattukalan on Janata Party ticket and became the Chief Minister of the State. In the 1980s, he formed the Lok Dal along with Chaudhary Charan Singh and started a platform called Naya Yudh. His campaign became very popular among the people and in the 1987 elections, he formed the government by winning 85 out of 90 seats in the State Assembly. In 1989 he joined the Janata Dal under the leadership of V.P. Singh and contested the Lok Sabha elections from Sikar and Rohtak and won from both places. One from Rajasthan and the other from Haryana. He became the Deputy Prime Minister in the V.P. Singh government.

Indian National Lok Dal (INLD)

The main politics of Haryana remained divided for a long time between the Congress and Devi Lal (whichever party he was in). In such a situation, the main regional party would be the one which Devi Lal was in. After leaving Congress, Devi Lal also remained associated with national parties like the Bharatiya Lok Dal, Janata Party and Janata Dal, but after differences with V.P. Singh, he revived the party again in the name of the Lok Dal. It had influence in some parts of Haryana and western Uttar Pradesh. In 1996, the name of this party was changed to Indian

National Lok Dal (INLD). In 1998 the party joined the National Democratic Alliance led by the Bharatiya Janata Party. In the year 2000, under the leadership of Om Prakash Chautala, the party formed the government with the BJP, but soon this alliance broke up and INLD distanced itself from the NDA. After that the party could not win any seat in the Lok Sabha in 2009, although it again contested the elections in alliance with the BJP. Om Prakash Chautala and his son Ajay Chautala were arrested in the year 2013 in the teacher recruitment scam during the tenure of Om Prakash Chautala. Both were sentenced to ten years each. In the year 2018, there was a split in the Chautala family, and Ajay Chautala's son Dushyant Chautala formed a separate Party in the name of the Jannayak Janata Party.

Jannayak Janata Party (JJP)

The formation of the Jannayak Janata Party was the result of mutual discord in the Chautala family of Chaudhary Devi Lal. This party was formed after separating from the Indian National Lok Dal. The 2018 Indian National Lok Dal rally: The reason for this in Gohana, in which jailed INLD leader Om Prakash Chautala's son and party leader Abhay Chautala accused his nephews Dushyant Chautala and Digvijay Chautala of being over-ambitious. Abhay Chautala expelled Dushyant and Digvijay Chautala from the party and also expelled his brother Ajay Chautala from the party for supporting them. After this, at a rally held in Jind in December 2018, Dushyant Chautala announced to contest the Lok Sabha elections by forming a separate party, the Jannayak Janata Party. Dushyant said that the name of the party is in honour of his great-grandfather and Deputy Prime Minister of the country, Chaudhary Devi Lal. The party followed the path shown by him.

In the October 2019 Haryana Assembly elections, JJP started its electoral politics as a regional party and won 10 seats in its very first election. Dushyant Chautala also got a big advantage of this limited success in the hung Assembly and became the Deputy

Chief Minister of the State by supporting the BJP. But the next election would be more testing for Dushyant. To remain with the BJP or not will be a tough decision to make.

Vishal Haryana Party

This party has the distinction of being the first official regional party of Haryana. This party came into existence shortly after the formation of Haryana. It was formed in 1967 by Rao Birender Singh who rebelled from the Congress and was also the Chief Minister for a few months (March 24, 1967–November 2, 1967). Rao Birender Singh broke away from the Congress and formed the Vishal Haryana Party, leading to the Aaya Ram and Gaya Ram phase in Haryana politics. Most of the Congress MLAs joined him and on March 24, 1967 he took oath as the Chief Minister. But Prime Minister Indira Gandhi soon dissolved the Assembly and President's Rule was imposed in the State. Rao Birender Singh has also been the Speaker of the Assembly. At that time Bhagwat Dayal Sharma was made the Chief Minister. Birender Singh's Vishal Haryana Party was in existence for almost 9 years. After that it merged with the Congress on September 23, 1978.

Haryana Lok Samiti

If we talk about the first regional party of Haryana, it started only in 1962, when Haryana was not a separate State and was only a part of Punjab. In 1962, Jagdev Singh contested the Lok Sabha elections by forming a Party called Haryana Lok Samiti. However, this party was not recognised by the Election Commission and he reached the Lok Sabha by winning the Jhajjar Lok Sabha seat as an independent candidate.

Haryana Vikas Party

The year in which Chaudhary Devi Lal changed the name of his party to the Indian National Lok Dal, in the same year 1996, the second 'Lal', i.e.Bansi Lal of Haryana also formed his own regional party. In 1996, the Congress led by Narasimha Rao was thrown out of power. There was a major change in the party and Sonia Gandhi was made the President of the party. Due to her foreign origin, many big leaders of the party did not agree to accept her as the President. One of them was Bansi Lal. He rebelled against the Congress and formed his own regional Party named Haryana Vikas Party and won the 1996 Haryana Assembly elections by playing a big bet with the BJP. He became the Chief Minister of the State and became famous and controversial at the same time because of his decision to ban liquor. He was the Chief Minister from May 11, 1996 to July 23, 1999. His government collapsed after the BJP withdrew support. In 2004, Bansi Lal again returned to the Congress and the Haryana Vikas Party merged with the Congress.

Bhajan Lal, the third 'Lal' of Haryana and considered to be an expert in manipulation, was also disillusioned with the Congress when the party contested Assembly elections under his name and Bhupinder Singh Hooda was made the Chief Minister of the State. After expressing his displeasure with the Congress several times in public forums, finally on December 2, 2007, he separated from the Congress and formed a separate party named Haryana Janhit Congress. In the 2009 Assembly elections, the party along with the BSP contested 87 seats in the State and won only six. Bhajanlal died in June 2011 and the leadership of the party passed to his younger son Kuldeep Bishnoi. Later five MLAs of the party also left him and joined the Congress. In the year 2013, when BJP declared Narendra Modi as the Prime Ministerial candidate, Kuldeep Bishnoi also supported him and included his party in the National Democratic Alliance. Haryana Janhit Congress fought the 2014 Lok Sabha elections in alliance with the BJP, but Kuldeep Bishnoi could not even win his seat in the Lok Sabha elections and lost to INLD's Dushyant Chautala.

Later in August 2014, Kuldeep Bishnoi announced to break his alliance with the NDA. He said that BJP has betrayed him by joining hands with INLD. In the 2014 Assembly elections, his party could win only two seats. Not seeing himself succeeding as a separate party, finally on April 28, 2016, he announced to join the Congress. In this way the journey of the Haryana Janhit Party lasted only for 9 years. But this was not the end of Kuldeep Bishnoi's political switching. He and his family again joined the BJP.

Haryana Lokhit Party

Haryana Lokhit Party is also a regional party with a limited base in Haryana. It was founded on May 2, 2014 by Gopal Kanda, an entrepreneur and politician embroiled in the controversial air hostess harassment case. Gopal Kanda had been trying to enter politics from Sirsa since 2006. He also grew closer to the Chautala family. In 2009, he also asked for a ticket but he did not get it from INLD. Kanda contested as an independent candidate and defeated the INLD's candidate. In this election, the Congress won 40 seats. Kanda emerged as the kingmaker and was appointed as a Cabinet Minister in the Hooda government. But on August 5, 2012, Geetika Sharma, a former air hostess of Gopal Kanda's airline, committed suicide. He wrote two suicide notes in which Kanda was accused of sexual harassment. Kanda was arrested in this case and he had to resign from the government. Kanda got bail before the Haryana Assembly elections in March 2014. After returning from jail, in May 2014, he returned to politics by forming the Haryana Lokhit Party. He also won the election by defeating INLD candidate Makhan Lal Singla.

Despite the formation of so many parties in Haryana, there is no stability there. In this state with ten Lok Sabha seats and 90 Legislative Assembly seats, a party is formed, remains functional and effective for a few years and then vanishes. If Om Prakash Chautala's INLD or Dushyant Chautala's Jannayak Party survive till date, then only one reason can be cited for it and that is the caste basis of these parties. But the vote bank of both the parties is Jat, hence the so-called national parties find it beneficial if the votes are divided into two or more parties. This would ensure better prospects for BJP and Congress. The Congress has formed its government here seven times. Devi Lal and his son Om Prakash Chautala have become Chief Ministers four times, but could complete the entire five-year term only once. And once Chaudhary Bansi Lal has also accomplished this feat. Bhupinder Singh Hooda also ran two governments under the banner of the Congress (2009-14), he also functioned more like a regional party and not like a national party. And before this, Bhajan Lal has also been the non-Jat Chief Minister of the State. Manohar Lal Khattar is running the BJP government for the last two terms.

Another characteristic of this small state politics is that the leaders here have influence over a particular region only. But the politics here runs in the name of Jat-support and Jat-opposition, albeit it does not go beyond this, and the equation keeps changing accordingly.

❑

29
Once Upon a Time - Strewn with Blood...

Heaven on earth. No one ever doubted these lines for Kashmir. Kashmir is so breathtakingly beautiful. The history of Kashmir dating back centuries has a long and glorious story. But the journey of time has many inscriptions on the pages of Kashmir - filled with both agony and ecstasy. No one knows when the beautiful leaves of poplar got strewn with blood. Various significant developments took place before and after India's independence that changed the predicament and course of Jammu and Kashmir—from the reverberating love songs in the valley to the horrific gunshots and human cries.

Jammu and Kashmir has a long political history from Maharaja Hari Singh to Dogra rulers, Abdullah and Mufti families, separatist leader, Syed Ali Shah Geelani. Shortly after Independence, on October 27, 1947, before signing the Instrument of Accession of the princely state of Jammu and Kashmir with India, Maharaja Hari Singh had both the imagination and the stubbornness of his independent country (the state). Actually Raja Hari Singh wanted to make his state a separate country from Pakistan and India. But the circumstances that occurred led to his change of stance to merge with India. Once Jammu and Kashmir was divided into five parts—Jammu, Kashmir, Ladakh we all know are in India but

Gilgit and Baltistan are under POK, i.e. Pak Occupied Kashmir. The Dogra Rajput rulers of Jammu are credited with creating a single state by binding these five parts with dauntlessness and gallantry. But if you want to get to the bottom of parties involved with Jammu and Kashmir, then it is necessary to understand the politics there.

The period of the State can be divided into three parts. Politics after independence, the advent of terrorism in 1989-90 and the abolition of Special Status of Jammu and Kashmir on August 5, 2019.

The first political party of Kashmir was the Kashmir Muslim Conference established on October 15, 1932. Sheikh Abdullah was its President, Chaudhry Ghulam Abbas as General Secretary and Maulvi Abdul Rahim as Secretary. At the launch of the party, in his Presidential address Sheikh Abdullah said that the Muslim Conference aims to fight for the rights of all the depressed sections of the society and not just the Muslims. In 1933, Sheikh Abdullah also formed a 9-member Committee whose purpose was to connect non-Muslims with the party, but the name of the party prevented it from being so. After this, Sheikh Abdullah, under the influence of Jawaharlal Nehru, called a special session of the Muslim Conference on June 24, 1938 to vote for changing the name of the party to National Conference.

Out of a total of 176 office bearers, 172 voted in favour of changing the name of the party. In this way the name of Muslim Conference was changed to National Conference. At the same time it was called that the deprived people of all caste and religion should join this party for the struggle against the monarchy of the Maharaja. American historian Burton Stein, who is credited with authoring many books on India, in his book—A History of India—writes that Kashmir had the desire to be an independent state but it was neither so old nor so large. It was like, say, Hyderabad. It was a reward given to an officer of the Sikh Empire for favouring the British after the defeat of the Sikhs in the First Anglo-Sikh War in

1846. At the time of partition in 1947, those in Pakistan were of the belief that 77 percent of the population in Kashmir is Muslim, so they will come with Pakistan. When the Maharaja showed hesitation, the Pakistani guerrillas tried to intimidate the Maharaja and force him to do so. When the Maharaja asked Mountbatten for help, he placed a condition that for this the Maharaja would have to propose a merger with India. (Stein, Burton, A History of India, Oxford University Press).

Immediately after independence, in 1948, after the dispute over Kashmir between India and Pakistan, this issue reached the United Nations. India accused Pakistan of annexing parts of Kashmir by force. The United Nations advised both countries to hold a referendum, which was never considered. Meanwhile, the first interim government was formed in Jammu and Kashmir and Sheikh Abdullah was declared the Prime Minister. A year later, in July 1949, Sheikh Abdullah, Mirza Afsal Baig, Moti Ram Bagra were made part of the Constituent Assembly and discourse began on Article 370 giving special status to the State. Soon on October 17, 1949, Article 370 was added to the Indian Constitution. This state of affairs continued till the Nehru era, but after Indira Gandhi came to power, Kashmir witnessed many incidents. In the year 1971, Pakistan had to face a humiliating defeat in the war with India and Bangladesh was formed. In 1972, the Shimla Agreement was signed between India and Pakistan wherein it was agreed to resolve the Kashmir dispute through talks. Two years later, in 1974, Sheikh Abdullah returned to the Valley and dissolved the Plebiscite Front (which was formed for a plebiscite) at the behest of PM Indira Gandhi. On February 24, 1975, Prime Minister Indira Gandhi announced that there was no scope for a plebiscite in Jammu and Kashmir. In June 1977, the Centre toppled the elected National Conference government in Jammu and Kashmir. However, in the Assembly elections that followed, the people again brought Sheikh Abdullah back to power with a majority. The politics of Jammu and Kashmir suffered a major setback when Sheikh Abdullah, who was popular, died on September 8, 1982. After his death, his son Farooq Abdullah became the Chief Minister of the province. In 1987, in the Assembly elections under his leadership, the National Conference returned to power, while the Muslim United Front (MUF) won only four seats. This was the occasion when MUF took a rebellious tone alleging election rigging. It is believed that this was the period when the foundation of terrorism was laid in the state.

Soon its effect was also visible in Jammu and Kashmir. Insurgent voices began to rise in the Valley and on December 8, 1989, the daughter of Mufti Mohammad Sayeed, the Home Minister in the Central Government, was kidnapped by the JKLF. In exchange for her release, five terrorists had to be released. After this, the Armed Forces Special Power Act (AFSPA) was implemented for the first time in Kashmir on July 5, 1990 and the army was given more power. However, only two weeks later there were attacks on Kashmiri Pandits in the Valley and a large number of Kashmiri Pandits were forced to leave the Valley and migrate to a safer place. On July 31, 1993, the Hurriyat Conference was formed in the State with a separatist attitude. In this, 26 organisations came together on one platform and raised their voice for freedom of Kashmir.

Assembly elections were held in Jammu and Kashmir in the year 1996. The National Conference got a majority in this election and Farooq Abdullah was again elected as the Chief Minister. On the other hand, on February 20, 1999, Prime Minister Atal Bihari Vajpayee's Lahore bus tour and the Lahore Declaration were signed, but the promise of peace was shattered in the same year when Pakistan infiltrated Kargil in India and captured it, but the Indian Army reclaimed it on July 26. India suffered loss of close to 450 soldiers in this short war, while between 2,900 and 3,100 of Pakistan's soldiers and its supporters were killed. Amidst these developments, on December 24, 1999, India's IC-814 plane was hijacked and taken to Kabul. In return for releasing the passengers, the terrorists demanded the release of dreaded terrorists Jaish Chief Masood Azhar, Ahmed Zargar and Sheikh Ahmed Umar Saeed. They were taken out of Kot Bhalwal Jail in Jammu and handed over to the terrorists. Jaswant Singh, the then Minister of the Government of India, took the terrorists to Kabul.

In the midst of the deteriorating situation in Kashmir, in May 2001, Prime Minister Atal Bihari Vajpayee constituted a Committee under the Chairmanship of former Minister K.C. Pant. This Committee recommended reducing the number of security forces in the valley and giving more autonomy to the State. Meanwhile, on October 1, 2001, a fidayeen attack on the Jammu and Kashmir Legislative Assembly in Srinagar resulted in the death of 37 people, 11 of them jawans. Two months later, on December 13, terrorists attacked the Parliament of India in Delhi and killed nine soldiers, however, five terrorists were also killed by the security forces.

The Janata Dal, which was once in power at the Centre, had disintegrated. In such a situation, Mufti Mohammad Sayeed, who was the Union Home Minister in the V.P. Singh government, also formed his own Party in 1999 named Jammu and Kashmir Peoples Democratic Party (PDP). In the year 2002, the party was also successful in forming the government in the State with the support of the Congress. It was part of the UPA alliance till 2009. In 2014, the PDP formed an alliance with the BJP and again formed a government in the State, which lasted until June 19, 2018 when the BJP withdrew support.

In the 2002 Assembly elections, no party got a majority but the PDP did better in the Valley while the Congress won 17 seats in the Jammu region. After much hesitation, Congress President Sonia Gandhi and PDP President Mufti Sayeed agreed to form a joint government. There was also an agreement to make the PDP Chief Minister for the first three years and the Congress Chief Minister for the remaining three years. Sayeed came up with the policy of 'Healing Touch' aimed at healing the wounds of the people of the valley. Meanwhile Manmohan Singh government came after the Vajpayee government at the Centre and on September 5, 2005, Prime Minister Manmohan Singh had a meeting with the Mirwaiz Umar Farooq faction of the Hurriyat Conference, which has been considered a moderate separatist faction. In this meeting, it was agreed to stop the violence and initiate talks, but then the Hurriyat Conference led by Syed Ali Shah Geelani rejected this meeting itself. Three years later, Ghulam Nabi Azad became the Chief Minister of the State. On May 31, 2006, with the intention of disturbing the atmosphere in Kashmir, Pakistani-backed terrorists attacked a bus of tourists from Gujarat using a grenade, in which 8 passengers lost their lives. Azad sent the tourists to Delhi in a special State plane, which earned him a lot of praise.

Meanwhile, news of PDP leader Muzaffar Hussain Baig coming close to Azad upset the PDP and he had to step down from the post of Deputy Chief Minister. A year later, in 2008, the PDP got furious over the grant of 100 acres of land to the Amarnath Shrine Board, and the dispute sparked violence across the State, in the Valley and in Jammu. The coalition government also collapsed after the PDP withdrew support. After this the situation in the valley worsened. In the year 2010, after the death of a Kashmiri youth by the security forces, the stone pelting started there. 112 people lost their lives in this violence. Then came the turn of the next election, with the support of the Congress, the National Conference government was formed and under the leadership of Omar Abdullah, efforts were made to restore peace. In the year 2011, the Chief Minister appealed to bring the youth into the mainstream by withdrawing the cases against 1,200 stone pelters.

In the politics of Jammu and Kashmir, the results of the Assembly elections in 2014 came in such a way that it implied a serious problem of representation on religious grounds. PDP got 28 seats, BJP 25, NC 15 and Congress 12 in the election. According to the seats, such a situation was being created that if PDP-NC-Congress came together in the government, then Hindus would not get an opportunity to appear in the government. After a long struggle, on March 1, 2015, after long talks, the BJP decided to form a coalition government under the leadership of Mufti Mohammad Sayeed. Senior BJP leader Professor Nirmal Kumar became the Deputy Chief Minister. There was opposition in the PDP to form the government with the BJP, however a government was formed. After the death of Mufti in January 2016, her daughter Mehbooba Mufti became the first woman Chief Minister of the State.

Terror resurfaces

During this, the security forces killed Hizbul Commander Burhan Wani, causing unrest in the valley lasting several months in which dozens lost their lives. On the other hand, on September 18, 2016, Jaish-e-Mohammed terrorists attacked the Army's Brigade Headquarters in Uri and killed 19 soldiers. The government was badly hit. India responded to this on September 28, 2016 when the Indian Army entered PoK conducting a surgical strike and killed a large number of terrorists and destroyed their base camps. Despite this, the terrorist incidents did not stop and on July 11, 2017, terrorists opened fire on a bus full of Amarnath pilgrims, killing 7 pilgrims.

On the other hand, in a big and dramatic political development, the BJP suddenly pulled out of the coalition government and the Mehbooba Mufti government came to an end. During this time Satya Pal Malik became the Governor of Jammu and Kashmir and the BJP tried to form the government with the parties of Kashmir. After six months, Governor's rule was imposed in the state. During the Governor's rule, on February 14, 2019, just before the Lok Sabha elections, terrorists carried out a major incident and killed 40 soldiers by attacking in Pulwama, Kashmir. Pakistan-based Jaish-e-Mohammed took responsibility for this attack, but on February 26, the Indian Air Force took revenge by airstrike on the Jaish camp in Balakot.

End of special status to Jammu and Kashmir

After a resounding victory in the Lok Sabha elections, on July 25, 2019, the new Home Minister Amit Shah indicated major decisions regarding Jammu and Kashmir and the Ministry deployed about 40,000 soldiers in addition to the Central Armed Police Forces in the terror-hit State. On the midnight of August 4, former Chief Ministers Mehbooba Mufti and Omar Abdullah were placed under house arrest, after which eyes were fixed on the next move of the Modi government. The very next day, Home Minister Amit Shah made a big announcement in Parliament to remove Article 370 from Jammu and Kashmir that flared up Indian politics. Along with this Article 35A was also abolished. By bifurcating the State, Jammu and Kashmir and Ladakh were made two separate Union Territories. The Opposition strongly opposed these decisions but the government called it a decision taken in the interest of the country.

A few months later, the Centre announced the election of District Development Councils in the State and its results declared on December 23 showed that the support of the people of Kashmir was with the National Conference, PDP and regional parties, while in the Jammu region the National Conference and the Congress gave a tough fight to the BJP in its stronghold. In these elections, the multi-party Gupkar alliance led by Farooq got 110 seats, the BJP 75, the Congress 26, Independents 50 and Apni Party, which is believed to be backed by the BJP, got 12 seats.

Geelani's departure

Syed Ali Shah Geelani was the biggest pro-Pakistan face of separatism in Kashmir and advocate of Independence of Kashmir. He was 92 years old at the time of his death on September 1, 2021 and was somewhat feeble. But there is no doubt that Geelani was more popular in the valley than the mainstream leaders Farooq Abdullah and Mehbooba Mufti. Thousands of people would gather at his call. Certainly, Geelani's departure has not only weakened the campaign of Jamaat-e-Islami and the Hurriyat for whom Geelani worked, but also the end of a chapter fuelling anti-India separatism.

Geelani's appeal had a tremendous impact on the Kashmiri youth. During the era of terrorism, Geelani had capitalised on his popularity in the valley and played a big role in turning the Kashmiri youth against India with his rhetoric. On an appeal by Geelani, the bustling Lal Chowk of Srinagar would drown in scary silence. Geelani's residence in Hyderpura in Srinagar was a major hub of activity. He was born on September 29, 1929 in Sopore. Till his death he stood firm on his demand for a plebiscite in Jammu and Kashmir and self-determination for Kashmiris.

Outside the Valley, people in other parts of the country would hardly know that Geelani was respectfully called 'Bob' i.e. Grandfather in the Valley. However, his counterpart and other separatist leaders also called him 'the hawk' as they alleged that Geelani's policies and ideas lacked flexibility, which did not lead to a final solution to the Jammu and Kashmir problem.

In fact, Geelani had also become an MLA thrice in the elections under the Election Commission of India from the Sopore constituency, winning thrice to the Jammu and Kashmir Legislative Assembly. However, after winning in 1972, 1977 and 1987, in 1990 with the onset of terrorism in Kashmir, Geelani became vocal against the elections and appealed to the public for its boycott. Despite his appeal, a large number of people took part in the Assembly elections and Panchayat elections of 2002 and 2008. There were also many critics of Geelani in Kashmir who alleged that Geelani instigated the youth of Kashmir to pelt stones, but himself has made both his sons doctors.

Geelani was the founder of the Hurriyat Conference, a hard-core group of separatist organisations in Jammu and Kashmir, and was the most influential leader of 26 separatist organisations.

However, Geelani broke away from the Hurriyat in 2003 and announced a separate organisation named Tehreek-e-Hurriyat. He was also placed under House arrest after the abrogation of Article 370. In June 2020, he disassociated himself from the Hurriyat.

Big faces in politics

Farooq Abdullah / Omar Abdullah: Sheikh Mohammed Abdullah's son Farooq Abdullah is the towering leader of the National Conference. Farooq, who was the Chief Minister for four times, is considered a cool man. From carrying actress Shabana Azmi as pillion rider on his bullet on the streets of Srinagar to playing tambola, singing bhajans at Asha Ram Bapu's programmes and dancing to film songs at parties, Farooq has had a different personality. His opponents have also been a fan of his personality. Senior Rajasthan Congress leader Sachin Pilot is the son-in-law of Farooq Abdullah.

He is the only leader in Jammu and Kashmir to have a personal identity with the leaders of political parties across the country, including major national political parties like BJP and Congress. He is as popular in the Kashmir Valley as in the Hindu-dominated areas of Jammu. This is the reason that in the DDC elections in late 2020, his Party National Conference got the support of the people in the BJP and Congress-dominated Jammu region and was successful in winning seats.

Farooq Abdullah's family is a kind of mini Hindustan. His wife Molly is a Christian while Farooq's daughter Sarah is married to Sachin Pilot, a Hindu. Payal Nath, wife of his son and former Chief Minister Omar Abdullah, was from a Hindu family, who now lives separately from him.

After the MBBS, Farooq went to London for medical practice, where he met Molly, who is a Christian from London. Before marriage, Molly was a nurse. Farooq and Molly have four children, three daughters and one son. The names of the daughters are Safia, Hina and Sarah while the son Omar Abdullah has been the Chief Minister.

Those very close to Farooq Abdullah, known for his controversial statements in politics, however, believe that Farooq truly loves India. Farooq is purely secular and has memorised more Hindu hymns than any Hindu leader can possibly claim. However, his statements create a storm in politics. As Farooq recently said that with the arrival of the Taliban, he hopes for good governance in Afghanistan and justice for all. Sometimes what he actually wants to say is misconstrued as something else.

He supports talks with Pakistan for peace in Kashmir, however, he has been a part of the BJP-led NDA to the Congress-led UPA. At present, Farooq, who is keeping distance from the BJP, is fighting to restore the status quo in Jammu and Kashmir before August 5, 2019 and is demanding the conduct of Assembly elections.

His son Omar Abdullah has also been the Chief Minister of the State. At present, Omar is the President of the National Conference. In 2000, Farooq handed over the responsibility of the party to son Omar Abdullah, who had previously served as Minister of State for External Affairs in the Vajpayee government from October 1999 to July 2001 in the NDA government. In 2009, he became the Chief Minister of the coalition government with the Congress and remained the Chief Minister of the state till 2015.

Sheikh Abdullah, popularly known as Sher-e-Kashmir, formed a political party called All Jammu and Kashmir Muslim Conference on October 15, 1932, with the support of Chaudhry Ghulam Abbas, although it was later renamed as Jammu Kashmir National Conference (JKNC). In the first election of September 1951, the National Conference won all 75 seats in the Assembly and Sheikh Abdullah became the Prime Minister of Kashmir. However, he was later dismissed and arrested. Even in 1965, the National Conference merged with the Congress amid many ups and downs. But after the 1977 elections, Sheikh Abdullah again became the Chief Minister of Kashmir and by then the party had its own separate identity. After Sheikh's death in 1982, Farooq Abdullah became the Chief Minister. Under Farooq's leadership, the party won the elections again in 1983 but Abdullah's brother-in-law Ghulam Mohammad Shah broke the party. Farooq's government was dismissed; Ghulam became the Chief Minister. After the 1987 elections, Farooq was again elected as the Chief Minister. In the 1996 elections, Abdullah won 57 of the 87 Assembly seats. Farooq's Party has been in favour of giving autonomy to Jammu and Kashmir.

Mufti Mohammad Sayeed/Mehbooba Mufti

Mufti Mohammad Sayeed was once one of the stalwarts of the Congress. He strengthened the Congress in Jammu and Kashmir but left the Congress in 1999 with his daughter, Youth Congress leader Mehbooba Mufti, and formed the Jammu and Kashmir Peoples Democratic Party (JKPDP). Mufti Mohammad Sayeed, who was once the Union Home Minister and then Chief Minister of Jammu and Kashmir, was also called the 'thinker' of the politics of Jammu and Kashmir.

His political journey started with the National Conference in 1950, but in 1959 he left the NC and formed the Democratic National Conference. He later merged with the Congress like the National Conference and became the Head of the Congress in Jammu and Kashmir. In 1987, he left the Congress also and formed the PDP. He became the Union Home Minister in the V.P. Singh government. In the 2002 Assembly elections, the PDP won 16 seats and formed the government with its own old party Congress and remained the Chief Minister for three years.

When Ghulam Nabi Azad became the Chief Minister, Mufti's daughter Mehbooba Mufti was offered to become the Deputy Chief Minister but she offered the position to the party's trusted senior leader Muzaffar Hussain Baig. After this PDP won 21 seats in the 2008 Assembly elections but this time the NC formed the government with Congress support. The PDP's performance in 2014 was the best when it won 28 seats, formed the government with the BJP and Mufti Sayeed became the Chief Minister. In the Lok Sabha elections too, it won a record 3 seats. But in 2016 Mufti died and his daughter Mehbooba Mufti became the Chief Minister. But this alliance did not last long and the government fell in 2018 after the BJP withdrew support. Mehbooba is currently part of the Gupkar alliance.

Mufti Mohammad Sayeed, who was an opponent of the National Conference and the Abdullah family and a strong Congress leader till 1999, has always been in favour of greater autonomy for Kashmir. The Mufti was in favour of giving Kashmir not freedom but more decision-making powers, contrary to the National Conference's demand for autonomy. While in the Congress, he never made adverse remarks about the Constitution but was in favour to pressurise Delhi to pay heed to the voice of the people of Kashmir. Like Abdullah, he demanded for talks with Pakistan. While in the Congress, Mufti was recognised as a different and big leader, and those who opposed Abdullah family politics in Kashmir joined him. During this time, he desired to form a separate Party. In 1999, he left the Congress and formed his own party, the PDP. The PDP has always been considered a political party with a divergence of opinion between the mainstream and the separatist ideology as it is supposed to be advocating for giving more rights to the people of Kashmir. The party has also been accused of supporting some terrorist organizations, however, the PDP leadership has denied this.

Despite being a uni-polar party in Kashmir politics, in 2017 the PDP surprised the country's political pundits when it formed a post-poll alliance with the arch-rival BJP to form the government. Mufti Sayeed headed this coalition government. After his sudden death his daughter Mehbooba Mufti also continued the alliance with BJP. The idea behind Mufti going with the BJP was that his image would improve by going with a Party of opposite ideology. However, the PDP is believed to have suffered adversely due to this in Kashmir. Some of their leaders left the party. However, in Kashmir, the PDP is still considered a political party with the second largest mass base after the National Conference.

Sajjad Lone/People's Conference

Sajjad Lone is the son of former separatist leader Abdul Gani Lone, who was assassinated in 2002 by unknown gunmen. Sajjad Lone once addressed Prime Minister Narendra Modi as his elder brother and called himself a friend of BJP. Even today, political experts consider him the 'face of BJP' in Kashmir in future. In 2018, when the BJP withdrew support to the PDP government, Lone had at one point reached the threshold of becoming Chief Minister. Then the BJP was preparing for its government by breaking the PDP and with the help of MLAs of other parties, but it did not fructify.

Lone's Party was a constituent of the PDP-BJP government and interestingly, Lone himself was a Minister in this government from the BJP's side. However, Lone's Party People's Conference had only two seats in the State Assembly. At that time senior PDP leader and former Deputy Chief Minister Muzaffar Hussain Baig was also prepared to support Lone. Lone is now with the Gupkar alliance led by Farooq Abdullah.

When the Central Government on August 5, 2019, abolished the Special Status of Jammu and Kashmir and withdrew Article 370, the status of the State was changed to a Union Territory. Along with this, Ladakh was separated from Jammu and Kashmir and it was also made a UT. Many leaders of the Valley were imprisoned for several months. The outline of the Gupkar was laid at the residence of National Conference President Farooq Abdullah when eight political parties of Kashmir held a joint meeting on August 4, 2019. In the meeting, these parties of Jammu and Kashmir announced to form this alliance against the

State policies of the central government. At that time, although the Modi government had not announced the withdrawal of Article 370 and Article 35A from the state, the deployment of the Army was increased. After the end of the special status of the state, these leaders again met at Farooq Abdullah's residence and announced the formation of an alliance which was called the Gupkar alliance. The coalition has made a Gupkar declaration, in which there has been a demand for the withdrawal of Article 370 and Article 35A. Not only this, they also demanded to restore the Constitution of Jammu and Kashmir and its statehood. With these demands made to the central government in the announcement, it was said, we will continue to fight till the old condition of the State is restored. The division of the state is absolutely unacceptable and we unanimously reiterate that without our unity, we cannot do anything. The declaration passed by the parties of this coalition further stated that the decisions of the Central Government on August 5, 2019, were unconstitutional, aimed at depriving Jammu and Kashmir of its rights and challenging the basic identity of its people. "We would like to assure the people that all our political activities will be on the way to the return of Jammu and Kashmir's status by August 4, 2019," the joint statement said.

The interesting thing is that BJP has described Gupkar as anti-national, but after the release of leaders this year, Prime Minister Narendra Modi and Home Minister Amit Shah held a meeting with all these parties in Delhi on June 24 regarding Kashmir.

In fact on August 22, 2020, seven political parties were together. The National Conference, PDP, People's Conference, Congress, CPI(M), People's United Front, Panthers Party and Awami National Conference participated in the meeting. However, the Congress later stayed away from it and also contested the DDC elections separately. At present, the Gupkar alliance is active and it is also possible that if Assembly elections are held, they will fight together.

❑

30
JMM - History of a Prolonged Struggle

Jharkhand has been identified with forests, trees, mountains, iron and coal mines and tribal communities. The tribal community, which wrote the story of a long struggle against exploitation and neglect, staged a movement for a separate State for more than five decades. In the Mughal period, this region was known as 'Khukra'. In the British era, it came to be known as Jharkhand. According to historians who considered mythology as part of history, Chhotanagpur was called 'Murand' in the Vayu Purana and 'Munda' in Vishnu Purana. Surrounded by forests and mountains, the wild region not only got historical and mythological recognition as Jharkhand, but in 2000, the Parliament of the country recognised a separate province with this name as the 28th state of the country. When the Bihar Reorganisation Bill, 2000 was passed by Parliament, this southern part of Bihar was separated from it and renamed as Jharkhand. The tribal community living in many parts of Jharkhand is known for their uniqueness. The north-eastern part of Jharkhand is called Santal Pargana. The tribal community living in this area adjoining Bihar and Bengal is called Santali. Apart from Santal Pargana, tribal communities in the northern region of Chhotanagpur are also called Santalis. On the other hand, the land area of Jharkhand spread over south and south-east is called Kolhan. The tribal community living here comes from the 'Ho' community. Apart from Ho, Munda and Santali also live here. The tribal community in the central and south-west of Jharkhand is called Munda and Oraon.

The story of Jharkhand Mukti Morcha is interesting. Jharkhand Mukti Morcha means Morcha formed for liberation. In Jharkhand, many parties emerged and vanished, but the Jharkhand Mukti Morcha stayed on. On February 4, 1972, the Jharkhand Mukti Morcha was formed in Kolanchal and witnessed many ups and downs on the way with a number of sharp twists and turns, and today the Jharkhand Mukti Morcha has reached a point without which Jharkhand politics has no power. The role of 'Trimurti' is considered to be of paramount importance in the formation of Jharkhand Mukti Morcha. 'Trimurti', i.e. Binod Bihari Mahato, A.K. Rai and Shibu Soren. The credit for the foundation of Jharkhand Mukti Morcha goes to these three personalities in its journey to liberate Jharkhand. Shibu Soren is now the only idol left in the trimurti. The other two companions could not walk farther in the way of life, but they gradually left the path of politics long ago.

The Jharkhand Mukti Morcha was formed taking inspiration from international thinking against exploitation, oppression and the "right to self-determination of nationalities" by renowned thinkers such as Karl Marx and Lenin. A.K. Rai was a native of West Bengal. He was a chemical engineer at the fertiliser factory in Sindri. In 1966, there was a strike by the workers and he quit his job quoting the strike as justified. He then joined the CPI(M) and started struggling for the workers. He contested twice from Sindri and became an MLA of CPI(M) in 1967 and 1969. But later, after differences with the party, he formed a Marxist Coordination Committee and contested under it and became an MLA in 1972. After coming in contact with Binod Bihari Mahato and Shibu Soren, he strongly supported the formation of Jharkhand Mukti Morcha in 1973. Ideologically, he continued to support the Jharkhand Mukti Morcha. He wrote many books of which Jharkhand to Lalkhand, New Direction of Jharkhand Movement and Jharkhand ek Colony were prominent.

Advocate Binod Bihari Mahato was not only a combative, struggling and pro-workers leader of the CPI(M) but also an educationist, a well-known lawyer and social reformer. Binod Babu was from Giridih, belonging to the Kurmi community. Not only was he educated, but also had a sound financial standing as he belonged to the khetihar family. The third person Shibu Soren hailed from Nemra village near Ramgarh (now Ramgarh is an independent district) in the then Hazaribagh district. Shibu Soren's childhood name was Shivcharan Manjhi. His father was Sobaran Manjhi, a teacher by profession, a freedom fighter against British Rule. He followed Gandhian philosophy. Shivcharan Manjhi was a 16-year-old student when the village's domineering contractors and moneylenders killed his father. This was the biggest event in Shibu Soren's life that turned the course of his life. After the murder of his father Sobaran Manjhi in 1957, Shibu Soren intended to surrender his life against exploitation and repression. His mother had said, "My son will definitely take revenge on these killers." He somehow completed his education up to matriculation, assuming the burden of his family which was then in a poor financial condition. He used to study as well as work as a labourer to run his family. He had cut the soil in the same Marafari (people knew Bokaro by this name only) and worked as a labourer in BSL. In 1966, Shibu Soren came out openly against the Mahajani system. Then he launched an agitation against the mahajans and the moneylenders. In many places, he harvested the crops of mahajans sowed in the tribal fields. In the campaign Shibu Soren received overwhelming support from tribals and natives. In 1969, the then President Dr. Zakir Husain promulgated an Ordinance. The Ordinance provided for the return of the land seized by tribals within 30 years from 1969.

Shibu Soren was also jailed several times during the agitation against moneylenders and mahajani practices. Shibu Soren also had to stay in Dhanbad jail in the same vein. In those days, noted IAS officer K.B. Saxena was posted as Deputy Commissioner District Officer of Dhanbad. DC (District Officer) K.B. Saxena was actually impressed by Shibu Soren's agitation. He wanted this young man to use his energy and leadership capacity in the right direction. Meanwhile, Shibu Soren had opened an ashram in Pokhria, a hilly area of the Tundi block of Dhanbad. Here he used to run a night school. He motivated the Santali community to be aware, to give up drugs and to study. Saxena suggested that Shibu Soren should focus his movement in rural areas. If you go to the cities, you will be caught. Under the 20-point programme, Saxena provided land-liberation of tribals, tractors for development of collective farming, night school, book-copy to tribal students and a jeep to Shibu Soren. Binod Bihari Mahato was contesting for the Dhanbad Lok Sabha seat from CPI(M) in 1971. It was during the elections that he met Shibu Soren at Jainamod in Bokaro. Binod Babu urged Shibu Soren to come together to campaign for his election. Shibu Soren agreed. Then Shibu Soren gradually came under the influence of Binod Bihari Mahato. After the Lok Sabha elections, Shibu Soren came to Dhanbad and started living with Binod Bihari Mahato. Inspired by Binod Bihari Mahato, Shibu Soren set up an organisation called 'Sonot Santal Samaj' to intensify the movement and took his movement from village to village. Binod Bihari Mahato had already formed the Shivaji Samaj in 1969 to educate, organise and sensitise the Kurmi community. Shivaji Samaj played a seminal role in the development of the society by removing the evils of the society, educating and sensitising the people. He opened schools in villages in the area where there were no schools. About 32 schools were opened in Dhanbad, Giridih, Bokaro and Hazaribagh areas. Binod Bihari Mahato created political awareness within the society.

On February 4, 1972, leaders of Binod Bihari Mahato's Shivaji Samaj and Shibu Soren's Sonot Santal Samaj met at the residence of Binod Bihari Mahato, a well-known lawyer and philanthropist of Kolanchal, at Dhanbad Chiragoda. The meeting was chaired by Binod Bihari Mahato himself, Shibu Soren of Sonot Santal Samaj, then MLA of Sindri A.K. Rai were specially present. Apart from this, former King of Katras, Purnendu Narayan Singh also attended the meeting. Shibu Soren's Sonot Santal Samaj and Binod Babu's Shivaji Samaj got merged. The merger of two social organisations created a new political party. Binod Bihari Mahato presided over the meeting and described the exploiting mafia section of society as his enemy. In 1971, he proposed the name of a new political party, referring to the role of 'Bangla Desh Mukti Vahini' for the liberation of Bangladesh and 'Kashmir Mukti Morcha'. Binod Bihari Mahato proposed the formation of a political party. All those present at the meeting agreed to the proposal. February 4, 1972 proved to be a historic day for Jharkhand.

A.K. Rai suggested the formation of a new political party as Jharkhand Liberation Front. Shibu Soren asked him the meaning of the Jharkhand liberation front. A.K. Rai translated it as- Jharkhand Mukti Morcha. Thus in Jharkhand, a regional political party 'Jharkhand Mukti Morcha' emerged which has now completed 50 years. Binod Bihari Mahato became the first President of Jharkhand Mukti Morcha. Former Raja Purnendu Narayan Singh and Shibu Soren were appointed as General Secretary and Vice Presidents respectively. Teklal Mahato and Chudamani Mahato were elected as Secretary and Treasurer. Then, on February 4, 1973, the first open session of the Jharkhand Mukti Morcha was held at the Golf Ground, which proved to be historic. More than one lakh people attended this session. By 7 pm, the number of participants in the session was increasing. Binod Bihari Mahato and Shibu Soren's jay-jaykaar echoed the entire Kolanchal. The slogans of creating Jharkhand a separate state which would be free from any exploitation were heard aloud.

Jharkhand Mukti Morcha General Secretary Shibu Soren moved several important proposals in the session. Among them were proposals such as making Jharkhand a new state, protecting the Chhotanagpur Tenancy Act and the Santal Pargana Tenancy Act, returning the land forcibly occupied by Mahajans and Sudkhors.

Beginning from Kolanchal the Jharkhand Mukti Morcha movement spread to Santhal Pargana, Kolhan and then all over Jharkhand. People associated with Jharkhand movement gradually joined Jharkhand Mukti Morcha. In Santhal Pargana, veteran leaders from their region like Simon Marandi, Suraj Mandal, Nirmal Mahato, Shailendra Mahato and Devendra Manjhi from Kolhan also joined JMM. Jharkhand Mukti Morcha President Binod Bihari Mahato due to his advancing age had shun active politics. Jharkhand Mukti Morcha was completely under Shibu Soren's command. When Shibu Soren became the President, Nirmal Mahato became General Secretary and Suraj Mandal Vice President. Nirmal Mahato, a young and strong leader of the region, was assassinated in 1987. After his murder, Shailendra Mahato was made the new General Secretary of the Morcha. The trio of Shibu Soren, Suraj Mandal and Shailendra Mahato remained the face of JMM for a long time. Political developments occurred. Four Jharkhand Mukti Morcha leaders Shibu Soren, Suraj Mandal, Shailendra Mahato and Simon Marandi were booked in an alleged bribery case during the Congress regime. All were arrested and sent to jail. Shailendra Mahato turned hostile. Later on, he joined the BJP. He was replaced by Sunil Mahato, another domineering leader of Jamshedpur. He was killed by naxalites in 2008. After that the Late Nirmal Mahato's younger brother Sudhir Mahato was made General Secretary of the party.

In Jharkhand, the ruling Jharkhand Mukti Morcha has become a youth team now. The supreme leader of Jhamumo is Shibu Soren. State Chief Minister Hemant Soren holds the post of Executive Chairman of Jharkhand Mukti Morcha. Among the other members of his family, Shibu Soren's elder daughter-in-law Sita Soren is the Central Vice President and youngest son Basant Soren is the President of the Youth Front of the Jharkhand Mukti Morcha. The Jharkhand Mukti Morcha has made a strong presence in the Bihar

Assembly, Lok Sabha, Rajya Sabha and Jharkhand Assembly. The Jharkhand Mukti Morcha has been gaining weightage in the electoral politics of Jharkhand as well as Bihar, Bengal and Odisha. The impact of the Jharkhand Mukti Morcha can be seen in the border areas of Bihar, Bengal and Odisha adjoining Jharkhand. Jharkhand Mukti Morcha is in power after winning the highest record of 30 seats in the 2019 elections to the Jharkhand Assembly (total seats 81, one nomination).

It is also true that the Jharkhand Mukti Morcha even after doing so much could not accomplish all that everyone expected. So far, 11 State Governments have been formed in Jharkhand. Five of them were led by the Jharkhand Mukti Morcha, while at two occasions the government was formed and run with the help of JMM. Shibu Soren emerged as pivotal in this game of politics. Shibu Soren himself became Chief Minister for three terms while his second son Hemant Soren ruled over the State for the second time. The Jharkhand Mukti Morcha aligned with Congress three times to form the government and lead the government, while two times it joined hands with BJP to form the government. Even at a time JMM supported independent MLA Madhu Koda and let him form the government. In 2005, he was in government only for 10 days. But his party never crossed the 41-majority mark alone.

The penetration of the Jharkhand Mukti Morcha is truly visible in the villages. On the other hand, the urban voters rely on the Bharatiya Janata Party. Looking at the Jharkhand Vidhan Sabha Result 2019, Jharkhand Mukti Morcha was able to form the government by winning 30 seats from the villages. Out of these, 20 are reserved seats, in which Scheduled Tribe candidates have won. Tribal leaders of Congress have won six reserved seats. Of the 81 assembly seats in Jharkhand, 28 seats are reserved for tribals in proportion to the population. Jharkhand Mukti Morcha and Congress hold 26 out of 28 seats; this is the biggest factor in the formation of the government. Ever since the Bharatiya Janata Party has been winning 14-15 seats out of these 28 reserved seats.

But the previous BJP government took many anti-tribal decisions, due to which the party had to bear the brunt in the elections. The tribals of Jharkhand consider the Chhotanagpur Tenancy Act and Santal Pargana Tenancy Act no less than any scripture. The previous BJP government angered the tribals by bringing up a proposal to change these laws. This made the tribal voters completely turn away from the BJP. Anyhow, the Bharatiya Janata Party has a strong hold in the urban region. The Jharkhand Mukti Morcha's roots can weaken politically only when the Bharatiya Janata Party can restore its faith in the villages, especially with the tribal community. Morcha Chief Shibu Soren is quite popular among Santal tribals. Jharkhand Mukti Morcha, by capitalising on this popularity, succeeds in getting maximum votes in the tribal areas. As long as Shibu Soren remains with Jharkhand Mukti Morcha, his party will get the votes of Santal Samaj. The aura of Shibu Soren inspires many people to come out of the village and countryside and reach the Assembly, to the Lok Sabha. Under his mentorship, both tribal and non-tribal people became leaders and made their mark.

Still it has been the influence of Shibu Soren's aura that many persons coming from remote villages have reached the Lok Sabha. It was his own ability and mettle that he has made his mark by becoming both a tribal and non-tribal leader. Shibu Soren's entire family is not only fully active in the politics of the state today but has also succeeded in making it to electoral politics. After Shibu Soren, his eldest son Durga Soren (now late) was elected to the Assembly thrice. His daughter-in-law Sita Soren has also become an MLA for the third time after his untimely demise. His second son Hemant Soren became an MLA for the third time and Jharkhand chief Minister for the second time. Shibu Soren's youngest son Basant Soren has also won the by-election. Shibu Soren's third generation is also preparing to enter politics.

Though JMM has a people's movement as its foundation, its leader has always been entangled in judicial cases. The political momentum of the Jharkhand Mukti Morcha was thwarted by these cases. Chirudih Naransanhar, Shashinath Jha murder and MP bribery scandal tarnished the political sheen of the Jharkhand Mukti Morcha. Shibu Soren also had to step down as Union Minister due to these cases.

Chirudih case: Jharkhand's much talked about leader and Jharkhand Mukti Morcha Supremo Shibu Soren has been acquitted after 32 years of legal battle in the notorious Chirudih massacre case. In 1975, there was a fierce conflict between two communities in a village called Chirudih in which 13 people were killed. Though Shibu Soren was not named in the preliminary report of the case, the charge-sheet filed in December 1979 named 69 people, including Shibu Soren. Thereafter, the matter was closed. But in 2004, the matter was reopened and a warrant was issued against Soren from the Jamtara Court. In the Jamtara court hearing, 14 persons including Shibu Soren were acquitted while 7 others were convicted.

Shibu Soren was sentenced to life imprisonment in 2006 in a lower Court in the murder of his personal secretary Shashinath Jha. But in 2007, the Delhi High Court quashed the lower Court's verdict. Shashinath Jha's family moved to the Supreme Court in 2007 against the verdict. But the Supreme Court granted a huge relief to Shibu Soren while upholding the Delhi High Court's verdict and dismissing the appeal of the Jha family and the CBI.

In 1993, to save Narasimha Rao's government of the Congress, four Jharkhand Mukti Morcha MPs, including Shibu Soren, were accused of bribery citing that money given to JMM Chief Shibu Soren and three erstwhile MPs - Suraj Mandal, Simon Marandi and Shailendra Mahato was a bribe. The four leaders had admitted during the Trial under the Prevention of Corruption Act that they had received money from the Congress Party in 1993 to vote in favour of the central government's vote of confidence. He was acquitted of bribery charges following the Supreme Court verdict in the case. The Supreme Court had then said that MPs have special exemption under Article 105 of the Constitution. This article deals with the rights and privileges of Parliament and its Members. It provides that no action will be taken in any Court against any MP in the matter of speeches or voting in Parliament.

Shibu Soren may be physically tired, but his existence in active politics is still a source of internal vigour for the Jharkhand Mukti Morcha. Hemant Soren is fully matured and ready to take over his long political legacy. Hemant Soren has learnt every trick of politics after he took over the Chief Minister's chair for the second time. Second generation leaders of the Jharkhand Mukti Morcha have gradually evolved. Daughter-in-law Sita Soren, younger son Basant Soren have now become adept players of electoral politics. Hemant Soren has formed a team composed of both veteran party leaders as well as youngsters. The Congress managed to achieve the best result ever on its own as it won the 2019 elections. In the Jharkhand Assembly, Congress has won the highest number of 16 seats so far. Hemant Soren, who is leading a 50-MLA government with coalition parties, is the leader of non-BJP parties.

But in the last two years, Hemant Soren is surrounded with many charges of corruption. Soren was accused of corruption in February by BJP MLAs, who said that the CM had issued a mining licence to himself in Ranchi's Angara block while in office. Governor Ramesh Bais, a former BJP minister, had referred the matter to the ECI and, depending on the election body's recommendation, will take a call on Soren's disqualification. There are also PIL's in the Jharkhand High Court demanding a probe by central agencies against the CM in alleged irregularities in mining allotments.

But no one can deny the role of Hemant Soren in Jharkhand politics in coming days, in power or without power.

Jharkhand Party

January 20, 1939 is a golden page, a memorable day in the history of Jharkhand. This day is marked with the expression of the emotional agony of Jharkhand's identity, existence and identity. Lakhs of tribal Jharkhandis had declared their battle for recognition on this day. A massive rally of All India Adivasi Mahasabha was held in Ranchi which was attended by a large number of men and women. On the same day, in the event of various tribal leaders at a large public meeting, Jaipal Singh was unanimously elected President of the All India Adivasi Mahasabha. The expert, combative leadership that Jharkhand was exploring was completed by Jaipal Singh Munda. Leading the Adivasi Mahasabha, Jaipal Singh, with political expertise and distinguished leadership capacity, gave a series of setbacks to the Congress by achieving tremendous success in the local bodies election. Gradually, the political expansion of the Tribal General Assembly continued. After completing his Class XII at Augustine College in 1920, he was admitted to St. Johns College, Oxford University, London, in 1922. At Oxford University, he completed his MA and achieved equal success in hockey. He played in many places by forming a hockey team of Indian youths. He was the captain of the Indian hockey team at the 1928 Olympics in Amsterdam and brought glory to India by giving India an unexpected victory in hockey matches. The Congress nominated Jaipal Singh as a Member of the Constituent Assembly in 1946 honouring his ability and agility. As a result of his initiative, struggle and continuous efforts, the Constitution provided for reservation for Scheduled Tribes.

Under Jaipal Singh Munda's skilled leadership the Adivasi Mahasabha in the southern part of Bihar had become a major political force in Chhotanagpur and Santhal Pargana. After the Independence of the country, Jaipal Singh, a member of the Constituent Assembly and President of the All India General Assembly, prepared a report on the States of Chhotanagpur, their merger and provincial unity, which was presented to the Constituent Assembly on March 15, 1948. In time, the Adivasi Mahasabha decided to formally assume itself as a political party to enrich its political character.

On December 31, 1949 and January 1, 1950, in a 02 day Sammelan at Karandih Maidan in Jamshedpur, attended by thousands of leaders, workers and general public, Adivasi

Mahasabha was renamed as the Jharkhand Party to act as a political one. Jaipal Singh Munda was appointed as the first President of the Jharkhand Party.

In 1952, the first Lok Sabha and Rajya Sabha were held across the country. The Jharkhand Party achieved huge success in these elections. In Bihar, Jharkhand Party won 32 seats in the Rajya Sabha. Jharkhand Party also bagged four seats in the Lok Sabha elections. In a way, the 1952 election result was a mandate for the State of Jharkhand. For ten years, the Jharkhand Party struggled hard for a separate state. But the Congress leadership of Bihar was not in favour of creating a separate state in Jharkhand. So, the entire Jharkhand Party, including Jaipal Singh, kept struggling. Meanwhile, several areas of Jharkhand were divided during the formation of the States of Bengal and Odisha. This was a blow to the proposal to form a separate State of Jharkhand. Manbhum area of Bihar was merged with Bengal. The struggle and movement politics of the Jharkhand Party did not attain anything significant.

Ten years later, on June 20, 1963, the Jharkhand Party merged with the Congress. Prime Minister Jawaharlal Nehru sent a proposal to Jaipal Singh to merge the Jharkhand Party with the Congress to make it possible to convince the Congress Party members to form the Jharkhand state. Pandit Nehru cited the example of Gujarat, Andhra Pradesh in support of his proposal. This was a golden chance for Jaipal Singh to build Jharkhand when the Prime Minister himself was taking the initiative to create a political atmosphere in this direction.

This initiative of Pandit Nehru and Jaipal Singh was welcomed by Bihar Chief Minister Pandit Binodanand Jha. On June 20, 1963, the Jharkhand Party merged with the Congress in Ranchi. A large public meeting was organised by the Jharkhand Party on the occasion. Odisha Chief Minister Biju Patnaik, Bengal's Praful Chandra Sen, Atulya Ghosh were present. Bihar Chief Minister Binodanand Jha and his cabinet members were present in the House. Jaipal Singh announced the merger of the Jharkhand Party with Congress.

Bihar Chief Minister Binodanand Jha inducted Jaipal Singh in his Cabinet after the Jharkhand Party merger with the Congress and was made Community Development Minister. But a month later, under the Kamaraj Scheme, Chief Minister Binodanand Jha had to resign from his post. K.B. Sahai was made the Chief Minister of Bihar after the incident. Congress leaders began designing their conspiracy. Jaipal Singh was removed from the post of Minister and replaced by his close aide Sushil Kumar Baghe as Minister. The Congress gradually started its policy of Divide and Rule within the party. Time changed. After Nehruji's death, a great chapter in history came to an end.

Jaipal Singh was later accused of selling away the Jharkhand movement since the Jharkhand Party merged with the Congress. The Jharkhand people did not accept the merger and refused to join the Congress. Jaipal Singh's aggressiveness before joining the Congress was now absent. Jaipal Singh's dream of Jharkhand State remained unfulfilled. Jaipal Singh won the 1967 general election from Khunti Lok Sabha as a Congress Party candidate. He was earlier a Member of Parliament of the Jharkhand Party in the 1952, 1957 and 1962 general elections. Jaipal Singh, who was plagued by the merger of the Jharkhand Party with the Congress and the continued neglect of the Congress Party, passed away on March 20, 1970 at his residence in Delhi. Addressing a meeting near Ranchi railway station on March 13, 1970, 11 days before his death, Jaipal Singh had said, "Merging the Jharkhand Party with the Congress was the biggest mistake of my life. I will return to the Jharkhand Party and Jharkhand will again strive for a separate State." But after that the Jharkhand Party could not retain its momentum and form.

The party's Central Executive has also become inactive. Enos Ekka, who was the last MLA of the Jharkhand Party, lost the 2019 elections. He is currently serving a jail term in a murder case.

❑

Political Parties of the North-East

31
The Government Supreme

North-East India is actually the seven states, also known as the Seven Sisters. These include Assam, Arunachal Pradesh, Manipur, Meghalaya, Mizoram, Nagaland and Tripura. You have already read about the politics of Assam and the regional parties in the previous chapter. In this chapter we will read about the regional parties of the remaining six states.

A research by V. Venkata Rao was published in The Indian Journal of Political Science (Vol. 48, No. 4, October-December 1987) titled Government and Politics in North-East India. It defined the North-East as a region that is bounded by Bangladesh, Bhutan and Tibet (China) and connects to the mainland with West Bengal and Bihar. It is a remote area surrounded by high mountains, beautiful green valleys and many small and big rivers.

Here we will try to understand the politics of the North-East along with its geography. First of all, out of these seven states let's talk about the politics and regional parties of Arunachal Pradesh .

Arunachal Pradesh

Arunachal Pradesh has only two Lok Sabha seats and a 60-member Assembly. National parties here are Indian National Congress and Bharatiya Janata Party. Apart from this, other parties of the country - National People's Party, National Congress Party, Trinamool

Congress Party, Trinamool Congress and Janata Dal (United) have also participated in the elections here. The main regional Party is the People's Party of Arunachal Pradesh (PPA). Apart from this, there are some parties, which were formed after breaking away from other parties. These include Arunachal Congress, Arunachal Congress (Mithi) and Congress Dolo.

The PPA was formed in 1977 by Beckin Pertin. Among its founding office bearers were Oken Lego and El Wanglet. At that time the P.K. Thungan government of the Congress ruled in the State. Tomo Riba also joined the PPA by resigning from the Thungan government and became the party's Vice-President.

Arunachal Congress also used to be a regional Party of Arunachal Pradesh, which was carved out of Congress. In 1996, Gegong Apang rebelled against the leadership of P.V. Narasimha Rao and formed a separate Party called Arunachal Congress in the State. 54 MLAs from the 60-member Assembly had joined the new party along with Apang. In the 1998 Lok Sabha elections, the party won both the seats in the State. After that the Arunachal Congress became a Founding member of the BJP-led National Democratic Front.

In 1998, there was a revolt in the Arunachal Congress also. Party MP Wangcha Rajkumar, who won from Arunachal East seat both in 1996 and 1998, accused Apang of running nepotism in the party, Because Apang had made his son Omek Apang in his place a Minister in the Atal government of the Centre. Apang expelled Rajkumar and five Ministers of the State, who supported him, from the party. One of these Ministers, Mukut Mithi, formed the Arunachal Congress (Mithi) and formed the government by taking along 40 MLAs with him. Surprisingly, both the Arunachal Congress and the Arunachal Congress (Mithi) both were in the Atal Government at the Centre, but just before the 1999 Lok Sabha elections, the Arunachal Congress (Mithi) merged with the Congress, while the Arunachal Congress contested the elections in alliance with the BJP. But this alliance lost in both the seats.

Apang's son Omek Apang from Arunachal West also could not win the election. Rajkumar, who was contesting on a Congress ticket from Arunachal East seat, defeated the BJP candidate.

The Lok Sabha elections were to be held in 2004, but before that on July 25, 2003, there was another split in the State unit of Congress and Congress (Dolo) was formed by Kameng Dolo, a Congress leader from Arunachal. Gegong Apang took advantage of this split of the Congress to form a new front called United Democratic Front, in which Parties separated from Congress and BJP along with 41 MLAs were shown to support and he took oath as the Chief Minister of the State. The result of all this exercise was that Apang along with all his 41 MLAs joined the BJP on August 30. With this, the BJP government was formed for the first time in the State and the entire term of the Congress (Dolo) Party was only one month and five days.

Though Apang joined the BJP along with the MLAs, the Arunachal Congress continued as a Party. Arunachal Congress announced to boycott the 2004 elections over the Chakma and Hajong refugees issue, but later contested the elections in alliance with the Congress. The Arunachal Congress merged with the Indian National Congress just before the 2009 elections.

Meghalaya

Along with the major national parties, regional parties also play a significant role in the politics of Meghalaya. There are many regional parties in this small State. These include United Democratic Party, People's Democratic Front led by P.N. Siem and A.L. Mawphlang, Hill State People's Democratic Party, Khun Hynwtrep National Awakening Movement, North East Social Democratic Party, Garo National Council and Meghalaya Democratic Party.

Apart from this, there are several other parties which fought political battles in Meghalaya but later disappeared or merged with some other party. In these, the All Party Hill Leaders Conference fought for the creation of Meghalaya. Meghalaya was earlier a part of Assam. This party later became the Hill People's Union. Similarly, the resulting All Party Hill Leaders Conference (Armison Marak Group) merged with the United Democratic Party (UDP). Other regional parties that merged into the UDP include the Hills People's Union, the Public Demands Implementation Convention and the Khun Hynwtrep National Awakening Movement (Pal Lyngdoh). In addition, some parties merged with the Congress, including the Meghalaya Nationalist Congress Party and the People's Democratic Movement Party.

The United Democratic Party was founded by E.K. Mawlong. It was established in 1997. In 1998, on behalf of the party, B.B. Lyngdoh became the Chief Minister with the support of his arch rival Indian National Congress. UDP had 20 MLAs and Congress 26 MLAs. There was an agreement between the two that the Chief Minister would change after two and a half years, but within two years, B.B. Lyngdoh was accused of scams and was replaced by E.K. Mawlong as Chief Minister with the support of the BJP and the Nationalist Congress. In December 2001 both parties withdrew support and Mawlong's government fell. Since then the politics of coalition started in Meghalaya. The UDP sometimes becomes a part of the Meghalaya Progressive Alliance and at other times of the North-East Democratic Alliance formed by the BJP for the North-Eastern States.

People's Democratic Front is also a regional party of Meghalaya. It was founded in 2017 by P.N. Siem and A.L. Mawphlang. Its base is in the two main tribes of Meghalaya, Khasi and Garo. The party won 4 MLAs in the 2018 Meghalaya elections. The party aligned itself with the BJP-led North-East Democratic Alliance.

The Election Commission also gives the status of a state-level party in Meghalaya to the Hill State People's Democratic Party (HSPDP). In 1968, Hoppingstone Lyngdoh rebelled against the All Party Hill Leaders Conference. Hoppingstone has been winning Assembly elections continuously since 1972. People affectionately call him Ma-Hopping. The HSPDP is part of the North-East Regional Political Front, an ally of the BJP-led National Democratic Alliance.

The North-East Social Democratic Party (NESDP) was formed just before the 2013 Assembly elections in Meghalaya. An interesting fact is that in the election, the party fielded only one candidate, Lambo Kling Myliam from Jirang and he also won with more than 42 percent votes.

Paul Lyngdoh, the leader of the Kerala Student Union, separated himself from the Khun Hynywtrep National Awakening Movement movement and founded the Khun Hynywtrep National Awakening Movement Party. However, the party did not last long. In 2011 it merged with the United Democratic Party.

Another Party in the State, the Garo National Council, was established in 1948 itself. Moody's Mark was its first President. This party was also a member of the Garo Hills State Movement Committee. It also raised the demand for a separate Garoland. The support base of the party is very small. Only in 1998 and again in 2013, it could win only one seat each in the Assembly elections. In the rest of the elections the party could not win any seat.

Nagaland

Nagaland is the State in the North-Eastern States, where all the national parties and the regional parties of the surrounding States also try their hand. These include Indian National Congress, Bharatiya Janata Party, Aam Aadmi Party, Janata Dal United, Nationalist Congress Party, Trinamool Congress, National People's Party, Lok Janshakti Party. Apart from these, two major regional parties are the Naga People's Front (NPF) and the National Democratic Progressive Party (NDPP and there are several smaller regional parties, including the Naga National Democratic Party (NNDP), the United Naga Democratic Party (UNDP). Nagaland was also a part of Assam earlier and became a separate State on December 1, 1963. During this time many political parties emerged in the State and disappeared. One Party was the National Convention of Nagaland, which merged with the Naga People's Convention. The Naga People's Convention also later merged into the Naga Nationalist Organization and the Naga Nationalist Organization further merged with the Congress. There was a Naga People's Party which later merged with the Nagaland People's Council. Another one was a Democratic Labour Party, whose political journey was too brief. The United Democratic Front broke into parts, the main part later became part of the Naga National Democratic Party, then the faction that called itself the Progressive (UDF-P) merged with the Congress. There used to be a Naga National Party which later merged with the Naga National Democratic Party.

The story of the Naga People's Front, the main regional Party of Nagaland, begins with the Naga People's Convention and the Naga People's Council. According to the Nagaland government's website nagaland.gov.in (https://webtest.nagaland.gov.in/nla/about-us/) until 1957, Nagaland was a district of Assam called the Naga Hills. In August 1957, the leaders of the various Naga tribes of the Naga Hills came together to form the Naga People's Convention (NPC). Its first session was held on August 21, 1957 at Kohima. Dr. Imkongliba Ao presided over it and a resolution was passed that the Tuensang Division of NIFA should be merged with the Naga Hills District to form a separate administration unit. The Government of India approved it on 1 December 1957. After this success, in 1963, a delegation of NPC met Prime Minister Jawaharlal Nehru. A 16-point agreement was reached that a separate State would be formed by the name of Nagaland. Thus, on December 1, 1963, Nagaland emerged as the 16th State of India.

Now we come back to the history of the regional politics of Nagaland which traces its roots to the Naga National Council. According to Shivani Kinkar Choubey's book Hill Politics in

North-East India, in April 1945, Naga Hills District Deputy Commissioner C.R. Pawbse by uniting the various Naga groups of the district formed The Naga Hills District Tribal Council. Soon it was changed to the Naga Club in February 1946, and it was renamed as the Naga National Council (NNC), turning it into a political organisation. (pages 74-77)

According to the Political Science Project India/Nagaz Paper of the University of Central Arkansas, on August 14, 1947, the Naga National Council declared Nagaland to be a separate country and declared Angami Japu Phizo as the President. Fijo also suggested holding a referendum. But it was not recognised. After this, taking a step further on March 22, 1956, the Naga National Council formed the Naga Federal Government and declared Skatu Swu as the President. Sane also formed his own armed organisation called the Naga Federal Army. To stop terrorism, the Indian government deployed Army in the State. After this Angami Japu Phijo dissolved the Naga National Council and fled to Pakistan in December 1956. Thereafter Pakistan started terrorist activities in the area by giving arms to the Naga militants against India between 1957 and 1971.

Local Naga leaders formed the Naga People's Convention (NPC) after terrorist activities increased in the region and the Naga National Council, a regional political forum, was dissolved. It played a major role in getting the Statehood of Nagaland separate from Assam. This Naga People's Convention later became the Naga Nationalist Organisation, which merged with the Congress.

But even after this, the terrorism in the State did not end. When Naga National Council leader Angami Japu Fizo was dreaming of separating Nagaland from India by hiding in Pakistan and England, at the same time his Party Naga National Council's John Bosco Jasoki strongly opposed Fizo saying that Nagaland is such a closed region, which is surrounded by hills on all sides and it does not even have enough resources of its own. Therefore, it is not wise to talk about making it a separate country. In such an open protest, Bosco was expelled from the Naga National Council. He founded the Naga National Party in 1964. He was also a two-term Chief Minister of Nagaland.

The Naga People's Front (NPF), the party that dominates the regional politics in Nagaland at present, has maintained its ground in both Nagaland and Manipur. Before 2002, this party was known as the Nagaland People's Council (NPC). It was renamed as Nagaland People's Front at the 9th General Convention of the party held in Kohima in October 2002. The Nagaland People's Party formed an alliance with the BJP-led NDA but backed Pranab Mukherjee, the Congress candidate for the Presidentship in 2012. In 2014, ten regional parties from the North-East came together to form the North-East Regional Political Front. It also included the Naga People's Front. This front of ten parties declared their support to NDA.

Manipur

Manipur may be a small State, but all the major political parties of the country try their luck there and apart from this there are also a large number of regional parties. The major parties of the country participating in politics here include BJP, Congress, National People's Party, Nationalist Congress, All India Trinamool Congress, Lok Janshakti Party, JDU, Janata Dal (S), RJD, Samajwadi Party, CPI, CPI(M), Revolutionary Socialist Party, All India Forward Bloc, Aam Aadmi Party, Shiv Sena, BSP and Republican Party of India (Ambedkar). The regional parties of the State include Manipur People's Party (MPP), Peoples Democratic Alliance (PDP), Meiyamagi Thogalloi Manipur (MTM), People's Resurgence and Justice Alliance (PRAJA), North East India Development Party (NEIDP), Nikhil Manipuri Mahasabha (NMM). Naga People's Front (NPF) and Naga National Party (NNP). There are also some extremist and Maoist organisations in the State, which is not the subject of our book.

National People's Party was founded on January 6, 2013 by the once Congress leader P.A. Sangma had parted ways with his ally Sharad Pawar's Nationalist Congress. Although the Election Commission gave it the status of a national Party on 7 June 2019. Along with forming the party, P.A. Sangma had also announced that his Party would be part of the BJP-led National Democratic Alliance. The same year the party contested the Rajasthan Assembly elections and won four seats under the leadership of Kirori Lal Meena. This was a major achievement for the newly formed Sangma's party. Thereafter, the party along with the BJP kept registering its presence in all the States of the North-East. It is part of the North East Democratic Alliance, which supports the BJP.

Manipur People's Party is the oldest regional Party in Manipur. On 26 December 1968, a faction in the Manipur unit of the Congress rebelled and established the Manipur People's Party as a separate one. The party's only major success came in the 2007 Assembly elections when it won seven out of 60 seats. In the 2009 election, the party won just one seat. After this, it allied with the BJP, but in the 2012 Assembly elections, the party could not win a single seat.

Another Party from Manipur which was born out of a long agitation, requires mention here. This party is the People's Resurgence and Justice Alliance (PRAJA). It was founded in the year 2016 by human rights activist Irom Chanu Sharmila known as Iron Lady of Manipur. Party leader Erandro Lishombaum, who had returned from Harvard University with a Master's degree in Public Administration. Irom Sharmila had fasted for 16 years against the Armed Forces (Special Powers Act) in Manipur. Ending this fast, the PRAJA Party was established on 9 August 2016. Its purpose was to provide an alternative with clean politics in the State. Irom Sharmila contested against Chief Minister Okram Ibobi Singh from Thobal in the 2017 State Assembly elections. Irom Sharmila got only ninety votes, while Ibobi Singh won with 18,649 votes.

Mizoram

Mizoram was also a part of Assam till 1972. After that it became a Union Territory and on February 20, 1987 it got the status as the 23rd State of the country. Besides the Congress and the BJP, two major regional parties in Mizoram politics are the Mizo National Front (MNF) and the Zoram People's Movement (ZPM). Apart from this there are some regional parties with limited mass base, Including Joram Thar, Ephraim Union, Ephraim Israel National Convention, Hamar People's Convention, Lai People's Party.There were many small parties which later merged with other parties. In these, the Mizo Union, Mizo National Front (Democratic) merged with the Congress. Mizo National Front (Nationalist), Citizen Common Front merged with Joram Nationalist Party. Parties such as the Maraland Democratic Front and the Reing Democratic Party joined the BJP.

The Mizo National Front was founded in 1961 by prominent Mizo leader Pu Laldenga. He also became the first Chief Minister of Mizoram. Behind the establishment of this party there is a whole saga of severe famine and plague in Mizoram, which the Government of Assam had failed to deal with. In the year 1959, the worst famine occurred in the Mizo hills, which is remembered as Moutam in the history there. Bamboo is cultivated on a large scale in Mizoram. That year the bamboo blossomed, causing a rapid increase in the rat population. After the bamboo seed ran out, the rats broke into crops and houses and huts. This not only destroyed the crops but also spread plague in the villages. People were digging roots from the forests and eating leaves to survive. Several people died. Laldenga was then the Secretary of the Mizo Cultural Society. In March 1960, he changed the name of the society to Moutam Front. This society demanded relief from the government and sought the attention of the public. In September 1960, Laldenga changed the name of the society to the Mizo National Feminine Front (MNFF). The party's popularity grew rapidly among Mizo youth and villagers. The organisation was renamed Mizo National Front (MNF) on October 22, 1961 and Laldenga became its President. The MNF also resorted to arms to get hold of the region and there were many murders. But MNF was not successful. Finally on January 30, 1986, Prime Minister Rajiv Gandhi signed the Mizo Agreement with the MNF.

Mizoram became a separate State in 1987 and Laldenga became its first Chief Minister. After Laldenga's death in 1990, former guerrilla leader P.U. Zoramthanga became the leader of the party. Zoramthanga was also the Chief Minister of the State for ten years. In 2008, the MNF suffered a major defeat and the party could win only three out of 40 seats. Before the 2014 Lok Sabha elections, the Mizo National Front became a part of the BJP-led United Democratic Front.

Tripura

At the time of independence, Hill Tipperah was part of the Regency Council until 1949 when partitioned. On September 9, 1949, the Queen Regent of Tripura signed the Treaty of Accession and Tripura became a Union Territory. It was given full Statehood in the year 1971. Apart from Congress and BJP, the Marxist Communist Party also has a decent hold in Tripura politics. The major regional parties here include the Indigenous People's Front of Tripura, the Indigenous Progressive Regional Alliance. There are also many smaller regional parties, including Twipra Dofani Sikala Sarvangni Motha, National Socialist Party of Tripura, Ganamukti Parishad, Janaganotantrik Morcha, Tripura Republican Manch etc.

Till the year 2000, the terrorist activities of the National Liberation Front of Tripura (NLFT) in Tripura were on a high scale. That year a Party called the Indigenous People's Front of Tripura (IPFT) contested the elections to the Tripura Tribal Areas Autonomous District Council. Terrorist organization NLFT announced that it will allow only Indigenous People's Front of

Tripura (IPFT) to contest elections. There were many murders and kidnappings during that election and apart from IPFT, only the Left Front fielded candidates in the election. IPFT won 17 out of 28 seats. Before the 2002 Lok Sabha elections, the Indigenous People's Front of Tripura and the Tripura Sub-Jati Juba Committee merged and the Indigenous Nationalist Party of Tripura (INPT) came into existence. In the 2003 Tripura Legislative Assembly election, INPT contested the elections in alliance with the Congress. INPT won six seats, but after the election, six MLAs under the leadership of Hirendra Tripura and Budhu Kumar Debbarma rebelled and formed a separate National Socialist Party of Tripura (NSPT). The NSPT formed a government in the State in alliance with the CPI(M). In 2005, there was another rebellion in INPT and young MLA Animesh Debbarma formed a separate Party named National Conference of Tripura. On February 25, 2019, Congress appointed Pradyot Bikram Manikya Deb Burma as the President of the Congress State unit. A few months later, Pradyot resigned from the party and formed the Tiprah Indigenous Progressive Regional Alliance (TIPRA).

In this way, except Assam in the North-East, there are a number of small parties with political instability. At the same time, the parties from other States of the country also try their luck by contesting elections here so that by getting the prescribed six percent votes in these States and winning one or two seats, they can achieve the status of a National Party.

❑

32
The Circular Politics of Loved Ones

According to James Minahan's Encyclopedia –'Ethnic Groups of South Asia and Pacific', Sikkim consists of two Limbu language words Su and Khyim. Su means new and Khyim means palace or house. According to the Tourism Department of the Government of Sikkim, the Tibetan name of Sikkim is Denjong, which means valley of rice. The Bhutia people call it Beyul Demajong, which means a hidden valley of rice. Sikkim's name also appears in Indian literature, Indrakil, which means the garden of Indra, the god of war.

Sikkim is a border State in the north-east of the country, bordering Tibet, Bhutan and Nepal. Sikkim was the Buddhist Namgyal Empire in the 17th century. In the British era, it got the status of Princely State. It then remained a country protected by India, but in 1975 there was a revolt against the King at the Chogyal Palace. The Indian Army suppressed this revolt and in a mandate the public voted against the monarchy and in favour of merger with India. Thus, in 1975, Sikkim became the 22nd State of India.

However, before independence, when the political movement for independence started in the country, the Sikkim State Congress was also established in Sikkim. Against this, the Sikkim National

Party came into existence in support of the Sikkim monarchy and the government, which was aimed at opposing the merger with India. In the December 1959 issue of The World Today, Warner Levy in his article entitled –'Bhutan and Sikkim: Two Buffer States', wrote that the Sikkim State Congress started a civil injunction movement against the monarchy. In 1950, an agreement was signed between Sikkim and India under which Sikkim was given the status of being protected by India. This was followed by India's control over Sikkim's foreign affairs, defence affairs and diplomacy and communication. The rest of the administrative autonomy remained with Sikkim.

According to the history of Sikkim, protests against the monarchy sparked in 1973 under the leadership of Kazi Lhendup Dorjee, a former member of the Sikkim Council. The protesters demanded that one person should be treated as one vote. In fact, the Bhutia-Lepcha population in Sikkim was only 25 percent and the remaining 75 percent were Nepalis. Therefore, the monarchy had made it a rule that a Bhutia-Lepcha vote was equal to that of six Nepalis. In 1973, there was a riot in front of the Chogyal Palace demanding that everyone's vote be treated equally. The monarchy asked for security from India. In 1975, the Prime Minister of Sikkim requested the Indian Parliament to give Sikkim the status of a State of India. Sikkim eventually became a State in India on May 16, 1975.

Coming to Sikkim politics and regional parties, there are two major regional parties, the Sikkim Democratic Front and the Sikkim Revolutionary Front. Besides, there are several regional parties having low mass-base such as Sikkim Sangram Parishad, Sikkim State Forum Party, Sikkim National People's Party, Sikkim United Front Party, Hamro Sikkim Party, Organization of Sikkim Unity, Sikkim Gorkha Party, Sikkim Schedule Caset League, Gorkha National Liberation Front and Sikkim Republican Party.

The Sikkim Democratic Front (SDF) was founded by Pawan Kumar Chamling in 1993. After that, in 1994, the party assumed power. Pawan Kumar Chamling was Chief Minister for more than 24 years from December 1994 to May 2019. He holds the record for being the longest consecutive Chief Minister in the country. Chamling was a Minister in the Nar Bahadur Bhandari Government of Sikkim Sangram Parishad between 1989 and 1992. Later, annoyed with Bhandari, Chamling formed the Sikkim Democratic Front on March 4, 1993. The party then won the Assembly Elections in 1994, 1999, 2004, 2009 and 2014. Chamling continued to be a popular leader due to peace and development work in the State. In the 2009 elections, the Sikkim Democratic Front had won all the 32 seats in the State Assembly. Though his Party split before the 2014 elections, his old colleague Prem Singh Tamang, more known as P.S. Gole, formed his own separate party, the Sikkim Revolutionary Front. As a result, the party came to power in the 2014 Assembly elections by winning 22 out of 32 seats. But within a year and a half, 7 out of 10 Opposition MLAs returned to Chamling's party.

But the results of the 2019 Sikkim Assembly elections were somewhat different. The Sikkim Revolutionary Front won 17 of the 32 seats in the State, the Sikkim Democratic Front won the remaining 15 seats and Chamling had to resign as Chief Minister. In August 2019, 10 leaders of the Sikkim Democratic Front left the party and joined the BJP, while after some time two more MLAs moved to the Sikkim Revolutionary Front. Chamling then became the lone MLA of the Sikkim Democratic Front.

The Sikkim Revolutionary Front Party was formed by a revolt in the Sikkim Democratic Front. P.S. Gole was the second prominent leader of the Sikkim Democratic Front after Chamling. He was a Minister in the Chamling government and by 2010 he became the main critic of Chamling in the party itself. As a Minister in the Chamling government, through his supporters he managed to form a new party, the Sikkim Revolutionary Front, in Soreng, on February 4, 2013,. Bharti Sharma was made its Executive Chairman. In September 2013, Gole was expelled from the Sikkim Democratic Front. As soon as he was expelled from the party, he became the President of the Sikkim Revolutionary Front. The party contested all the seats in the State in April 2014 and won 32 seats. Former State Chief Minister Nar Bahadur Bhandari also extended his full support to him and his party Sikkim Sangram Parishad did not field any candidate. The Sikkim Revolutionary Front formed an alliance with the BJP ahead of the September 2014 by-election. The Sikkim Revolutionary Front contested the 2019 Assembly Elections in association with the BJP. Gole became the Chief Minister of the State by winning 17 of the 32 Assembly seats.

The story of the Sikkim Sangram Parishad begins with the Sikkim Janata Parishad. The Sikkim Janata Parishad was founded by Nar Bahadur Singh Bhandari in 1977. The party won a majority in the 1979 elections and Nar Bahadur Bhandari became the Chief Minister. In 1981, the Sikkim Sangram Parishad merged with the Congress and Bhandari continued as the Chief Minister of the Congress. But in 1984, he rebelled and parted ways to launch a new party called the Sikkim Sangram Parishad. In the 1985 State Assembly elections, the Sikkim Sangram Parishad won 30 of the 32 seats and Nar Bahadur Bhandari became the Chief Minister again. In 1989 also, the Sikkim Sangram Parishad won and Nar Bahadur Bhandari continued as Chief Minister. But in 1994, his own ally Pawan Chamling seized power from him by forming a separate party. In 2004, the Sikkim Sangram Parishad could not win a single seat. Nar Bahadur Bhandari then merged the Sikkim Sangram Parishad with the Indian National Congress. He became the President of the Congress State Committee but in 2013 he parted ways with the Congress and re-formed the Sikkim Sangram Parishad.

The Sikkim Rajya Manch Party was founded on December 7, 2017 by Roop Narayan Chamling, younger brother of the then Chief Minister of Sikkim Pawan Kumar Chamling. Roop Narayan Chamling stood as an independent candidate against the will of his brother Pawan Chamling to contest the bye-election for Yangong seat in Sikkim on September 16, 2014 and he also won by defeating Sikkim Democratic Front candidate Kumari Manjer. Pawan Chamling never forgave his younger brother for this and expelled Roop Narayan Chamling from the party. Roop Narayan remained in the Assembly as an independent MLA and on December 7, 2017, he formed his new party Sikkim Rajya Manch Party. In the March 2019 elections, the Sikkim State Forum Party formed an alliance with the Sikkim Progressive Alliance but could not win a single seat.

Another regional party in the State, the Sikkim National People's Party (SNPP), was formed after a break up with the Congress on October 10, 2008. Biraj Adhikari and Delay Namgyal Barfungpa were members of the Sikkim Pradesh Congress Committee. The State Unit of the Congress was then led by Nar Bahadur Bhandari. In 2006, Biraj Adhikari got into a dispute with Nar Bahadur Bhandari and left the Congress and joined the Sikkim Himali State Council. In October 2008, when Adhikari was expelled from the Sikkim Himali State Council also, he formed his own separate party called the Sikkim National People's Party. Adhikari became the party President and Delay Namgyal also joined him. However, there was no significant mass base of the party; it did not register itself with the Election Commission as a political party. So, its candidates fight elections as independent candidates.

The country's great footballer Bhaichung Bhutia founded the Hamro Sikkim Party on May 31, 2018. However, before the formation of the party, Bhutia had already started his political innings with the Trinamool Congress. Bhutia was influenced by the Aam Aadmi Party and formed the Hamro Sikkim Party to fight against the alleged corruption of the Pawan Chamling government in the State. He was joined by several senior leaders of the Sikkim Democratic Front and the Congress State. In January 2019, the party formed an alliance with the Sikkim Revolutionary Front and the BJP. The party fielded 22 candidates in the election but could not win a single one.

The 1994 Organization of Sikkim Unity was formed by other smaller parties of the State demanding reservations for the Nepali-speaking population. Jigme N. Kazi's Party could not create much influence despite raising the issues regarding the interests of the majority of Nepalis. The Sikkim United Front Party, the party of Narendra Adhikari, formed on June 25, 2018, holds the status of a registered but unrecognised regional party with the Election Commission.

❑

Goa

33
Everything is Fair – for Power

Think of the most attractive yet small state in the country and the name of Goa instantly comes to mind. After ruling Goa for 450 years, the Portuguese handed it over to the Indian administration on December 19, 1961. Currently BJP Chief Minister Pramod Sawant is in power in the 40-seat government in the State having an excellent literacy rate of 88 percent. Goa has two Lok Sabha seats and one Rajya Sabha seat.

But the dilemma associated with small states is also rooted with Goa. There has always been a predominance of regional parties. The BJP, which took over the reins from the Congress and formed the government along with other allies, after the 2022 election results and forming the government there, faces many challenges.

It is very difficult to ascertain the stand of any political party here. More than the history of the party, there is a leader's move that is more important. So, we will also talk about the prospect of any party according to its leaders.

Maharashtrawadi Gomantak Party

The Maharashtrawadi Gomantak Party in Goa has been like a pivot for the BJP. The BJP had won 4 Assembly seats in 1994 in alliance with the long-time ruling MGP. It may be assumed that the political upliftment of the BJP in Goa has taken place at the cost of the MGP.

But the 2022 Assembly election results changed it all. The alliance that the Maharashtrawadi Gomantak Party (MGP) entered with the Trinamool Congress did not bear any favourable results. TMC gained nothing and Gomantak also could win just 2 seats and was left with no option but to support BJP. In the 2017 Assembly elections also, MGP broke ties with BJP before elections and joined hands with the Goe Suraksha Manch (GSM) and Shiv Sena to fight elections. It had won only 3 seats in 2017.

It has to be remembered here that the Gomantak Party had formed its first government in Goa after its liberation from the Portuguese and remained in power for 16 years until its own leaders parted ways with the party. Earlier, the Maharashtrawadi Gomantak Party had also given two Deputy Chief Ministers to Goa as Ramakant Khalap and Ravi S. Nayak. When the Maharashtra Gomantak Party came to power on December 20, 1963, party founder Dayanand Bandodkar became the first Chief Minister of Goa. It was Dayanand who was sworn in as Chief Minister for the second time in the 1967 Assembly elections. After completing this term, he became the Chief Minister of Goa for the third time on March 23, 1972. Shashikala Kakodkar of MGP then took over as Chief Minister till April 27, 1979.

The MGP's main support-base was the lower class vote bank, which never got a stake in power in the Portuguese era, but after the 1990s, Sudden's party could not hold its flock together and today the vote bank has slipped to the BJP. His party had won three seats in the 2017 election; it imposed a condition on the BJP that it would support only if Manohar Parrikar was removed from the Centre and made Chief Minister in the State. The BJP was forced to accept this condition. Sudeen also became Deputy Chief Minister but as soon as two of his colleagues turned to the BJP, Sudeen also lost the Deputy Chief Minister's post. After the 2022 elections, Sudden has again sided with BJP.

Goa Forward Party

Vijai Sardesai is the Supremo of the Goa Forward Party formed on January 25, 2016. The party came into the limelight when it fielded its candidates in only 4 seats in the 2017 Assembly elections and managed to win three. The party was formed by Prabhakar Timble. He became its first President and appointed Dr. Renuka da Silva as Vice President and Mohandas Loinkar as State Secretary. The party got coconut as an election symbol. Vijai Sardesai is currently the Deputy Chief Minister of Goa. When neither the BJP nor the Congress got a majority in the 2017 Assembly elections, two Goa Forward Party MLAs and Vijai Sardesai supported the BJP in an alleged manipulation. It was Vijai Sardesai who campaigned against the BJP throughout the election. Party president Prabhakar Timble resigned after the Goa Forward Party MLA supported the BJP-backed government. Vijai Sardesai was sworn in as Cabinet Minister in the Manohar Parrikar government on March 14, 2017. Vinoda Palinkar and Jayesh Salgaonkar from Goa Forward Party were also made Cabinet Ministers. It may be recalled that when the Goa Forward Party was formed on January 25, 2016, Vijai Sardesai did become its mentor but did not officially join. The reason was the Anti-Defection Law. But on January 16, 2017, he officially joined the Goa Forward Party.

Vijai Sardesai had earlier emerged as an independent MLA in 2015. His performance in and outside the Goa Assembly brought him into the limelight. Vijai then led his panel to victory in the Margaon Corporation elections 2015. Though Vijai was also accused of Lewis Berger bribery, it could not be proved.

Born on June 14, 1970 at the home of Jaywant and Lakshmibai in Buenos Aires, Argentina, Vijai Sardesai received his BSc degree in 1992 from Dr. Bala Saheb Sawant Konkan Krishi Vidyapeeth. Vijai's father Jaywant worked with the UN as a scientist. After graduating, Vijai entered the real estate dealer's business and married Usha Sardesai. Vijai Sardesai started his political career with student politics in Goa. He became Chairman of the Goa University Student Council. He then took over the reins of the Congress and became the President of the Goa Pradesh Youth Congress. Sardesai then became a councillor from the Margaon Municipal Council. When the Congress did not give Vijai Sardesai a ticket from the Fatorda Assembly in 2012, he decided to quit the Congress and contested as an independent candidate from the Fatorda Assembly and won.

The Goa Forward Party's manifesto in Goa in 2017 and 2022 included free WiFi across Goa, zero tolerance on drug trade, 80 percent jobs for local youth, reduction in prices of fish, rice, pav, establishment of employment promotion board, passing new laws for the status of a special state of Goa, increasing Goa's participation in the tourism and mine sectors and nationalisation of rivers of Goa. But the 2022 Assembly election results put a brake on its aspirations when it was confined to just one seat.

The United Goans Democratic Party, once a strong contender for power in Goa and popular among Christians there, is now in a dormant state. The party, led by Churchill Alemao, is reduced to a situation where its two leaf election symbol is also seized. The party won only one seat in 2007 and not a single one in the 2012 elections. So there are Goa Suraksha Manch, Goa Praja Party, Goa Suraj Party, Goa Vikas Party and Goa Democratic Front. As the name suggests, Goa security forum is Subhash Velingar's party and Subhash has been associated with the Sangh in the past. Their main issues have been - withdrawal of grants from English medium schools and giving priority to Kannada and Marathi language studies. The same has been the case with the Goa Development Party. The party, which has one MLA, is currently part of the NDA once had 4 percent vote share in the State. In Goa, people often joke that there is a party in every locality with a plethora of founders but dearth of impact.

❑

34
Much Ado About Little Things

Just as an ordinary Indian feels jubilant to wander around in Puducherry, Puducherry politics is also somewhat playful. In this small region of four districts, on one side there is spirituality, tranquillity of Aurobindo Ashram, peace of dancing Dolphins, on the other there is no political regime untainted with corruption. In this Union Territory - from Pondicherry to Puducherry (meaning-new village), every Chief Minister's tenure has brimmed with controversies.

Pondicherry's first Chief Minister Edouard Goubert, a Pro-French leader, was appointed by the Congress government on July 1, 1963. Goubert and Lambert had earlier founded the French India Socialist Party in Pondicherry in 1947. Edouard Goubert was known as Papa Goubert in Pondicherry. Edouard later merged his party with the Indian National Congress. On August 23, 1964, Puducherry was given its first Chief Minister by the Congress after the assembly elections. V. Venkatasubba Rediyar was made Chief Minister. At that time, the People's Front Party sat in the Opposition. Congress forms the government by winning a total of 22 seats.

V. Venkatasubba Reddiar became the Chief Minister of Puducherry twice in which he served for 2 years 228 days in the first term and 196 days in the second term. Meanwhile, the

Congress had handed over the charge of Puducherry to M.O.H. Farook for 332 days.

Due to instability, President's rule was imposed in Puducherry on September 18, 1968, which lasted for 180 days. Dravida Munnetra Kazhagam, who came to power thereafter, and M.O.H. Farook, who joined the DMK from the Congress, got a second chance to become Chief Minister on March 17, 1969. He also became the first Chief Minister of Puducherry to hold the Chief Ministership for nearly five years in this government. On January 3, 1994, President's Rule came into force once again in Puducherry.

At this juncture balance of power tied and Subrahmanyan Ramaswamy was made the fourth Chief Minister of the State from All India Anna Dravida Munnetra Kazhagam (AIADMK). But in the first term, he was able to hold the Chief Minister's post only for 22 days (March 6, 1974 to March 28, 1974). This was followed by the President's Rule in Puducherry. It lasted for 3 years and 96 days. But then, when the elections were held, Subrahmanyan Ramaswamy came back to power. He was sworn in as Chief Minister on July 2, 1977. Afterwards, DMK, Congress and All India NR Congress took turns to rule the UT. N. Rangaswamy of the new party All India NR Congress (Namathu Rajyam meaning: Our Raj) formed his government in 2011. N. Rangaswamy had earlier become the Chief Minister of the State from the Congress Party. On May 16, 2011, when he was sworn in as Chief Minister for the second time, he assumed charge for 5 years and 20 days. However, on June 6, 2016, the Congress returned to power. Narayanasamy's dispute with the then Lieutenant Governor Kiran Bedi is one of the most controversial in history. Samy held the post till February 22, 2021.

The fall of Narayanasamy's government was no big deal. In the nearly 50-year history of the Union Territory, 5 governments have fallen here before without completing their term. Only four Governments have been able to run full tenure. Owing to the small size of Assembly, MLAs keep changing parties and as a result, many coalition governments could not complete their term due to strife among the constituent parties. The governments that completed their term include the Farook-led Congress government of 1985, the Congress government led by V. Vaithilingam of 1991, the N. Rangaswamy-led Congress government in 2001 and the Rangaswamy-led AINRC Government of 2011.

The governments which have not been able to complete their term include the DMK-CPI coalition government (1969), the DMK (1974 and 1977), the DMK-Congress government (1980), the DMK-Janata Dal government (1990) and the Narayanasamy-led Congress-DMK coalition government. In 1974, there was also a clash between the then Chief Minister Ramaswamy and the then Lieutenant Governor Chhedi Lal belonging to the AIADMK Party.

In fact, as a regional party, there have been DMK's governments, we are limiting ourselves to and we are not discussing the National Parties (like Congress and the BJP) here. In Puducherry, the only regional party was the All India NR Congress, which had a Chief Minister. But NR Congress Chief N. Rangaswamy has been an old stalwart of politics. N. Rangaswamy became Chief Minister for the first time in Puducherry in 2001. His emphasis was on many populistic programmes which made him popular but led to opposition in the Congress Party. In 2008, the Congress replaced Rangaswamy with V. Vaithilingam as Chief Minister and in 2011 N. Rangaswamy formed the All India NR Congress. Within 3 months of the formation of the new party, he won 15 seats in the Assembly elections (total seats 30, nomination 3) held in the State. In this election, Congress got 7 seats and AIADMK 5 seats and DMK 2 seats and Others got 1 seat. Rangaswamy became Chief Minister for the second time. The mid-day meal scheme launched by Rangaswamy in Puducherry was highly appreciated.

In the 2021 Assembly elections, The AINRC made alliance with the NDA and again took the oath of office as Chief Minister office after defeating the Congress. AINRC got 10, BJP 6 seats.

This gave NDA a majority in the 30-seat Union Territory. The Congress was reduced to only 2 seats. The Congress constituent DMK also got only 6 seats.

N. Rangaswamy has a speciality. He formed a new party and re-formed the government in just 3 months. He lost his first Assembly election in 1990 but Rangaswamy, who has contested 10 assembly elections so far, managed to win 8 times.

Coming to the Lok Sabha elections, Puducherry has only one Lok Sabha seat. From 1967 to 2019, the Congress has won the Lok Sabha seat 11 times. The BJP managed to win the Puducherry Lok Sabha seat only in 2009 and 2014 because of its constituent parties. But the road ahead is not easy. Both the parties have made huge promises and it is not easy to live up to them.

All India Anna Dravida Munnetra Kazhagam, Amma Makkal Munnetra Kazhagam, Dravida Munnetra Kazhagam, Naam Tamilar Katchi and Puducherry Munnetra Congress are among the parties contesting in Puducherry. Puducherry Munnetra Kazhagam was established on May 11, 2005 which was merged with the Congress in 2009. It was established by P. Kannan. The Naam Tamilar Katchi was established in 1958 by S.P. Adithaner. At present, Siman is the prominent leader of Naam Tamilar Katchi, who holds the post of Chief Coordinator of the party.

The DMK has been a major contender for power here. In fact, the DMK has considered Puducherry as an extension of Tamil Nadu in a way. It joined hands with the Congress in 2021 for power. But the NDA, along with the All India NR Congress, made it to sit in the opposition again.

❑

PART - 3

FROM THE PAGES OF HISTORY

From Independence till 1967

35
The Unchallenged Nehru Era

The period since independence of the country till 1967 is considered to be the Nehru era of Indian politics. After a long spell of slavery, the country breathed in the fresh air of freedom. The people who had suffered exploitation had high expectations from Nehru and the Congress. After independence, in 1951-52, the first Parliamentary Elections and the Assembly elections were won by the Congress all over. The Congress had won a total of 364 out of 489 seats in Parliament. In the first general election, the Congress got 45 percent votes, or more than half of the votes were divided among other parties. There was considerable enthusiasm in the first election, so there were large-scale parties. In the first general election, 53 parties and 533 independent candidates contested.

The Election Commission had also shown full generosity. It had also given National Party status to Parties which had an impact only in two to four districts. There were Parties which had the status of a national party but contested over a single seat. Leaving aside the Lok Sabha, when it was contested for the same State Assembly, the number of its candidates did not reach the tens. Under the existing definition, we can call such parties regional parties only. However, many parties were recognised as regional Parties, such as 10 registered regional Parties along with 9 national parties, contested the Assam Assembly elections in March 1952.

Two leaders in the Nehru Cabinet in the post-independence interim government also contested the 1952 elections by forming a separate Party. One of them was Shyama Prasad Mukherjee, who separated in October 1951 and founded his party Jan Sangh. Ambedkar, the Law Minister of the country, had formed a Scheduled Caste Federation and participated in this election independent from the Congress. Other major parties included Acharya Kripalani's Kisan Mazdoor Praja Parishad, Ram Manohar Lohia and Jayaprakash Narayan-led Socialist Party and Communist Party of India. But none of them could pose a major challenge to the Congress in the elections. But some regional parties started making an impact even in the Nehru era. One of them was the Shiromani Akali Dal in Punjab. Although there were differences and divisions, it had a good hold on a section of Punjab. Similarly, the Dravidian Munnetra Kazhagam emerged in the south. Though it did not participate in the first elections of 1952, it struck an electoral chord in 1957. You have read about these two parties in detail in the other chapters.

The first election was also held through a different process. There were one MP each in 314 parliamentary seats, while 86 seats were two MP seats. Voting was held for a general caste MP and a Scheduled Caste or Scheduled Tribe MP. That is, the voters double cast their votes. This system was changed in the 1960s and reserved seats were separated.

After the condition in which the British left the country, restructuring was necessary. Under the State Reorganisation Act, 1956, the State of Ajmer was incorporated in the State of Rajasthan on 1st November, 1956. Bhopal was a separate state then, but four years later, on November 1, 1956, it was merged with Madhya Pradesh. After Independence, Mumbai was also a separate province with 317 Assembly seats. It was connected to Mysore State on November 1, 1956.

We now take a glance at the regional parties which participated in the general elections and Assembly elections held in 1951-52 after Independence. Though these do not include parties like Shiromani Akali Dal and Dravida Munnetra Kazhagam, you have read about them in detail in the separate chapters.

Lal Communist Party Hind Union

The Lal Communist Party Hind Union was a regional political party in Punjab which lasted four years in all. It was formed on January 5, 1948 under the leadership of Teja Singh Swatantra. Most of its members were underground revolutionaries active against the British government in the Pepsu (Patiala and Eastern Punjab State Union) area. In the 1952 Pepsu Assembly elections, the party contested 5 seats and won one seat. In Punjab also, it fielded its candidates in 9 seats and won one. The party's election symbol was the locomotive. However, soon after this election, the party merged with the Communist Party of India (Bhakiyu). Ajmer Sandhu has mentioned the party in many places in his book 'Baba Bhuja Singh, An Untold Story'. According to him, it was formed in 1948 after breaking from Bhakiyu. It was formed by about 300 officials at a four-day conference held from January 5-8, 1948 at Nakodar in Jalandhar district. The party had 1,500 active members. Kirti and Gadari did not like some of the policies formulated by the CPI High Command, so they parted ways and formed their new party. The party used to publish its mouthpiece called Lal Jhanda in three languages Hindi, Punjabi and English. Teja Singh was also the editor of the Swatantra Lal Jhanda. The party men believed in the armed movement even after independence. After its formation, the Lal Communist Party had sent a group of its fighters led by Pandit Kishori Lal to liberate Goa from the Portuguese. One party worker, Karnal Singh Isaru was killed in the clash. The party had a firm hold among the poor farmers in the Pepsu region. The party was also accused of inciting poor farmers to launch an armed movement. The agitated farmers started killing the zamindars. In 1949, some fighters of the party clashed with the police in Kishangarh and killed a sub-inspector. They hold-up the village also. The army was then sent to the spot. A two-day clash with the army killed six party fighters and arrested 26 workers. As the arrest of its leaders intensified, Teja Singh Swatantra went underground. Teja Singh's name also came up in a bank robbery in Rae Bareli. Arrest warrants were issued against most of the party leaders. Some party leaders then talked about a re-merger with the CPI, though Teja Singh Swatantra opposed it. The CPI, displaying a liberal attitude, approved the merger and a meeting led by Lal Party leader Dalel Singh Wala decided to merge with the CPI. Arrest warrants of leaders other than Teja Singh were cancelled, they were brought into the mainstream. However, many activists, including Baba Bhuja Singh, refused to join the CPI and started the naxalite agitation. Most of the Naxalites in Punjab were old workers of the same Party.

Uttar Pradesh Praja Party

The party was formed by the zamindars of Uttar Pradesh in 1951-52 against the Congress Zamindari Abolition policy. On May 14-15, 1950, a conference called the All India Democratic Convention was organised in Lucknow by zamindars. They were of the view that a Conservative political party should be formed. The Conference sought civil liberties and maintaining the right to property. Referring to the Conference in the Reeves Peter book - The Lords and Government in Uttar Pradesh—A Study of Their Relations Until Zamindari Abolition, the Chief Organiser of the Conference, Sir Jagdish Prasad, called for pro-West foreign policy and advocated strong opposition against leftism and land reforms. This was followed by some more Conferences and at the two-day Conference on April 5-6, 1951, the Zamindar Union officially announced the formation of the Praja Party. Jagdish Prasad became its first Chairman. In the 1952 Uttar Pradesh Assembly elections, the party fielded its candidates in 55 out of 430 seats and won only one seat. The party also contested the Lok Sabha elections in six seats but without much success. It was only after this election that the party disappeared.

Pururushrathi Panchayat Party

The Pururushrathi Panchayat Party can also be called a small-influence regional Party. The party was formed in June 1951 by Sindhi refugees led by Kaka Tilok Chand after the partition of the country. S.N. Sadasivan's 1977 book—Party and Democracy in India mentions Tilok Chand and his party on page 59. Ajmer was a separate province when the country became independent. It had 30 Assembly seats. The headquarters of Pururushrathi Panchayat Party was built at Khari Khul in Ajmer. The party was formed with the objectivc of social and economic development of the Sindhi community. In the Ajmer Assembly elections held on March 27, 1952, 6 out of 30 seats were fielded by Pururushrathi Panchayat. The party also won three of these seats. Arjandas, Parasram and Bhimdas became MLAs for the first time on behalf of the party. In 1956, Ajmer province was merged with the State of Rajasthan under the Reorganisation of States Act. After that, there is no mention of Purusharthi Panchayat.

Garo National Council

The Garo National Conference was formed in 1946 before independence. Moody's Mark was its first Chairman. The party was formed demanding the formation of a separate Garoland state for the people of Garo Hills in Meghalaya. In 1948, the Garo National Conference was renamed as the Garo National Council. On March 27, 1952, out of 105 seats in the Assam Assembly, 4 seats were contested by the Garo National Council and three seats were won. The Council had a major success when two districts of Assam were separated and the State of Meghalaya was made on January 21, 1972. These two districts had one Khasi Hills and Jayantia Hills and the other Garo Hills. The party became a constituent of the All Party Hills Leaders Conference in the 1972 elections, which formed the government by winning 32 of the 60 Assembly seats in the first election held on March 9, 1972. The party is still a constituent of it.

Khasi Jayantia Darbar

There is not much information about this party now. It was constituted on the issues of the people of Khasi and Jayantia Hills of the present Meghalaya. But after independence, in the first Assembly elections in Assam two parties of the people of the region were formed. The other party was the Khasi-Jayantia Federated State National Conference. In 1952, Khasi-Jayantia contested four seats and won one seat, while Khasi-Jayantia Federated State National Conference (KJFSNC) contested on a single seat and won. KJFSNC was formed in 1946 and demanded from the British authorities that the Khasi-Jayantia Federal State be created in Assam. This was mentioned on page 12 in Chapter 2 of C.R. Lyngdoh's book - Visiting Traditional Institutions in the Khasi-Jayantia Hills. He writes that the party wanted more sovereignty for the people of the region within Assam itself. In the 1952 elections, A. Ale of KJFSNC won a big victory by contesting from the Nongpoh Assembly constituency with more than 57 percent votes.

Sarbadal

The Sarbadal or All People's Party was a regional party in Assam, formed on May 8, 1945, in Dibrugarh on the demands of the prominent Ahom community of Assam. It was then considered a major challenge for the Indian National Congress in the State. The All India Muslim League, Tribal League and Ahom Sabha played a key role in its formation. The Kachari, Mutok and Deuri communities of Assam were also associated with the party in the name of Hindutva. At that time, a large number of tea garden labourers were associated with this party. After Independence, the party won 3 seats and one seat on the Titi Bar in the 1952 Assam Assembly elections. He then contested the 1957 and 1962 Assembly elections. In 1967, the party was renamed as the Sarvabad Shramik Sabha, but failed to win any seat.

Mizo Union

Mizo Union, which contested the first election of 1952 from Assam, was also a regional party. It had contested three Assembly seats in Assam and won all three. Mizo Union is considered to be the first party of the people of Mizoram. It was established in 1946 at Aizawl, now the capital of the State of Mizoram. Like Meghalaya, Mizoram was then part of Assam province. During British rule, it was considered to be a political force of Lushai Hills. Lushai Hills is the old name of Mizoram. It had won the Mizoram Zilla Parishad elections held in 1951 after Independence. It continued winning till 1957, 1962 and 1966. This was followed by Mizoram as a separate Union Territory on January 21, 1972 followed by a separate full statehood on February 20, 1987. But for a long time it has not been a separate party. The party merged with the Congress in 1974.

All India Hindu Mahasabha

According to the name, it was an All India Party, but it had an impact in only a few regions of the Hindi strip. In 1952, the All India Hindu Mahasabha contested 9 of the 30 seats in the Bhopal State Assembly elections. Bhopal was a separate state then, but four years later, on November 1, 1956, it was merged with Madhya Pradesh. Similarly, in the central India province, the party contested over 33 seats and won 11. The Sarvdeshak Hindu Mahasabha was formed in 1915 on the lines of the formation of the Muslim League in 1906. In the sixth session of the General Assembly, it was renamed as the All India Hindu Mahasabha in 1921. In 1933, a political party emerged as the All India Hindu Mahasabha. The Hindu Mahasabha had organised itself in Punjab, UP, Bihar, Bengal, Central Province and Berar and Bombay Presidencies. In the book on the Hindu Mahasabha - Hindu Mahasabha in Colonial North India, 1915-1930: in the Constructing Nation and History-Lekh Prabhu Bapu writes on page 40 that although leaders who had separated from the Congress in the Hindu Mahasabha were the first to come, it never supported the country's freedom movement against the British. Even in the Civil Disobedience movement of Mahatma Gandhi of 1930, the Hindu Mahasabha was absent. In 1937, the Hindu Mahasabha joined hands with the Muslim League to form governments in Sindh, North West Frontier Province and Bengal. On page 103 of the same book, he writes that the Hindu Mahasabha had openly boycotted the British Quit India Movement. Vinayak Damodar Savarkar was the President of the Hindu Mahasabha at that time. The party made a consistent presence in Parliament till the 1967 elections. After that, it managed to win a seat only in 1989 and none after that.

Jharkhand Party

The Jharkhand Party registered its strong presence in Bihar province from the very beginning as a regional party. In the 1952 Bihar Assembly elections, the party contested over 53 seats and won 32 seats and was the main opposition party. The party was formed by Justin Richard in Ranchi on March 5, 1949 with the demand for a separate State for the tribals of Jharkhand. Later, prominent tribal leader Jaipal Singh Munda also joined it. Munda was the first elected President. In 1955, the Jharkhand Party had submitted a memorandum to the State Reorganisation Commission seeking separate statehood for Jharkhand, but the Commission rejected the demand because the tribals of the entire region did not have a common language, not even the tribal majority. Jaipal Singh Munda's popularity declined after the Commission rejected the demand for a separate state and the party won only 20 seats in 1962. Disappointed, Jaipal Singh Munda merged his party with the Congress in 1963. The merger did not go down well with many other party leaders. In 1968, they parted ways with Jaipal Munda and the Congress to form their own party. David Munjani formed the All India Jharkhand Party on May 19, 1968, while Justin Richard formed the Hull Jharkhand Party on December 28, 1968.

Chhotanagpur and Santhal Pargana Janata Party

As the name suggests, this party was a regional party formed for the development of the people of Chohtanagpur and Santal Parganas. Chohtanagpur is a plateau area between Ganga and Mahanadi valley. At present, it is in Jharkhand. In the first Assembly elections in Bihar in 1952, Chohtanagpur and Santhal Pargana Janata Party contested over 38 seats and won 11 seats.

All India Ram Rajya Parishad

It was a party of Hindu nationalists founded by Swami Karpatri on April 18, 1948. The party had also won 3 seats in the 1952 Lok Sabha elections. The party had contested over 29 Assembly seats in Bihar that year, winning only one of them. In Madhya Pradesh, the party contested over 35 seats and 3 candidates won. In the central India state, the party contested 39 seats and won two seats. The Central Province of India was merged with Madhya Pradesh in 1956, one of its districts was given to Mandsaur, Rajasthan. The party's influence in Rajasthan and Hindi belt also strengthened in the later days. It also won two seats each in the 1957 and 1962 Lok Sabha elections. It was then merged with the Bharatiya Jana Sangh in 1971. The party launched an agitation against the Hindu Code Bill and against cow slaughter in 1966.

Lok Sevak Sangh

The party was formed on the demands of the people of Purulia region. In 1952, it also contested over 12 seats for the Bihar Assembly and won 7. The party is mentioned on page 133 of Anis Kumar Majumdar and Bhanwar Singh's book - Regionalism in India Politics. The party's full name was Manbhum Lok Sevak Sangh. It was formed in 1948. In fact, freedom fighters Nirbhay Chandra Dasgupta and Bibhuti Dasgupta launched a social movement in the 1930s, against untouchability, exploitation of tribals and Dalits in Manbhum region after their release from jail. The movement was inspired by Gandhiji's idea of swaraj and social reforms. Its leaders had come out of the Congress itself. These leaders played a major role in the Quit India Movement in Purulia district. Out of these, Bibhuti Dasgupta and Arun Ghosh wanted the Bengali language to be encouraged in South Bihar also. The men had parted ways against the Congress promoting Hindi. The party had also won two seats in the 1952 Lok Sabha elections. In 1956, under the Reorganisation of States Act, Bengali-speaking areas including Purulia in Bihar were given to West Bengal. The Lok Sevak Sangh marched on a 480 kilometre long walk from Pakbidh village in Manbhum district to Kolkata in protest. Police arrested several leaders and dispersed the protesters. In the West Bengal Assembly elections in 1962, the party contested from all the 11 Assembly constituencies in Purlia region and won four seats. Before the 1967 elections, the Lok Sevak Sangh became part of the United Left Front, a left-wing coalition. Its leader Bibhuti Dasgupta became the Panchayat Minister. The party parted ways with the United Front ahead of the 1971 Bengal Assembly elections. In the Purlia region, it contested over 11 seats but won only one. It was then that the party began to collapse. Most of its prominent leaders joined the CPI(M).

All India Gantantra Parishad

It was a regional party in Odisha. It was founded in 1950 by Rajendra Narayan Deo of a royal family in Odisha. However, the party was formed by the Utkal Praja Parishad which was formed in 1948. Earlier, in the general election, the party had won 6 seats in the Lok Sabha. In 1952, the party won 31 seats in the Odisha Assembly and one seat in the Bihar Assembly. In the 1957 Odisha elections, the All India Ganatantra Parishad won 51 seats and its leader Rajendra Narayan Singh Deo was the Leader of the Opposition. However, in 1962, the political party merged with the Odisha unit of the Swatantra Party.

Bharatiya Kisan Mazdoor Party

It was a Marxist-minded Party in Maharashtra, which had a significant influence in three or four districts which still remain intact. The party was formed on June 13, 1948. It had more than one lakh members before Independence. In the 1952 Mumbai Assembly elections, the party contested 87 seats and won 14. It showed great strength in the Hyderabad State elections, with 10 of its 21 candidates winning.

Kaamgaar Kisaan Paksh

The party was formed in November 1951 after breaking up with the Bharatiya Kisan and Mazdoor Party. In the 1952 Bombay Assembly elections, it fielded its candidates in 33 seats, out of which only two won. Its leaders were close to the ideology of the Communist Party of India. Its prominent leaders were Nana Patil, Datta Deshmukh and D.S. Wagh who was called Kakasaheb Wagh. Earlier, the party had fielded three candidates in the Lok Sabha elections, none of which could win. The party soon split into two factions over the Communist Party issue. One was a Lal Nishaan Gut led by Patil and the other was called the Lal Nishaan Party led by Deshmukh.

Schedule Caste Federation

The Scheduled Caste Federation was founded by Dr. B.R. Ambedkar. However, he had earlier formed the Independent Labour Party on August 15, 1936 against Brahmanism and casteism. Being an ethnic-minded party, the Left leaders then neither supported nor welcomed it. In 1937, the Independent Labour Party contested over 17 seats in the provincial election and won 14. Later, the Congress Socialist Party also came forward in its support. Ambedkar founded the Scheduled Caste Federation in 1942. It contested from 37 Assembly constituencies in the

Bombay Assembly elections in 1952. The party won only one seat. Similarly, it fielded 9 candidates in the Himachal Pradesh Assembly elections and only won one seat. Five out of 24 candidates won in Hyderabad State. In the Mysore Assembly, 2 out of 7 candidates managed to win. On September 30, 1956, Dr. Ambedkar dissolved the Scheduled Caste Federation and formed a new organisation, the Republican Party of India. In the 1957 Lok Sabha elections, the Republican Party won 9 seats. However, since then, the party has been continuously breaking down and forming new parties. More than 50 parties have so far broken out from the lead party. The leaders who emerged from it formed their new parties. Among them are the Bahujan Samaj Party formed by Kanshiram and the Republican Party (A) of Ramdas Athawale.

Krishikaar Lok Party

In fact, the Agricultural Lok Party was a regional Party in Hyderabad state. It was formed in April 1951. Its leader Acharya N.G. Ranga had split from the Hyderabad State Praja Party and formed the party. It had contested elections in some states. It won one seat in the country's first Lok Sabha elections.

In the Madras Assembly elections in 1952, the party contested over 63 seats and won 15 seats. It had also fielded 16 candidates in the Bombay Assembly elections, out of which only one won. Its founder N.G. Ranga joined the Swatantra Party formed by C. Rajagopalachari on June 4, 1959.

Tamil Nadu Toilers' Party

John L. Variano, Jean-Luke and J.R. Viramma's book Viramma: Life of an Untouchable refers to the Tamil Nadu Toilers' Party. On page 293 the party is said to have been formed by the Vanniyar community of Tamil Nadu in 1951. However, the Vanniyar community could not remain united. The Tamil Nadu

Toilers Party was formed under the leadership of South Arcot of Madras Presidency and S.S. Ramasamy Padachi of Vanniyar in Salem district, while Vanniyars from Northern Arcot district and Chengalpattu formed the Commonweal Party led by M.A. Manickavelu, a lawyer by profession. In the 1952 Lok Sabha elections, 4 MPs of the Tamil Nadu Toilers' Party were elected. In the Madras Assembly elections also, the party contested over 34 seats and won 19. The Commonwell Party contested over 13 seats and won 6.

Madras State Muslim League Party

At present it is known as the Indian Muslim League Party and is a regional Party of Kerala and Tamil Nadu. At present, the Election Commission gives it the status of a regional party in Kerala. It was part of the Congress-led United Democratic Front in Kerala in the 2019 Lok Sabha elections. In Tamil Nadu also, as a Secular Progressive Alliance, it has an alliance with the Congress and is part of the UPA alliance at the national level. In 1952, in the Madras Assembly, the party contested 13 seats in the name of the Madras State Muslim League and won 5.

Justice Party

The Justice Party was an organisation of liberals from South India. It was formed on November 20, 1916 in the Madras Presidency during British rule. It was led by Dr. C. Natesa Mudaliar, T.M. Nair and P. Theagaraya Chetty, non-Brahmin leaders from the south. In 1944, Periyar E.V. Ramaswamy raised the party to his self-respect movement and linked it to his social organisation Dravidar Kazhagam. In this way, politically, this party ended. However, some rebel members of the organisation contested the 1952 election calling themselves the real Justice Party. In the Madras Assembly elections, the Justice Party contested over 9 seats and won one.

Saurashtra Khedut Sangha

In fact, this party was born out of the Kisan Andolan of Saurashtra. Its leader Ratibhai Ukabhai was a member of the Indian National Congress. He had strong support from the Liu Patidar community. Initially, the Khedut Sangh was a farmers' unit of the Congress in the Saurashtra region. But with the Congress leadership not supporting the formation of the organisation, it carved for itself an image separate from the Congress movement. Samajwadi Party leader Jaswant Singh Mehta supported the Khedut Sangh from outside. The members of this organisation bore Leftist inclination. They started calling the Congress a zamindar and a pro-urbanization party. When the first elections were held in Saurashtra after independence, the Khedut Sangh was the main opposition party before the Congress. Khedut Sangh fielded its candidates in 37 of the 60 seats in Saurashtra state, though only one of them won. In 1966, the party merged with the Swatantra Party.

Travancore Tamil Nadu Congress

In the British era, Travancore had the status of an empire. Malayalis were the majority and Tamil a minority in this State. Tamil organisations felt that they were discriminated against on the basis of language and education. Tamil leaders staged agitations and formed political parties demanding the formation of a separate Tamil Nadu state. One of them was the Travancore Tamil Nadu Congress. After independence, the states of Travancore and Cochin were merged into separate Travancore-Cochin states. In the first Assembly election of Travancore-Cochin in 1952, the party contested over 15 seats and won 8 and joined power in alliance with the Congress in the State, but within a year and a half, the two began to have differences. The government collapsed and in the second election held in 1954, the party won 12 seats and started an agitation to include Tamil-dominated areas of the State in the Madras Presidency. In many places, the movement turned violent. In 1956, the State Reorganisation Commission separated Tamil-dominated areas from Travancore and Cochin and merged them into the Madras State. The party merged with the ruling Congress in 1957 after the demands were accepted.

Cochin Party

It was a regional party in Cochin, formed in 1949. The party was formed to protest against the inclusion of Cochin in Travancore. Its slogan was 'Cochin only of the Cochinis'. S.N. Sadasivan, referring to the party on pages 61-62 in his book—Political and Administrative Integration of Princely States—writes that the party was right-wing. Its slogan was a Separate Cochin state with an election symbol as a flower. In the 1952 elections in Travancore-Cochin, the party fielded candidates in 12 seats, out of which only one won. However, the party disappeared in the second election held in the state in 1954. Its leaders and workers joined other parties.

Kerala Socialist Party

Kerala's freedom fighter Mathai Manzooran founded the Kerala Socialist party in Kozhikode on September 21, 1947. Though this was a small regional party, the front line leaders of this party had great respect among the people. Other prominent leaders included freedom fighter, writer and labour leader N. Srikant Nair and Left writer and columnist K Balakrishna, freedom fighter G. Janardhan Karup etc. In the Travancore-Cochin Assembly elections in 1952, the party contested over 10 seats and won one. In Kerala in 1967 when E.M.S. Namboodiripad formed a United Front alliance with the Left parties in which the Kerala Socialist Party was also included. In 1970, the party won only one seat. Then he formed an alliance with the CPI(M).

Uttar Pradesh Revolutionary Socialist Party

It was a regional Left Party in Uttar Pradesh, formed in 1951. Uttar Pradesh leader Jharkhand Rai of the Revolutionary Socialist Party had a difference of opinion with the party. He considered the Communist Party closer to his ideology. So he parted ways and along with his supporters formed the Uttar Pradesh Revolutionary Party.

In Uttar Pradesh, in 1952, the party contested in alliance with the Communist Party of India and the Bolshevik Party of India. Candidates fielded in 9 seats in the State, out of which only one won. It was after this election that the party merged with the Communist Party of India. It was officially announced at a party conference in Mau in November 1952.

Bolshevik Party of India

According to H. Chaudhary's book—Leftism in India—the Bolshevik Party was formed in 1939. Though its leaders were earlier part of the Communist Party of India, the leaders differed with the CPI over Netaji Subhas Chandra Bose. N. Dutta Majumdar and others wanted the CPI to support Netaji, who broke up with the Congress and formed the All India Forward Bloc. He was also against the CPI leaders' inclination towards Gandhianism. So, a separate party was formed. It had its Headquarters in Nagpur but played an active role in the labour movements in West Bengal. It also had a small stake in communist governments in West Bengal after independence. Though the Election Commission had given the National Party of India the status of a national party in the 1951-52 elections, it had fielded only one candidate in the Lok Sabha elections. Sudha Rai was given a ticket from Barrackpore. After independence, the party fielded candidates in 8 seats in the West Bengal Assembly elections but did not win any of them. In 1969, for some time, the party got a chance to partner with the Left government in Bengal, but later it was weakened by the party's rifts within it. In 1914, it rejoined the Left Front.

❑

1967- 1975

36
The Onset of the Indira Era and the Rise of Regional Parties

In the 1967 general election, the Indian National Congress was hit hard in seven States for the first time. In the last five years, the Congress had lost two of its Prime Ministers Jawaharlal Nehru and Lal Bahadur Shastri. Some crafty stalwarts of the Congress entrusted the leadership to Indira Gandhi assuming her as a dumb doll, but this resulted in a split in the party. Deputy Prime Minister Morarji Desai made no attempt to hide his displeasure at giving command to Indira. In 1966, he had openly staked a claim against Indira Gandhi for Party leadership. Apart from the Left, the right-wing parties like Jan Sangh and Swatantra Party seemed to be emerging as new forces after the wrap-up of the Nehru era of politics. It was a period of rapid emergence of regional parties. Many regional parties were functioning well and emerging as new regional forces. Dravida Munnetra Kazhagam (DMK) had defeated the Congress in the Madras Presidency. The Congress had won only three Lok Sabha seats while the DMK had won 25 seats. Several regional parties emerged in this election. In Punjab, the Shiromani Akali Dal led by Parkash Singh Badal emerged as a new political force.

In the 1967 elections, the Congress, under Indira Gandhi, proved itself potent and came to power, but was finding adjustment difficult with the senior leaders in the party. By 1969, the Congress got split into two. A faction expelled Indira Gandhi from the party but most Congress MPs came out in support of Indira Gandhi. The Election Commission, called the Indira-led faction, the Indian National Congress (R), also considered it a successor to the old party. The rebel 31 MPs formed the Indian National Congress (Organisation) led by K. Kamaraj. The Congress split gave rise to new parties in many States.

Bangla Congress

The Bangla Congress was formed in 1966 by freedom fighter Ajoy Mukherjee. The party came to the fore after the split in the Bengal unit of the original Indian National Congress and formed the government in Bengal in 1967 in association with the Left Front. Ajoy Mukherjee became Chief Minister. In 1966, several Party leaders raised discontent over the food movement against Bengal Chief Minister and Congress leader Praful Chandra Sen. Among those who opposed Chief Minister Praful Sen were Ajoy Mukherjee, Pranab Mukherjee, Siddharth Shankar Ray, A.B.A. Ganikhan Chaudhary and Abha Malti. In the 1967 Assembly elections, Ajoy Mukherjee defeated Chief Minister Praful Sen by contesting against him. The Bangla Congress fielded 80 candidates, out of which won 34. The party also contested 7 seats in Bengal in the 1967 Lok Sabha elections and 5 of its candidates won. However, this Government lasted only from March 15, 1967 to November 2, 1967. In 1969, midterm elections were held in the State. In this election, the Bangla Congress once again fought over 49 seats and won 33 seats in a United Front with the Left. Ajoy Mukherjee once again became the Chief Minister of this United Front government. But this time too, he could not complete his term. His Government was able to function only till July 30, 1970. With this, the Bengal Congress began to plunge rapidly. In the

1971 Lok Sabha elections, the party fielded 14 candidates but won only one seat. After the 1971 elections, the party merged with the Indian National Congress.

Odisha Jan Congress

Dr. Harekrushna Mahatab was a stalwart of the Congress from Odisha. He had participated in the freedom struggle in a big way. He was also associated with Gandhiji's Salt movement and went to jail several times. People knew him as Utkal Kesari. Mahatab was the first Chief Minister of Odisha from 1946 to 1950 and then from 1956 to 1961. In his second term, he is remembered for merging Princely State Cuttack and Bhubaneswar with Odisha. In 1962, he was sent from State politics to the Centre. He won the Lok Sabha elections from Angul. He was made Vice President of the Congress in 1966. He did not agree with the reins of the Central government of Congress going into the hands of Indira Gandhi. He returned to State politics. So, in the same year, he resigned from the Congress and formed his own regional party under the name of Odisha Jan Congress. The party also contested the 1967 Lok Sabha elections but could not win a single seat. Mahatab himself won the Assembly election in 1967, 1971 and 1974. The party eventually merged with the Janata Party in 1977.

Kerala Congress

Home Minister P.T. Chacko was thrown out of the Cabinet by the then Congress Chief Minister R. Shankar after a sex scandal came to light in Kerala in 1963. Chacko died a few days later. Angered by this, 15 political associates of Chacko brought in No-Confidence Motion led by K.M. George. George and R. Balakrishna Pillai then formed a separate Kerala Congress. Its other prominent leaders included M. Kurovinkunal, M.P. Pillai. The party also contested the Lok Sabha elections in 1967 but failed to win a single seat. After the death of K.M. George in 1976, there was a tug of war between two young leaders K.M. Mani and P.J. Joseph and senior leader R. Balakrishna Pillai over the party's ascendancy. Pillai was secluded and just before the 1977 Kerala Assembly elections, Pillai formed a separate party, the Kerala Congress (Balakrishna Pillai). Two years later, in 1979, K.M. Mani also parted ways to form the Kerala Congress (Mani). The media then started calling the Joseph-led Kerala Congress the Kerala Congress Joseph. In 1985, Mani and Pillai merged their parties with the Kerala Congress again. In 1916, the Kerala Congress became part of the BJP-led National Democratic Alliance (NDA).

Akali Dal Sant Fateh Singh

In 1962, Sant Fateh Singh formed a separate Akali Dal, Sant Fateh Singh, in the tug of war over Panthak politics in Punjab. His main political tussle was with Master Tara Singh, another senior leader of Panthak politics in Punjab. Master Tara Singh's Akali faction was called Akali Dal-Master Tara Singh. The supremacy in the Shiromani Gurdwara Parbandhak Committee was the bone of contention between the two. In October 1962, Akali Dal Saint Fateh Singh won the Gurdwara Parbandhak Committee election and held control of it. In January 1965 Management Committee elections, the party won 90 seats while Master Tara Singh's Party got only 45 seats. In the 1967 Punjab Assembly elections, the party won 24 seats and formed the first government in the State under the leadership of Justice Gurnam Singh. In the 1967 Lok Sabha elections also, the party won 3 seats. In November 1967, the party merged with the Shiromani Akali Dal. Akali Dal-Master Tara Singh did not win a single seat in this Lok Sabha election.

All Party Hill Leaders Conference (AHLC)

Williamson Apang Sangma, who launched an agitation after the country's independence for the State of Meghalaya to separate from Assam, convened a conference in 1960 to unite Garo, Jayantia and Khasi leaders and make a collective demand for a separate State. There the groups agreed to forget about their differences and formed consensus. The result of this consensus was the All Party Leaders' Conference. Williamson Apang Sangma became its first Chairman. In fact, at the same time, Assam Congress Chief Minister Bimal Prasad P. Chaliha declared Assamese as the official language. This had created a lot of resentment among the people of the mountains in the eastern parts of the State. It united Garo and Khasi leaders to agitate against the Congress and demand a separate Meghalaya State. In the 1967 Lok Sabha elections, the party won one seat. But after the formation of a separate Meghalaya State in 1970, the same Party had power till 1982 and in the meantime it gave four Chief Ministers to the State.

United Goans Party

The United Goans Party was a regional party in Goa, founded in 1963 by Dr. Jake de Sequeira. Dr. Sequeira is also known as the Father of Opinion Polls. There were different opinions whether Goa should be allowed to remain a Union Territory or merge it with Maharashtra. Then, on January 16, 1967, Dr. Sequeira conducted the first opinion poll in Goa to help the Central Government arrive at a decision. Sequeira, however, was playing politics of the opposition. In September 1963, Sequeira formed the United Goans Party, comprising of four parties, Álvaro de Loyola Furtado's Party Partido Indiano, JM D'Souza's Govan National Union, United Front Govans and The Goanchu Paksh, working for the separate identity of Goa. Dr. Sequeira became its first Chairman. The Goanchu Paksh was his own Party. However, Alvaro de Loyola Furtado was considered to be the brain behind the new party. In the 1963 Goa elections, the United Goans Party fielded 24 candidates, winning 12 of them. In this way, it became the main opposition after the Maharashtrawadi Gomantak Party there. After conducting the 1967 Opinion Poll, the United Goans Party split. Furtado formed a separate Party, United Goans

(Furtado). The main Party became the United Goans (Sequeira). In the 1967 Lok Sabha elections, United Goans (Sequeira) won a seat in Goa. The Sequeira faction had then received the election symbol. There was another split in the party in 1977. Dr. Sequeira's son Erasmo de Sequeira joined hands with Chaudhary Charan Singh's Bharatiya Lok Dal. Before deciding on this, he had not even taken other leaders of his party into confidence.Thus, the party was again divided into two factions, the Sequeira Group and the Naik Group. With this, the party started to decline. In the next Assembly elections, Sequeira Group won just three seats and Naik Group won 10 seats. By 1989, the party was no longer in a position to win a single seat and merged with the Congress. However, in 2016, A. Monserate, popularly known as Babush, re-formed the United Goans Party.

Democratic National Conference

Ghulam Mohammad Sadiq, the Prime Minister and Chief Minister of Jammu and Kashmir, separated from the National Conference and established the Democratic National Conference in 1957. Ghulam Mohammad Sadiq was the Cabinet Minister in Jammu and Kashmir between 1947 and 1953 when the first Government of the National Conference was formed under the leadership of Sheikh Abdullah.

Naga National Organisation

After 1956 in the Naga region of the North for nearly a decade, Terrorist activities continued to be carried out from the East. Pakistan. On March 22, 1956, the Naga National Council formed the Naga Federal Government (NPG) and the Naga Federal Army, describing the region as autonomous. Sketu Svu was declared President. The Government of India deployed troops in the region. As the conflict escalated, Angami Japu Fijo, its first Chairman, in

May 1956, dissolved the Naga National Council and fled to East Pakistan itself. Pakistani forces started providing weapons and help to naga rebels. Meanwhile, the Naga People's Convention (NPC), led by Imcongliba Ayo, tried to solve the problem. Prime Minister Jawaharlal Nehru signed an agreement with Ayo on June 12, 1960 to make Nagaland a State. The State was formed on July 30, 1960 with 42 Assembly seats. An Interim government was decided to be formed under Ayo's leadership. But Naga militants shot him on August 22, 1961, and he died two days later. Parliament approved the proposal to form the State of Nagaland on August 21, 1962. On December 1, 1963, the new State came into existence and P. Shilu of the Naga National Organisation (NNO) became its first Chief Minister. The State held its first Assembly elections in January 1964 and the Naga National Organisation won 33 out of 46 seats. In the 1967 Lok Sabha elections also, the Naga National Organisation had won one seat. Subsequently, in the 1969 Assembly elections also, NNO won 22 seats and formed the government. NNO lost power in the 1974 elections. The United Democratic Front (UDF) government was formed in the State. After that, the team disbanded.

Bharatiya Kranti Dal

Chaudhary Charan Singh's name is counted among the three prominent Congress leaders in Uttar Pradesh between 1952 and 1967. He was constantly in discord with the party on farmers' issues. He was eventually expelled from the party in 1967. Then, in October 1967, Chaudhary Charan Singh formed his own separate party, the Bharatiya Kranti Dal, in Lucknow.

Raj Narayan and Ram Manohar Lohia had inspired him to separate from the Congress and form a new party. The Bharatiya Kranti Dal contested the 1971 Lok Sabha elections and won one seat. The party got 2.18 percent votes. After the 1977 elections, the party merged with the Janata Party.

Telangana Praja Samiti

The demand for a separate Telangana State had been rising since Independence. Ananthula Madan Mohan formed a regional party called Telangana Praja Samiti in 1969 to intensify the struggle for a separate State. However, the party was soon captured by Mari Chenna Reddy. The party won 10 Lok Sabha seats in the 1971 general election. After winning so many seats, the party merged with the Congress. P.V. Narasimha Rao became the Chief Minister and the dispute over a separate State was completely suppressed. Later in 1983, Pratap Kishore reconstituted the party.

Utkal Congress

In 1969, when the Congress central leadership fought for supremacy, it also had an impact in Odisha (now Odisha). Congress leader Biju Patnaik joined the Congress (R) in support of Indira Gandhi. But in the 1970 Rajya Sabha elections, both the party candidates lost. It was blamed on Biju Patnaik. His relations with the central leadership deteriorated and he resigned from the Congress on April 6, 1970 and formed a separate Party in the name of Utkal Congress. In the 1971 Lok Sabha elections, the party won one seat and 32 seats in the Assembly elections. Later in 1974, the party joined the Bharatiya Lok Dal formed by Chaudhary Charan Singh.

Vishal Haryana Party

The party was formed in 1967 by Rao Birender Singh in revolt against the Congress. It was the first regional party in Haryana. Haryana separated from Punjab and became a separate State on November 1, 1966. Bhagwat Dayal Sharma of Congress became the first Chief Minister of the State. Rao Birender Singh was also elected Congress MLA from Pataudi seat and became Speaker in the first Assembly.

But soon he rebelled against the Congress and formed the Vishal Haryana Party. Most of the Congress MLAs joined him and on March 24, 1967, he was sworn in as the second Chief Minister of the State in place of Bhagwat Dayal Sharma. But Indira Gandhi dissolved the Assembly and imposed President's Rule in the State. In 1971, the party contested the Lok Sabha elections and Rao Birender Singh won from the Mahendragarh seat and reached the Lok Sabha.

On September 23, 1978, after the Emergency, Rao Birender Singh merged the Vishal Haryana Party with the Congress (I).

Maharashtrawadi Gomantak Party

The Maharashtrawadi Gomantak Party was the first party to form the government after the Portuguese lost control of Goa in 1961. After the liberation of Goa with the efforts of India, the first elections were held there in 1963.

The party was in power in Goa from 1963 to 1969. It had a mass base among non-Brahmin Hindus. The party was founded by Dayanand Bandodkar. He became the first Chief Minister on behalf of this party. The Maharashtrawadi Gomantak Party is now part of the National Democratic Alliance (NDA).

Muslim Majlis

It was a regional party in Uttar Pradesh. It was founded in 1968 by Abdul Jamil Faridi. The party is mentioned in Laurent Geyer's book--Muslims in Indian Cities --Transactions of Marginalisation. In the 1971 Lok Sabha elections, the party fielded its candidates for the first time but not a single one won. But in 1977, two Party MLAs won seats in the Uttar Pradesh Assembly elections. However, it contested the election on the symbol of Janata Party. By 1992, the party had turned into the All India Muslim Majlis. In 1992, Party President Omar Kazmi staged a protest against the Demolition of the Babri Masjid. He launched the Caravan-e-Insaf (Nyaya Yatra) parallel to the Rath Yatra of BJP leader L.K. Advani. In 2002, the Muslim Majlis became a part of the Awami Morcha.

Lok Raj Party

Thakur Sen Negi, who entered politics from the bureaucracy, and Jai Bihari Lal Khachi, who came into politics from being a student leader from Shimla, formed the Lok Raj Party in 1967. The party contested the Lok Sabha elections in 1971 but did not win any seat. However, a year later, in the 1972 State assembly elections, the party fielded 16 candidates. Both Negi and Khachi managed to win their respective seats. No other party candidate could win. But after five years, the two leaders parted ways. Khachi joined the Congress and Thakur Sen Negi joined the Janata Party.

Manipur People's Party

The regional party of Manipur was also born out of rebellion in the Congress. On December 26, 1968, N. Sovakiran split from the Indian National Congress and formed the party. He was the Chief Minister of the party thrice in Manipur. It later became part of the North-Eastern Regional Political Front. This front went with the NDA.

Swatantra Party

The party was actually the result of division and ideological opposition in the Congress. It was founded on June 4, 1959 by C. Rajagopalachari. Rajagopalachari alleged that the Indian National Congress is completely dominated by Nehru. The trend of Socialism and State control is increasing in the party. According to HL Erdman's book The Swatantra Party and Indian Conservatism, published by Cambridge University Press, the

1959 Swatantra Party formed a right-wing opposition in India. The party soon became the main opposition party in Parliament. It soon merged several right-wing regional parties in the country. Most of the leaders of this party had left the Congress. Among them was Tanguturi Prakasam Pantulu, a freedom fighter and Chief Minister of Madras Presidency and new Andhra Pradesh. The third prominent Party leader was Minosher Rustom, known as Meenu Masani, and a three-time Swatantra Party MP from Rajkot in Gujarat. Farmer leader N.G. Ranga was made the first President of the party. The party had two senior leaders from Punjab- Darshan Singh Feruman and Udham Singh Nagoke. Nagoke was also the jathedar of the Akal Takht and a member of the Rajya Sabha. Another big name was Ghanshyam Vyas who distinguished himself as a writer named Kanhaiyalal Maniklal Munshi. The party in its Nagpur resolution had demanded that the country abolish the licence raj and start a market-based economy. Though it was considered a right-wing Party, the Swatantra Party was not a party of Hindu nationalist ideology or any cult-based ideology like the Bharatiya Jana Sangh. The party had soon made its mark as a national party.

❑

1977 to 1990

37
Janata-Indira-Rajiv Era

On June 25, 1975, after Prime Minister Indira Gandhi declared an Emergency in the country, there was a burst of outrage against the government. Autocracy and arbitrariness of Indira and her son Sanjay Gandhi had added to the anger within Congress also. The entire opposition came together against the Congress as a Janata Gathbandhan (People's Alliance). Rift and differences were also visible in the Congress. Many senior leaders like Babu Jagjivan Ram, Hemwati Nandan Bahuguna, Nandini Satpathy quit Congress. They contested the 1977 election jointly. The opposition contested under the banner of Janata Party on the symbol of Lok Dal. Most of the regional parties in the country merged with the Janata Party. Therefore, not many regional parties were visible in this election, but at the same time, two new regional powers such as Anna Dravida Munnetra Kazhagam and Prakash Singh Badal's Shiromani Akali Dal in Punjab also emerged. We have explained these two parties in detail in the other chapter. Only a handful of regional parties tried their luck in the 1977 elections with their independent existence, but they could hardly make much of an impact.

After the elections, a government led by Morarji Desai was formed but it failed to complete the term. Raj Narayan played his cards and Janata Dal got divided into two groups. Chaudhary Charan Singh became Prime Minister with the support of Congress but could not run the government through. In 1980, for the first time, mid-term elections were held in the country. The Congress returned to power. Indira emerged stronger. During this period, a few more parties were formed out of Congress, such as Congress (Urs), Congress (Jagjivan) and also Janata Dal (S), which called themselves National Parties, but with limited area of influence. In 1978, Akali organisations passed the Anandpur resolution to strengthen their political hold in Punjab. It called for greater autonomy for the State, but the seeds of separatism that grew from it further resulted into terrorism in Punjab. Indira Gandhi lost her life to this terrorism and in 1984 elections were held once again in the country. Riding on the sympathy wave Rajiv Gandhi gained the largest majority. Most of the regional parties also suffered major setbacks in this election. But five years later, the opposition reunited. In 1979, many regional parties contested, but public opinion was polarised in three parts. In such a situation, apart from Tamil Nadu, Punjab and north-east, the regional parties could not put up a great show. In this election, the Indian Republican Party, The Karnataka State Riota Sangh, Gorkha National Liberation Front, Jharkhand Party, Manipur People's Party, Humanist Party Of India, Cookie National Assembly, Uttar Pradesh Republican Party, Amra Bengali, Tharasu Makkal Mandaram, Shoshit Samaaj Dal, Uttarakhand Kranti Dal, Jammu and Kashmir Panthers Party, Karnataka Gana Parishad, Tamilar Kazhagam, Hal Jharkhand Party, Manipur People's Party, All India Gorkha League, West Odisha People's Front, West Bengal Socialist Party, Gujarat Janata Parishad, Punjab People's Party, Bharat Makkal Congress and dozens of parties like the Deccan Congress, Punjab Kairo Dal contested but could not make any mark.

Muslim League (Opposition)

On January 19, 1973, Abdurrahiman Bafaki Thangal, leader of the Indian Muslim League, who went on Haj, died in Mecca. It was only after his death that the infighting started in the party's

Kerala Unit. The reason for this discord was that Omar Bafaki Thangal and Ch. Mohammad Koya both exerted their control over the party. The controversy escalated when the Indian Muslim League reached an agreement with the Indian National Congress. In protest, in May 1975, six party MLAs voted against the party whip in the Assembly. When expelled from the party, they formed a separate one-Muslim League (Opposition), led by Omar Bafaki Thangal. The party entered into an agreement with the Marxist Left Front in Kerala. The party contested the 1977 elections with the CPI(M) but the party itself could not win any of the seats. However, the party managed to win three seats in the Kerala Assembly elections the same year. It left the Left Front in 1985 and merged with the Indian Union Muslim League on August 3, 1985.

In the 1980 Lok Sabha elections, the Indira Congress returned with a huge majority by winning 353 seats. The opposition, which came together in the Emergency, was now fragmented into several parties. The Congress was also constantly in breaking down mode thereby new parties were formed. Therefore, in the 1980 elections, many regional parties once again dominated the scene.

Tripura Up-jati Juba Committee

In fact, it was an organisation of tribal youth of Tripura, called the Tripura Up-jati Juba Committee. It was formed on June 10, 1967, but ten years later, in 1977, it took the form of a political party and contested the Lok Sabha elections. However, the party did not get any major success in the elections. It came to the party first in the 1988 elections. The Tripura Upajati Juba Committee contested the election in association with the Indian National Congress and of the 60 seats in the states together both won 31 and formed the government. Out of these, seven seats were won by the Tripura Up-jati Juba Committee. However, the party dissolved in 2001 and merged with Bijoy Kumar Harangkhaul's Party, the Indigenous Nationalist Party of Twipra (INPPT).

Indian National Congress (URS)

In July 1979, the then Chief Minister of Karnataka and Congress leader D. Devraj Urs was infuriated by Sanjay Gandhi's growing dominance over the affairs of the party and resigned. He was accompanied by MLAs from Karnataka, Kerala, Maharashtra and Goa. Indian National Congress Urs became a new party under his leadership. Many of the leaders who accompanied Urs were big names. These included Yashwantrao Chawan, Dev Kant Barua, Keshu Brahmanand Reddy, Sharad Pawar, A.K. Antony, Sarat Chandra Sinha, Priyaranjan Das Munshi and K.P. Unnikrishnan. The party contested the 1980 Lok Sabha elections and won 13 seats. But soon the party got split further. Devraj Urs joined Chandrashekhar's Janata Party. Yashwanta Rao Chawan, Brahmanand Reddy and Chidambaram Subrahmanyam made way to Indira Congress. In Kerala, A.K. Antony parted ways with Congress Urs and formed Congress (A). Sharad Pawar became the President of the party in 1981 and changed the name of the party to Indian Congress (Socialist).

Janata Party (Secular)

Whether it was a national party or a regional party or just a masquerade, whatever you may call it, this party gave a Prime Minister to the country. After that, a Lok Sabha election was also officially contested in the name of the same party, though those who contested the 1980 Lok Sabha elections in the name of this party had formed their own party under a different name but could not get recognition from the Election Commission. We are talking of the Janata Party (Secular) formed by Raj Narayan on July 28, 1979. It was formed by splitting the Janata Party. The leadership of the main Janata Party had gone into Chandrashekhar's hands. Rajnarayan and Chaudhary Charan Singh launched a separate party and formed the government with outside support of the Congress and Charan Singh became the Prime Minister of the country. Though Charan Singh changed the name of the party to Lok Dal before the 1980 Lok Sabha elections, the 1980 election had to be fought in the name of Janata Party Secular due to non-recognition from the Election Commission. The party won 41 seats and became the second largest party after the Congress in the Lok Sabha.

People's Party of Arunachal

The People's Party of Arunachal is a Regional Party in Arunachal Pradesh, which aligned with the BJP-led NDA in 2016. It was founded on March 10, 1977 by Baikin Pertin, the first MP from Arunachal. Pertin then joined hands with the ruling Janata Party at the Centre. However, the friendship did not last long. Pertin went to the Congress. He was a Congress MP in the Lok Sabha and was the leader of the People's Party of Arunachal in the State. Though his party contested the Lok Sabha elections independently in 1980, it did not win. Pertin himself lost. However, PPA could achieve major success only in 1979. Tomo Riba became the first Chief Minister from the party and ran the government for a total of 47 days. The party suffered through various ups and downs for a long time. The party experienced good times in December 2015 when the then Chief Minister of Aruna Chal Pradesh Kalikho Pul left the Congress with 30 MLAs and joined the People's Party of Arunachal and formed the government along with the BJP. Since then, from 2016, the party remains an ally of the NDA.

Sikkim Janata Parishad

It was founded in 1979 by Nar Bahadur Bhandari, leader of the Sikkim Sangram Parishad. The party formed the government by winning 17 out of 32 seats in the 1979 Sikkim Assembly elections. Nar Bahadur Bhandari became the Chief Minister. He was the first Chief Minister of Gorkha origin in India. He succeeded in getting Nepali language included in the Eighth Schedule of the

Constitution. He was the Lifetime President of the Indian Nepali Language Federation. He is also known as the creator of modern Sikkim. In the 1980 Lok Sabha elections, the party contested a seat in the state and enjoyed a one-sided victory with 61.65 percent votes. The party merged with the Indira Congress in 1981, but Bhandari again formed a separate party called Sikkim Sangram Parishad in 1984. His wife Dil Kumari Bhandari became the President of the party after the death of Nar Bahadur Bhandari on July 16, 2017.

Sikkim Congress (Revolutionary)

The party, which existed for just two years from 1979 to 1981, finds mention by Jigme N. Kazi in his book Sons of Sikkim: The Rise and Fall of the Namgyal Dynasty of Sikkim. The Sikkim Congress (Revolutionary) was formed by Ramchandra Paudial just before the Sikkim Assembly elections in 1979. Out of 32 Assembly seats, the party contested over 27 seats that year and won 11 seats. The party also contested the 1980 Lok Sabha elections from the Sikkim seat but did not succeed. However, the party got more than 22 percent votes. Despite doing well in its first election, the party could not stay for long. In 1981, the party's winning MLAs moved to the Sikkim Democratic Congress and the party collapsed.

Sikkim Prajatantra Congress

The longest serving Chief Minister of Sikkim and founder of the Sikkim Democratic Front, Pawan Chamling, in 1978 formed a Regional Party called the Sikkim Democratic Congress. The party did not get any major success initially. In the 1979 Sikkim Assembly elections, the Sikkim Prajatantra Congress candidate was in the fray in all the 32 seats in the state but only 4 of them won. It also contested the 1980 Lok Sabha elections and got less than 10 percent votes. In the 1985 Assembly elections, the party contested only 14 seats. Chamling himself then moved to the Sikkim Sangram Parishad and thus the party collapsed.

Congress (Jagjivan)

It was also a short-lived Party that lasted from 1981 to 1986 only. It was carved out of the Indian National Congress (Urs). Party leaders Devraj Urs and Jagjivan Ram were adamant on dominance over the party. Jagjivan Ram tried to form his own faction in the All India Congress Committee (Urs). He convened a meeting of his confidants and announced the expulsion of Party President Devraj Urs from the party. In the same vein, Devraj Urs also convened a meeting of the Committee and expelled Jagjivan Ram from the party. After being expelled from the party, Jagjivan Ram formed his own separate party, the Indian National Congress (Jagjivan). The party contested the 1984 elections. Despite a unilateral wave of sympathy for the Congress arising out of Indira Gandhi's assassination, Jagjivan Ram's party managed to win a seat. However, with the death of Jagjivan Ram in 1986, the party also ended.

Doordrishti Party

Spiritual Guru Baba Jai Gurdev founded the Doordrishti Party in Ahmedabad on March 24, 1980 with the slogan of bringing in social reforms and spiritual advancement of the people. The party contested three consecutive Lok Sabha elections. In 1984, the party contested over 97 seats, 288 seats in 1989 and 321 seats in 1991, but did not win a single seat and the vote percentage remained almost negligible. Then, in 1997, the party decided to withdraw from politics. It was a national Party, but its devotees were the only mass-base (Janadhaar) of the party. In Uttar Pradesh, the party had a limited mass base.

Plain Tribals Council of Assam (PTCA)

In fact, it was an extremist organisation formed in 1966. Samar Brahma Chaudhary and Charan Narjari had launched a terrorist agitation demanding the formation of a caste-based state Udayachal under the banner of Plain Tribal Council of Assam by uniting tribals and Scheduled Castes. In 1968, the organisation boycotted the Assam elections. Though the Centre had agreed to set up an autonomous Council, PTCA refused to accept it. This was followed by a separate agitation by the All Bodo Student Union demanding Bodoland in the State and Bodo agitators started protesting against the PTCA's demand. However, the Plain Tribal Council later returned to electoral politics. It contested the Lok Sabha elections in 1984 and won a single seat.

Patli Makkal Kachi (PMK)

It is a Regional Party in Tamil Nadu formed by S. Ramdas in 1989. The Vanniyar community, which is part of the Other Backward Classes (OBCs) in north Tamil Nadu, dominates here, just as Yadavas and Kurmis in north India. S. Ramdas was the leader of the Vanniyar community. In 1987, the community launched an agitation in Tamil Nadu demanding reservation. The agitation escalated to such a large scale that law and order across the state was paralysed for nearly a week. Several thousand trees were cut down on all the roads. More than 1400 houses belonging to the Dalit community were damaged. At that time there was the AIADMK government led by M.G. Ramachandran. 21 protesters were also killed in police firing. Till this time S. Ramdas had the identity of a social worker of the Vanniyar community. This movement made him a leader. He founded a separate Party Patli Makkal Kachi (PMK) on July 16, 1989. The party fielded candidates in the Lok Sabha elections held in November that year but could not win a single seat. Prior to the 2004 elections, the party became part of the Democratic Progressive Alliance led by the DMK and the Congress and participated in power between the State and the Centre. Later, it also became a part of UPA-1. In 2014, the PMK left UPA and joined hands with the BJP-NDA.

❑

1991-2003

38
Minority Governments and the Rao-Atal Era

The country entered the last decade of the century amidst a turbulent atmosphere of Mandal-Kamandal movement and blur of political instability. As Prime Minister, V.P. Singh had failed and Chandrashekhar turned out to be a temporary one, the former Prime Minister Rajiv Gandhi was assassinated. There was a need for new leadership. Politics was no longer mere social service. Tickets for the parties were allegedly being sold. In such an atmosphere, there were many parties which appeared only in one election. By the second election, they changed into another party. There was a mushroom growth of many new regional parties and Dal across the country in every election season.

Joint Loka Parishad, Sarva National Front, Tharsu Makkal Mandram, Yuva Vikas Party, Jawan Kisan Mazdoor Party, Prootist Block of India, Soshit Samaj Dal, Odisha Vikas Parishad, All India Hindustani Revolutionary Samajwadi Party, Asom Jatiyatabadi Dal, Socialist Party (Ramakant Pandey), Vidarbha Praja Party, All India Gram Parishad, All India Secular Party, Desi Kisan Party, Azad Hind Fauj (Government), Samdarshi Party, Lok Party, Socialist League of India, All India Urdu Morcha, All India Ram Rajya Parishad (Vasudev Shastri Atul), Pandav Dal, All India Desh Bhakti Morcha, Marx Angeles, Leninist Community

Health Association, Adarsh Lok Dal, Desh Bhakta Party, All India Bharat Desam Party, Mukt Bharat, National Revolutionary Party, Entire National Army, Grama Munnetra Kazhagam, Navbharat Party, Labour Party of India (VV Prasad), Thyaga Marumalarchi Kazhagam, Purvanchal National Congress, All India Mahila Dal, Lokhit Morcha, Cheluva Kannada Nadu, Azad Party, Hindu Shiv Sena (AK Brahmbat), Rashtriya Unnatshil Dal, Senior Citizens National Party of India, Socialist Labour League, MGR Munnetra Kazhagam, Mahabharata People's Party, Janata Congress Party of India, All India Hindu Shakti Dal, All India Socialist Party, Jai Mahakali Monitoring Committee, Kannada Desh Party, Bharatiya Dhruv Labour Party, Vishal Bharat Party and Jan Ekta Morcha, all these parties are those who contested the 1991 Lok Sabha elections and most of them lost their identity just after a single election. They got between one and zero percent of the votes. Many details are not available about most of these parties. Those involved have also forgotten them. The length of the ballot papers was surprisingly increased as new parties emerged in the election season. The flow of black money into politics was increasing. The need for a variety of electoral reforms was being felt.

At the same time, T.N. Seshan became the Chief Election Commissioner. He identified more than 100 shortcomings in the then election process of the country and revamped the entire election process. Under the shadow of those reforms, the 1996 Lok Sabha elections were held. The Congress government led by Narasimha Rao had become notoriously infamous for corruption. The BJP was fast emerging and many regional parties had emerged powerful enough to influence the course of politics at the Centre.

However, despite all the electoral reforms, new and smaller parties continued to be launched. In the 1996 elections, there was also a party called the Indian Nationalist Party which got a total of 53 votes. Besides, Jan Ekta Morcha, Bharatiya Sarva Kalyan Kranti Dal, Manav Samaj Party and Labour Party of India (V.V. Prasad) were also parties which got less than 100 votes. All

India Democratic People's Federation, All India Jagruk Nagrik Dal, Federation Sabha, Hind Kisan Mazdoor Party, Purvanchal National Congress and Kranti Dal got less than 200 votes.

From 1999, the Atal era of Indian politics emerged. The BJP formed the NDA government. But even during this time, smaller regional parties continued to emerge. During this period, there were some regional parties which made their mark. We are referring separately to the parties that made some recognition between 1991 and 2003.

Janata Dal (Gujarat)

This political party resulted from a split in the Gujarat unit of the Janata Dal in October 1990. The new party was formed by Chimanbhai Patel and Chhabildas Mehta. Chimanbhai Patel was then the Janata Dal leader and Chief Minister of the Janata Dal-BJP alliance-government in Gujarat. But on October 25, 1990, the alliance broke up. Chimanbhai Patel then formed the Janata Dal (Gujarat) with 70 MLAs and formed the government with the support of 35 Congress MLAs and remained Chief Minister till his death on February 17, 1994. After the death of Chimanbhai Patel, the Janata Dal (Gujarat) also merged with the Congress. The Janata Dal (Gujarat) also contested the 1991 Lok Sabha elections and won one seat.

Natun Asom Gana Parishad

The party was the result of a tug of war between Praful Kumar Mahanta and Bhrigu Kumar Phukan for leadership in the Asom Gana Parishad. Fukan was the Home Minister of Assam and Asom Gana Parishad MP Dinesh Goswami was then the Union Law Minister. The two formed a separate Party Natun Asom Gana Parishad due to their displeasure with Praful Kumar Mahanta. Other prominent Party leaders were Brindavan Goswami and

Pulkesh Barua. The party also contested the Lok Sabha elections in 1991 but did not succeed in a single seat. Later, in 1994, Bhrigu Phukan was made the Executive Chairman of the Asom Gana Parishad and the Natun Asom Gana Parishad was merged with the Asom Gana Parishad.

Autonomous State Demand Committee

In the 1990s, Communist leader Jayant Rongpi formed the new party Autonomous State Demand Committee from the People's Democratic Front. Its members were originally Marxist-Leninists. The party contested the Lok Sabha elections in 1991, 1996 and 1998 but without any success. After that it broke down in two parts and a large part of it left marxist-Leninist ideology and joined the BJP.

Shiromani Akali Dal (Amritsar)

On May 1, 1994, Akali leader Simranjit Singh Mann, considered an extremist, split from the Shiromani Akali Dal and established the Shiromani Akali Dal (Amritsar). He was accompanied by Captain Amarinder Singh, Brother Manjit Singh, Colonel (R) Jasmer Singh Bala, Surjit Singh Barnala and Jagdev Singh Talwandi. All of them unanimously elected Simranjit Singh Mann as the President. The party won a seat from Sangrur in 1999. After that, the party could not win any seat. Other prominent leaders, except Simranjit Singh Mann, also parted ways with the party.

Tamil Manila Congress (M-TMC)

The party was formed in 1996 in the Tamil Nadu unit of the Congress by G.K. Moopanar's revolt. Most of the leaders of the State Congress unit had come with Moopanar. The revolt was launched by Moopanar in 1996 to protest against the Congress' alliance with the AIADMK. During Narasimha Rao's government,

Moopanar's image had become that of a political strategist and a trouble shooter. He lived the life of a common man even while in power. So, he commanded a lot of respect among the general public. In 1996, 20 party MPs were in the Lok Sabha. In 1999, Moopanar refused to support the BJP-led government in the Lok Sabha on a vote of confidence. After that, the Vajpayee government fell by one vote. After the death of Moopanar, his son G.K. Vasan was elected President of the party. Then, in 2002, the party merged with the Congress. Vasan parted ways with the Congress on November 3, 2014 and once again formed the Tamil Manila Congress (TMC). However, the party did not get any success in the State in the 2016 Assembly elections.

Samata Party

George Fernandes and Nitish Kumar parted ways with the Janata Dal in 1994 to form the Samata Party. However, in 2003, the party split once again and a large part of it separated as the JD(U) led by Nitish Kumar. But Brahmanand Mandal and Raghunath Jha continued to hold together with the Samata Party. Later, Raghunath Jha also left the party but Brahmanand Mandal continued to keep the 'Mashaal', the party-symbol, high. The 1996 election was contested by the Samata Party in alliance with the BJP and it won 8 seats. Six of these seats were in Bihar. It won 12 seats in the 1998 Lok Sabha elections. Ten of them were in Bihar and two in Uttar Pradesh. In October 2003, Party President George Fernandes announced its merger with the JD(U), but Brahmanand Mandal retained a distinct identity of the party, but after that the party did not get any significant success in any election.

Haryana Vikas Party

As the name suggests the party was a regional party in Haryana. The party was formed by Haryana Congress leader Bansi Lal and his son Chaudhary Surendra Singh after Sonia Gandhi became

Congress President in 1996. The party managed to form the government in the State after the Assembly elections. Bansi Lal also came into the limelight due to liquor ban. But soon Bansi Lal's government collapsed as ally BJP withdrew its support. This was followed by the merger of Bansi Lal's Party with the Congress on October 14, 2004.

Bharipa Bahujan Sangh

The party was formed by Prakash Ambedkar on July 4, 1994. The party was formed separately from the Republican Party of India. The party lasted for nearly 25 years. In 2019, it merged with the deprived Bahujan Aghadi. The party did not succeed in the 1996 Lok Sabha elections but fielded 34 candidates in the 1999 elections. Prakash Ambedkar himself won from Akola. He lost the 2004 Lok Sabha elections from the same seat. Then, in 2019, Prakash Ambedkar formed a separate party called the new party, the deprived Bahujan Morcha.

Apna Dal

The party was founded on November 4, 1995 by Dr. Sone Lal Patel, Kurmi leader of Varanasi region. Sone Lal Patel was once considered a very close political ally of the BSP leader Kanshi Ram. He was one of the founding members of BSP along with Kanshiram. Sone Lal Patel, who was annoyed over Kanshiram's overt attention to his female political associate Mayawati, had parted ways and formed his own party. Apna Dal is believed to be quite influential in Varanasi and Mirzapur region. The party's electoral politics shone somewhat in 2002 when Bahubali Atiq Ahmed won the election from Allahabad seat on the party ticket. After that, the party did not get much success in the state elections. Sone Lal Patel died in a car accident in October 2009. Within 20 days of his death, his elder daughter Anupriya Patel married Ashish Singh. In March 2014, the party entered the BJP-led

National Democratic Alliance. Anupriya Patel became a Minister in the Modi government at the Centre.

Majlis Bachao Tehreek

The party was formed in Telangana in 1993. Amanullah Khan had formed the Majlis Bachao Party following differences with AIMIM President Sultan Salahuddin Owaisi. After the split, the party won two seats in Chandrayangutta and Yakutpura in the state Assembly elections. Amanullah Khan died on November 10, 2002. After that his son Dr. Khayyam Khan became the party President.

Gondwana Gantantra Party

The party was formed in 1991 by Hira Singh Markram for the rights of Gond, the main tribe of central India. The purpose of the formation of the party was stated that 80 percent of the population is labourers, farmers and unemployed, facing injustice incessantly. Therefore, the struggle for our rights is inevitable. In Uttar Pradesh, the GGP fielded 8 candidates in 2002 but got less than a total of 12,000 votes. The party fielded 61 candidates in the Madhya Pradesh Assembly elections next year and three of them won. In 2018, the Gondwana Republic Party entered into an agreement with the Samajwadi Party.

Janata Dal (Secular)

The party has regional party status in three states of Karnataka, Kerala and Arunachal Pradesh. It was formed in July 1999 by former Prime Minister H.D. Deve Gowda. Deve Gowda had parted ways with the Janata Dal and formed the party over some differences. The party had managed to win one seat in the Lok Sabha elections the same year. In 2004, the party's star shone favourably and it became part of the ruling coalition in the State. It then joined hands with the Congress from 2013 to 2018 to partake in power.

Dravida Munnetra Kazhagam of Marumalar

It is a regional party of Tamil Nadu and Puducherry. It was founded on May 6, 1994 by Vaiko, separated from the Dravida Munnetra Kazhagam. Vaiko was considered a threat to party Chief Karunanidhi in the DMK. During the Sri Lankan civil war, Vaiko extended his full support to the Tamils and LTTE living there. The party had won four seats in the 1999 Lok Sabha elections. The party contested the 2019 Lok Sabha elections in association with the DMK and won one seat.

Rashtriya Lok Dal (RLD)

The party, which has influence in a part of western Uttar Pradesh, was founded in 1996 by Chaudhary Ajit Singh, son of former Prime Minister Chaudhary Charan Singh. The party had won two seats in the 1999 Lok Sabha elections. In the 2002 Uttar Pradesh Assembly elections, the party fought alongside the BSP and formed the government. Mayawati had two cabinet ministers in the party's government. In the 2004 elections, RALOD contested with the Samajwadi Party and won three seats. The 2009 Lok Sabha elections were fought in alliance with BJP and won five seats. The party could not win any seat in the 2014 and 2019 elections. The Jat community, considered to be the vote bank of the party, went with the BJP in large chunks after the Muzaffarnagar riots which dented the party-base. After Chaudhary Ajit Singh died from Corona on April 20, 2021, his son Jayant Chaudhary holds the command of the party.

Pyramid Party

The party was founded in Rishikesh on February 25, 1999 by Brahmarishi Patriji for a very different purpose. B.V. Reddy was made its Founding Chairman. The party's objective was - by 2012, to propagate the science of meditation all over the world, to find happiness in everything, to find the science behind spiritual subjects and promote vegetarianism, to create a new generation of miraculous thinkers, to establish centres of the Pyramid Young Masters Association all over the world. The party contested the 1999 elections but all the candidates together got a total of 31,699 votes.

Maraland Democratic Front (MDF)

MDF used to be a regional party in Mizoram. It was formed in 2003 by P.P. Thawala, a leader from Mara community of Mizoram. The party had influence in the southern part of the State. Mara Autonomous Council was also run in collaboration with Congress. In 2003, the party contested two Assembly seats in the state and the party's founding President P.P. Thawala emerged victorious. The party remained a separate party in the state for 14 years but on July 12, 2017, Thawala merged the party with the BJP.

❑

39
From Manmohan to Modi Continued....

With the turning of the new century, the country looked forward to a new dawn. The BJP's Shining India's Rathchakra was rejected by the Indian masses, echoing the tragedy of the Kargil war. Congress emerged as the single largest Party with 145 seats, with no party having a majority, a coalition government was formed under the leadership of Manmohan Singh.

This was the era when regional parties became extremely powerful in politics at the Centre. The Ministries were allotted not at the will of the Prime Minister but as per wishes of the regional parties. Several new parties also jumped into the 2004 general election. Some were created at the last moment just before the elections and their whereabouts are not known to anyone now. Many parties did not get even one percent of the total votes. One such party, Kannada Nadu Party, was formed in Karnataka by Vijay Sankeshwar and after the 2004 elections it joined the Janata Dal Secular. Hari L. Khoday, a businessman from Karnataka, formed a party named Urs Samyuktha Paksha on January 16, 2004 before the Lok Sabha elections in the name of safeguarding the rights of the backward classes and saving the legacy of Devraj Urs, once the Chief Minister of Karnataka. It fielded three candidates in the 2004 election. All three in total got only 33,128 votes. Other similar parties include Prabuddha Republican Party, Tamil Desiak Katchi, Kosi Vikas Party, Chhattisgarhi Samaj Party, Savarna Samaj Party, Shivrajya Party, Manuwadi Party, Rashtriya Hamara Dal, Parivartan Samaj Party, Rajasthan Vikas Party, Lokpriya Samaj Party, Youth and Student Party, Pichhda Samaj Party, Nari Shakti Party, Shikshit Berozgaar Sena, Bharatiya Ekta Dal, Janmangal Paksha, Sanatan Samaj Party, Rashtriya Garib Dal, Phule Bharti Lok Party, Maharashtra Rajiv Congress, Vijeta Party, Jansatta Party, Niswarth Seva Party, Manav Jagriti Manch, Awami Party, Akhand Party and many more like this.

The Congress contested the 2009 election with Manmohan Singh as their Prime Minister's face and won a majority on its own. For the last five years, this election had limited the strength of the regional powers that had been bargaining with the Manmohan Singh government. However, in this election also many new parties jumped in the election-field but vanished after the election. They got a meagre number of votes and are not worth the mention. The 2014 Lok Sabha election was a battle of prestige between the then Gujarat Chief Minister Narendra Modi and Congress President Rahul Gandhi which Narendra Modi won unilaterally. He emerged as a National Leader and became the Prime Minister of the country. There was polarisation across the country. This election restricted the power of regional parties. The Congress' disintegration had begun long before this election. In Andhra Pradesh, in the year 2011 itself, Y.S. Jagan Mohan Reddy formed a separate party YSR. In this way the Congress was weakened in one of its major strongholds in the South. You have read about this party in detail in the previous chapter.

The 2019 election was fought against the backdrop of the Pulwama incident and the air strikes on Pakistan, which gave a one-sided majority to the BJP again led by Prime Minister Narendra Modi. In this election, not only regional parties, the status of national parties like Congress also dropped.

Lok Janshakti Party (LJP)

Lok Janshakti Party was founded on November 28, 2000 by Ram Vilas Paswan, a leader of the Dalit community in Bihar, after parting ways with Janata Dal (United). Along with Paswan, his brother Ramchandra Paswan, Captain Jai Narayan Prasad Nishad, Ramesh Jigajinagi also quit JD()U and joined him. Paswan was a Minister in the Atal Bihari government but before the elections in 2004, he allied with Congress and RJD. The party was also successful in winning four Lok Sabha seats in Bihar. The next year in 2005, the party also won 29 seats in the Bihar Assembly elections. But in the 2009 Lok Sabha elections, Lok Janshakti Party left the UPA and formed a fourth front with RJD and Samajwadi Party and could win only one seat in this election. In the same year, the LJP suffered a major setback when the entire Jharkhand unit of the party joined the Congress. In the 2010 Bihar elections too, the party won only 3 seats. Out of these, two MLAs of the party later joined JD(U). On 27 February 2014, the Lok Janshakti Party joined hands with the BJP and after a gap of 12 years became a part of the NDA again. In this Lok Sabha election, the party won seven seats in Bihar. But in the 2015 Assembly elections, the party could win only two seats. Ram Vilas Paswan breathed his last on October 8, 2020, just before the Bihar Assembly elections and his son Chirag Paswan, with his son Chirag as Party President. It contested the Assembly elections alone against all JD(U) seats and did not win a single seat. In 2021, there was a huge uprising in the party against Chirag Paswan. Five MPs of the party parted ways under the leadership of his uncle Pashupati Kumar Paras. The Speaker of the Lok Sabha accepted Paras as the Leader of the LJP in the House. (You have already read this in detail.)

Telangana Rashtra Samithi (TRS)

It is a regional party of Telangana, founded by K. Chandrashekhar Rao on April 27, 2001. Chandrashekhar Rao was then a member of the Telugu Desam Party and also the Deputy Speaker. The party's single agenda was the creation of a separate Telangana State with Hyderabad as its capital. The party performed well in the first Lok Sabha elections of 2004, winning five seats. It also won six seats in the State Assembly elections. This party was progressing fast. In 2001, within six months of its formation, it had won one-third of the Mandal Parishad Territorial Constituencies (APPTC) and one-fourth of the Zilla Parishad seats. In the 2009 elections, the party entered into a pact with the BJP and became a part of the NDA. But in this Lok Sabha election, the party could win only 2 seats. In the year 2014, the party contested the Lok Sabha and Assembly elections on its own and registered a major victory in Telangana. The party won 11 of the State's 17 Lok Sabha seats and formed its government by winning 63 of the 119 Assembly seats. Chandrashekhar Rao was the lone star campaigner from the party in this election who held more than 300 rallies. The TRS got an even bigger success in the 2018 elections, winning 88 of the 119 seats in the State Assembly. In this way the TRS as a regional party has emerged as a major political force. (We have discussed its emergence in detail in the previous chapter.)

Suheldev Bharatiya Samaj Party (SBSP)

It is also a regional party claiming influence in a part of Uttar Pradesh, Purvanchal and some districts of Bihar. The Headquarters of this party is also in Ballia district. It was founded in 2002 by Om Prakash Rajbhar, a leader of the Rajbhar community. In the 2004 Lok Sabha elections, the party fielded 14 candidates and overall got nominal votes (0.07 percent). In the 2009 elections also, all its 20 candidates had their deposits forfeited. In the 2012 Uttar Pradesh Assembly elections, the party fielded 52 candidates, out of which only four were able to save their security deposit. The 2017 Assembly election was fought by the Subhasp together with the BJP. The party won 4 seats and Omprakash Rajbhar was made a Minister in the Yogi Government. During the 2019 Lok Sabha elections, there was a rift in the relationship between the BJP and the SBSP. The sitting on the fence attitude is the characteristic of this party.

Bharatiya Navshakti Party (BNP)

This party lasted a decade. Its main activity was limited to Dadra and Nagar Haveli and South Gujarat. This party was formed by Mohanbhai Sanjibhai Delkar, a seven-time MP from Dadra and Nagar Haveli. Delkar had contested elections on the ticket of Congress and sometimes on BJP ticket. He was also in the Janata Party led by Morarji Desai. Delkar was the leader of the Silvassa tribe and advocated for its rights. He contested the 1999 Lok Sabha elections as an independent and formed the party—Bharatiya Navshakti—afterwards. The BNP contested the Dadara and Nagar Haveli Panchayat elections in the year 2000 under alliance with the Congress and captured the Gram Parishad by winning 10 out of 12 seats. The 2004 election was won by Delkar fighting from his party with outside support from the UPA. The party merged with the Congress before the 2009 elections.

Lok Bhalai Party (LBP)

This party was a regional party of Punjab, which was formed in 1999 by former Union Minister Balwant Singh Ramuwalia. During those days the illegal human trafficking racket (Kabootrabaazi) was rampant in Punjab. The youth of Punjab were lured with a promise of sending them abroad and then dumped in African, European and Gulf countries. In return, lakhs of rupees were extracted from them. Similarly, the lives of many young women were ruined in the name of getting married to youths settled abroad. Ramuwalia formed the Lok Bhalai Party and raised the voice of such people harassed by travel agents. Politically, the party could not make a mark. It merged with Shiromani Akali Dal (Badal) in November 2011.

Rashtriya Samaj Paksha (NSP)

National Society Party or Rashtriya Samaj Paksha is a regional Party of Maharashtra launched in 2003 by Mahadev Jankar who entered into politics with BSP under the leadership of Kanshi Ram. Kanshi Ram made him the Chief of Yashwant Sena in Maharashtra. Yashwant Sena was not a political organisation, it was a cultural organisation. Therefore, Jankar formed the Rashtriya Samaj Paksha in 2003 to fulfil his political aspirations. The party fielded 12 candidates in 2004 but none could win. Jankar contested from Madha Lok Sabha seat in 2009 and ranked third. In 2014 he contested from Baramati against Supriya Sule and finished second. After that the party became part of the BJP-led National Democratic Alliance. By winning the election from the Legislative Council in 2015, he also became a Minister in the Devendra Fadnavis-led BJP government in Maharashtra.

Rashtriya Parivartan Dal

This party was founded by D.P. Yadav, known as the mafia don of western Uttar Pradesh charged with drug smuggling and murder. At some point of time, he was considered very close to the Samajwadi Party and Mulayam Singh Yadav. He joined the BJP before the 2004 Lok Sabha elections, but was soon sidelined after a dispute. After that he formed his own party named Rashtriya Parivartan Dal. In the 2007 Assembly elections, Rashtriya Parivartan Dal won two seats. D.P. Yadav himself won from Sahaswan and his wife Umlesh Yadav from Bisauli. After that this party merged with Mayawati's Bahujan Samaj Party.

Jharkhand Disom Party (JDP)

This party was formed out of a split in the BJP in Jharkhand. BJP MP Salkhan Murmu formed this party in 2002 by breaking away from the BJP, raising the issue of the interests of the tribal people. The party demanded that tribals should get more quota and reservation in Jharkhand. In the 2004 elections, JDP fielded four candidates from West Bengal, two from Bihar and one from Jharkhand. In Maharashtra, this party supported Raj Thackeray's Maharashtra Navnirman Sena. In 2014, Murmu merged the party with the BJP.

Ekta Shakti

Ekta Shakti Party was founded by a former bureaucrat Virendra Verma before the 2004 elections.Talking of his own political legacy, his father Ram Varma had been a leader of the Bharatiya Jana Sangh. Virendra Verma belonged to the Roh community of Haryana, who claim its roots are associated with the Marathas. Ekta Shakti fielded three candidates from North Haryana in the 2004 Lok Sabha elections but with no success. In 2009, Virender Verma contested against Dr. Arvind Sharma of Congress in the Karnal Lok Sabha seat and got defeated. The party merged with the BJP before the 2014 elections.

Party of Democratic Socialism (India) (PDS)

The PDS was founded in 2001 by Saifuddin Chowdhury, a CPI(M) leader from West Bengal. At the same time, Sameer Putatundu was expelled from the CPI(M). He too joined this new party. In the same year, in the Bengal Assembly elections, the party fielded 98 candidates, but none could win. The party overall got only 0.6 percent of the votes. The party has been accorded regional party status in West Bengal by the Election Commission.

Samta Samaj Party

In 2003, owing to some differences, Bahujan Samaj Party President Mayawati expelled the party President of Madhya Pradesh unit Phool Singh Baraiya from the BSP. On October 30, 2003, Baraiya formed a separate Party. Another leader expelled from the BSP, Sant Kumar, became the Vice-President of this party. In Punjab, Darshan Singh Jethumajra was made its President. The party contested the 2004 Lok Sabha elections and got only 0.02 percent of the votes. After that in the year 2007, this party merged with Ram Vilas Paswani's Party Lok Janshakti Party.

Praja Rajyam Party (PRP)

The Praja Rajyam Party was founded on August 2, 2008 by Telugu film actor Chiranjeevi. On August 26, 2008, when he held his first meeting in Tirupati, Andhra Pradesh, it drew lakhs of people. The party flag and agenda were announced in this meeting. Former Minister Talu Devendra Goud also merged his Party Nava Telangana Praja Party with Praja Rajyam Party. Devendra Goud was made the Vice President of Praja Rajyam Party. In the year 2009, the party fielded candidates on 294 seats in the Andhra Pradesh Assembly elections. Of these, only 18 won. Chiranjeev himself contested from two seats Tirupati and Palakolu and won only from Tirupati. In 2011, Chiranjeev merged the party with the Congress.

Desiya Murpokku Dravida Kazhagam (DMDK)

DMDK is a regional party of Tamil Nadu. It was founded on September 14, 2005 by Tamil actor Narayana Vijayaraja Alagaraswamy, popularly known as Vijayakanth. In the 2006 Assembly elections, the party contested all 234 seats in Tamil Nadu and secured 10 percent of the total votes, but only Vijayakanth could win his seat, the rest were defeated. Similarly, in the 2009 Lok Sabha elections, the party contested all the 39 seats in the State, even though no candidate won, but the party's support base increased. In the 2011 Assembly elections, the party became the main opposition party by winning 29 seats. Vijayakanth became the Leader of the Opposition. Before the 2014 Lok Sabha elections, the party entered into an alliance with the BJP and became a part of the National Democratic Alliance.

Jharkhand Vikas Morcha (Prajatantrik)

Jharkhand Vikas Morcha (Prajatantrik) was a regional party of Jharkhand, which existed for about 14 years. It was formed by former Jharkhand Chief Minister Babulal Marandi on September 24, 2006. Earlier Marandi was a prominent leader of BJP in Jharkhand but he felt that he was not given his due importance in BJP. The party managed to win one seat in the 2009 Lok Sabha elections. But the Modi wave of 2014 left him empty handed. In February 2015, 6 MLAs of the party also joined the Bharatiya Janata Party. On February 17, 2020, about 10 months after the 2019 elections, Babulal Marandi also joined the BJP and merged the entire Party with it.

Haryana Janhit Congress (HJC)

It was a regional party of Haryana. Bhajan Lal, a prominent leader of the Haryana Congress and considered to be master-manipulator, was upset with the party High Command for naming Bhupinder Singh Hooda as Chief Minister whereas the party had contested the election with his face as the Chief Minister. His displeasure was not satiated even after son Chandramohan was named Deputy Chief Minister. On December 2, 2007 he parted ways with Congress and formed Haryana Janhit Congress.The influence of the party was limited to Hisar and Fatehabad districts. The party contested the 2009 Assembly elections together with the Bahujan Samaj Party. The party contested 87 seats out of 90 and won 6 seats. Earlier in May 2009, the party had also won one seat in the Lok Sabha elections. Bhajan Lal passed away in June 2011. The command of the party came to his son Kuldeep Bishnoi. As soon as the BJP declared Narendra Modi as its Prime Ministerial candidate in 2013, Kuldeep Bishnoi declared his party's support.

The party fought the 2014 elections in alliance with the BJP, but Kuldeep lost this Lok Sabha election to Dushyant Chautala. In August 2014, Kuldeep Bishnoi broke the alliance with the BJP and joined hands with the Haryana Jan Chetna Party, the party of leader and entrepreneur Vinod Sharma. Together they fought the 2014 Assembly elections and won only two seats. Seeing no success as a separate Party, Kuldeep Bishnoi joined Congress on April 28, 2016 and Haryana Janhit Congress got merged with the Congress.

Bahujan Vikas Aghadi

Actually its original name in Marathi is Vasai Vikas Aghadi. It was formed by Hitendra Thakur, who was once a Congress MLA raising the issues of Vasai rural area of Virar. However, after leaving the Congress, he had also won two elections in this region as an independent candidate. In the 2009 Lok Sabha elections, Party leader Baliram Jadhav reached the House by winning from Palghar. In the same year, in the Assembly elections of Maharashtra, the party won two seats in Boisar and Nalasopara. The party was successful in winning three seats in the 2014 Assembly elections. Hitendra Thakur was also among the winners. In the 2019 elections too, the party could win only three seats. However, the party could not win any seat in the Lok Sabha elections.

Mahaan Dal

It is a party of Western Uttar Pradesh. It was formed by Keshav Dev Maurya to bring his section of society to power and for their betterment. In 2009, the party also contested the Lok Sabha elections but did not get any success. Maurya declares candidly that his party favours no ideology. Their aim is to do good to their community by coming to power. In the 2014 Lok Sabha elections, the Mahaan Dal tied up with the Congress and contested from Badaun, Nagina and Etah seats, but the party lost all three seats.

The party claims that it has the support of Shakya, Maurya and Kushwaha votes. The party stood to its earlier stand in the 2019 elections as well.

Jaago Party

Actually this party is registered by a non-political organisation. It was formed in August 2007. Deepak Mittal was elected its leader. It was registered with the Election Commission in 2008. The party's promise is freedom from reservation and free education for all. In the year 2008, the party contested the Rajasthan Assembly elections on 26 seats but without any success. The party contested 2009 Lok Sabha elections, 2013 Rajasthan Legislative Assembly and 2014 Lok Sabha elections. The slogan of the party is "come! Let's end crime, corruption and reservation".

Kosal Kranti Dal (KKD)

It is a regional Party of Odisha. It was formed in 2007 by Pramod Mishra, a leader of Kosal region. With the formation of the party, it was announced that 10 districts of western Odisha should be merged to form a separate Kosal Pradesh. Kosli language should be given the status of the national language. However, the demand for a separate Kosal State from Odisha started rising only in the 90s of the 20th century. Supreme Court lawyer Prem Ram Dubey was the first person to officially raise this demand and submit a memorandum to the President. Dubey formed an organisation named Kosal Sammelanhi. He also brought out a regional newspaper named Kosli Khabar and formed the Kosal Sena. His campaign also got support from BJP MLA Balgopal Mishra then. The party also contested the Lok Sabha elections in 2009 but met with no success. Otherwise, the Aam Aadmi Party, which emerged from the movement in Delhi and Punjab, had rapidly become a new force.

Rashtriya Lok Samata Party

It was a regional party of Bihar. JDU leader Upendra Kushwaha formed this party on January 4, 2013 by resigning from JDU and leaving Rajya Sabha membership. He accused JDU leader and Bihar Chief Minister Nitish Kumar that his model of development of Bihar has failed. However this party did not last very long. Eight years later, on March 14, 2021, the party merged with JDU. Upendra Kushwaha again became a supporter of Nitish Kumar. The 2014 election was contested by the Rashtriya Lok Samata Party in alliance with the BJP and won three seats. After that in the 2015 Bihar Assembly elections, the party contested 23 seats and won two.

Peace Party

A surgeon by profession Mohammad Ayub had formed this party in 2008 in Uttar Pradesh. In the 2012 Uttar Pradesh Assembly elections, it became the sixth largest Party in the State by winning three seats. This party was formed with a declaration to protect the rights of Muslims and Dalits in the State. The party could not win a single seat in the 2017 Assembly elections. After that cases were registered against several party leaders under the National Security Act (NSA).

Quami Ekta Dal

This party was founded in 2010 by Mukhtar Ansari, named the Bahubali leader of Uttar Pradesh. The party also contested the 2014 Lok Sabha elections but with no success. On June 21, 2016, Mulayam Singh merged this party with the Samajwadi Party, but his son and the Chief Minister of the State, Akhilesh Singh, opposed it and did not accept the merger.

Jana Sena Party (JSP)

It is a regional party of Andhra Pradesh and Telangana, formed by Tollywood actor turned politician Pawan Kalyan on March 14, 2014. The objective of the party was - to fight for the rights of every common man. In the 2014 Lok Sabha elections, Pawan Kalyan gave the slogan of 'Remove Congress, Save the country' in Andhra Pradesh and Telangana and supported the BJP and Narendra Modi. Despite this, the party failed to win any Lok Sabha seat. In 2019, the party contested from all 175 seats in the State Assembly. Pawan Kalyan himself fought from two seats but did not win any. His party's R.V. Prasad Rao was successful in winning the Rojol Assembly seat.

Vanchit Bahujan Aghadi

This is a party from Maharashtra. It was formed by Dalit leader Prakash Ambedkar on March 20, 2018. The party entered into an agreement with All India Majlis-e-Ittihadui Muslimeen in September before the 2019 Maharashtra Assembly elections, which it broke before the elections. The party single-handedly contested 234 seats in the State but did not win a single one. However, the party got 4.6 percent of the total votes. It stood second under 10 Assembly constituencies.

Makkal Needhi Maiam (MNM)

This regional party of Tamil Nadu was founded by actor Kamal Haasan, a popular name of Tamil and Hindi cinema, on February 21, 2018. Its aim is to unite the six States of the South and make them a big power. In the 2019 Lok Sabha elections, the party could not win any seat but managed to garner 3.78 percent votes. In 2021, the party contested over 154 seats in Tamil Nadu and 22 seats in Puducherry but without any success.

❑

PART -4

THE FUTURE

40

The Ifs and Buts of the Future

Will we witness a repeat of 2019 before the next Lok Sabha elections? That is, on the one hand, there will be the BJP and on the other hand, there will be a scattered opposition. Every party will be contesting elections separately and after the results are out, will they be holding their heads and mourning? Or there will be an Alliance beforehand in 2024. Obviously, if an Alliance is formed, there has to be Congress in a pivotal position. Since 2024 is far away and a month or even a week's time matters in politics, but the big question is-to be or not to be and this entails many small but crucial questions. There have been instances that whenever a coalition is formed, it may seem formidable but as the government begins functioning, only then its challenges and problems or even strengths emerge.

Even after the 2022 assembely elections, one thing is certain that if the opposition unites to form a coalition, it cannot be formed without the Congress. Now it is for the Congress to prove that it has the ability to lead the alliance. There are other reasons for this. After all, if a party is capable of winning 100+ seats, it is the Congress. If the BJP takes any party as a challenge, it is the Congress. But are the opposition parties other than the Congress prepared to come under the parasol of the Congress? Seems unlikely to happen. It is clear that these other parties or regional parties will surely influence the politics of the next few years. And this will certainly decide the Sensex of the regional parties.

Assembly elections are scheduled to be held in 11 states before the end of 2023. Congress and BJP are facing each other in a straight fight in more than a dozen of these states. But by registering a smashing victory in Punjab Assembly 2022 elections AAP is seemingly very hopeful of giving a tough fight. Under Priyanka Gandhi as General Secretary, the Congress may not have gained anything in these elections but it is not ready to sit quietly in UP and play second fiddle to the Samajwadi Party. The arch rivalry of SP and BSP is already written wide on the walls and both have suffered its consequences but at the same time only God Almighty himself can unite them. Although, in Bihar, Nitish Kumar‘s new action has brought some hope for the opposition.

Though Prashant Kishor (PK) must have been disappointed with the 2022 results, a few months before the results he had said that there would be no third or fourth front. Something different needs to be thought of… something new. Is PK thinking something new? only PK knows. But one thing is certain. There will only be a second front. Once upon a time there used to be Third and Fourth Front when there was one front in the form of Congress in the country and another front in the form of BJP. Now on one side there is BJP and on the other side all those who are against the BJP and are hell bent on defeating BJP. However, apart from this, there are some parties which are neither with Congress (Opposition) nor with BJP. But such parties are neither uniting separately to oust BJP nor are they likely to have any such intention. But does it seem like a situation now that those who intend to defeat the BJP in 2024 will be able to work on some strategy with consensus or will they be doomed in the darkness of the 2022 results .. and will then hold hurried meetings by the end of 2023? Then the stake will be fixed and the partnership will also be decided there. There is a blunt question here, is the Congress prepared to become a scapegoat in the share? Congress has already lost a lot in these stakes. It has to be seen here what policy needs to be adopted where there is already an old partnership and what could be done where there is none. For example, in Tamil Nadu, there is an old partnership with the DMK, where it will be necessary to follow the coalition-dharma. Imposing itself there will not work. In Jharkhand also the Congress may say that Chief Minister Hemant Soren should confine himself to the State but leave more seats to Congress in the Lok Sabha elections.

The latest incidents suggest that the Congress is pushing to prove itself rather than imposing itself on the opposition parties or playing second fiddle to them. In UP, it was said some time ago that the Congress was keen on a compromise with Akhilesh Yadav and Akhilesh Yadav was not even taking the calls of the Congress High Command. But in the current situation, Lakhimpur Kheri incident has given Priyanka Gandhi a political edge to say that she is a woman and ready to fight tough. In the 2022 assembely election, The Congress tried a campaign to carve its own new vote bank by announcing 40 percent seats to female candidates. It is also seen as a break into the caste-based politics of Akhilesh Yadav and Mayawati and Hindutva politics of the BJP, provided sincere efforts are made and 2022 elections results are not mourned any more. In UP there was a straight fight and the vote bank of Congress slipped to 2.3 percent. Even 97 percent of its candidates had their deposits forfeited. In fact, in UP, the Congress has only two options left with no vote bank to take over. Dalit Jatav once used to be with Mayawati, OBC Yadav supported Akhilesh, (most of them are still with the respective parties). But many of them are with the BJP now. Savarna castes had already been with the BJP (non-Yadav OBC and non-Jatav Dalit). Parties were relying upon a shift in Brahmin votes but in the 2022 elections they did not seem to take any risk either. Congress chose not to take any risk.

In Bihar, Congress approved of the same by fielding separate candidates in the by-elections to the Assembly in two seats. Lalu Yadav of the RJD got agitated over this action and attitude of the

Congress and called Congress 'names' which we would not even like to mention here. But things are changing after Nitish Kumar's eight term of chief ministership.

The Congress fielded its own candidate in the by-election to the Lok Sabha seat of Dadra Nagar Haveli also, with Shiv Sena fielding separate candidates. As the baton has changed in Maharashtra, Congress is not on the bargaining side. Some of these examples show that the Congress is not ready to become a scapegoat. Its altered image in UP and Bihar is indicating further and perhaps its next step will be West Bengal, where it has once ruled and has come down to zero.

A harsh fact is that the Congress is facing many challenges from within itself. G23 has been raising questions on any defeat or victory. The same thing happened after the 2022 elections. And now perhaps the party is in no hurry to come to power. It wants to tend to its ground first so that it can reap the harvest on time i.e. in the 2024 Lok Sabha elections. It may not even be in the mood that someone else may cultivate its ancestral land and then bargain to write a lease. In fact, Congress should have done this after the humiliating defeat in the 2014 Lok Sabha elections and should not have worried about the 2019 Lok Sabha elections. Had Congress started preparations for 2024 in 2014 itself, a lot of homework would have been completed by now. But it is also true that the Congress is compelled to walk under the patronage of the Gandhi family. The Gandhi family needs to have its doors open. (By the way, it has more doors leading out of its court.)

If the Congress is up to it, a major reason behind all this is the opportunistic attitude of the regional parties. After winning the Assembly elections for the third time in Bengal and defeating BJP in an Arvind Kejriwal style, Mamata Banerjee came to Delhi and met opposition parties, she also met Sonia Gandhi. There was no apparent desire from her to become Prime Minister, the aim was to overthrow the Modi government, she made such sacrificial statements too. She, though, avoided statements that hinted at

Congress being the pivot of unity for the opposition. But three months later, she brought in Filario, a Congress leader and once Chief Minister in Goa into her party. Former Mahila Congress President Sushmita Dev was also taken into her fold and sent to the Rajya Sabha and also entrusted with the responsibility of Tripura. Similarly in Manipur she has started breaking in. People may think about what Didi of Bengal, which has 294 seats, has to do with 40-seat Goa. Also, not many Bengalis live in Goa. In Goa, the Aam Aadmi Party was in the fray on one side and Mamata Banerjee on the other. AAP even got two seats but ended the chances of Congress. TMC won none but both parties damaged Congress. In Goa, it seemed that the BJP was writing the script of the opposition. Do the regional parties think that by 2024, the more states they are in power or whichever has even a small number of seats, the greater will be the chances of its leader becoming the Prime Minister? After all, the country has seen V.P. Singh, Chandrashekhar, Deve Gowda, Gujral and Charan Singh becoming prime ministers. But is the Congress only left with the role of making the likes of Gujrals and Chandrashekhars as the Prime Minister?

The question now is- what is the ideal situation. Talking about Trinamool leader Mamata Banerjee's Khela Hobe style, even if the team is yet to take shape, the purpose is clear and the adversary is fixed. For the majority of regional opposition parties, The enemy is Prime Minister Narendra Modi and the aim is to remove him from power in 2024. Mamata Di herself, Stalin in Tamil Nadu, Nitish Kumar of JDU and Lalu Yadav of RJD in Bihar, Uddhav Thackeray of the Shiv Sena in Maharashtra and Sharad Pawar of NCP, Arvind Kejriwal in Delhi- Punjab and Gujrat, Hemant Soren in Jharkhand, Chandrababu Naidu in Andhra Pradesh, Kumaraswamy of JDS in Karnataka, Left Front in Kerala, Akali Dal in Punjab, Farooq Omar Abdullah and Mehbooba Mufti in Jammu and Kashmir, apart from Chandrasekhar Rao in Telangana and Akhilesh Yadav in UP, Rahul Gandhi-Priyanka Gandhi all want to oust Narendra Modi in 2024. It is crystal clear that these parties on their own cannot single-handedly even touch Modi. Barring the Congress, none can send more than 40 MPs to the Lok Sabha in any case including UP which has 80 seats. The Congress is the only party with the potential to reach the hundredth mark.

It is noteworthy that BJP alone won 282 seats in 2014 and 302 in 2019. So it is certain that if they wish to defeat BJP they will have to do this in unison, in any case, Congress inclusive. In addition, regional parties will have to perform their best. This endeavour has two aspects. One is to use its full potential in their states or, say, in the original State. Two the regional parties will have to shun those states where they have a meagre stronghold and focus on their original one. Now the question is about the strength the regional parties have and whether they are energised enough to reach the finishing line in the 2024 race. However, this applies to the Congress also, which has to decide where to insist and where to resist. Here, we are talking about the General Elections, that is, the Lok Sabha elections.The catch here is even in the Assembly elections, if the Congress leaves the ground for the opposition parties, it will neither have an organisation nor a dedicated worker to contest the Lok Sabha elections.

Besides Congress there are four parties or say leaders which can contribute as a good footing to the opposition-Mamata Banerjee in West Bengal and M.K. Stalin in Tamil Nadu and Akhilesh Yadav in Uttar Pradesh. However, the Samajwadi Party's performance in the 2022 Assembly elections has made a place for itself. The Aam Aadmi Party may have fewer seats but the recent surge in its performance will surely make it the epicentre of central politics. Bengal has 42 Lok Sabha seats. Mamata had won 22 seats even after BJP's stupendous performance in the last Lok Sabha elections. The BJP got 18 seats though the party was once upon a time confined to Darjeeling in Bengal. But these seats have now come down to 16. Babul Supriyo quit the BJP as he left the Asansol Lok Sabha seat and joined Mamata. It is believed that by 2024, some other BJP MPs may also join TMC. Now the question is whether the Congress and the Left Front, which were decimated in the Assembly elections, should forget Bengal. Or will the complete field be left unopposed to Mamata Banerjee? Can Mamata win all the 42 out of 42 seats or at least cross the number 35? It seems that the Congress made a big mistake by fighting the Assembly elections in alliance with the Left parties. Mamata was ready to compromise with the Congress then. Rahul Gandhi was also said to be keen but Bengal Congress leader Adhir Ranjan Chowdhury stood firm and Rahul Gandhi bowed down. If the Congress had compromised and agreed to contest thirty-five seats, the relationship with Mamata would have improved. If the Congress had won half of these seats, it would have been a saving grace. Mamata would have given one or two Rajya Sabha seats to the Congress. The possibility of a dignified agreement with the Congress would have been alive and kicking for the forthcoming Lok Sabha elections and above all Mamata would not have been planning to ransack the Congress in Goa and Manipur.

However, Mamata's supporters and a large part of the opposition believe that Mamata's role is not going to be confined to Bengal alone. Prashant Kishore has been igniting this desire in Mamata's heart very often. After giving the BJP a beating in Bengal, Mamata has become an ideogram which could be useful in creating an undertone against Modi in other states. Mamata's Hindi is passable; she attacks her opponents brutally in her speeches. She is a Kali Maa and Durga Maa worshipper, who renders a flawless Chandi path.. This image can be useful to the opposition in parts of the North Indian region but they have to work really hard towards it. Mamata also knows that if this image is not created prior to 2024, the BJP can perform well in Bengal despite all its weaknesses.

It is necessary to break the Tina factor. If the people of Bengal realise that there is no alternative against Modi, they will vote in the name of Modi. There is a new trend in many states where if they vote for their preferred regional party within the state then change their preference in the Lok Sabha elections. Modi has been voted for by his supporters and despite all the difficulties, at the moment, there is no ground to think otherwise. His voters are bubbling with the spirit of nationalism. Thus if Mamata has to win over 90 percent Lok Sabha seats in Bengal, she would have to show to the voters of Bengal that there is a National Front to present an alternative to Modi. When the voters of Bengal observe there is Congress also in the Front and with Mamata Di by their side, they may rethink their perception about Modi.

The Congress may be somewhat unflustered that even though the leaders in North India are vying to become Prime Minister, South India does not pose such a challenge. Here it is adopting the strategy of give and take. That is, it plays second fiddle to the regional parties in the Assembly elections and seeks their help in a big way in Lok Sabha elections where it is the main contender. Let us understand it with the example of Tamil Nadu. The DMK is in power there. Stalin is the Chief Minister and his anti-Modi attitude is apparent. The characteristic of Tamil Nadu voters is that they give bumper seats in the Lok Sabha elections to the same party that they choose for the State. That is why, from Atal Bihari Vajpayee to Manmohan Singh's minority governments, they have banked heavily on 40 Lok Sabha seats in Tamil Nadu (Tamil Nadu 39, Puducherry one). Jayalalitha was in power at the time of Atal Bihari Vajpayee and was with the NDA. Manmohan Singh headed the government with the DMK. Stalin has the potential to become a major player in 2024. His alliance included the Congress, the Left Front, and some very small parties. The DMK had given only a few seats to the Congress in the last Assembly elections. Only 25. The Congress had no means to bargain.

In the Lok Sabha elections also, Stalin seems to be on a similar path and will give only those seats to fellow parties, including Congress, which are weak seats for him and there is some hope for other parties. They will try to win 35 plus seats out of 40.Tamil

Nadu does not have the same compulsion as Bengal. Here, Modi's party is considered to be a Hindutva-vadi party and the Dalits and OBCs politics prevail in Tamil Nadu. So to the voter here it hardly makes any difference whether there is an alternative available against Modi or not.

Accordingly, Stalin has to keep his flock together intact. He is also working in this direction. He is the one who took the matter of OBC reservation in the Centre's quota seats in the NEET Examination to the Madras High Court. When the youth from Tamil Nadu were lagging behind in the NEET examination, he managed to get passed a resolution in the Assembly that their State would not hold a NEET test. Stalin may benefit from this in the Lok Sabha elections. Moreover, if Stalin helps to strengthen the anti-Modi front in other states of South India, people there may take it seriously.

In Karnataka, Deve Gowda's party JDS has been the king-maker in the Assembly elections. Last time, the Congress had won two and a half times more seats than the JDS, but Deve Gowda's son H.D. Kumaraswamy became the Chief Minister. Out of 28 seats in Karnataka, JDS will have to perform best in Vokkaliga-dominated seats. The problem is that the Congress is also strong in bits and pieces here. The Congress has been getting some votes for Lingayat, Vokkaliga, OBC, Dalits, though the Congress vote percentage is not affected but it is not able to win seats because a large section of the Lingayat vote goes to BJP and Vokkaliga to JDS. Depending upon Yeddurappa's mood, who has been forcibly retired from BJP's active politics,--annoyed or happy--depending upon whether his sons get a handsome ransom, would reflect upon JDS Congress. But in Karnataka, Congress is not in a mood to leave any stone unturned. Latest is Rahul Gandhi took "initiation" into the Lingayat sect, which is considered a separate religion by its followers.

The story is interesting in Andhra Pradesh. Chandra Babu Naidu and Congress are staunch Modi-opponents. The Congress has been consumed by the regional parties and the BJP is not able to do what it intends to. Then there is Jagan Mohan Reddy who is neither with the BJP nor against it. The Opposition's first challenge is to bring Jagan Mohan into its camp. Jagan Mohan occupies more than three-fourths of the majority in the Assembly. Most of the 25 Lok Sabha seats are likely to come under their fold. But why would Chandrababu Naidu believe so? At the moment it is difficult to even think that he will surrender his stronghold to Jagan. And if he does so, then what would be left for his son Nara Lokesh? The point to ponder here is that casteist calculations have a huge influence in Andhra.

In 2009, YSR had asked Sonia Gandhi to give him a free hand in distributing tickets, with a two-thirds majority in the Assembly and it would bring 38 seats out of 42 seats in the Lok Sabha (42 seats in the United Andhra Pradesh and after Telangana was formed, 25 seats went to Andhra Pradesh and 17 seats to Telangana). Sonia agreed with that and YSR kept his promise. Jagan Mohan Reddy may have had to endure an ungraceful exit from the Congress in a big way, but there is no permanent friend or foe in politics. But the fact is Jagan is closer to the BJP camp.

Something similar can be said for neighbouring Telangana. KCR also came out of the Congress. The aggressive manner in which the BJP contested the Municipal elections in Hyderabad has created a stir in the KCR camp. KCR feels that first BJP will capture the votes of Congress and then will snatch its vote-bank. KCR is looking for more political space in Telangana. In Telangana, seat arrangment between KCR and Congress is not easy. Congress does not want to open the door for agreement.

With 48 seats Maharashtra has the highest number of Lok Sabha seats after UP, Sharad Pawar, Uddhav Thackeray and the Congress stay firm by 2024 and forget their differences, go on a 'defeat Modi' campaign. But the fact is after assuming power in Maharashtra, BJP is armed with a new lieutenant i.e. Chief Minister Eknath Shinde. Though any state-specific development for governance may not be a development for the future. It would be premature to project it as the formula for 2024.

After the bumper victory of the BJP, Mayawati is pushed to the corner and Akhilesh Yadav is unable to decide his future course and where to manipulate now. Akhilesh Yadav got the biggest blow in 2022. Akhilesh's vote share may have increased in 2022, but will he be able to retain it seems very difficult. In such a situation, Akhilesh Yadav will have to redesign his style of politics. Like inclusive politics, politics of working together, the politics of sharing, etc. If the opposition fights together they can win some seats, if not, they are bound to doom. It remains to be seen whether Akhilesh has learnt this lesson or not. But the fact is Akhilesh has to learn the art of having partners. Om Prakash Rajbhar is not in his camp nor is his uncle Shiv Pal yadav. On the other hand, It will not be easy to say that the Muslim vote bank will be able to abide by him completely. Akhilesh should not forget here that in 2019, when Akhilesh and Mayawati were united, Amit Shah had directly set a target of fifty percent votes. Surprisingly, his voter, his worker also grasped this and almost voted this much. One more thing has to be kept in mind here. The big parties of the Opposition have also started thinking ahead and apart from the Congress. They are now more keen on agreement with the parties that have flourished in different parts of the states rather than partnering with the Congress. (BJP is also doing the same). Uttar Pradesh and Bihar are current examples of this trend. RLD, Nishad Party, Suheldev Party and Mahan Party are such examples.

But in the 2024 elections, the biggest focus will be on the Aam Aadmi Party. It is not easy for the Aam Aadmi Party to decide its enemy number one, Congress or BJP. The bumper victory in Punjab has awarded him this courage. It is true that its count in the Lok Sabha is negligible but the enthusiasm in its vote bank can spoil the chances for any party. Now AAP is trying to increase its national base. It may not immediately eye the 2024 elections, but would like to be the centre of the Opposition's politics.

Finally, let's talk about the Congress which had 20 percent of the votes in the last Lok Sabha elections, i.e. around twelve crore votes. (BJP got more than 23 crore votes). Mamata, Sharad Pawar, Akhilesh and Mayawati did not get as many votes as Congress. This is the basic strength of the Congress. By the way, in 2024, the Congress has only a few states like Himachal, Rajasthan, Haryana, Chhattisgarh, Madhya Pradesh, Goa and Gujarat where it is directly competing with the BJP. That is, around 140-150 seats. But there is no guarantee that the entire opposition will stand with the Congress on these seats. (This understanding is very unlikely to come by.) Anyway the Congress will have to showcase its full strength in these seats and it will have to win more than half the seats. Only then will the Congress be able to reach a hundred in the country altogether. But it is certain that the Congress will have to work really hard, it will have to show strategic intelligence. The Congress, which is currently struggling, staggering and searching for its ground, will be able to do so, cannot be said right now. And the rest of the Opposition will not want to leave their own stronghold either, so everything is at stake for both sides.

As of now, the rising mercurial aspirations of Arvind Kejriwal and Mamata Banerjee may pose a challenge for BJP but are they potential enough? Interestingly, Nitish Kumar's new Avtaar is also worth watching. Currently, both UPA and NDA have 16 constituent regional parties each. The 2024 Lok Sabha elections may be the testing ground of their vigour.

❑

PART -5

OVER & ABOVE

41
Election Symbol and Recognition

In electoral politics, the election-symbol has been of great importance. Parties have been working hard on this. From 1952 onwards, Congress continued to be recognized with the pair of two bullocks and this process continued for almost twenty years. In the year 1972 when Congress (I) (i.e. Indira) was formed, a cow and a calf together were its electoral symbol. But this could last for only five years. After that, Congress is being identified by the 'Hand', though there are not many takers of blessings from this hand. The Jana Sangh's "diya" had been burning dim since independence, but after its merger with the Janata Party (symbol-farmers with plows) and then later split, now the Bharatiya Janata Party is identified with a lotus flower and is in full bloom. In the 2019 Lok Sabha elections, if BJP was a party of 22 crore votes, Congress is not much behind with 12 crore voters, though has fewer seats.

For ten to twelve years of independence, the electoral process continued relying on the initially made rules, but in 1960, a law regarding its rules and regulation was passed by the Parliament.

There are different rules for national and regional parties regarding election symbols and the symbol is not changed unless it is requested to do so on behalf of the parties or in case of any dispute. This happened several times with the Congress and even when several parties merged into one, the symbol was also changed on a need basis.

Similarly, there are separate rules for recognition of regional parties and different rules for national ones. Presently there are 8 National Parties, 54 Regional Parties and 2,796 Registered Parties in the country.

According to Section 6 (b) of the Election Symbols (Reservation and Allotment) Order, 1968, a party is granted the status of a national party when that party by contesting elections in four or more states in the Lok Sabha or Assembly elections in each of these states received 6% or more of the total valid voting votes. Also at least its minimum four candidates have been elected to the Lok Sabha.

The second condition for becoming a national party is that the party concerned has won two percent of the total seats in the Lok Sabha election. Also, its candidates must hail from at least three states.

According to the third condition, the party should have state party status in at least four states. On fulfilling any one of these three conditions, the Election Commission of India grants the status of a national party to the said party.

❑

42

National and Regional Parties in India

8 recognised national parties				
Party's Name	**Founded in**	**Founder(s)**	**Leader(s)**	**Election Symbol**
All India Trinamool Congress AITC	1998	Mamata Banerjee	Mamata Banerjee	
Bahujan Samaj Party BSP	1984	Kanshi Ram	Mayawati	
Bharatiya Janata Party BJP	1980	Syama Prasad Mukherjee (as Bharatiya Jana Sangh) Atal Bihari Vajpayee, L. K. Advani	J.P. Nadda	
Communist Party of India CPI	1925	Shripad Amrit Dange, S.V. Ghate, Muzaffar Ahmed, Singaravelu Chettiar, Shaukat Usmani etc.	D. Raja	

Commu-nist Party of India (Marxist) CPI(M)	1964	P. Sundarayya, E. M. S. Namboo-diripad Jyoti Basu	Sitaram Yechury	
Indian National Congress INC	1885	Allan Octavian Hume	Rahul Gandhi	
National People's Party NPP	2013	P. A. Sangma	Conrad Sangma	
Nationalist Congress Party NCP	1999	Sharad Pawar, P. A. Sangma, Tariq Anwar	Sharad Pawar	

54 recognised state parties[4]				
Party's Name	**Founded in**	**Leader(s)**	**Recognised in state(s)/UT(s)**	**Election Symbol**
Aam Aadmi Party AAP	2012	Arvind Ke-jriwal	Punjab, Delhi	
All India Anna Dravida Mun-netra Kazhagam AIADMK	1972	O. Panneer-selvam Edappadi K. Palaniswami	Tamil Nadu, Puducherry	
All India For-ward Bloc AIFB	1939	Debabrata Biswas	West Ben-gal	
All India Maj-lis-e-Ittehadul Muslimeen AIMIM	1927	Asaduddin Owaisi	Telangana	

All India N.R. Congress AINRC	2011	N. Rangas-wamy	Puducherry	
All India United Democratic Front AIUDF	2004	Badruddin Ajmal	Assam	
All Jharkhand Students Union AJSU	1986	Sudcsh Mahto	Jharkhand	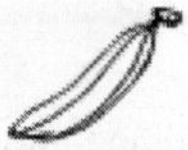
Asom Gana Parishad AGP	1985	Atul Bora	Assam	
Biju Janata Dal BJD	1997	Naveen Patnaik	Odisha	
Bodoland Peo-ple's Front BPF	1985	Hagrama Mohilary	Assam	
Communist Party of India (Marxist–Le-ninist) Liber-ation CPI(ML)L	1974	Dipankar Bhattacharya	Bihar	
Desiya Mur-pokku Dravida Kazhagam DMDK	2006	Vijayakanth	Tamil Nadu	
Dravida Mun-netra Kazhagam DMK	1949	M. K. Stalin	Tamil Nadu, Puducherry	

Goa Forward Party GFP	2016	Vijai Sardesai	Goa	
Hill State People's Democratic Party HSPDP	1968	Hopingstone Lyngdoh	Meghalaya	
Indian National Lok Dal INLD	1996	Om Prakash Chautala	Haryana	
Indian Union Muslim League IUML	1948	Sayed Hyderali Shihab Thangal	Kerala	
Indigenous People's Front of Tripura IPFT	2009	Mevar Kumar Jamatia	Tripura	
Jammu & Kashmir National Conference JKNC	1932	Farooq Abdullah	Jammu and Kashmir	
Jammu and Kashmir National Panthers Party JKNPP	1982	Bhim Singh	Jammu and Kashmir	
Jammu and Kashmir Peoples Democratic Party JKPDP	1999	Mehbooba Mufti	Jammu and Kashmir	
Janata Dal (Secular) JD(S)	2016	H. D. Deve Gowda	Arunachal Pradesh, Karnataka, Kerala	

Janata Dal (United) JD(U)	1999	Nitish Kumar	Arunachal Pradesh, Bihar	
Jannayak Janata Party JJP	2003	Dushyant Chautala	Haryana	
Janta Congress Chhattisgarh JCC	2018	Renu Jogi	Chhattis-garh	Farmer Ploughing (within square)
Jharkhand Mukti Morcha JMM	1972	Shibu Soren, Hemant Soren	Jharkhand	
Kerala Con-gress (M) KC(M)	1979	Jose K. Mani	Kerala	
Lok Janshakti Party LJP	2000	Chirag Pas-wan	Bihar	
Maharashtra Navnirman Sena MNS	2006	Raj Thac-keray	Maharashtra	
Maharashtrawa-di Gomantak Party MGP	1963	Deepak Dha-valikar	Goa	
Mizo National Front MNF	1961	Zoramthanga	Mizoram	
Mizoram Peo-ple's Confer-ence MPC	1975	Lalhmangai-ha Sailo	Mizoram	

Naga People's Front NPF	2002	T. R. Zeliang	Manipur Nagaland	
Nationalist Democratic Progressive Party NDPP	2017	Neiphiu Rio	Nagaland	
Pattali Makkal Katchi PMK	1989	S. Ramadoss	Puducherry	
People's Democratic Alliance PDA	2012	B.D. Behring	Manipur	Crown
People's Democratic Front PDF	2017	P. N. Syiem Auspicious L. Mawphlang	Meghalaya	
People's Party of Arunachal PPA	1977	Kamen Ringu	Arunachal Pradesh	
Rashtriya Janata Dal RJD	1997	Lalu Prasad Yadav, Tejashwi Yadav	Bihar Jharkhand	
Rashtriya Lok Dal RLD	1996	Jayant Chaudhary	Uttar Pradesh	
Rashtriya Lok Samta Party RLSP	2020	Upendra Kushwaha	Bihar	

Rashtriya Lok-tantrik Party RLP	2013	Hanuman Beniwal	Rajasthan	
Revolutionary Socialist Party RSP	1940	Manoj Bhat-tacharya[35]	Kerala West Ben-gal	
Samajwadi Party SP	1992	Akhilesh Yadav	Uttar Pradesh	
Shiromani Akali Dal SAD	1920	Sukhbir Singh Badal	Punjab	
Shiv Sena SS	1966	Uddhav Thackeray	Maharashtra	
Sikkim Demo-cratic Front SDF	1993	Pawan Kumar Chamling	Sikkim	
Sikkim Kranti-kari Morcha SKM	2013	Prem Singh Tamang	Sikkim	
Telangana Rashtra Samithi TRS	2001	K. Chan-drashekar Rao	Telangana Andhra Pradesh	
Telugu Desam Party TDP	1982	N. Chan-drababu Naidu	Andhra Pradesh Telangana	
United Demo-cratic Party UDP	1997	Metbah Lyngdoh	Meghalaya	

United People's Party Liberal UPPL	2015	Urkhao Gwra Brahma	Assam	Tractor Driving Farmer
Yuvajana Sramika Rythu Congress Party YSRCP	2011	Y. S. Jaganmohan Reddy	Andhra Pradesh Telangana	
Zoram Nationalist Party ZNP	1997	Lalduhawma	Mizoram	

❑

43
House Strength of Various Assemblies

Sr. no.	Assembly	House strength
1.	Uttar Pradesh Legislative Assembly	403
2.	West Bengal Legislative Assembly	294
3.	Maharashtra Legislative Assembly	288
4.	Bihar Legislative Assembly	243
5.	Tamil Nadu Legislative	234
6.	Madhya Pradesh Legislative	230
7.	Karnataka Legislative Assembly	224
8.	Rajasthan Legislative Assembly	200
9.	Gujarat Legislative Assembly	182
10.	Andhra Pradesh Legislative	175
11.	Odisha Legislative Assembly	147
12.	Kerala Legislative Assembly	140

13.	Assam Legislative Assembly	126
14.	Telangana Legislative Assembly	119
15.	Punjab Legislative Assembly	117
16.	Chhattisgarh Legislative Assembly	90
17.	Haryana Legislative Assembly	90
18.	Jammu and Kashmir Legislative Assembly	85
19.	Jharkhand Legislative Assembly	81
20.	Delhi Legislative Assembly	70
21.	Uttarakhand Legislative Assembly	70
22.	Himachal Pradesh Legislative Assembly	68
23.	Arunachal Pradesh Legislative	60
24.	Manipur Legislative Assembly	60
25.	Meghalaya Legislative Assembly	60
26.	Nagaland Legislative Assembly	60
27.	Tripura Legislative Assembly	60
28.	Mizoram Legislative Assembly	40
29.	Goa Legislative Assembly	40
30.	Puducherry Legislative Assembly	33
31.	Sikkim Legislative Assembly	32

❑